英語文学テクストの語学的研究法

菊池繁夫・上利政彦［編］

TOWARDS
THE LINGUISTIC
AND PHILOLOGICAL
STUDY OF ENGLISH
LITERARY TEXTS

九州大学出版会

Towards the Linguistic and Philological Study of English Literary Texts

Edited by Shigeo Kikuchi
        Masahiko Agari

Kyushu University Press

まえがき

　今回の企画が編者の間で一定の形を得たのが 2011 年秋である。その目的として，研究者が「語学」的見地から文学テクストを論じるにあたって，高いレベルの「論文」を書くための指針となるように，その方向性を示すことにあった。

　我が国で「語学的に文学テクストを論じる」という時，その視点の取り方は，かなり雑多なものである。従来は文献学的 (philological) な，したがって社会背景なども含めた文学テクストの研究を指した。言語学 (Linguistics) は自然言語を扱い，文学テクストには関心を示して来なかったため，語学的にテクストを読むという時には，言語学的なものはこの範疇に入ることはなかったが，執筆者の一人である Geoffrey Leech 氏もあげている Roman Jakobson の 'Linguistics and Poetics' (1960) の論文あたりを境として，つまり 20 世紀半ばあたりから，文学研究の戦列に加わるようになった。その二者に加えて，文学，非文学を問わずテクストの言語的スタイルの研究に特化した分野も存在する。それが文体論 (Stylistics) と呼ばれる研究分野であるが，この分野は英語では，文学テクストのみを扱った研究分野を指す場合と，文学および非文学テクストを扱った分野を示す場合がある（この文体論の区分に関しては pp. 3–4 を参照）。これら文献学，言語学，文体論の三者の研究の共通の視点は「言葉」であるが，それらを包括的に呼称する用語は英語にはない。本書では，従来から我が国で広く用いられてきた「語学的」という用語を用いたい。

　したがって，本書で「語学的」という場合には，これら文献学 (Philology)，言語学 (Linguistics) および（狭義および広義の）文体論 (Stylistics) の三者を包含した上位語としての意味合いを持たせてある。本書の第 1 部では，この三者のうち文体論 (stylistic) 的な観点からのものに重点を置いた。言語学的 (linguistic) なものは文学テクストを扱ったもののみが，この第 1 部に入れてある。もうひとつの社会的な現象も視野に入れて文学テクストを論じる文献

学的 (philological) なものもここに収めている。第2部では，上位語としての「語学的」観点から，文学テクストを論じた論文の解題を行った。第3部では研究のサンプルとして編者達の論文を収めた。第4部では語学的文学研究に必要な辞書に含まれる情報の読み方について論じている。以上の方針に基づいて，各部の概観を下に見てみる。

　まず第1部「文学テクストを語学的に読むとは」の「語学的文学論の通時的および共時的広がり」（菊池繁夫）では表題通り，文学テクストの研究がどのように行われて来たかを主に文体論の観点から歴史的および現代の共時的視点を提供することを目的としている。文学テクストの語学的研究という場合，この長い伝統を持つ文体論と呼ばれる分野は必須の分野で，それを通時的・共時的に概観しておくことは，今後のこの領域の研究の発展に指針を与えるという意味で意義があると考えたからである。文体論に重点が置いてあるとはいえ，その方法論は言語学および文献学の方法も取り入れながら行われて来たことはいうまでもない。

　第2部「文学テクストを語学的に読む：論文解題」では，文学テクストを語学的に論じた代表的な論文の紹介を行っている。新聞などの非文学テクストも，広義の文体論研究として文学テクスト研究に負うところが大きいため，ここに含めてある。目的は，この領域を研究する方々にとって必須の論文を紹介し，研究の参考にしてもらいたいという編者の願いからである。書籍の解題は今まで行われているし，本書の第1部でも言及されているが，論文のみに関しての解題は初めての試みであると思われる。この分野は古いテクスト研究，したがって文献学的な研究から発展したということもあり，元来ヨーロッパ大陸およびイギリスで主に文体論という形で発展した。アメリカでは，例えば古英語で書かれた*Beowulf*や，中英語でのGeoffrey Chaucerの作品，初期近代英語で書かれたWilliam Shakespeareの作品などを読むための，その作品の語学的な研究は必要なく，初期の例えばWashington IrvingやJames Fenimore Cooper，のちのNathaniel HawthorneやWalt Whitmanなどでも，同時代的 (contemporary) なテクストであったため，作品の内容に焦点を当て

た，アメリカ文学の文学的 (literary) な研究という領域が成立した。他方，アメリカ大陸での不明な言語といえば先住民族が使っている言語で，それの言語学的な研究という分野が確立した。このように，アメリカでは，文学研究と言語学という形で二極化してしまい，イギリスでのように文学テクストの語学的研究という分野が発展しなかった。こういった文学および非文学の語学的研究は，イギリスで大きく発展して来た。そのため，この語学的なテクストの論文解題については，3人のイギリス人学者にお願いをした。Lancaster 大学の Geoffrey Leech 教授，Birmingham 大学の Michael Toolan 教授，East Anglia 大学の Jean Boase-Beier 教授である。タイトルはそれぞれ 'The best of the bunch: Ten articles on literary stylistics' (Geoffrey Leech)，'A sample of memorable articles on stylistics and text analysis from the past fifty years: A personal selection and commentary' (Michael Toolan)，'Articles relating to stylistics and translation' (Jean Boase-Beier) となっている。3人とも「文体論」というタイトルを用いられているが，扱われている論文は上位語の「語学的」と呼ぶにふさわしいものである。我が国における論文解題「日本の論文でテクストを読む」は編者の1人の菊池繁夫が担当した。なお，この書物の校正中に，我が国のスタイル研究に多大の貢献をされた，寄稿者の1人である Geoffrey Leech 教授が他界された。心よりご冥福をお祈りいたします。

　第3部の「文学テクストの語学的研究の試み」は以下の4つの章よりなっている。

　「ジェイムズ・ジョイスの『ユリシーズ』と2人の歩くキャンドル」(菊池繁夫) では，難解と言われる James Joyce の大作 *Ulysses* (『ユリシーズ』) の表現の中に作者の発話意図 (author's intent) を探ることを目的としている。この作品は，作者の発話意図において先行する *Dubliners* (『ダブリン市民』)，*A Portrait of the Artist as a Young Man* (『若き日の芸術家の肖像』) との連続の中にあり，Joyce によって意識的に作り出された文脈の中に表現を置くことによって作者のそれに迫ることができることを見る。従来の研究では，作品中の個々の表現に詳細な註を付けるという形がとられていたが，本論文では先行する作品群を横断的に見ることで，物語中の発話者である登場人物を越え

て，本来の発信者である Joyce の「声」に迫ろうとするところに意義がある。

　方法論としては，作品をひとつの文法上の節 (clause) として見ることで，機能主義言語学のいうところのテクスト部門 (textual component) のうち発信者の関わる「主題―題術」(Theme-Rheme) 関係をテクスト中に求める。ジョイスの *Dubliners*（『ダブリン市民』）および *A Portrait of the Artist as a Young Man*（『若き日の芸術家の肖像』），そして *Ulysses*（『ユリシーズ』）と続く作品群を3つの同一のメッセージを伝達しようとする節と見るわけである。これらの中に，共通に，節に相当する人工的なコンテクストが相似的に存在し，その中に置かれた発話は，この「主題―題術」関係に沿っていることを見ることで，作者の発話の意図に迫ろうというわけである。なお，この章は，日本学術振興会の科学研究費助成事業 基盤研究 (C)（「James Joyce 作品における談話的主題化の問題」研究者番号：70204831）の研究の一部である。

　以下の3つの試論は近代初期の文学テクストにおけるモデルとテクストの重要性を再確認させてくれよう。

　「詩語の継承と排除――マロリーの用語に関して――」（上利政彦）は，近代前夜（1460年代）を含む文学テクストの言語を，伝統の継承と排除の視点から観察することを目的とする。近代初期に出版された *Songes and Sonettes*（『歌とソネット』），通常 *Tottel's Miscellany*（『トテル詩選集』）(1557)(*SS*) に現れる OE 詩語を遡り，*Beowulf* から ME 頭韻詩，Malory と Caxton へと衰退の過程を辿る。*SS* では OE・北方いずれの由来かは不明ながら，散文 Malory には ME 頭韻詩に拠る「限定使用」とその後 Caxton 同様の「排除」が見られる。これは地域言語から一般言語へ移行する英語近代化の影響によると思われる。Malory の散文英語の歴史的再検討を促す現象であろう。

　「モデルとテクスト――『トテル詩選集』翻訳詩から――」（上利政彦）では，英国最初の秀歌集 *SS* (1557) から，古典・当代のモデルに拠りながら独自性を発揮する翻訳詩，古典の題材を用いこれを凌駕せんとする自立詩を選び，躍動する人文主義精神に迫る。

　伝統の継承と排除は古典模倣論の実践に典型的に見られよう。模倣は，英国では16世紀半ば以降18世紀初頭まで創作原理であったと言われる (C. S. Lewis)。「文学テクストの重層性――『失楽園』最終部について――」（上利政

彦）はモデルに教わりながら依拠したことを隠す「模倣」を Milton がキリスト教化して実践したことを *Paradise Lost*（『失楽園』）の例から示す。

　第 4 部の「歴史辞書を読む」の「語学研究における辞書の役割——初期の英語辞書を中心にして——」（和田章）は文献学的な観点から歴史辞書の見方を示しているが，その目的と意義は以下の通りである。
　現代の英語辞書でなく初期時代の英語辞書を中心に，語学研究における辞書の役割を考える。語を歴史的感覚で理解する契機となり得るのではと思うからである。平たくいえば，語の今の姿は，時の流れの中で形成されたことが，幾分なりとも，実感できるだろう。そのような実感があれば，この選択に意義があろうし，なければ，本論の目的は達せられない。
　本章では初期時代の英語辞書は，英語辞書のひとつの頂点である 1755 年の Samuel Johnson, ed., *A Dictionary of the English Language* 以前の英語辞書とする。選んだ英語辞書を 2 区分し，揺籃期の Cawdrey (1604) から Coles (1676) までの難語辞書 6 点と，Kersey (1702) と Bailey (1721) の一般語を含む辞書 2 点を中心に，適宜他の初期時代の辞書および現代の辞書も援用する。これらの辞書には，言語のあるがままの姿を記述する現代の辞書編纂の基本方針は通用しない。編者が選択した語からなる辞書である。一方の難語辞書は，非難解語は除外して，外来語を中心とする難解語を平易な言葉で解説した。他方，一般語を含む辞書といっても，見出し語の語釈に用いられながら，見出し語にならない語は続出する。見出しにならない語，簡単な語釈，詳しい語釈にはそれなりの理由が見て取れる。これらの辞書では，言語使用者にとって馴染みの薄い語の方が詳しく扱われ，言語の中枢を占めるありふれた語や語形成要素は簡単に扱われるか無視される。かような編集の辞書から，語は歴史が形成すると気づくはずである。
　初期近代英語期のこれらの辞書では，17–18 世紀の発想に直に触れることができる。例えば，地球は，宇宙の中心点にあるから center で表されている。Artery（動脈）には血液に加え，vital spirits（生気）が流れており，生気が体外に洩れて流れ落ちると生き物は息絶える。これらの事実は，歴史的原理で編纂された *The Oxford English Dictionary*（*OED*）からも読み取ることができ

る。しかし，whale は mammal ではなく fish であり，cataract（白内障）は humour（体液）の異常現象であるとの見方が過去にはあったとの言及は *OED* にない。四季語のうち 17 世紀の難語辞書の見出しにあるのは autumn のみで harvest と語釈されている。秋の平易語は harvest であり autumn はまだ難語であったことが窺える。このことを *OED*, autumn から読み取ることはできない。現在の英語の四季語は，spring, summer, autumn/ fall, and winter であるとの今の言語体系の中での理解に加えて，四季語それぞれの成立の歴史は異なることを理解すれば，語は歴史を背負って今を生きていることを実感する端緒となるだろう。横の広がりの記述言語学的体系の理解に加えて，縦に貫く歴史的理解があれば，語の重層的理解へと深まるということである。

　書式に関してはおおまかな統一を図ったが，それ以外は各執筆者に任せた。表記は「日本語訳（外国語）」を中心としたが，外国語で書かれた部分をとくに重要視したい場合，あるいは日本語が定着していない場合は「外国語（日本語訳）」とした箇所もある。索引も同様で，またイギリス人の研究者の用語は英語で引く形にしてあるので，同一概念が日本語索引と外国語索引の 2 箇所に載っている場合もある。紛らわしいとお考えの方もあるであろうがご容赦願いたい。文献上の名前は索引に載せていないので，必要な場合は各セクションの文献をご参照願いたい。

　本書の出版に関して関西外国語大学学長谷本義高氏より貴重な御指導を賜った。心よりお礼申し上げる次第である。
　なお，本書の出版を快諾していただいた九州大学出版会編集企画委員会，ならびに出版に至る過程で様々なアドバイスをいただいた尾石理恵氏および編集部の方々に心から感謝申し上げる次第である。

編　者

目　次

まえがき ……………………………………………編　者　　*i*

第1部　文学テクストを語学的に読むとは

語学的文学論の通時的および共時的広がり …………菊池繁夫　　*3*

第2部　文学テクストを語学的に読む：論文解題

イギリスの3人の学者による論文解題について ……菊池繁夫　　*82*

The best of the bunch: Ten articles on literary stylistics
………………………………………………Geoffrey Leech　　*89*

A sample of memorable articles on stylistics and
text analysis from the past fifty years:
A personal selection and commentary …………Michael Toolan　　*97*

Articles relating to stylistics and translation
……………………………………………Jean Boase-Beier　　*123*

日本の論文でテクストを読む ………………………菊池繁夫　　*139*

第3部　文学テクストの語学的研究の試み

ジェイムズ・ジョイスの『ユリシーズ』と
2人の歩くキャンドル ……………………………………菊池繁夫　*209*

詩語の継承と排除
　　――マロリーの用語に関して――………………………上利政彦　*231*

モデルとテクスト
　　――『トテル詩選集』翻訳詩から――…………………上利政彦　*249*

文学テクストの重層性
　　――『失楽園』最終部について――……………………上利政彦　*267*

第4部　歴史辞書を読む

語学研究における辞書の役割
　　――初期の英語辞書を中心にして――……………………和田　章　*283*

　索　引……………………………………………………………………　*339*

第 1 部

文学テクストを語学的に読むとは

語学的文学論の通時的および共時的広がり

菊池繁夫

はじめに

語学的な文学研究は，多くは言語学的であろうと文献学的であろうと，文体論と呼ばれる分野で行われて来た。したがって，この章では，「文体」(style) および「文体論」(Stylistics) の定義から始めようと思う。

まず我々は「文体」(style) を研究する学問が「文体論」(Stylistics) であると認識している。ところが実際はそう簡単ではない。というのが，文体と呼ばれる言語現象と文体論が研究対象とする言語現象が異なる指示対象を持つことがあるからである[1]。

その違いは，2つの用語の示す言語現象が，一般的な言語現象を全て含むか，あるいは文学における言語に特化しているかによって生じている。まず違いの概略を述べるとこうなる。文体の概念を先に見た方が分かりやすいので，それを先に見る：

(1) 文体1：全ての言語現象の文体
(2) 文体2：文学の中で用いられた言語現象としての文体

---

1) 豊田 (1981) では「文体」という用語は用いられず一貫して「スタイル」という言葉が用いられている。従来は「文体」という用語で「書かれた言葉」をもっぱら扱ってきたが，発音も重要な側面であるとして，より広い領域をカバーする「スタイル」という用語を用いることにしたという。それに加えて，豊田はスタイルという用語を，文学のみならず，全ての言語現象の文体という意味で用いている。したがって，彼の文体論は広義の文体論である。言語現象を示す用語としては，本論では従来からの「文体」という用語を用いる。

これによって文体論がカバーする領域にも 2 種類が出てくる：
(1) 文体論 1：全ての言語現象の文体を扱う（「文体の研究」もしくは広義の文体論とでも呼べるもの）(study of style)
(2) 文体論 2：文学の中で用いられた言語現象としての文体を扱う（狭義の文体論にあたる）(Stylistics)

いずれも 1 の方が対象が広く，2 の方が狭い。研究対象としての文体という時には 1 の広義の文体を，文体論の対象としての言語現象は 2 の，文学言語を指す。

ここで以上の関係を，文法を左端に置く形で図示してみる[2]：

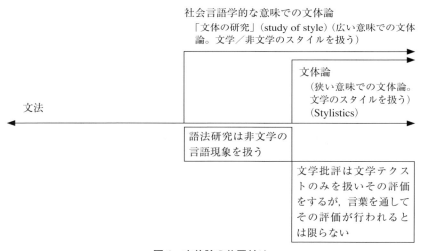

図 1　文体論の位置付け

Fowler (1987) と Wales (2001) によると，文体とは文学であるとそうでないとを問わず，言語形式と非言語状況が交錯する地点である。つまり文体 1 である。したがって，この文体 1 の研究は文体論 1 となり，文学であるとな

---

2) 文体論は類似の領域を扱う文学批評とどのような関係にあるかについては Wales (2001: 372) が次のように述べている：'In many respects, however, stylistics is close to literary criticism and practical criticism'.（しかしながら多くの点において，文体論は文学批評や実践批評に近い。）

いとを問わず，あらゆる言語の表現様式を扱うことになる。
　ただし，彼らは「文体論」という用語は文学の言語，つまり文体2を扱う領域であるとする。Fowler (1987) によると文体論の対象領域は文学批評がカバーする領域と同じであって，主に文学テクストを現代言語学の方法でもって扱う。つまり領域的には文学を扱う狭義の文体論である文体論2となる:

> Stylistics ... is the application of theoretical ideas and analytic techniques drawn from linguistics to the study of literary texts.　　(Fowler 1981: 11)
> 文体論は言語学からの理論的概念や分析手段を文学テクストの研究に応用することである。

> The term 'stylistics' or 'linguistic stylistics' has come to designate any analytic study of literature which uses the concepts and techniques of modern linguistics,...　　　　　　　　　　　　　(Fowler 1987: 238)
> 「文体論」もしくは「言語学的文体論」(linguistic stylistics) という用語は，現代言語学の概念やテクニックを用いる全ての文学の分析的研究を示すようになった。

上記の引用では Linguistic Stylistics という用語が用いられているが，linguistic の部分は文体論の方法論を示す。この Fowler の主張は彼が自らの「文体の研究」を文学にのみ限定しているということではない。というのが，Fowler はニュースの言語の分析に，その方法論を用いているからである。この場合には，Fowler は「文体の研究」を文学テクスト以外のものにも行っているというべきであろう。
　そして我々が普通「文体論」(Stylistics) という時には，この伝統的である方の「文学テクストの分析」のことを指す。Toolan (1996: viii–x) も文体論とは文学の言語以外のものを扱ってもよいとしながらも，中心は文学言語であると述べている:

> Stylistics is the study of the language *in* literature.　　(Toolan 1996: viii)

文体論とは文学で用いられた言語の研究である。

> ... Stylistics is crucially concerned with excellence of technique; traditionally, its attention has been directed to such excellence of craft in works of literature, but clearly there is no intrinsic reason why it cannot equally be used in the study of excellence of craft (and, conversely, of mediocrity of craft) in other fields such as advertising, political discourse, legal pleading, and pop-music lyrics. (同 ix–x)

文体論は優れた技法に関心を持つ。そして伝統的に，その関心は文学作品の優れた技巧に注意を払ってきた。しかし，文体論が，宣伝，政治的談話，法律上の弁論，そしてポップミュージックの歌詞といった他の分野における，そういった優れた技法（そして，逆に言えば劣った技法）の研究に同様に用いられることをその本質として妨げるものではないことは明らかである。

(Toolan は初めの引用の前に 'the term (Literary) Stylistics' (p. viii) という言い方をしているが，この場合の literary は文体論の対象とする領域を指す) 彼は文体 (style) という語を使わず，一貫して「技巧」(craft) という言葉を使っているが，文体と同じものと考えてよい。そしてこの技巧という語は文学・非文学を問わず使用されているところから，広い意味での文体，つまり文体 1 である。

Leech and Short (1981) の場合も同じである。文体を広義の文体，つまり文体 1 としながら，伝統的には文学の文体，つまり文体 2 としている:

> In the broadest sense, STYLE can be applied to both spoken and written, both literary and non-literary varieties of language; but by tradition, it is particularly associated with written literary texts, and this is the sense of the term which will concern us. (Leech and Short 1981: 11)

もっとも広い意味では文体という用語は，話された言葉と書かれた言葉の両方に対して，また，文学と非文学の言語の両方の変種に対して用いられる。しかし，伝統的には，文体という語は特に書かれた文学テクス

トに対して用いられ，我々が最も関心を持つのは，文体という語のこの意味である。

そして文体論に関しては以下のように定義する：

> Stylistics (or the study of style) has typically ... been concerned with *literary* language. 　　　（Leech and Short 1981: 38）（イタリクスは著者）
> 文体論とは（あるいは文体の研究は）典型的には文学言語を対象とする。

彼らも文体論とは主に文学言語の文体の研究ととらえている。

　少し時代が遡るが，Crystal and Davy (1969) などにおいても，同様の定義がなされている。彼らによると，まず文体とは概ね以下の2つを指すとされる：

> Style may refer to some or all of the language habits of one person — as when we talk of Shakespeare's style (or styles)...
> 　　　　　　　　　　　　　　　　　　　　　　　　　（Crystal and Davy 1969: 9）
> 文体は，例えば Shakespeare の文体（あるいはいくつかの文体）という時のように，1人の人物の言語習慣の一部，もしくは全てを指すと見ることができる

> ... style may refer to some or all of the language habits shared by a group of people at one time, or over a period of time, as when we talk about the style of the Augustan poets, the style of Old English 'heroic' poetry...
> 　　　　　　　　　　　　　　　　　　　　　　　　　（Crystal and Davy 1969: 10）
> 文体とは，古典主義詩人達の文体や古英語の英雄詩の文体といった，ひとつの時期において，あるいはひとつの時代において，ひとつのグループの人々によって用いられた言語習慣の一部か，もしくは全てを指すと見ることができる

このように見た後で，彼らは文体論を，以下のように，一般的には広義の文

体論の文体論 1 を指すが，もっぱら狭義の，文学の文体論である文体論 2 を指すと定義する：

> ... the aim of stylistics is to analyse language habits with the main purpose of identifying, from the general mass of linguistic features common to English as used on every conceivable occasion, those features which are restricted to certain kinds of social context; to explain, where possible, why such features have been used, as opposed to other alternatives; and to classify these features into categories based upon a view of their function in the social context.　　　(Crystal and Davy 1969: 10)
> 文体論の目的は，考えられるあらゆる場合において用いられるものとしての英語に共通な言語特徴の一般的なまとまりの観点から，ある種の社会的文脈に限定されている諸特徴を見出すという主たる目的を持って言語習慣を分析することにある。また，可能な場合には，他の可能な選択肢が選ばれないで，なぜそのような特徴が用いられたのかを説明することにある。そしてまた，それらの特徴を，社会的文脈の中で果たす機能の観点に基づいて，いくつかのカテゴリーに分類することにある。

> It (=Stylistics) is not concerned solely with literary language, although its techniques are most widely used in this context;...
> 　　　　　　　　　　　　　　　　　　　(Crystal and Davy 1969: 90)
> 文体論は文学言語のみに関係しているわけではない。ただ，文体論の用いる分析技術は，この分野において最も広く用いられている。

文体の定義の方では主に文学の言語の文体を指すと断っていないことに注意がいる。それに対して，文体論の方は，ここに示されたように，もっぱら文学の言語を対象とするとしている。

　まとめれば，上に見て来たように，文体は広く言語現象を指し，文体論の方は，主に文学の言語の研究ということになる。それも，20 世紀の初頭からの現代言語学の中で発展して来た分析手段を用いて「文学表現」の様式を扱う分野ということになる。

このように文体の指し示す指示対象の方が文体論の研究対象よりも一般的に指示対象が広いのは，文体という言葉は，はるかギリシャ・ローマにまで遡り，したがってその歴史の中で多義となって来たのに対して，文体論という言葉は比較的新しい学問用語として発達して来たからである。次の節では文体の対象とする領域ではなくて，文体そのものをどうとらえるかという点に焦点を当てながら，文体論を通時的に，その後共時的に概観してみたい。

1　文体論の通時的概観[3]

1.1　文体論の源流を求めて

独立した研究分野としての文体論は 19 世紀に確立した。*Oxford English Dictionary*（On-line 版）（以下 *OED On-line*）によると，'stylistics' という語は 19 世紀に初例が記載されている：

> **stylistic**
> **B**. *n*. The science of literary style; the study of stylistic features. Also (more commonly) **stylistics** *n*. [see -IC *suffix*]
>
> [1846 J. E. WORCESTER *Universal Dict. Eng. Lang.*, *Stylistic*, the art of forming a good style in writing; a treatise on style.]
> 1883　P. SCHAFF et al. *Relig. Encycl.* II. 965　Giving proper place to New Testament stylistics and rhetoric.

したがって文体論は 19 世紀に確立し始めた学問体系としてよいが，それの扱う「文体」（style）の概念はギリシャ・ローマにまで遡る。

---

[3]　この文体論の歴史を記述するにあたって，戦前の文体論の歴史については山本（1938）が大変参考になった。

'Style' という語自身はラテン語の 'stilus' という語から来ており，それは 'a stake or pale, pointed instrument for writing, style of speaking or writing'（*OED*（初版））とあるように多義的であって，現在に至るまで，多くの意味を含み，いまだに変化し続けている。

特に言語学が大きく発展した 20 世紀の初頭以来，その発達に伴って，この 'style' という語は広く用いられ始め，意味があいまいとなっている。前節であげた定義は現代という時点での文体（および文体論）の定義であるが，そこに至る過程を歴史的に見ると，例えば以下のように異なった定義がなされて来た：

    Stil... individueller geistiger Ausdruck　　　　　　（Vossler 1904: 16）
    文体とは個人の精神が表現されたものである

    ... le style est l'homme meme　　　　　　　　　（de Buffon 1922: 24）
    文体とはその人そのものである

    ... le choix, c'est-à-dire le style　　　　　　　　（Marouzeau 1941: 10）
    選択，それが，つまり文体である

Marouzeau にとって文体とは「選択」という言葉に反映されているように以下にもその考えが反映されている：

    la langue comme la somme des moyens d'expression dont nous disposons pour mettre en forme l'énoncé, le style comme l'aspect et la qualité qui résultent du choix entre ces moyens d'expression.　（Marouzeau 1941: 10）
    言表に形を与えるために我々が用いる表現手段の総体としてのラング。一方，それら表現手段の間の選択から生じる側面や性質を備えたものとしての文体。

Enksvist の定義はこうである：

The style of a text is the aggregate of the contextual probabilities of its linguistic items　　　　　　　　　　　　　　　　　　　(Enkvist 1964: 28)
あるテクストの文体とは，そのテクストの言語単位が持つ文脈的な可能性の総体である

Enkvist の定義は分かりにくいが，豊田 (1991: 56–57) によると，「『通常の用法』，つまり 'norm'（基準）に 'contextually related'（文脈に関連する）という語を冠して文脈とかかわる頻度を考慮に入れようと」する試みであるとされる。

さて，Enksvist よりも少し時代が下る Crystal and Davy (1969) の定義をもう一度短くまとめて引用すると以下のようになる：

Style may refer to some or all of the language habits of one person ... In a similar way, style may refer to some or all of the language habits shared by a group of people at one time, or over a period of time...
　　　　　　　　　　　　　　　　　　　　　　(Crystal and Davy 1969: 9–10)
文体とは1人の人物の一部または全部の言語習慣を指すと言えよう…同様に文体とはひとつの時期において，あるいはひとつの時代においてあるグループの人々によって共有された言語習慣の一部または全部を指すこともある

Fowler (1987) においては，文体とは言語形式と非言語的な条件が交わるところに生じる表現様式のことである：

A style is a manner of expression, describable in linguistic terms, justifiable and valuable in respect of non-linguistic factors.　(Fowler 1987: 236)
文体とは言語学的用語で記述され，非言語的な条件の点から正当化され価値を持つ表現様式である。

オランダの文体論学者 Verdonk は以下のように定義する：

A set of conscious or unconscious choices of expression, inspired or in-

duced by a particular context　　　　　　　　（Verdonk 2002: 121）
（文体とは）特定の文脈によって刺激された，あるいは引き起こされた表現の意識的もしくは無意識的な選択の集合を示す

これらの文体の定義は一見様々に異なる定義のように見えるが，一般論として，文体の定義はどの部分に焦点を当てるかによって大きく 2 つのカテゴリーに分類できる。
　ひとつのカテゴリーは
（1）　言語の特定の実現の仕方
である。こちらの代表者は，その源流に位置する学者として Charles Bally や Jules Marouzeau がいる。もうひとつのカテゴリーは
（2）　発信者の心的態度
である。Karl Vossler や Leo Spitzer はこのカテゴリーの源を代表している。

1.2　文体論の 2 つの流れ

これらの 2 種類の文体研究の流れは 19 世紀の von Humboldt に始まるが，その前に，さらにギリシャ・ローマの時代までその歴史を遡ってみる。
　古典ギリシャの人々の間では文体論的なストラテジーはレトリックの対象であった。Guiraud（1955）には以下のように述べられている：

> L'ensemble des procédés de style était chez les Anciens l'objet d'une etude spéciale, la rhétorique qui est un art du langage, une technique du langage considéré comme un art.　　　　　　　　（Guiraud 1955: 10）
> 文体的な手法の集合は，古代の人々にとっては，言語の技法であり，また芸術とみなされる言語の技術であるレトリックという特別な研究領域の対象であった。

レトリックとは，聴衆に印象づけ彼らに影響を及ぼして，ある種の行動をうながす，あるいはそれに反対させる言語の使用法であるが，Aristotle（384–322

BC)は，そこでの言葉の用いられ方を文体としている．文体論の最初の理論家はAristotleと言ってもよく，彼にとって，そもそも文体とは「話し方」のことである：

> We have therefore next to speak of style; for it is not sufficient to know what one ought to say, but one must also know how to say it,...
> (*Art of Rhetoric*, 345)
> 我々はしたがって次に文体について語る必要がある：というのが，我々は何を言うかを知っているだけでは不十分であり，いかに言うかについても知っておく必要があるからである

Guiraud (1955: 11) によると，このレトリックは中世には文法や方言学と共にリベラル・アーツの3分野 (the *trivium* of grammar, logic and rhetoric) のひとつとなる．

19世紀および20世紀になると，言語学に基づく文体理論が登場する．源流はドイツの言語学者であり哲学者であったWilhelm von Humboldtである．19世紀の初頭，彼は，そのvon Humboldt (1876) において機能的文体論を論じた．言語における2つの側面であるergon（出来上がったもの）とenergeia（創造過程）の区別をしたのはこのvon Humboldtである．彼はこう述べる：

> Sie (=the language) selbst ist kein Werk (*Ergon*), sondern eine Thätichkeit (sic) (*Energeia*)　　　　　　　　　　(von Humboldt 1876: 56)
> 言語自体，出来上がったもの (*Ergon*) ではなく，活動 (*Energeia*) である

この19世紀におけるergonとenergeiaの二分法から，先に述べた文体論の大きな2つの潮流が生じることとなる．

ひとつは，スイスの言語学者Ferdinand de Saussure（例えばde Saussure 1966 [1916] を参照）と，その弟子のフランス人言語学者のCharles Bally (Bally 1952 [1935], 1963を参照）である．20世紀前半に始まるSaussure–Ballyの流れがここから始まる．もうひとつはイタリアの哲学者のBenedetto Croce（例えば

Croce 2006 [1902] を参照のこと）とドイツのロマンス語学者 Karl Vossler（例えば Vossler 1904, 1925 を参照）の流れで，それに Leo Spitzer を加えて，まとめて Vossler–Spitzer のラインが始まる。ここから上に述べた，文体論として「(1) 言語の特定の実現の仕方」と「(2) 発信者の心的態度」を見る2つの潮流が始まるわけである。

この2つの流れは分析の方向性において異なる。まずひとつ目の Humboldt–Saussure–Bally の流れは以下のような分析の方向を取る：

general → collective (→ individual)

この方向性では，一般的なものから集団的なものを見ようとする。ただし，Bally は個人的なものをその分析対象に加えなかった点は注意を要する。右端までは追究しなかったのである。現代でも言語学者が，その理論の説明に文学作品からの引用を行うが，彼らは決して，その作者独自の文体にまでは迫らない。例えば村上春樹からの日本語の引用をしても，村上独自の文体に迫るわけではない。その一歩手前で止まるわけである[4]。

他方，後者の Humboldt–Croce–Vossler–Spitzer の流れは逆の分析の方向性を取る：

individual → collective (→ general)

こちらは個人的なものから集団的なものへの方向性で，こちらの方は一般化

---

[4] 山本（1940: 57-58）は文法論が文体まで迫り得ない点について，西田幾多郎の「猫も死んでしまった」という文章を引用しながら次のように述べている：「それを或人は批評して『死んだもの』が他にもあるのだから『猫も』といつたところで何も不思議はないではないか…これを敢えて文體的といふのは當らない，と言つた人がある。かういふ解釋を私は文法的だと言ふのである。…文體論が問題にするのは，かかる一片の助詞が，西田博士の筆にかかつて，如何なる機能を生じ，如何なる價値を表はすか，の問題である。博士の鋭敏なテニヲハの使ひ方や，博士の人間らしい一面が，此の助詞に表現されてをり，かやうな語法に博士の人格を如實にみるのは，「も」を文法の一隅から探し出して説明するのでは分からない。」

を求めなかった。

　少し脱線になるが，この初源の段階で，これら2つの文体論の方向性とも，文学的および非文学的なものの区別をしていないということは心に留めておく必要がある。20世紀も後半あたりになって言語使用域（register）の概念が芽生えるまでは，この文学的および非文学的なテクストの区別はなされない。

　さて，Ferdinand de Saussure は von Humboldt の理論を構造主義の方に押し進めたもので，規則の体系である langue とその規則と体系が具体的に実現したものとしての parole を区別した。その弟子にあたる Charles Bally は，独自の記述的文体論を発展させた。Bally の考えによると，文体論は，ひとつの言語の中において，出来事とそれを言語化した表現の関係を記述するものであった。したがって，彼の文体論もまた表現的文体論（Expressive Stylistics）と呼べるものである。

　Bally は文体論を，de Saussure の言語学を表現的な文体上の事実の面に応用するものとみなした。したがって，彼の文体論は，langue の概念を最も抽象度の低いレベルにまで拡張するが，しかし決して parole の領域にまでは入らないのである。彼は parole の段階に入る手前で分析を止める。Langue の最も抽象度の低いレベルには文学言語が位置しているが，Bally の文体論は言語事実を記述するのみで，したがって，体系の中に存在する言語現象，あるいはこう言ってよければ，個人の言語使用にまでは行きつかない言語事実のみを扱う。Bally（1952）からひとつ例をあげてみる：

　　—Une lettere, père Azan?
　　—Oui, Monsieur, ça vient de Paris.
　　Il était tout fier que ça vînt de Paris, ce brave père Azan; moi pas, etc.

　On sent que l'interlocuteur de père Azan a été frappé, comme le lecteur, de la forme *ça vînt* et qu'il veut lui en laisser la responsabilité（il était tout fier que *ça vînt*）; c'est que cette syntaxe est le symbole d'une culture imparfaite; en l'entendant, on s'aperçoit que celui qui l'emploie doit être un homme du peuple ou un paysan, et elle provoque un sentiment ou un jugement de valeur portant, non sur les choses dites, mais sur celui qui les dit.

... celle-ci (=la stylistique) ne s'y attache que si l'expression entendue symbolise un milieu social (par exemple le peuple), ou une forme déterminée ou générale de la vie, ainsi un âge (par exemple l'enfance), ou une forme spéciale de pensée (par exemple la pensée scientifique).

(Bally 1952 [1935]: 59–60)

「『手紙かい，アザン小父さん。』

『へい，旦那，こらパリからめえりましたんで。』

彼はこらパリからめえりましたんで大得意であった，この好々爺のアザンぢいは。僕は然らず。」

これを読むと，アザンぢいの話相手が讀者と同じく語形 *ça vînt*「こらめえりましたんで」に驚き，その責任をぢいさんに押附けようとしてゐるさまが (il était tout fier que *ça vînt*「こら」) まざ〳〵と眼に浮ぶ。ほかでもない，この統辭法は敎養の不足の象徵であるからだ。それを聞けば，それを用ひた人間が下層民か田舎者かに相違ないと思はれ，その言葉遣は言はれた事柄よりも言つた人間に對して或る感情ないし價値判斷を起させる。

…文體論は，人から聞いた表現がさる社會的環境なり（例へば民衆），生活の一定の一般的形態なり（年齢の如き，例へば兒童期），社會的關係の一形態なり（例へば結婚生活），思想の特殊形態なり（例へば科學的思想）を象徵するときならでは，それに執心しないのである。

(小林英夫（訳）『言語活動と生活』岩波書店，1941)

Bally の文体論もしたがって，langue の文体論と呼んでいいであろう。

　Bally の弟子である Jules Marouzeau と Marcel Cressot は，その狭い文体概念を拡張した。これら 2 人の弟子は Bally が話された言葉に対して行った分析を書かれた言葉に対して行った。Bally (1963) は話された言葉のみが，その言語の唯一信頼するに足る実現であると述べている：

Quant à la *langue parlée*, dans le sens restreint du mot, c. à d. la *langue de la conversation* ou *expression familière*, il faut se garder d'y voir un mode d'expression idéal, une langue déduite par abstraction des tendances

générales du langage; c'est au contraire une *réalisation* concrète de ces tendances, c'est la seule langue réelle et vivante qui existe.
(Bally 1963: 29)（イタリクスは著者）
話された言葉に関して言えば，狭い意味では，つまり会話，あるいは身近な表現に関して言えば，そこには理想化された表現様式があると見るべきではなく，つまり，そこには，その言語の一般的な諸傾向を抽象化した言葉が存在すると見るべきではなく；これら言語的諸傾向の具体化したもので，その具体化したものこそが唯一存在する生きた言語なのである。

このBallyの話された言葉に対する概念を拡張しながら，Marouzeau (1941) とCressot (1947) は，ひとつの書かれた言葉の文体論，すなわち書かれたフランス語の文体論を完成させた。

Von Humboldtから影響を受けたもう一人のフィロロジストはKarl Vosslerである。Vossler (e.g. 1904, 1925) はCroce (2006 [1902]) の美学の影響のもとで，言語学的美学を打ち立てた。彼は，言語を対象物と見る実証主義者に対して，言語表現は個人による純粋な創造物であるとみなされるという観念主義 (idealism) の立場を取る。

Vosslerの考えによると言語とは，音，形式，そして統語といった全てのレベルにおける個人の美的な創造という観念的な行為であるとした。

Vosslerの主張するところによると，古典ラテン語における，例えば格や受動形や未来形といった総合的な形式は，ロマンス語においては，表現上の必要性から，その分析的な形式によって取って代わられた：

man nach stärkeren, eindeutigen Ausdrücken des Wollens, des Sollens, des Müssens trachtete (Vossler 1925: 66)
意思と当為と義務をより強く明確に表現することが求められた。

彼は文体的な必要性が先にあり，それが文法的な変化を引き起こすと見るのである：

Den Sprachgebrauch, insofern er individuelle Schöpfung ist, betrachtet die Stilistik. Der inductive Weg aber führt vom Individuellen zum Allgemeinen, vom Einzelfall zur Konvention. Nicht umgekehrt. Also erst Stilistik, dann Syntax!　　　　　　　　　　（Vossler 1904: 16）

言語の使用を，それが個人の創造物である限りにおいて観察するのが文体論である。しかしながら，帰納的方法とは，個人的なものから一般的なものへ，個別のケースから慣習へと向かうものである。その逆ではない。したがって，初めに文体論があり，その後で統語論が来るのである。

　Vossler にとっては文体とは 'individueller geistiger Ausdruck'（個人的な精神的表現）（Vossler 1904: 16）であって，それが歴史的な文法変化を引き起こすと見ているわけである。

　Guiraud（1955: 64）の意見ではこうである。Leo Spitzer は Vossler と共に 'la linguistique idéaliste de l'école Vossler–Spitzer'（Vossler–Spitzer 学派の観念的言語学）を提唱するものとされているが，実際には彼はその文学テクスト研究において Bally の実在論（positivism）と Vossler の観念論（idealism）という文体論の二つの流れの折衷をはかろうとしたとする。確かに Spitzer はこう述べている：'möchte ich einen positiven Idealismus oder idealistischen Positivismus verfechten'（私は実証的観念論あるいは観念的実証主義を擁護したいと思う）（Spitzer 1961 [1928]: XI）。Guiraud の見方ではそうではあるが，Spitzer はやはり Vossler と方向性を同じくすると見たい。彼は，'an individual style'（個別の文体）を認めることは可能かと問いかけながら，文体とは個人の作家がその時代の変化を感じて，それを新しい言語表現で表そうとした，その表現を指すとする：

The individualistic stylistic deviation from the general norm must represent a historical step taken by the writer ... it must reveal a shift of the soul of the epoch, a shift of which the writer has become conscious and which he would translate into a necessarily new linguistic form.
　　　　　　　　　　　　　　　　　　　　　（Spitzer 1962 [1948]: 11）

一般的な基準からの個人の文体的逸脱は，その作家による歴史的な一歩

を表していなければならない。その文体的逸脱は，その時代の魂の変化，その作家が意識をするようになった変化であり，彼が必然的に新しい言語形式で表そうとした変化を示していなければならない。

彼の視点は，したがって，ある時代において新しい文体の生まれる瞬間に向けられている。その瞬間こそ 'an individual style' の生まれる場面だとするのである。この視点は現代では Adamson (2010) の Shakespeare 論などに受け継がれている[5]。

Spitzer は実際の文体論研究においては，個々のフィロロジカルな事実と全体としてのテクストの間を行き来する，いわば帰納的−演繹的方法が取られるべきだとする。例えばフランスの作家の Gustave Flaubert には次のような文体的特徴がある。彼は pâlir (消える) の代わりに apalir (ゆっくりと消える) を用いるが，これは 'apalir mit seinem Präfix *a-* drückt Annäherung an einen Zustand aus' (接頭辞の *a-* の付いた apalir はある状態への接近を表現する) からである (Spitzer 1961 [1928]: 8)。Flaubert は，また，pourrir (腐る) や pâlir (消える) などの *ir-* 動詞を用いるが，これは 'die *ir-*Verba drücken ein Werden aus' (*ir-* 動詞は段階的な変化を表す) からである (8)。そして s'échapper (逃げる) から新語として作られた s'irradier (放射状に広がる) などを用いている (9):

> ... im Dienste des »faire du réel écrit«, wie Flaubert selbst sagte, im Dienste desselben »Dynamismus« oder der »description en mouvement«,..., der Wiedergabe der dynamischen Intensitäten durch den Stil, einer Art abgeleiteten Lautmalerei, die den Vorgang der Außenwelt sprachlich porträtiert: ein ähnlicher Effekt wie das Partizip in *il vit la carriole s'éloignant* zum Ausdruck für allmähliches Entschwinden! Flaubert hat sich sprachliche Mittel geschaffen, um Dämpfung der Realität, ein Decrescendo

---

[5] Sheffield 大学の Sylvia Adamson 教授は 1996 年 9 月に 'Linguistics and Literary History Conference' を Simon Alderson, Joe Bray と共に Cambridge 大学の Trinity College で開催している。この学会のタイトルは Leo Spitzer 著の *Linguistics and Literary History: Essays in Stylistics* から取られていて，Leo Spitzer に捧げられたものである。

zu malen, wobei er nur Keime, die in der Volkssprache bereit lagen, zu entwickeln brauchte. 　　　　　　　　　　（Spitzer 1961 ［1928］: 9）
　Flaubert 自身が述べたように「文章を生き生きとしたものにする」ために，「ダイナミズム」すなわち「描写を動的なものにする」ために…，文体による動的な力強さの再現，すなわち外界の流れを言語的に描写する一種の派生的な擬音：それは，il vit la carriole s'éloignant（彼には荷車が去って行くのが見える）における分詞と同様に，徐々に消え去って行くことを表現するための効果を与える。Flaubert は，現実の緩和，すなわちデクレッシェンド的な図を描くための言語的手段を作り出したのである。そして，その時には，彼は一般民衆の言語の中にすでにある萌芽を発達させることだけを必要としたのである。

　これら Spitzer の論じた Flaubert 流の動詞（apalir, pourrir, s'irradier）は，その中核的意味に多少のずれを生じている。Spitzer はさらに一歩進めて，Flaubert がこれらの動詞を用いたのは，物語の中で実際に起こっている変化の様相を描きたいという願望に動機づけられていると主張する。この場合は，ひとつの文体効果は動詞の 3 種類の文法的用法によって実現している。ここに文体および文法の相互作用を見ることができるとする。Guiraud は Spitzer は実在論と観念論の折衷と述べたが，Spitzer は個人の文体に迫ることを目標としていることから，やはり Vossler の観念論の流れの中にあると見てよい。
　ロマンス語の研究に心理学的な方法を用いることを拒んだのは Vossler の弟子である Eugen von Lerch である。彼は，その文体研究において 'ästhetische'（美学的）および 'soziale'（社会的）なアプローチと共に 'historische'（歴史的）な視点を導入した（von Lerch 1930: 22）。Von Lerch (1930: 22) によると，例えばドイツ語の *er frug*（彼は尋ねた）は廃れることはなかったが，その理由は 'die starken Präterita altertümlicher und daher edler klingen als die schwachen'（弱変化の er fragte 彼は尋ねた）よりも強変化の過去形の方がより古く響き，したがってより高貴な響きがあるからである。
　一般的な言語構造の現れとしての「言語の特定の実現の仕方」としての文体を論じる Sassure–Bally ラインと，「発信者の心的態度」としての文体を研

究する Vossler–Spitzer ラインの間にあって，特に言語における collective な民族精神の現れに心理学的に関心を持ったグループがある。それは，ドイツのフィロロジストにして哲学者である Heymann Steinthal と，同じくドイツの心理学者にして生理学者である Wilhelm Wundt で，共に von Humboldt の理論にしたがって，言語の心理学的研究，つまり概念と言語の平行性についての研究を展開した。Steinthal (1881) は，文学作品に現れた個人的および人工的な形式は思考の論理形式にしたがっているとの想定の下で独自の文体論を発展させた。Wundt (1901) は民族心理学の観点から言語と民族精神の平行的な関係を論じた。そして，そこには 2 つのタイプの言語構造，すなわち 'gegenständliches Denken'（関係的な考え方）に基づく 'attributiv'（限定的）な構造と，'zuständliches Denken'（静的な考え方）に基づく 'pradikativ'（述語的）な構造という 2 つの言語構造があるとした (Wundt 1901: 447)。彼は Homer においては多くの並列的な文が用いられ，それは客観的に関係性を持たせて出来事を記述するのに適していて，その文構造はギリシャ精神を示しているとした (Wundt 1901: 312)。

Wundt の理論に基づいて文体論研究を進めたのが Fritz Strohmeyer, Max Deutschbein そして Philipp Aronstein の 3 人である。

Strohmeyer は epithet の研究で有名である。Strohmeyer (1924: 91–97) によると，感情は一語のみにおいて，あるいはひとつの語群においてまとまりをなしている。それに対して，提言はひとつの思考の表現であるとした。したがって，Strohmeyer は前置形容詞とその名詞用法にひとつの概念を認めている一方で，後置形容詞には，ひとつの提言の価値があるとしている。彼は，フォーマル，インフォーマルを問わずフランス語からその例を集め，ドイツ語のそれらに相当する語と比較し，それによってフランス語の 'Gesamtbild'（全体像）をつかもうとした。

Max Deutschbein はその視点において心理学的である。彼はこう述べる：

> Um also der Eigenheit eines sprachlichen Phänomens einen besonderen sprachlichen Ausdruck zu geben (meist herbeigeführt durch starke Gefühlserregung), wählt die Sprache die stilistisch wertvollere Form, z. B.

das Abstraktum oder das substantivierte Adjektivum. Man vgl. z. B.:
　a）in der dunklen Nacht verlor er den Weg
　b）in der Dunkelheit der Nacht...
　c）im Dunkel der Nacht...　　　　　　　　（Deutschbein 1932: 108）

（それは，大抵は強い感情によって引き起こされるのだが）ある言語現象の特異性に特別な言語表現を与えるために，言語は文体的により価値の大きい形式，例えば，抽象名詞ないしは名詞化された形容詞などを選ぶ。以下を比較参照すること：
　a）暗い夜に，彼は道に迷った
　b）夜の暗がりの中で，彼は道に迷った
　c）夜の闇の中で，彼は道に迷った

Deutschbein はこういった例として *Beowulf* からの例をあげる：

483 Grendles gūþe *mid gryrum ecga*.
　グレンデルの攻撃 剣の恐怖でもって

ここでは，gryre（恐怖）が対格の gryrum として使用されているが，「恐ろしい剣」の形ではなく「剣の恐怖」という風に抽象名詞の gryre を用いて強い感情を表している。逆に名詞が形容詞的に用いられ出した例として，Deutschbein（1932: 108–109）は 'choice' 'dainty' 'commonplace' 'cheap'（本来は purchase の意味）のような抽象的名詞が形容詞となった例をあげる。いずれにせよ，初め新鮮であったこれらの語は，ステレオタイプ化することで，その文体的価値を失う。
　Philipp Aronstein は，英語の性質を調べる上で，英語が持っている特異性を見ることが大切であり，そのためには英語と他の言語の比較をすることが最良の方法であると述べる。したがって彼は，英語とドイツ語の比較研究を行う。彼によると，擬人化の用法はドイツ語よりも英語の方が少ない。これはイギリス国民が物事を客観的に見ることを好むことによる。例を見ると：

Der Satz 'Ein prächtiger Buchenwald nahm ihn auf' (Hauff, 'Das Bild des Kaisers') könnte English sehr wohl übersetzt werden: *A forest of magnificent beeches received him*. Ein solcher Ausdruck würde aber nicht wie im Deutschen sachlich sein, sondern poetisch, '*flowery*', wie der Engländer mit ironischer Ablehnung sagen würde, und an dieser Stelle unpassend klingen. Der englische Übersetzer (M. A. Faber, *Tauchnitz Collection of German Authors,* vol. 11, p. 160) sagt deshalb prosaisch: *He entered a forest of magnificent beeches*. Die englische Sprache, nicht der einzelne sprechende Engländer, ist weniger poetisch als die deutsche; sie neigt weniger zur Belebung des Leblosen, zur Personifikation, sie stützt sich weniger als diese auf Anschauung und Phantasie und mehr auf die kühle reflektierende Betrachtung. (Aronstein 1926: 11)

'Ein prächtiger Buchenwald nahm ihn auf'(見事なブナの森が彼を受け入れた)(Hauff, 'Das Bild des Kaisers'(「皇帝の肖像画」))という文は次のようにスムースに英語に翻訳できよう：*A forest of magnificent beeches received him*(大きなブナの木々が彼を迎えた)。しかしながら，そのような英語表現はドイツ語でのように散文的ではなく，イギリス人ならアイロニーを込めて拒絶して 'flowery'(華麗)と言うように，詩的で，そして，その表現はこの点において不適当である。したがって，このM. A. Faberというイギリスの翻訳家(M. A. Faber(訳) *Tauchnitz Collection of German Authors*, vol. 11, p. 160)は散文的に *He entered a forest of magnificent beeches* としている。個々のイギリス人がというわけではないが，一般的に英語という言語はドイツ語よりも詩的ではない。英語は，生命のないものに生気を与えたり，擬人化したりすることに対する関心がより低く，ドイツ語よりも直観は想像に頼るところが少なく，冷静な反省的観察に頼るところがより大きい。

WundtはHumbolt流の概念を取り入れて，内部言語形式は外部言語形式と同じくらい具体的で実在するものであり複雑な心理的結合体であるということ，また，この内部言語形式は本質的には言語そのものであって，それにはその言語を使用する民族の独特の精神が現れていて，このことは，他の現れ方，例えば建築や生活習慣や，社会的慣習，その歴史などにその民族精神が現れているのと同じことなのであるとした。Aronstein (1926) は，このWundt

の言葉を引用しながら，文体論を次のように定義する：

> Die Stilistik in diesem Sinne betrachtet also die Sprache als Organ und Ausdruck der Geistesorganisation eines Volkes und umfaβt alle ihre Erscheinungen, soweit sie diese widerspiegeln. （Aronstein 1926: 4）
> この意味での文体論は，したがって，言語を一つの民族の精神構造の器官であり表現であると見る。そして，文体論はその言語のあらゆる現象を，それが民族の精神構造を反映している限りにおいて，対象として取り上げる。

　ロマンス語圏ではBallyの記述的文体論の影響を受け，ドイツではVossler–Spitzer流の観念的で個人的な文体論の影響を受けたのに対して，20世紀初頭において，ロシアでは形式主義（Formalism）と呼ばれる新しい文学運動が起こった。
　19世紀における文体論の流れは上に述べたように，大きく2つに大別できよう。ひとつは文法的なるものから始まり，集団的なものを通って個人的なものに迫ろうとする流れ。2つ目は，逆の流れで，個人的なものから始まり，集団的なものを通って，文法的なものに迫ろうとする流れである。そして，この中間にWundt一派が位置する。
　言語の一般的構造（structure）の現れとしての文体に関心を示したSassure–Ballyのグループ，個人的（individual）な文体に関心を示したVossler–Spitzerの観念的文体論，集団的（collective）な民族的な文体に関心を示したWundtの心理学的文体論，それに最近の文体論的潮流をTaylor and Toolan（1996: 88）の樹形図に加えると，この文体論という語が広く使われ出した時代からの概略を描いてみることができる（図2）。
　20世紀に入ってからの文体論の発展は，大きく前半と後半の2つの時期に分けられる。20世紀の前半には，今見て来たように文体論はヨーロッパ大陸で発達し，後半には英米で発展を見た。こちらは次の節で述べる。
　この20世紀後半までの文体論に関しては，注意しておくべき事柄がひとつある。それは，このあたりまでは，研究者の間で文学テクストを現代で言

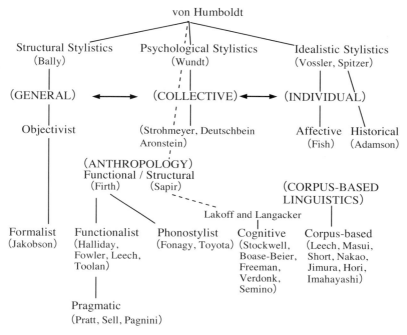

図2 文体論の歴史

う言語コーパスと見ていたということである．文学テクストにおける話し言葉の部分は，そのまま自然言語の話し言葉と同一であると見ていた．そのため，文体論の定義において，主に虚構の言語を対象とするといった表現はこの20世紀後半までは見られない．話された言葉と書かれた言葉の区別はしていたが，文学と非文学，あるいは虚構と非虚構，といった側面での言語使用域（register）の区別をしていないのである．上のBallyのpère Azan（アザンぢい）の会話の部分はフィクションであるため自然言語のやりとりとは特性を異にするという特別な認識はBallyにはなかった．

さて，上で述べたように，20世紀の前半には，Saussure–BallyとVossler–Spitzerの2つの大きな伝統的流れがあった．後半になると，アメリカでの記述言語学（Descriptive Linguistics）の興隆を受け，アメリカでその言語学の知見を借りた文体論が発達する．この後半は，我々と同時代の文体論研究の時

期である。

　現代の文体論研究の大枠は以下となる。1959 年に T. A. Sebeok がアメリカのインディアナ大学で文体論の大会を開催し，その成果は 1960 年に T. A. Sebeok (ed.) *Style in Language* としてまとめられた。ここに掲載された代表的論文は Roman Jakobson の 'Linguistics and Poetics'（言語学と詩学）で，これは，このインディアナ大学での文体論の大会で Jakobson が retrospect として話した内容が活字となったものである。この大会以後のいくつかの代表的文体論研究は Weber (1996) にまとめられている。

　1960 年代には代表的な言語理論の生成文法が，1970 年代になると談話分析と語用論が文体分析に有効な分析手段を提供した。1970 年代の文体論研究は，Fish (1980) の情動的文体論（Affective Stylistics）や Iser (1974) の受容理論（Reception Theory）のように，テクストよりは読者に重点を置いた文学理論に影響を受けた。最近は認知言語学（Cognitive Linguistics）や，その一分野である関連性理論（Relevance Theory）から文体論は影響を受けている。その流れを端的に表明したのが Ronald Carter である。1997 年には The Poetics and Linguistics Association (PALA) の第 17 回大会が 'New Rhetoric' という標語のもとでイギリスのノッティンガム・トレント大学で開催されたが，ここでノッティンガム大学の Ronald Carter の文体論研究における認知言語学的側面の重要性を強調し，'PAST 20 years—sociolinguistic-driven (discourse grammar) vs. PRESENT—psychologically-driven (poetics of mind)'（過去 20 年の，談話分析のような社会言語学志向の文体論と精神の詩学とでも呼べる心理学志向の文体論の大きな 2 つの流れ）と述べ，この認知理論への傾向を主張した。

　次の節では，こういった語学的文学言語の研究の流れをさらに詳しく述べてみたい。

2　文体論の共時的概観

　文学言語と非文学言語の違いが明確に意識されていなかった 20 世紀前半以前と異なり，後半では，その相違点は明確になっている。戦前に盛んであっ

た民族精神などの視点は姿を消し，言語使用域 (register) といった社会言語学的な枠組みがより明確になり，その最も個人的デリカシーの高い位置に狭い意味での文体論が位置する（「図1　文体論の位置付け」を参照）。

　Crystal and Davy (1969) は，文体をある種の言語変種とみなす：

> Linguistics is the academic discipline which studies language scientifically. Stylistics, studying certain aspects of language variation, is therefore essentially a part of this discipline.　　　　（Crystal and Davy 1969: 9）
> 言語学は言語を科学的に研究する学問分野である。文体論は，言語変種のある種の側面を研究するが，そのことにより，本質的に言語学の一部ということができる。

このように現代言語学の観点からの文体への伝統的なアプローチは，文体というものを言語的特徴の集合と見て，文学作品を方言などのような，ひとつの言語使用域 (register) と見るところにある。この点では，20世紀の前半と比べるとひとつの進展ではあるが，やはり，文学言語の特性を包括的にとらえるには至っていないと言える。同様に，文体に対する多くの文学的アプローチの方を見てみると，こちらは，文学言語を登場人物の思想を伝達する媒体ととらえ，結果として，特定の状況もしくは特定の文学テクストにおける特定の表現に焦点を当てて来た。そして，文学という文脈の中でその言語の一般的特徴をとらえては来なかった。

　文学テクストを対象とする狭い意味での文体論 (Stylistics) の目的は，そのテクストの形式的諸特徴を記述するにとどまらず，その形式的諸特徴がいかなる機能的な意味合いを，その文学テクストの解釈上持つのかを見て行くところにある。言い換えるならば，文体論の役割は文学的効果を言語的諸特徴と結びつけるところにある。そのような役割のために，文体の研究は方法論として言語学のモデルやその用語を用いることになり，その方法論は非文学テクストにも応用が可能なため，文体の研究は語法研究 (usage studies) がカバーする領域をも包含し，広い意味での文体論 (the study of style) が成立することとなった。以下では文学テクストを対象とする狭い意味での文体論

(Stylistics) と，自然言語を対象とし社会言語学の一部を構成する広い意味での文体の研究 (the study of style) がいかに重なるものであるかを見たい。

2.1　個人的文体 (Stylistics) と社会言語学 (Sociolinguistics) としての文体の研究 (the study of style) との相違

社会言語学的な広い意味での文体の研究は，一つの言語集団の言語慣習の一部としての言語テクストにおける形式的特徴を記述することにある。James Joyce の *Dubliners* の中に収められている 'Two Gallants' は 'The *grey warm* evening of August' (イタリクスは筆者) という形容詞を重ねた表現で始まっているが，これなどは語法的には of August は in August の方がより自然であるとしても，文体的にはこの作品全体の文体にふさわしく新聞などに多い記述的な散文の特徴を示している例と言えよう。They evening of (in) August, *grey and warm* と形容詞群を後置すれば詩的な文体となる。

　文体論においては，形容詞のそういった前置の用法 (The *grey warm* evening of August.)，もしくは後置の用法 (The evening of August, *grey and warm*.) は，それが文学テクストにおいて現れる限りにおいて，つまり，それがそのテクストの中で文学的意義を持つ限りにおいて狭い意味での文体論 (Stylistics) の問題である。そして，この用法は作者の文体という観点から，および，ある文学集団の一部としてのテクストの文体の観点から論じられる。

　もしそのテクストの言語的特性が社会における一つの集団もしくは一つの時代を反映していると見られるなら，その場合は，それら言語特徴は狭い意味での文体論 (Stylistics) ではなく，社会言語学的な文体の研究 (the study of style) の対象となる。例をあげてみよう。John Milton の *Paradise Lost* と *Paradise Regained* に 'battle proud' (不遜な戦い) という句が現れる (*Paradise Lost*, Book I, 43) が，これはラテン語から影響を受けた形容詞後置の例である。この両方の作品のタイトルは NP + Past Participle の形式を持っていて，'Lost' 'Regained' は名詞の後ろに置かれているが，これらは分詞形容詞として後ろに置かれたというよりは，むしろ，文体的に言って，現代英語の新聞のヘッドラインに用いられているような 'Kennedy Shot; Condition Critical' (ケネ

ディ撃たれる 重体）と同じ用法である。つまり，'Kennedy Shot' の 'Shot' のように 'Lost' と 'Regained' が分詞の叙述的用法（predicative use of past participle）として用いられているのである。日本語訳をあえてすれば 'Paradise Lost' は形容詞のように「失楽園」ではなく，叙述的に「楽園失われたり」とでもなろう。ただし 'Kennedy Shot' と 'Paradise Lost' は発生的には異なり，'Paradise Lost' の Lost を叙述的に名詞の後ろに置く用法は，新古典主義の文体（neoclassical style）で，ルネサンス期に広まった古典ラテン語や古典ギリシャ語の分詞に基づいた文体なのである。同種の例は 19 世紀の Percy B. Shelley の 'Prometheus Unbound'（プロメティス，解き放たれたり）や現代英語の 'Batman Unmasked'（バットマン，正体見えたり）に見られる。現代の用法では，形容詞は 'The Lost World'（秘境）のように通例名詞の前に置かれる。（ただし，ここでの 'Lost' の意味は 'Paradise Lost' の 'Lost' とは異なる。）'Paradise Lost' の 'Lost' は分詞形容詞ではなく分詞の叙述的用法であると述べたが，後置された分詞形容詞の方の例を Milton で探せば，'And to the fierce contention brought along / Innumerable force of spirits *armed* / That durst dislike his reign ...'（*Paradise Lost*, Book I, 100–103）（イタリクスは評者）（激しき戦いに，彼の支配を好まぬ数多の武装の天使らを導けり）における 'armed'（武装した）があるが，これは分詞形容詞なので，韻律の関係で '... has regained *lost* Paradise'（*Paradise Regained*, Book IV, 608）（イタリクスは評者）（失いし楽園を取り戻せり）や，'I who ... now sing / *Recovered* Paradise'（*Paradise Regained*, Book I, 1–3）（イタリクスは評者）（回復せし楽園を称えて謳う）のように前置されることもある。こういった分詞が前置されるか後置されるかなどは，それが Milton などの文学テクストに現れる限りにおいて文体論の問題であり——したがって，その用法は文学的価値判断に関係してくる——，そして，その用法は作者の文体，そのテクストの文体，そのテクストが属する集団の文体といった観点から論じられることになる。それに対して，それが新聞などの，社会におけるある集団に特有の，もしくはある時期の言語特徴であるならば，それは社会言語学的な意味での文体の研究において論じられることとなる。ただし，主語と動詞の一致の問題のように「選択」の余地のないものは文体論にも語法研究にも属さず，文法研究の問題となる。

これらの差はひとつには対象となる表現が，文学テクストか非文学テクストのどちらにあり，その表現の最終的な発信者（encoder）（＝作者）の言語的な特徴を論じるのか，それともその発信者の属する集団を論じるのかで変わってくる。文学テクスト内の表現を論じ，その最終的発信者（＝作者）の言語的特徴をとらえようとする場合は文体論の領域となる。
　こういった点をもう少し例をあげて見てみる。
　下の James Joyce の *Ulysses* で Leopold Bloom が語る台詞の中で，イタリクスの部分に注目してみよう。この部分で，Leopold Bloom は腹をすかした男の食べ方は怒った男の食べ方に似ていると感じている：

> Chump chop from the grill. Bolting to get it over. Sad booser's eyes. Bitten off more than he can chew. Am I like that? See ourselves as others see us. *Hungry man is an angry man*. Working tooth and jaw. Don't! O! A bone!　　　　　（Joyce *Ulysses*, Episode 8, 161）（イタリクスは評者）

焼いた羊の肉のかたまりだ。そいつを食べてしまおうとして丸呑みにする。悲しそうな酒飲みの目だ。食べ切れないほどのかたまりを食いちぎってやがる。俺もやはりこうだろうか？　他人がこちらを見る目で自分を見るがいい。腹がすけば腹が立つのさ。歯と顎を働かせて。やめろ！　あ！骨まで食べようとしている！

Staten (1997) によると *Ulysses* は身体的および言語的な解体が描かれている作品である。Staten はこう述べる：

> ... the digestive process is a form of decomposition, and in one sense *Ulysses* is a stomach or tomb in which language breaks down into its constituent units— ... mimesis as the isomorphism between two decompositional series, one involving language and the other the body.　　　（Staten 1997: 380–392）

消化する過程は解体の一形態である。そして，ある意味，*Ulysses* は胃袋ないしは墓のようなものであって，そこでは言語がその構成要素に分解される…いわば2つの解体作用は，ひとつは言語を，他方は身体に関係している同形をなしている擬態である。

'Hungry man is an angry man' においてはこの2つの解体作用が生じている箇所と言えよう。まず，'hungry' という語は，食べるという行為において消化と解体の両方に関係している。言語的解体の方はどうであろうか？ 'Hungry man is an angry man' は元来 'A hungry man is an angry man' という格言に由来している。*Ulysses* では最初の不定冠詞 'a' が略されている。あるいはこう言ってよければ，冠詞は言語化していないと言ってもよい。というのは，Joyce の意識の流れ (stream of consciousness) においては，言語規則に支配される以前の状態にある言語が記述されているからである。それによって身体と言語の不確実な状態が表現されている。上の文章では，名詞句は電報や新聞の見出しのように冠詞を持っていない。

'Hungry man is an angry man' は Leopold Bloom の内的独白 (interior monologues) の文体に沿っているように思われるが，この文章は Joyce の文脈においては文体的に意味を持つ表現である。そういった，ある作家においてのみ重要な文体的特徴——ここでは解体および／あるいは身体と言語が最終的な形を取る前の不確かな状態を表現するゼロ冠詞であるのだが——，その文体的特徴は狭い意味での文体論 (Stylistics) の研究対象であって社会言語学的な文体研究の対象ではない。もしゼロ冠詞が電報や新聞の見出しのような社会的な言語使用域との関連で論じられると，このゼロ冠詞という言語的特徴は後者の文体研究の対象となる。次の例もそうである。

河井 (1984: 62–69) で論じられた Charles Dickens の 'in short' (つまり) という句も，文学テクストで用いられた表現ながら，文体論 (Stylistics) と文体研究 (the study of style) の両方において重要なものである。これは Tanaka (1991: 27–37) で論じられた Fanny Burney 作の *Evelina* (1778) での用法についても同じである。例えば，そこで論じられた過去分詞の代わりの過去形 (having *rode* so far in vain) の用法なども，同じく両方の領域にまたがる。文体論の観点から見ると，河井の論じた *David Copperfield* の Micawber は，何か言おうとしてためらう時にこの句を用いる。そして，このためらいが，結果として，この人物は置かれた状況を的確に把握していないことを示している。この種の文学的に重要な文体を見る時には，*OED On-line* が 'in short' の定義として示している 'a summary statement' という視点だけでは不十分である。

それに対して，語法研究においては，この句は他の類似の句，例えば *OED On-line* の 'in short' の定義にあるような 'briefly' や 'concisely' との関連で論じられることになろう：

a. ***in short*** (also *Sc.* †***at short***): briefly, concisely. From the 18th c. onwards used only as parenthetical phrase, introducing or accompanying a summary statement of what has been previously said.

次の 'after' は社会言語学的な広い意味での文体研究 (the study of style) で扱われることとなる。この前置詞は元 Nottingham 大学教授の Walter Nash が，前に触れた The Poetics and Linguistics Association (PALA) というイギリスの文体論学会の第 17 回大会で論じたもので，下の例で見るように時間列において後という関係を示すというよりは原因・結果を示す前置詞として用いられている。Nash によればこれはタブロイド版新聞の特徴的な前置詞の使用法である：

A young tennis star has been zapped *after* developing 'Nintendo elbow' from playing too many computer games.（Nash 1997）（イタリクスは評者）
1 人の若いテニスの選手が，コンピュータゲームをやり過ぎて「ニンテンドー肘」が高じ，そのため敗退することとなった。

このタブロイド版では 'due to' や 'because of' など原因・結果を示す前置詞句の代わりに時間の経過を示す 'after' が用いられていて，それによって選手が Nintendo Wii Sports Tennis をし過ぎたために本番のテニスの試合で敗北したことが表現されている。このような用法はタブロイド版新聞の言語的特徴なのだが，もしこの表現が文学テクスト内のタブロイド版新聞の表現として現れると，その場合はこの 'after' のそのテクスト内での効果を見ることになる。

このように，英語での Stylistics という用語は時には広い意味で用いられており，その場合は文学テクストにおける使用法のみならず，社会言語学的

な文体研究をも包含する (Crystal and Davy 1969; Bex 1996)，この章の初めでも述べた，広い意味での文体論も包含する。この意味においては，文体論は大変広い領域をカバーすることになるので，むしろ社会言語学に極めて近くなる。

　ここで，註 2) で触れた，文体論と批評との関係も簡単に見ておく必要があろう。本来の狭義の，文学テクストの文体論について言えば，批評との比較では，文体論は文学を扱う点において批評の領域と重なるが，言語学的方法を用いる点において文学批評とは異なると言えよう。

　文体論 (Stylistics) はこのように文学および非文学テクストの分析に用いられるが，以下では現代における研究の代表的なものを見ておく。文学テクストを対象としているものは，ほとんどが狭義の文体論のみにおいて扱われるもので，van Dijk のように文学テクストを生成する理論から談話分析 (Discourse Analysis) への方向性を示す分析例は，社会言語学的な広義の文体論の色合いが濃くなる。

2.2　現代の文学言語研究の広がり

形式主義 (Formalism) と呼ばれる，文学言語の形式面を見れば文学言語の特質が分かるとしたグループが，戦前にロシアで現れ，ロシアフォルマリズム (Russian Formalism) と呼ばれた。この文体論は形式文体論 (Formal Stylistics) と呼んでもよい。彼らは，読み手の，テクスト内の媒体 (medium) の形式に対する意識を高める特徴を持ったものが文学作品であるとする。Shklovsky (1990: xviii–xix, 6–12) は異化 (estrangement (ostranenie) もしくは de-familiarization) が芸術作品一般の特質であるとする。詩では韻などが異化された要素となる。

　Fowler (1986: 72) は，このロシアフォルマリズム (Russian Formalism) の伝統にある 2 人のうちの 1 人である Jan Mukařovský を 'Prague School poetic theory' (プラーグ学派の詩学) を代表する者，Roman Jakobson を 'the founder of modern linguistic poetics' (現代言語学的詩学の創設者) と呼んだ。この Mukařovský–Jakobson 理論のうち前者 Mukařovský の中心的理論は前景化 (foregrounding) であり Jakobson のそれは平行性 (parallelism) である。

同じ形式主義 (Formalism) の系列にあり，最も注目されて来たのが，この Jakobson (1960) の詩学 (Poetics) と呼ばれる文学理論で，この原理は，上に述べた T. A. Sebeok (ed.) *Style in Language* (MIT Press, 1960) に収められた 'Linguistics and Poetics' (言語学と詩学) と題する論文に短く述べられている。すなわち，文学言語とはメッセージの形式に焦点化する機能を持った言語のことである：

> The set (*Einstellung*) toward the MESSAGE as such, focus on the message for its own sake, is the POETIC function of language.
> 　　　　　　　　　　　　　　　　　(Jakobson 1960: 356)（イタリクスは著者）
> メッセージそのものへの指向，メッセージそのものへの焦点合わせは，言語の詩的機能 poetic function である。
> 　　　　　　　　　　　　　　（川本茂雄（監）『一般言語学』みすず書房，1973）

続けて彼は，この特性は文学テクストにのみ内在する特性ではないと述べる：

> The poetic function is not the sole function of verbal art but only its dominant, determining function, whereas in all other verbal activities it acts as a subsidiary, accessory constituent.　　　(Jakobson 1960: 356)
> 詩的機能は言語芸術の唯一の機能ではなく，ただその支配的，決定的な機能であり，反面，他の言語活動においては副次的，付随的な成分として活動する。　　　　　　　　　　　　　　　　　　　　　　（川本同上）

　このメッセージ自身へ焦点化するメッセージが文学言語であるとする視点は Hymes (1968: 117) や Cook (1989: 24–26, 1994: 153–154) でも支持されている。このように形式文体論は文学および非文学の両領域を扱うことになり，Jakobson の唱える詩的機能 (poetic function) も文学テクストにのみ限られた機能ではないが，彼の詩学 (Poetics) は主に文学テクストである詩を扱っている。その分析例は Mouton から出ている彼の全集第 3 巻である *Selected Writings III: Poetry of Grammar and Grammar of Poetry* (Mouton, 1981) や *Language in Literature*（eds Krystyna Pomorska and Stephen Rudy）（Belknap, 1987）に，フランス語訳としては *Questions de Poétique*（Seuil, 1973）にまとめられている。最近では Margaret Thomas（ed.）*Roman Jakobson:Critical Assessments of Leading Linguists*（Routledge, 2014）（4 Volumes）の Vol. 3 は Jakobson の詩学（Poetics）に捧げられていて，彼の著作集である上記 *Selected Writings III: Poetry of Grammar and Grammar of Poetry* のレビューから始まり，書き下ろしの論文，過去の Jakobson の詩学（Poetics）を支持する，あるいは批判的な論文が掲載されている。Jakobson の主な分析例は，我が国では川本茂雄（編）『ロマーン・ヤーコブソン選集 3』（大修館，1985）で読むことができる。Jakobson の代表的な分析例は何と言っても人類学者の Claude Lévi-Strauss と共に Charles Baudelaire の 'Les Chats'（猫たち）を分析した Jakobosn and Lévi-Strauss（1962）であろう。これほど議論として取り上げられた語学的文学論はないのではなかろうか。次には Laurence Jones との共著で Shakespeare のソネット 'Th'Expence of Spirit' を論じた Jakobson and Jones（1970）であろうか。Jakobson の方法論については批判も起こった。2 つあげると，ひとつは Michael Toolan で，Toolan（2008）では Jakobson（1960）の詩学の中心部分を一言で言えば 'repetition lies at the core of verbal art'（反復が言語芸術の核にある）であるとしながら，Toolan は 'I am very doubtful of the possibility of reducing verbal art to "scientific" and rule-governed description and explanation'.（言語芸術を「科学的」で規則に支配された記述や説明に還元できるとは思わない。）としている。もう 1 人は Paul Werth で Werth（1976）では Jakobson の注目する詩的言語の反復を批判して次のように述べている：

> It seems quite clear that the various types of distribution countenanced by Jakobson as parallelistic and poetic…, appear in the unlikeliest of contexts (a telephone directory, for example, will display the most remarkable patterns of repetition in syntax, lexical items and phonology). Obviously the mere existence of such patterns guarantees neither their effectiveness nor their meaningfulness. （Werth 1976: 54）

ヤコブソンが平行的および詩的としている様々な形式の分布は，詩的と

はとても言えないような文脈で生ずる。(例えば電話帳は最も顕著に統語，語彙そして音韻面での反復を示す。) 明らかなことであるが，そういったパターンは，あるからといって，それらに効果も有意味性も保証しない。

このように述べ，続けて，言語は 'a finite ... inventory of signs' (60) (有限の記号の目録) から項目を選択するので，'repetition is a fundamental linguistic principle' (60) (反復は言語の基本的な原理である) として Jakobson の詩の原理を批判している。なお，花輪光 (編)『詩の記号学のために—シャルル・ボードレールの詩篇「猫たち」を巡って』(書肆風の薔薇, 1985) には，この Jakobson and Lévi-Strauss (1962) の 'Les Chats' (猫たち) の分析の訳と，それをめぐっての Michael Riffaterre, Georges Mounin, Nicolas Ruwet, Léon Cellier らの論文が収められていて，Jakobson の方法論を批判的に見る上で必読の書である。

　Jakobson が依拠した静的な形式論に対して，派生 (deribation) という動的な概念を導入した文法が Noam Chomsky による文文法 (sentence grammar) としての生成文法 (Generative Grammar) である。これに拠った文学言語の研究も 1970 年代には現れた。James P. Thorne がその 1 人で，Thorne (1970: 190–191) では Raymond Chandler の *The Lady in the Lake* を論じて，'*I Verb Phrase and I Verb Phrase*' (イタリクスは著者) が繰り返される高度に 'repetitive' (191) な文体と呼んでいいが，そのことは，表層で省略される 2 つ目の 1 人称主語が深層構造では存在することが分かって初めて了解されるとした。そしてこの反復が 'the mood of aimless, nervous agitation' (191) (何に向けられているとも知れない神経質な高ぶった気持ち) を伝えているとしている。生成文法 (Generative Grammar) を用いた文体分析は Jacobs and Rosenbaum (1971) という形でも現れたが，本家の生成文法そのものと異なり発展しなかった。ただ，このアプローチは次に見るように文学的文もしくは文学テクストそのものの生成を記述しようとするテクスト文法 (Text Grammar) へ引き継がれる。

　以下でテクスト (text) から談話 (discourse) へという流れを見て行くが，こ

の2つの類似した概念の定義をしておく必要がある。いくつかの定義がある中で Cook (1994) のものが分かりやすい：

> テクスト (text) の定義：'The linguistic forms in a stretch of language and those interpretations of them which do not vary with context'. (Cook 1994: 24)（言語のひとつの連鎖における言語形式，および文脈 (context) によって変化しない，それら形式の解釈のことである。）

> 談話 (discourse) の定義： "Discourse', as opposed to text is a coherent stretch of language in use, taking on meaning in context for its users, and perceived by them as purposeful, meaningful, and connected. This quality of perceived purpose, meaning and connection is known as 'coherence'. 'Discourse analysis' is the study and the explanation of this quality of coherence. A discourse is a coherent stretch of language'. (Cook 1994: 25)（Text に対する discourse とは，言語使用における一貫した (coherent) ひとつの言語の連鎖で，その言語使用者にとって context 内で意味を持ち，そしてその使用者によって意図と意味を持ち，連鎖している状態であると感じられるものを指す。この意図と意味と連鎖がある状態が「一貫性」(coherence) である。Discourse Analysis は，この一貫性の質についての研究と解明の作業である。ひとつの discourse は言語のひとつの一貫性を持った連鎖のことなのである。）

> 文脈 (context) の定義：'In the narrow sense it refers to (knowledge of) factors outside the text under consideration. In the broad sense it refers to (knowledge of) these factors and to (knowledge of) other parts of the text under consideration, sometimes referred to as 'co-text''. (Cook 1994: 24)（（文脈とは）狭い意味では，当該テクストの外部にある要素（の知識）を指す。広い意味では，文脈は，これらの要素（の知識）を指し，また時に 'co-text' と呼ばれる，当該のテクストの他の部分（の知識）を指す。）

これらをまとめるとテクストとは形式的なまとまり，つまり結束性（cohesion）を持った言語の連鎖で，談話とは文脈（context）内に置かれたテクストのことで，こちらは一貫性（coherence）に関係してくる。本書では各執筆者は概ねこの定義に沿った形でテクストを論じている。
　談話とテクストの関係で見ると，形式を論じるテクスト理論の方が先行して，それもヨーロッパ大陸でテクスト言語学（Text Linguistics）という形で発達した。全体として理論から文脈重視の自然言語の分析の方向性を取っていて，一貫して虚構の文学テクストについての成果は多くはない。出発点となったのはオランダの van Dijk（1972）で，この学位論文で彼は Chomsky の生成文法の影響のもと，文の集合を意味と形式の両面から統合する上位の構造としてマクロ構造（macrostructures）（＝textual deep structure），つまりテクストレベルでの深層構造，という概念を考えた（131ff.）。そして文学規則（literary rules）のもとで文学性（literariness）（van Dijk 1972: 163, 193）を持ったテクストを生成する文学テクスト文法（Literary Text Grammar）を提唱した。これらの概念を用いて，彼は Ross（1970）にならって T → Tql + Prop（T はテクスト，Tql は Test qualifier，Prop は Proposition），Tql → Perf + Mod（Perf は Performative，Mod は Modal）のモデルを考えた（301）。このうち Mod で Fiction か Fact かが決定される。この段階での，その方法論の問題点は，池上（1975: 465–466）でも指摘されているように，生成された文の集合が表層上でまとまった連鎖をなしているという保証はないということである。この点は Gerald Prince の Prince（1982: 145）は，生成された文間に物語性（narrativity）を要求している点で優れている。van Dijk（1976）では生成文法の枠組みではとらえ切れない多くの文学的現象があるとして統語理論から離れ始め，文学現象の説明に Grice（1975）の協調性の原則（Cooperative Principle）を紹介している。van Dijk（1977）では連続した命題間の一貫性（coherence）は，それらの指示する事実間に原因・結果のような関係性があることが前提となるという点を打ち出し，van Dijk（1972）の理想状態でのテクストの生成という視点から，より文脈を重視した方向に進んだ。その後は，さらに文脈中心の方向に進み，イデオロギー分析を目指す批評的談話分析（Critical Discourse Analysis）（CDA）の方向へ舵を切っている。例えば移民の話などでは，Labov and Waletzky（1967）の

ナラティブの分析の単位である「紛糾」(Complication) により重点が置かれるといった分析を行っている (van Dijk 1984, 1987)。その後 van Dijk (2005) ではラテン諸国でのレイシズムについて論じている。例えばメキシコでの 'racist discourse' (99) について，スペイン人とネイティブ・アメリカンの先祖を持つ混血スペイン人 'mestizos' について語る中産階級の女性の言葉を報告している。彼女によると，彼らは 'superstitious' で 'people who do not to work'，また 'uncivilized' で 'backward' である (100)。この本では文字テクストとしての新聞への言及はあるが，文学テクストへの言及は姿を消している。彼は全体の方向としては，理論から Norman Fairclough 達の批評的談話分析や Roger Fowler の批評的言語学 (Critical Linguistics) に近づいて行ったというべきであろう。

　van Dijk のようにナラティブの内容 (the narrated) の分析論者が談話分析に移行するのは大堀 (2004: 250–255) が指摘しているように，言語学において談話分析が興ったことと並行している。

　テクスト言語学 (Text Linguistics) は，ドイツとオランダでも生成文法の影響のもとで発展した (Petöfi (1973), Rieser (1973), Ihwe (1973))。しかし，テクストの生成は複雑になりすぎで，最終的にテクストを生成する 'formal systems' (Ihwe 1973: 302) はあきらめられた。こちらも文学テクストへの貢献は見るべきものがない。

　テクストの生成と並行して，テクストの表層に関心を向けた学者もいた。ひとつは結束性の概念で，それは Halliday and Hasan (1976) から始まる。その原理は Hendricks (1976), Quirk et al. (1985) でも詳しく論じられている。Halliday and Hasan (1976) で認められている結束性を実現する装置は 5 種類が考えられている：reference, ellipsis, substitution, lexical cohesion そして conjunction である。Cook (1989) では一貫性 (coherence) との関連から結束性 (cohesion) が論じられていて，大変分かりよい説明となっている。Cook (1989: 14) は結束性を「形式的な連結」(formal links) として (1) 言語形式 (verb forms), (2) 平行性 (parallelisms), (3) 指示方言 (referring expressions), (4) 反復および語彙連鎖 (repetitions and lexical chains) (語彙連鎖は反義性 (antonymy), 集合—元の関係 (set–element), 全体—部分の関係 (whole–part), スキーマ

(schema) から成る），(5) 置換 (substitution)，(6) 省略 (ellipsis)，(7) 接続 (conjunction) の 7 種類をあげている。Alan A. Milne の *Winnie-The-Pooh* は 'Here is Edward Bear, coming downstairs now, bump, bump, bump, on the back of his head' で始まり，'Edward Bear ... his head' には 'his' という代名詞が使われており（(3) 指示表現），それに加えて Edward Bear–head は (4) の語彙連鎖のうち全体―部分の関係にあると言えるが，その日本語訳の「クマくんが…頭を階段にぶつけながら」（石井桃子訳）ではクマ―頭の (4) の whole–part の関係しかないと分析することができる。この結束性に対して文脈的連結 (contextual links) と言えるものが一貫性 (coherence) で，結束性を実現する装置はなくても含意 (implicature) などで連結されている発話同士には一貫性 (coherence) があるとする。我が国の研究では Koguchi (2014) が Dickens の *A Tale of Two Cities* における人称代名詞を，この結束性の観点から数量的に分析している。結束性のひとつである反復は片見 (2011) において，中英語から近代英語にわたる説得の技法として研究されている。

　De Beaugrande and Dressler (1981) も同様にテクスト言語学の観点からテクストに迫っている。彼らはテクスト性 (textuality) の 7 つの基準を示している：結束性 (cohesion)，一貫性 (coherence)，意図性 (intentionality)，容認可能性 (acceptability)，情報性 (informativity)，場面性 (situationality)，テクスト間相互関連性 (intertextuality)。これらは Searle (1969: 33f.) にならった構成原理 (constitutive principles) で，彼らによるとこれら 7 つの基準を満たしたものがコミュニケーションとしての「ひとつのテクスト」(a text) ということになる。これらを満たした上でさらに，Searle (1969) にならってテクストによるコミュニケーションをコントロールする統制原理 (regulative principles) として効率性 (efficiency)，有効性 (effectiveness)，適切性 (appropriateness) を考えた。ただ文学テクストも非文学テクストも通常はこれらを満たしているので，ある作家の文体を論じる場合には，これらの条件がどのように応用されているかを見ることになろう。例えば，ある作家の文体は一貫性よりも形式的なまとまりである結束性に頼る傾向があるといった風に。

　全体として形式的なテクストへの関心から，文脈も含めた談話へと関心は移って来たと言えよう。文脈が考慮されるところから，当然そこに秘められ

たイデオロギーにも向けられるようになって行ったのである。この談話への関心は，次のナラティブの説明の後で詳しく述べる。その前に，ナラトロジー (Narratology) という形で発展したテクストそのものへの関心を見てみる。

テクストの形式の追究は，ナラティブの文法という形で発達した。20世紀後半でのナラティブ研究の発達に大きな影響を与えたのは，20世紀の前半に活躍したロシアの民族学者の Vladimir Propp (1968 [1928]) で，Propp (1968 [1928]) では登場人物 (dramatis personae) の物語中の機能 (functions) に基づいて，物語の類型論を展開した。現代風に言えば，登場人物の意味役割 (semantic roles) の研究を進め，物語の統語論 (彼によれば形態論) を展開した。彼は例えば The Swan-Geese Tale と呼ばれるロシアの民話は次の機能から成るとした (99): $\gamma^1\beta^1\delta^1 A^1 C \uparrow \{[DE^1 \text{ neg. F neg.}] / d^7 E^7 F^9\} G^4 K^1 \downarrow [Pr^1 D^1 E^1 F^9 = Rs^4]^3$。この中でたとえば β の機能は「家族の一員がいなくなること」で，これらの機能を同じくするものは個別の物語を超えて同一の役割をする。例えば以下の (1)〜(4) は別の物語に属しながらも同一の役割を持つ：

(1) A tsar gives an eagle to a hero. The eagle carries the hero away to another kingdom. / (2) An old man gives Súčenko a horse. The horse carries Súčenko away to another kingdom. / (3) A sorcerer gives Iván a little boat. The boat takes Iván to another kingdom. / (4) A princess gives Iván a ring. Young men appearing from out of the ring carry Iván away into another kingdom, and so forth.　　　　(Propp 1968 [1928]: 19–20)
(1) 皇帝がヒーローにワシを与える。ワシはヒーローを別の王国に連れて行く／(2) 一人の老人がスチェンコに馬を与える。馬はスチェンコを別の王国に連れて行く／(3) 魔法使いがイワンに小さな船を与える。船はイワンを別の王国に連れて行く／(4) お姫様がイワンに指輪を与える。指輪から現れた若者達がイワンを別の王国に連れて行く。

ブルガリア出身の Tzvetan Todorov は Boccaccio の中世物語集である *Décaméron* (『デカメロン』) の構造を Propp 同様に統語的観点 (後で述べる Greimas のように意味論的ではなく) から分析し，「レシ，物語」(the récit) の文

法の目的を次のように述べた：

> Notre objet est constitué par les actions telles que les organise un certain discours, appelé le récit　　　　　　　　　　　　　(Todorov 1969: 10)
> 我々の目的は，レシ (the récit) と呼ばれる談話 (discours) を構成する行為群にある

Todorov はナラティブの統語的側面に注目し，ナラティブは命題 (proposition)（例えば，«Jean vole de l'argent»（ジャンはお金を盗む），«Le roi tue son petit-fils»（王は孫を殺す）など）と，シークエンス (sequence) と呼ばれる命題の連鎖からなるとした (Todorov 1969: 19–20)。これをもとに彼は *Decameron* の中の，恋人を桶に隠す Peronella の物語を分析しているが，Jonathan Culler が Culler (1975) でその分析を短くまとめているのでそれを用いると次のようになる：

> X commits a misdeed → (socially required consequence) Y should punish X → X desires to avoid punishment and therefore acts to modify the situation → X is not punished　　　　　　　　(Culler 1975: 216)
> X が不当な行為をする → (社会的に要求された結果) Y は X を罰しなければならない → X は罰を逃れようとし，そのために状況を変えようとする → X は罰を逃れる

この分析によって Todorov は，この物語は，罰せられるべきでない者が罰せられようとした，失われた平衡性を取り戻す構造となっており，したがって，この物語の趣旨は社会に対する個人の優越を説いているとする。

　このアプローチにはいくつかの批判がある。Jonathan Culler からの批判としては，文化的モデル一般がこの形を取るので，こういった構造はこの物語に特徴的なものではないとする：'... anything that modifies a situation will receive the same structural description,...' (Culler 1975: 217)（状況を変えようとするものは，同様の構造を持つ）。たしかに「平衡性」の概念は先にあげた Propp (1968 [1928]: 92) でも「不幸からの回復」(liquidation of misfortune) と呼ばれ，

Lévi-Strauss (1972 [1958]: 224) の神話分析でも「媒介」(mediation) という概念で登場し，そこでは現実における越え難い対立 (生と死など) が物語という想像の中で解消されるとしているし，それは Aristotle (1995: 49) に始まり I. A. Richards に引き継がれる，芸術を通して人は心の平安を得るというカタルシス論 (catharsis) に通じるものがある (Richards 1926: 113, 245)。

Todorov への批判をもう 1 人あげる。Seymour Chatman は現代のフィクションは二項対立で成立していないとする：'The worlds of modern fiction and cinema are not two-valued, black and white, as are the Russian fairy tales and the *Decameron*'. (Chatman 1978: 92) (現代のフィクションや映画の世界は，ロシアの民話や『デカメロン』のような二項対立や白や黒の世界ではない。)

フランスの構造主義的ナラトロジストである Claude Bremond は体系文法 (Systemic Grammar) のシステム (system) のようなものをナラティブに導入して，話のあるポイントでは進む方向に選択肢を与え，Propp 流の線形モデルに動的な要素を持ち込んだ (Bremond 1964, 1966)。

こういったナラティブの統語論的分析は，現代の社会言語学者の William Labov による自然ナラティブの分析でも見られる。Labov and Waletzky (1967) は個人の経験を語るナラティブの分析を行い，次のような時系列的構造を発見した：

Orientation–Complication–Evaluation–Resolution–Coda
(Labov and Waletzky 1967: 32–41)
導入―紛糾―評価―解決―終結

ただし，Labov and Waletzky の社会言語学的分析は，その対象が自然ナラティブである点に注意をしないといけない。ここでは，'I had dogs that could do everything but talk'. (Labov and Waletzky 1967: 14) (話すこと以外なら何でもできる犬を数匹持っていた。) と語るナレーター (narrator) と，Hemingway の 'Cat in the Rain' で 'She held a big tortoise-shell cat pressed tight against her...' (170) (彼女は大きな三毛猫をしっかりと抱いていた) と語るナレーター (narrator) は性質が異なることに注意すべきである。前者では作者とナレーターは同一

であるが，後者ではこの2つは理論上別で，つまり後者のナレーターの背後には作者のHemingwayがいることを忘れてはならない。そうしないとLabov流のナラティブの分析をそのまま文学テクストに当てはめるということをしてしまうからである。文学のナラティブでは，ナレーターの語る世界の中で「紛糾」(Complication) に見えるものが，作者の視点からすると「評価」(Evaluation) や「解決」(Resolution) であったりすることがあるのである。

Propp, Todorov, Labov and Waletzkyとナラティブの統語論を見てきたが，これらの分析に共通する問題が，このナレーターと作者の二重性である。PropやTodorovの分析では発信者が1人の自然ナラティブと発信者が二重になっているフィクションのナラティブの区別をしていなかったし，LabovとWaletzky達はもともと，その分析は小説などの分析のためのものではないことは十分心得ていた[6]。

リトアニア生まれのフランスの記号学者 Algirdas J. Greimas の「行為者モデル」(Actantial Model) (Greimas: 1983 [1966]) は，Propp の機能的意味を持った「登場人物」(dramatis personae) に基づくもので，以下の3つのペアから成る6つの「行為者」(actants) からできている：(1) 主体 (Subject)（対象 (Object) に向けられる王子など）／対象 (Object)（救い出される姫）；(2) 派遣者 (Sender)（王など行為を促すもの）／受益者 (Receiver)（主体 (Subject) と対象 (Object) の結合で利益を得る者で王など）；(3) 助力者 (Helper)（魔法の剣，馬，勇気など）／対立者 (Opponent)（魔法使い，竜，王子の疲れなど）。Proppや Lévi-Strauss と同じく，Greimas もナラティブでは最初の秩序の破壊が起こった後，それが後に回復されるとした。

神話や民話の分析者達は，語られた物語世界内の構造を分析しようとした

---

6) 精神分析を文学テクストに応用する人達もこの間違いを犯している。Wilhelm Jensen の *Gradiva* を Freud (1990 [1907]) は精神分析的に論じ，主人公の妄想は，幼馴染の友人への抑圧された欲望から来ているとした。Wilson (1962 [1938]) は Henry James の *The Turn of the Screw* をフロイト流に分析し，この作品は Governess（住み込み家庭教師）が性的に抑圧されているため幽霊を作り上げ，自分のフラストレーションを隠蔽しようとしているとしている。この2つの分析は自然ナラティブと虚構ナラティブの混同から生じていて，誤って作品中のナレーターをあたかも現実世界のナレーターのようにひとつの人格を持った者として扱っている。

のであって，その物語世界をメッセージとする談話の構造ではない。これは自然言語の談話や虚構言語の文学テクストと異なり，メッセージの発信者（文学作品の場合は作者）が不明なため，このような方法論が取られることとなったのである。

　先に大堀（2004: 250–255）を引用して，「語られるもの」（the narrated）から「語り」（narration）への研究のシフトが起こったのは談話分析の発達によるということを述べたが，Gérard Genette は，この点に焦点を当てたフランスの代表的ナラトロジストの1人である。Genette（1980 [1972], 1988 [1983]）ではテクストを3つの垂直的ナラティブレベルに分けて，その複数性を強調した。3つのレベルとは次の通りである。Genette が例として用いている Abbé Prévost の *Manon Lescaut* から例をあげてみる：

（1）物語世界外的（extradiegetic）：*Manon Lescau* 内のナレーターであり「私」である Renoncour 侯爵が「作者」として回想録を書く行為
（2）物語世界的（diegetic），もしくは物語世界内的（intradiegetic）：Renoncour 侯爵の回想録の中で語られた出来事で，第2のナレーターであり Manon に惚れた騎士の Des Grieux が，Renoncour 侯爵に向かって顛末を語る行為が，その出来事にあたる。ナレーターの Des Grieux や，ナレーティー（narratee）である Renoncour 侯爵，彼が Pacy の街で見た Manon はこの世界にいる
（3）メタ物語世界的（metadiegetic）：騎士 Des Grieux が Renoncour 侯爵に向かって語った出来事で，Des Grieux 自身や Manon や他の登場人物などはこの世界にいる

この枠組みは，いわゆる枠物語を論じるのに適していよう。ただ（3）の meta-diegetic なレベルで登場する人物がまた別の出来事を語った場合，さらに（4）のレベルを設定するのかなど問題点がある。基本的には，発信者（encoder）としての実際の作者と，作者が虚構として語る内容としての虚構の世界が存在し，ナレーターはこの後者の世界に含まれる。ただ，Short（1996: 260）が述べているように1人称ナレーター（first-person narrator）の場合は物語世界内の

登場人物―登場人物 (character–character) のレベルに近づき，3人称ナレーター (third-person narrator) の場合は作者―読者 (author–reader) の物語世界外のレベルに近づく。この Short のような意見はあるにしても，基本的には，発信者 (encoder) (＝作者)―受信者 (decoder) (＝読者) のレベルと，発信者によって語られる虚構の世界 (the narrated) という，2つのレベルのみが存在すると思われる。

ちなみに Susan S. Lanser は，虚構テクストの外側に Lanser (1981) で「虚構テクスト外の声」(extrafictional voice) と呼ぶレベルを設定した。Lanser によればこの「虚構テクスト外の声」がテクストが作り出す様々な声を最終的に支配していて，この最終的な支配権を持つ声は Wayne C. Booth が Booth (1961) で導入した「含意された作者」(Implied Author) と同一であるとした[7]：

... the narrating voice is equated with the textual author (the extrafictional voice or «implied author») unless a different case is marked—signaled—by the text. What is important here is that from the extrafictional voice provides the information to formulate an 'implied' author.

(Lanser 1981: 151)

語る声は，当該テクストによって明確となっているか，もしくは記号的に示されている場合を除き，テクストの作者 (虚構テクスト外の声もし

---

[7]「含意された作者」(Implied Author) というのは Booth (1961) に始まるが，テクスト中心の New Criticism (新批評) が興るに連れて実在の作者が後退し，替わりに，テクストから得られる情報に基づいて読者が構築する「含意された作者」が考え出された。Leech and Short (1981) および Short (1996) で示された虚構談話の枠組みでは「含意された作者」の概念は不要とされている。Toolan (1988: 78) も '... the pictures we have of authors are always constructions, so that all authors are, if you like, "inferred authors"'. (作者について我々が描く像は常に作り出されたものであるので，全ての作者は，もしこう呼んでよければ「推論された作者」である。) として，含意された作者という概念に反対している。Fludernik (1993: 61–64) でも不要とされている。筆者も単に「作者」としてよいと思われる。というのが，現代作家のようにその作家に関する情報が多く手に入る場合 (Booth の言う作者) と，Shakespeare のようにほとんど手に入らず，作品から推論して作者像を構築しなければならない場合 (Booth の言う含意された作者) とがあっても，手に入る情報量は相対的なものであるので，実際問題として両者の間には明確な違いを認められないからである。

くは「含意された作者」）と同一である。ここで重要なことは虚構テクスト外の声は含意された作者を形作るための情報を提供していることである。

ナラトロジーと言えば，Monika Fludernik も重要である。Fludernik (2009) では「全知全能」(omniscience) を示すナレーター，Stanzel (1984 [1979]) の用語では「作者的ナレーター」(an authorial narrator) は，フィクションの世界の一部ではなく，その上に立つ。先にあげた Genette の用語で言えば「物語に参加しない，物語世界外的ナレーター」(a heterodiegetic and extradiegetic narrator figure) (135) であるとされる。George Eliot の *Silas Marner* や Henry Fielding の *Joseph Andrews* のナレーターがこれにあたる。このタイプのナレーターは，19世紀に起こり20世紀に発達した，登場人物の知覚を通してフィクションの世界を見る「反射体モードのナラティブ」(reflector-mode narrative) (130) の技法に取って代わられる。モダニズム (modernism) の代表とされる James Joyce の *A Portrait of the Artist as a Young Man* や Henry James の短編ではナレーターが全知全能ではなく，この「反射体モードのナラティブ」であると Fludernik は主張する。ナレーターの歴史的発達に関しては，本書の論文解題で取り上げた Saito Yoshifumi 'Fiction as historical discourse: Diachronic analysis of the narrative structures of English fiction' (*POETICA* 58, 2001) でも詳しく論じられている。ナラトロジーの中でも，道木 (2009) は，アイルランドというコンテクストの中に位置する一種の記号として，James Joyce の作品の中で生きる人々を論じている。

ナラトロジーの包括的なものとしては David Herman の編になる *Narratologies: New Perspectives on Narrative Analysis* (Ohio State University Press, 1999)，David Herman, Manfred Jahn and Marie-Laure Ryan（著）*Routledge Encyclopedia of Narrative Theory* (Routledge, 2007) と H. Porter Abbott（著）*The Cambridge Introduction to Narrative* (Cambridge University Press, 2002) がある。

ナラトロジーにおいても，物語世界である「語られた世界」(the narrated) から，メッセージの発信者およびそのメッセージの形に重点が移って来てい

るのが分かるが，それはこの分野でも，虚構テクスト内での談話とは言え，研究対象が談話の方向へ移って来ているのである。

　談話分析は自然言語の文脈を考慮に入れるため，文学テクストへの応用が難しい部分もあるが，大いに期待できる分野である。例えば，山崎（2014）では自然言語の談話における because の用法に着目し，「並列的な *because* 節が，相手の反応に応じて即興的に行うターンの維持・獲得・拡張などのマネジメント…に深く関わっている」(45) とする。このような視点は，文学テクストにおける登場人物の characterization の研究への応用が期待される。談話分析が応用されている例としては，我が国では，第2部で解題を行った福元（2010）が Shakespeare 作品の 'Look you' 等の呼びかけ語に着目し，その談話標識的機能の有無を論じている。松井（2010）も同じく談話標識を論じていて，J. D. Salinger の *The Cather in the Rye* における 'I mean' の機能を分析している。平山（2012）では，類似の，'me thinks' の考察を15世紀の書簡集である *The Paston Letters*（『パストン家書簡集』）において行っている。脇本（2001）は Goldsmith の *The Vicar of Wakefield* における会話部の考察を行っている。Sando（2002）は松井（2010）と同じく *The Catcher in the Rye* における Holden の speech を論じている。

　この談話の観点から，広い意味での文体論として通常の話（common talk）にも文学テクストに特有の創造性（creativity）があると主張するのは Carter（2004）である。彼は次のように述べて，文学テクストに見られる創造性は文学という分野に限られたものではなく，日常言語の中にも広く行き渡っているとしている：

> ... the ubiquity of creative language ... creativity is an all-pervasive feature of everyday language.　　　　　　　　　　　(Carter 2004: 13)
> 創造的言語の偏在性…創造性は日常言語に深く浸透したものなのである。

　このように述べて，文学テクストのスタイルに特有とされて来た創造性を，次のような日常言語にも見出している：

For example, a petrol company in Ireland goes by the name of *Emerald Oil*. Interpretation of the effects of this name require a knowledge that green (emerald) is the colour associated with Ireland and that Ireland is often referred to as the 'Emerald Isle', but most particularly that an Irish accent renders the word 'isle' as 'oil', ... (Carter 2004: 21)

例えば，アイルランドの石油会社で *Emerald Oil* と呼ばれているものがある。この名前の持つ効果の解釈には緑色「エメラルド」はアイルランドに結びついた色であり，アイルランドはしばしば 'Emerald Isle' (エメラルド色の島) と呼ばれることがあることを知っておく必要がある。それに加えて，アイルランドのアクセントでは 'isle' (島) を 'oil' (オイル) と発音することを知っておかねばならない

Rebecca Hughes も，また，自然言語の特徴を文学言語の中に見て，両者の密接なつながりを主張する。彼女は自然言語に通常存在する談話上の特徴である「通常の非流暢的特徴」(normal non-fluency features) は文学言語では現れないが，もし現れるとどうなるかを論じて，その文学テクストの発話は次のような特徴を示すことになるとしている：

hightened emotion ... such as anger, fear or uncertainty ... mental disturbance (Hughes 1996: 52)
高ぶった感情，例えば怒りや恐れ，あるいは不安など…心理的な動揺

この指摘は大変重要で，自然の発話ではあるのが当然の特徴ながら（したがって無いとおかしい），無いのが普通の文学テクストで現れると「高ぶった感情」や「とまどい」などを示してしまうというのである。この説を用いると，次の Dickens の *David Copperfield* からの一節は「通常の非流暢的特徴」のひとつである「割り込み」(interruption) の好例と言えよう：

"You were speaking about its being a girl," said Miss Betsey. "I have no doubt it will be a girl. I have a presentiment that it might be a girl. Now child, from the moment of the birth of this girl—"

"Perhaps boy," my mother took the liberty of putting in. (7)
　「そういえば，生まれる子は女の子らしいとお言いだったね」とミス・ベッチーが言った。
　「そうだ，きっと女の子だよ。なんだか，そうに違いないって気がするんだもの。でね，お前，女の子が生まれたら，すぐそのときからね…」
　「いいえ，多分男の子だと思うんですの」母は思いきって言葉を挟(はさ)んだ。
　　　　　　（中野好夫（訳）『デイヴィッド・コパフィールド』（1）新潮文庫，1967）

「割り込み」（interruption）は自然談話では通常の特徴なので，自然談話で現れても何も示さないが，ここではDavidの母の高ぶった感情を示しているのである。

　談話の分析は言語学から発達したため自然言語の分析が中心ながら，文学テクストの分析にも影響を及ぼしている。1950年代のアメリカの言語学者Zelig Harrisによる自然言語の研究から発達した談話分析は，イギリスではThe Birmingham School of Discourse Analysisと呼ばれる，Sinclair et al. (1972) やCoulthard (1985) を中心とした，教師と生徒達の間で交わされるやりとりの分析へと発展した。こちらは全体の構造をtop-down的に論じる形を取る。アメリカでは会話分析（Conversation Analysis）の名称で呼ばれ，逆にbottom-up式に個々の言語現象から見て行き全体の構造に迫ろうとした。例えばFAMILYといった「成員カテゴリー化装置」（membership categorization devices）でboyやmotherといった家族関係の語句のグルーピングを行い，テクスト内にまとまりを見出して行く。こういった試みの中心にいたのがSacks (1972) やGumperz (1972) を中心としたグループで，これにイギリスのCoulthard (1985) も加わる。

　テクスト一般における談話分析とは「批評的」（critical）なものと「非批評的」（non-critical）なものの2つがある。前者として批評的談話分析（Critical Discourse Analysis (CDA)）をあげることができる。CDAとはToolan (1997: 83) によれば 'one form of a justifiably reflective and suspicious inspection of how discourses shape and frame us'（どのように談話が我々を形作り，また型には

めるかの考察を，当然のことながら深く批判的に行うひとつの方法）で，Widdowson (1995: 157) が指摘しているように，テクストに込められた 'ideological bias'（イデオロギー上の偏見）を取り出そうとする傾向がある。CDA は主に自然言語のテクストの分析に重点を置いているので，文体論とは領域を異にしている。CDA の創始者としては Lancaster 大学の Norman Fairclough をあげることができよう。Fairclough (2001 [1989]) は言語と社会制度との関係を論じたものであり，Fairclough (2000) は Tony Blair と Gordon Brown 両党首が率いた時期のイギリス労働党が用いるレトリックを論じたものである。Toolan (1997) は CDA は 'thoroughness and strength of evidence in its argumentation' (83)（議論において徹底性と証拠上の確かさ）が必要であるとしながらも 'I am very much more in favour of CDA' (84)（CDA に私は好意的である）としている。Fairclough (2001 [1989]) の初版より遡ること 10 年前，East Anglia 大学の Roger Fowler が Fowler et al. (1979) で提唱した批評的言語学（Critical Linguistics）も CDA と同一の方法論と射程を持つと言えよう。その Fowler は Fowler (1991) で，それは副題として *Discourse and Ideology in the Press* とあるように，新聞のイデオロギーを扱っている。例えば *The Sun* の 1985 年 12 月 31 日版の社説では次のような文が載っている：'Yet there is no mention of Bob Geldof in the *dreary* New Year Honours List'. (Fowler 1991: 38)（イタリクスは著者）（しかし，ボブ・ゲルドルフの名前はこの退屈な新年勲爵士団リストにはない）。Bob Geldof はアイルランド出身の慈善家のミュージシャンである。ここで用いられている 'dreary'（退屈な）という形容詞は 'projecting values on the subjects of discourse' (41)（談話の主題に価値観を投影している）とする。また新聞の見出しに 'PC shot boy from 9 inches' (71)（PC は Police Constable の略で「巡査」に相当）のように 'shot' という行為の動作主（Agent）が明示的に示されていれば，それは 'implying clear responsibility' (78)（（行為者の）責任が明確であることを含意する）という働きがある。それに対して 'A boy of five was shot' のように受動文にして動作主を隠すと 'mitigate the accusation' (72)（非難を和らげる）とする。'Allege'（断言する）の代わりに 'allegation' (79)（断言）とする名詞化も，参加者（participants）が非明示的になり，'time'（時）や 'modality'（法性）の表示を欠く 'mystification' (80)（あいまい化）する働きを

持った構文となる。もちろん受け身構文も名詞化も科学論文で発達し，個々の科学者によらない客観性を示す用法として受け入れられて来たが，新聞などで社会的出来事を示すため用いられると書き手のイデオロギーを示すようになる。理論的には Halliday and Martin (1993) を参照のこと。このように CDA は非文学の分析をもっぱらとするのではあるが，Fowler (1995) では社会的視点を持つ George Orwell の文学テクストを分析することで，テクストに込められたイデオロギーを抉り出そうとしていて，CDA の手法が文学に当てはまらないわけではない。Fowler (1995: 168) には，Orwell の *Animal Farm* は 'impersonal'（非人称的）で 'a personal voice'（個人的声）もしくは 'a dominating narrator'（支配的ナレーター）の存在が希薄になっていて，それはテクスト外の読者に語りかける単数や複数の 1 人称ナレーターが存在せず，'those kinds of'（そういった）のような一般化が無く，modality（法性）に関しては判断や評価を示す 'may' や 'should' などが少ないなどで実現されている，とある。我が国では Sakauchi (2004) などがこの流れに連なる。

　フェミニスト文体論 (Feminist Stylistics) も，この CDA と呼ばれる批評的談話分析のひとつと考えることができる。フェミニズム文学は 19 世紀後半から 20 世紀前半に活躍したイギリスの作家 Virginia Woolf に始まり，その哲学的面は 20 世紀を通して活躍したフランスの哲学者 Simone de Beauvoir から始まるとされているが，フェミニズムが言語論として論じられ始めたのは 1970 年に入ってからである。Lakoff (1975) と Mills (1995)，そして Tannen (1990, 1994) を，その代表的なものとしてあげることができよう。その分析は，CDA 同様，自然言語に向けられており，我々が言語を操るその仕方には制約があるとするが，文学テクストにも 'phallocentric'（男性中心主義的）な傾向が表れているとする。こういった点は，隠れたイデオロギーをテクストの中に読み取るということなので，批評的言語学や CDA の一分野と考えることができよう。

　この文学テクストにイデオロギーを読み取るという傾向はポスト構造主義の文学理論にもうかがえる。Terry Eagleton もその 1 人である。彼の考える，言語の集合としての文学テクストとは社会に根ざしたもので，意味はそういっ

たテクストと密接に結びついている。彼によれば文学的価値とは言語のイデオロギー的な使用のことである：

> What we have uncovered so far, then, is "that these value-judgements themselves have a close relation to social ideologies".
> (Eagleton 1983: 16)

したがって，我々が今まで明らかにして来たことは，これらの価値判断自身は社会的なイデオロギーと密接な関係にある。

20世紀を通して活躍したフランスの言語学者 Émile Benveniste は，言語とは発信者の I と受信者の you の間に意味が形成されるシステムのことであるとした (Benveniste 1966: 260)。ロシアの哲学者である Mikhail Bakhtin はこの Benveniste に影響を受けながら，発信者よりも受信者の you を重視した。彼によれば Tolstoy の作品では，作者の言葉は主人公について語っている (Bakhtin 1984 [1929]): 56)，それに対して，Dostoevsky の作品では作者は主人公にあたる人物について語っているのではなく，その人物と共に語っている (Bakhtin 1984 [1929]: 63) とする。ただ，ここで彼の言う作者とはナレーターのことで，自然言語のコミュニケーションの枠組みを論じた Benveniste の影響を受けたために，Bakhtin は物語の語り手であるナレーターを，そのメッセージの発信者 (encoder) の I，つまり作者であると思いこんでいる。Dostoevsky の作品はどれほど 'dialogic'（対話的）であろうとも Tolstoy の作品の持つコミュニケーションの枠組みと変わらず，作者が人物と共に語るというのは比喩でなければ錯覚である。

Benveniste の発信者 I と受信者 you の間で成立するコミュニケーションの枠組みで述べると，Roland Barthes のポスト構造主義的文学テクスト分析は Bakhtin よりもさらに進んで，Barthes (1968 [1967]) の «La mort de l'auteur»（「作者の死」）と題する論文では受信者の you を重視し，発信者 I は死んだとした。したがって作者の伝記的事実は意味を持たないことになる。Barthes によると全ての人が意味を作り出し，したがってテクスト内の意味は複数存在し，様々な読みが可能となる。テクスト内のコードさえも複数である。19世

紀のフランスの作家である Honoré de Balzac の *Sarrasine*(『サラジーヌ』)という作品を分析した，1970年出版の *S/Z* で Barthes は，この作品には「行動のコード」(Code des Actions)，「解釈学的コード」(Code herméneutique)，「文化的あるいは参照のコード」(Codes culturels ou de références)，「意味素，すなわち，コノテーションの記号内容」(Les Sèmes ou signifies de connotation)，「象徴の場」(Le Champ symbolique) の5つのコードがあるとした。これらのコードを用いて彼は *Sarrasine* の最初の一文を分析している。Barthes (1970) に掲載されている *Sarrasine* の書き出しはこうである:

> J'étais plongé dans une de ces rêveries profondes qui saisissent tout le monde, même un homme frivole, au sein des fêtes les plus tumultueuses.
> (Barthes 1970: 227)

> 私は深い夢想に耽っていた。それは，もっとも騒々しい宴会の中でも，すべての人を，軽薄な男でさえも捉えるあの夢想であった。
> (沢崎浩平(訳)『S/Z バルザック「サラジーヌ」の構造分析』みすず書房, 1993)

Sarrasine というタイトルから，これは人物の名前であると分かる。これが解釈学的(herméneutique)コードで，これによって「サラジーヌとはだれか?」という謎を提供することになる。さらに，この名前は *-e* で終わっており，このことからこの名前は女性の名前であると分かる。象徴的(symbolique)コードでは 'rêveries'(夢想) というのは現実と対比されている。このようにして，テクスト内の5つのコードを探りながら *Sarrasine* に Balzac が本来は抱いていなかったかも知れない意味を付与していく。Barthes は意味の複数性は全てのテクストに内在していると主張する。彼はこのように深く隠された意味をテクスト内に読み取る自由が読者の側にあることを示しながら，また，そこにテクストを読む 'plaisir'(快楽) が存在するとする。

伝統的な学問からの Barthes への反論を一つ。チョーサー学者である Derek Pearsall は，Pearsall (1992) で，以下のように述べて生身の人間である作者の人生の情報の重要性を述べている:

... I have to assert ... that the experience of writers' lives, outer and inner, is the matter of their writings in a most significant manner. Knowledge of a writer's life does not "explain" his writings,... but it does provide an important context for understanding them. I do not imagine that MM. Foucault and Barthes,... would wish ... to think of their own texts as detached from their own persons,... and they would acknowledge how what they write is the product of what they themselves are and have benn and are desirous of being. (Pearsall 1992: 4–5)

…こう主張しなければならない。すなわち書き手が人生で経験したことは，外面的なことであれ内面的なことであれ，きわめて重要な意味において，その書き物の内容そのものなのである。書き手がどのような人生を生きたかを知っておくことは，その書いたものを説明しないとしても，その書いたものを理解する上で重要な文脈を提供するのである。私はフーコー氏やバルト氏が，自らが書いたものが彼ら自身から引き離された存在だとは思わないであろうし…彼らは，いかに彼らが書いたものが，自らあるところのもの，あって来たところのもの，そして，あろうと望むところのものであることを認めるであろう。

　19世紀から20世紀前半までの作者に意味の源泉があるとするテクスト理論に続いて，20世紀中間以降は新批評 (New Criticism) や Roman Jakobosn の構造主義文学理論におけるように，作者からテクストである作品に焦点を移した。意味の源泉はテクストであるとしたのである。やがて，閉じた概念としての構造主義の言うテクストは他のテクストや読者には開かれているということになり始める。そして今見たように，Barthes は生身の作者を「死んだ」とすることで作者を追放し，さらには構造主義が唱えていた有機的統一体としてのテクストも捨て，意味の源泉はテクストの受信者に在りとしたのである。
　情動的文体論 (Affective Stylistics) は少し趣を異にする。批評家がある種の表現へ反応するためには，その批評家の感情的な反応が不可欠だとする，批評家の感情に基づいた文体論のことである。Weber (1996) によるとこの情動的文体論の提唱者の1人は Stanley Fish (Fish 1980) である。情動的文体論者

にとっては形式的に自己完結した文学テクストは存在しない．文学テクストは読まれて，つまり，感情的な反応を持って読まれて初めて存在する．批評家は読者であるので，やはり読者中心主義と言ってよかろう．同じく読者中心の理論を立てた Iser (1974 [1972]) との違いを述べると，Fish は読むという経験は全ての読者に共通であるとするが，美学的反応理論 (Theory of Aesthetic Response) の提唱者である Iser (1974 [1972]) は Fish の情動的文体論から分離し，文学テクストの中のギャップ (gaps) は異なる読者が異なる形で読んで埋めると主張する．

　社会的なコミュニケーション手段としての音声言語の研究から文学テクストに光を当てているのが，音声文体論 (Phonostylistics) である．Quirk (1982: vii) では 'a style of pronunciation' (発音のスタイル) という表現も用いられている．言語の音声上のスタイルに注目した豊田昌倫は，豊田 (1981) において文体は語や文のレベルにおいてだけではなく，あらゆる言語レベルにおいて論じることができるとして，音韻から文に至るレベルでの分析を行い音声面を文体論に含めている．彼は音声面での文体を特に重視し（豊田 2012, 2013a, 2013b, 2014），Toyota (1981) のひとつの章は音声面での文体分析にさかれている．彼は，どのように実際の社会方言と地理的方言が文学作品に反映されているかを分析することによって，文学と非文学の文体の双方に光を当てている．本書でも我が国の論文改題において『英語青年』に「現代英語のスタイル」として連載された豊田 (1997–1998) を取り上げている．この文体分析の方法は Ivan Fónagy (Fónagy 1991) に始まると言っていいであろう．最新の音声文体論の論文は Jobert (2014) に見ることができる．

　Roman Jakobson が行ったように作品から言語形式を客観的に引き出すという流れを，Jakobson 自身は言語の詩的機能に注目していると言っているが，別の機能主義言語学から機能主義的な文体論が発達して来た．

　その別の機能主義的文体論 (Functional Stylistics) の主要な提唱者はもちろん M. A. K. Halliday である．Halliday の体系機能文法の枠組みを，その言語学的批評理論に取り入れている Roger Fowler も機能主義的文体論者の 1 人と見ていい (Taylor and Toolan 1996: 89)．文体分析の一例として，Halliday (1971) は，William Golding の *The Inheritors* は 'clauses of action, location or mental process'（動作，位置あるいは心的過程を表す節）を効果的に用いていて，心的過程を表す節に関しては，'is expressed by a finite verb in simple past tense'（単純過去時制の定形動詞によって表現されており），ほとんど 'all of the action clauses describe simple movements (*turn*, *rise*, *hold*, *reach*, *throw forward*, etc.'（全ての動作を表す節は単純な動き (*turn*, *rise*, *hold*, *reach*, *throw forward*) を描写している）。それによって，小説を支配しているネアンデルタール人の世界観を作り出しているとする。

　他の機能主義的文体論者としては Hausenblas (1993) と Chloupek (1993) がいる。前者は，'conveyance and exchange of information'（情報の伝達と交換）がなされるコミュニケーションの構造は文学テクストの中で実現しており，そして 'thematic means'（主題的手段）は '"carried" by linguistic means, constitute a higher level of the semantic structure of communication' (Hausenblas 1993: 52–53)（言語的手段によって「運ばれ」，そして高度なコミュニケーションの意味構造を構成する）と主張する。Hausenblas は高度な意味レベルを設定したことで，それをしなかった Halliday や Fowler とは異なっている。この種の，高度なレベルの構造は，本書の論文解題でも取り上げてある Kikuchi (2010) での *Hamlet* 論でも論じられている。この構造は文学テクストにおける意味作用を研究するに際しては不可欠の視点である。Chloupek (1993: 113) が 'functional styles'（機能主義的文体）を 'relatively established sets of means of expression intended for the basic function of communication'（コミュニケーションの基本的機能を果たすための比較的確立された表現手段のまとまり）と規定しているように，Hausenblas は，例えば，'the motive of sharing grief which is an essential component of a letter or telegram of condolence'（弔辞の電文の基本的要素である悲しみを共有しようとする動機）は様々な言語的手段で表現でき，またそのうちのいくつかのものは確立していると主張する。もしこの種の機能的文体を慣習的と表現するなら，非慣習的で作者に特有な機能的文体も論じることができよう。

　機能的 (functional) という概念に関係のある文体論として文学語用論 (Literary Pragmatics) がある。この理論では，例えば，Sell (1991: 223) が述べているように，ポライトネスは，その表現のある文脈の中での機能ということでなけ

れば達成できないとする。Sell はこの視点から Tennyson の詩を分析し，その詩は，詩人が同時代人へ過度の敬意を払う形で書かれたと主張する。Pagnini (1987: 9) もこの文体分析を行う 1 人であるが，彼の分析は形式的記号とテクスト外文脈を考慮してなされていて，言語表現の中で言語によって作り出された 'the "subject" of semiotics' (記号的な「主体」) と 'the real subject' (実際の主体) の両方を論じている。

　言語データを収集する方法がコンピュータの発達に伴い格段に進歩した。20 世紀の前半に活躍した Otto Jespersen の文法書で収集された言語データは主に文学作品からのものであるが，この時代には文学作品が言語コーパスと考えられていたのである (八木 2007)。コーパス文体論 (Corpus Stylistics) では，文体論学者は示差的な，普通のあるいはまれな語の出現頻度を計算し作者の文体を計測する。この文体論の代表的なものとしては Semino and Short (2004) や，我が国では Masui (1964)，Jimura, Nakao, Matsuo, Blake, and Stubbs (2002)，田畑 (2003)，本書でも論文解題を行った Hori (1999, 2004)，水野 (2006)，Ohno (2010, 2015)，石川 (2014) をあげることができよう。Chaucer の *Melibee* におけるワードペアの分布から，その様々な読みを探ろうとする Tani (2010) も興味深い。瀬良 (2014) では川端康成の『雪国』の英語訳 *Snow Country* (Seidensticker 訳) の感情表現に焦点を当て，コーパス分析ソフトウェア Wmatrix を用いて，それら表現の意味分析を行っている。Shiina (2005) では，初期近代英語の喜劇における vocatives (呼格の語) の使い方をコーパスという量的な視点と，ポライトネスなどの理論の 2 つの観点から分析している。Nishimura (1999) も Chaucer の強意副詞について分析を行っている。Nishio (2010) では，Yamamoto (2003) で Dickens のイディオムの変化は change → development → stability の形を辿るとされていたものを，そのコロケーション (collocation) の計量的精査から，4 つ目として stability の次に比喩的な意味を持つに至る deviation の段階を設定している。例えば 'steam up' などがそれにあたる。Matsuura (2009) も Sir Philip Sydney が periphrasis (迂言法) を好む点を計量的に分析している。類似の方法を用いてベイコン (Sir Francis Bacon) の *Essays* のスタイルを分析しているのが西岡 (2004) で，*Essays* の文体は Ciceronian 風 (キケロ風の荘重なもの) ではなく，単純な等位節を用いた

ものであるとしている。Fuami (2003) も計量的な方法を一部に用いながら，18 世紀の文学テクストで使用されている主格／目的格の使用法から 18 世紀テクストを研究している。なお Dickens に関しては，山本忠雄博士 (1904–1991) が，The Dickens Lexicon 作成のために作成した約 6 万枚のカードをもとに，高機能インターフェイスを備えた Dickens Lexicon Digital の作成が現在進行中である。このプロジェクトは，広島大学と熊本大学出身の研究者を中心とした 24 名の研究者によるプロジェクトである。2017 年までには Web 上で部分的に公開される予定である。コーパス言語学において利用できるコーパスに関しては「コーパス言語学―主なコーパス」(http://home.hiroshima-u.ac.jp/wisdom/corpus_ling/corpus02.html) と Corpus Linguistics: 'A Practical Introduction' (http://www.as.uni-heidelberg.de/personen/Nesselhauf/files/Corpus%20Linguistics%20Practical%20Introduction.pdf) に詳しい。

先に，Nottingham 大学の Ronald Carter は，文体論研究ではこの 20 年間における社会言語学的な談話分析から認知言語学に重点が移ったと述べたと書いた。その認知言語学 (Cognitive Linguistics) に基づく認知文体論 (Cognitive Stylistics) に関しては，まず認知的文体分析を先導する形で 'mind style' (精神的文体) という概念を提唱した Fowler (1996 [1986]) をあげなければならない。この精神的文体を Fowler (1977) は以下のように定義している：

> The study of mind style therefore involves the identification of linguistic patterns that accounts for the perception of a distinct world view during the reading of a text. The notion of 'patterns' is particularly important here. Mind style arises from the frequent and consistent occurrence of particular linguistic choices and structures within a text.
>
> (Fowler 1977: 2)

したがって，精神的文体の研究は，テクストの読みの最中に明確な世界観を認識する，その認識を説明する言語パターンを特定することを含む。「パターン」の概念は特にここでは重要である。Mind style は特定の言語的選択と構造がテクストの中で繰り返し現れるところから生じる。

Fowler の言う精神的文体とはおおまかに定義された概念で，その概念は 'a

particular point of view of things created by language'（Leech and Short 2007: 28）（言語によって作り出された特定の視点）と理解してよいと思われる。この認知的視点は「図2　文体論の歴史」に示されたSapirにまで辿ることができるが，現代の認知文体論の先駆けとなるものである。

　Fowlerに続いて，イギリスではSemino and Swindlehurst (1996)，Semino and Culpeper (2002)，Stockwell (2002) そして Boase-Beier (2003, 2004a, b, c)，アメリカではLakoff and Turner (1989)，我が国ではNakao and Iyeiri (2013) がこの認知文体論的なテクスト分析を行っている。また本書の論文改題でも取り上げた池上 (2011, 2012)，山梨 (2012) も認知言語学のこの分野への貢献を示唆している。浜田 (2007) は民族詩学 (folk poetics) を提唱し「文体に関する民族理論 (folk theory) の一種」であるとする。

　認知文体論の試みは，オランダの文体論学者Peter Verdonkの論文集であるVerdonk (2013) に見ることができる。この論文集は1983年のUlrecht大学での講演で分析したWilliam Blakeの詩 'London' から始まっている。この時期のVerdonkの詩の分析は，どのように詩が読者にとって日常言語と異なるものになっているか（異化 (defamiliarization)）を示すことにあった (Verdonk 1984)。この分析方法は，それ以後の論文に継続的に用いられているが，収録された最も新しい論文であるVerdonk (2010) ではTed Hughesの 'Hawk Roosting'（「憩う鷹」）を分析している。詩は次のような連で始まる：

　　I sit in the top of the wood, my eyes closed.
　　Inaction, no falsifying dream
　　Between my hooked head and hooked feet:
　　Or in sleep rehearse perfect kills and eat.
　　わたしは森のてっぺんに止っている，
　　目を閉じたまま。何もせず
　　鉤のくちばしから鉤の爪先にいたるまで
　　偽りやすい夢など微塵もない。
　　或いは　眠っている間に　完璧な殺害と
　　食事を幾度も下稽古する。

(片瀬博子（訳・編）「憩う鷹」『テド・ヒューズ詩集』土曜美術社，1982)

ここでは異化の視点に加えて，認知言語学で言う図 (figure) と地 (ground) の観点が入ってくる。彼はこう述べる：

> ... the theory of figure–ground organization provides yet another rational explanation for all the foregrounded patterns of sound, syntax, grammar and diction that captivated my attention when reading this poem. By the way, our hawk also makes use of the very same faculty when, in full flight, it targets its prey (the figure) in a large open field (the ground).
> (Verdonk 2010: 166)

その上，図と地の理論は，この詩を読むに際して私の注意を引いた音声，統語論，文法そして言いまわしの前景化されたパターン全てを理性的に説明するもうひとつ別の原理を提供する。ところで，この鷹も地上の大きな平原（地）で，その獲物（図）を全力飛行で狙う時には同様の能力を用いている。

この精神的文体に迫った研究として Nakao (2012) がある。Thackeray の *Barry Lyndon* を分析し，主人公の Redmond Barry の発話における 'confidence'（確信性）に epistemic modality（認知的法性）を通して迫っている。Fowler (1995: 49) では George Orwell の文体としては 'foregrounded modality'（前景化された法性）とでも呼べるものがこの作家の 'a defining feature of his personal voice' (49)（個人的声の特徴）であるとしているが，Nakao (2012) はこの研究に連なるものである。Matsutani (2001) は Jane Austen の作品における法性を論じていて，特に会話部分での 'most probably' のような法助動詞と副詞の連結の解釈により Austen の精神文体に迫ろうとする点が興味深い。キーワードを通して作者の精神文体に迫ろうとするもうひとつの論文は上利 (2003: 35–40) である。ここでは Malory が，*Le Morte d'Arthur*（『アーサー王の死』）において 'appeyche' という唯一の語を卑劣な Mark 王に使わせた，その意図に迫っている。Sakemi (1997) では，Chaucer はスタンザを単位として *Troilus and Criseyde* を展開しているので，スタンザ内には時制上の一貫性が必要と

考えたという観点から 'went(e' を preterites として用いたとして，また篠田 (1977) は 'Cursor Mundi' の副詞の位置からこの作者の意図の表れとしての文体に迫っている．

　認知文体論のもうひとつの成果は，メタファー (metaphor) 論である．そのメタファー論を文学言語の分析に応用した例を2つ述べる．メタファーを間主観的で無意識的な認知的なプロセスとする Lakoff and Turner (1989: 27) は Shakespeare の Sonnet 73 の詩の分析において，'first four lines evoke the PEOPLE ARE PLANTS metaphor'（最初の4つの行は「メタファー：人々は植物である」を喚起する）としている：

　　That time of year thou mayst in me behold
　　When yellow leaves, or none, or few, do hang
　　Upon those boughs which shake against the cold,
　　Bare ruined choirs, where late the sweet birds sang.
　　きみが私のなかに見るものは一年のあの季節，
　　寒気におののく木の枝から黄いろい葉が落ちつくし，
　　残っても二，三枚，先ごろまでは鳥たちが美しくうたい，
　　いまは，裸の，朽ちた聖歌隊席となりはてたあの季節．
　　　　　　　　　　　　　（高松雄一（訳）『ソネット集』岩波書店，1986）

Lakoff と Turner によると，「メタファー：人々は植物である」は，PLANT（植物）スキーマの構造を MAN（人間）という領域にマッピング (mapping) したもので，そのことにより，両者の生命のサイクルの間に対応関係が生じるというものである．例えば，黄色い葉は老年を表している．

　2つ目の認知言語学の応用例としては，散文の例として Semino and Swindlehurst (1996) をあげることができる．彼らは Ken Kesey の *One Flew Over the Cuckoo's Nest* におけるメタファー化を分析し，1人称ナレーター Chief Bromden の 'mind style' がいかに展開して行くかを論じている：

　　The development of Bromden's world view is marked in part by a rejection of the machinery metaphor and in part by the expression, through

metaphor, of his new belief that the machines can be beaten.
(Semino and Swindlehurst 1996: 21)
　Bromden の世界観は，部分的には機械のメタファーが，部分的にはメタファーを通しての機械は打ち負かせるという新しい信念の表明が，その特徴となる。

ここでいう「機械」とは，機械化された病院という組織，そしてアメリカ全体が機械化されていることをメタファー的に示している。
　そのほか我が国でのメタファー研究として，欽定訳聖書の研究に応用した橋本功が著名である (橋本 2010, 2011)。もう 1 人は瀬戸賢一で，彼は通常の日本語のメタファー表現 (瀬戸 1995) のみならず，特に日本語の味言葉の中に潜むメタファー的思考を追究するというユニークな研究も行っている (瀬戸 2003, 2005)。散文への応用例としては Dickens の *Great Expectations* におけるメタファーを探った Funada (2009) が，将来的な展開も含めて有望である。
　認知的な分析，すなわち広義の文体論の研究としては，関連性理論 (Relevance Theory) の提唱者である Sperber and Wilson (1995)，その後，Carston and Uchida (1998), Pilkington (2000), 東森・吉村 (2003), Clark (2014) が，この種の分析に大きな貢献をしている。文学テクスト研究への貢献を見てみると，Sperber and Wilson (1995: 224) では関連性理論の文学理論の中核を成す「詩的効果」(poetic effects) について，それは詩作品などにおける意味の多重性を説明する装置であるとする：

Poetic effects, we claim, result from the accessing of a large array of very weak implicatures ... Stylistic differences are just differences in the way relevance is achieved. One way in which styles may differ is in their greater or lesser reliance on poetic effects,...　　(Sperber and Wilson 1995: 224)
我々の主張は，詩的効果は…広範囲にわたるごく弱い推意を呼び出すことから生じるということである。文体上の差異は関連性の達成の仕方における差異なのである。文体の異なり方の一つは，詩的効果への依存度の大小にあり…　(内田聖二他 (訳)『関連性理論―伝達と認知』研究社，1999)

Sperber and Wilson（1986: 222）を引用する Uchida（1998: 176）の言葉を借りれば，詩的効果（a poetic effect）とは 'an utterance which achieves most of its relevance through a wide array of weak implicatures'（弱い推意の大きな集合を通して最大の関連性を達成する発話）の効果のことである。例えば William Wordsworth の *Daffodils*（「水仙」）の冒頭の 'I wandered lonely as a cloud' には「雲のようにさまよった」という表意に対し，推意としては強いものはなく，いくつかの弱い推意（weak implicatures）が推論できる。Wordsworth は読者が想像力を駆使していろいろな意味を推論してくれることを想定して，意図的に多くの推意の生じる一文を作ったということになる。そしてこの詩的効果の存在が詩という文学テクストの特徴であるとする。Pilkington（1994: 9）は関連性理論について 'it can offer genuine theoretical explanations for the linguistic choices that poets make'（それは詩人が行う言語選択に関して真の理論的説明を提供することができる）としているが，文体論学者の Michael Toolan からの反論もある（Toolan 1998, 1999）。Toolan（1998: 68）では Barbara MacMahon による関連性理論による Browning の詩の分析について（MacMahon 1996），理論部分の説明は無くても，それだけで優れた論文であるとしている。また同じ論文で，関連性理論は 'rehabilitate a "language as code" picture'（「コードとしての言語の像」を修復）しようとしているにすぎないとする。本書で論文の解題を行っている翻訳論の Jean Boase-Beier は 'the style reflects its author's choices and unconscious influences, and is also the basis for the cognitive effects on the reader'（Boase-Beier 2011: 163）（文体は作者の行う選択と無意識の影響を反映し，また読者に与える認知的効果のベースでもある）として，その翻訳理論としては，'a theory of communication—Relevance Theory—is sufficient'.（Boase-Beier 2011: 81）（コミュニケーションの理論である関連性理論があればよい。）と，この理論の価値を積極的に肯定している。

　認知言語学を応用したもうひとつ興味深い理論が出た。Werth（1999）はテクスト世界理論（Text World Theory）と呼ばれる視点を提唱し，テクストと呼ぶ概念を理解する仕方を示してくれている。この理論を発展させた文献としては Gavins（2007）と Semino（2009）がある。テクスト世界（Text World）とは人間の頭の中で構成される心的表象（mental representation）のことである。

この理論の基本的な考え方は，人間は，作者と読者の間に成立する談話を心的表象として構築することで処理し理解するというものであり，この理論は，その表象（representation）の分析手段を提供する。

　ここで文体理論やテクスト理論から離れ，その応用面を見てみたい。

　教育的文体論（Pedagogical Stylistics）の方面で活躍している大御所の Widdowson (1975) は文体論を文学教育と言語学の橋渡しをするものと位置付けている。豊田昌倫も文学教育での文体論の教育的効果を強調していて，文体論は言語への我々の感受性を高めるとする (Toyota 2001)。斎藤兆史の創造的文体論（Creative Stylistics）もこの文体論の効果を強調している (Saito 1997)。Ronald Carter (Carter 2004) と Rebecca Hughes (Hughes 1996) は口語的文体，文学的文体，そして文体教育の3つの出会う地点としての文体論を論じている。これら領域においては広い意味での文体論と言語教育の2つが交わっているとする。Teranishi, Saito and Sakamoto (2012) も同じく，三島由紀夫と俳句を例に出しながら，文学作品を味わう上において文体の精査がいかに重要かを説いている。小迫 (2010) は，英語教育において文学テクストをどのように交差させるかを論じた論文集である。その中でも田淵 (2010) は Roald Dahl の言葉を引用して，文を越えたレベルの「プロット」教育の重要性を説いている。魚住 (2009) も graded readers の比較分析の中で，原作のプロットがどのように反映されているかという点への関心を見せている。村上 (2014, 2015) もテクストの構成を重視する。Hall (2014) では，Henry Widdowson, Ronald Carter および Mick Short の EFL 論を紹介した後，将来この分野が考慮すべき事柄として，従来はテクストに重点が置かれて来たが 'the dynamics of classrooms' (248)（教室のダイナミズム）といった方面にも関心が向かうべきだとしている。気鋭の研究者による文学テクストと英語教育の関連を論じたものとしては西原 (2013) があり，文学コミュニケーションという点から，「気づき」に重点を置いた，文学テクストを用いた英語教育を提唱している。この「気づき」は奥 (2012) でも文体論の役割として重視されている。

　ここで代表的な語学的文学論の入門書を3冊紹介しておく。本書の論文改題でも執筆をお願いした Lancaster 大学の Geoffrey Leech と，その同僚の Mick Short によって書かれた文体論の代表的入門書 *Style in Fiction: A Lin-*

guistic Introduction to English Fictional Prose（Longman, 1981）を忘れるわけにはいかない。Roman Jakobson の *Poetry of Grammar and Grammar of Poetry*（Roman Jakobson Selected Writings Vol. 3）（Mouton, 1981）や *Language in Literature*（Belknap, 1987）などが韻文の文体を扱ったものとすれば、こちらは副題にもあるように散文を扱ったものである。韻文の方は、Geoffrey Leech がこの本に先行して *A Linguistic Guide to English Poetry*（Routledge, 1973 [1969]）を出している。*Style in Fiction* の概略を述べると Part One: Approaches and Methods（1 Style and choice, 2 Style, text and frequency, 3 A method of analysis and some examples, 4 Levels of style）と Part Two: Aspects of Style（5 Language and the fictional world, 6 Mind style, 7 The rhetoric of text, 8 Discourse and the discourse situation, 9 Conversation in the novel, 10 Speech and thought presentation, 11 Stylistics and fiction 25 years on, 12 'The Bucket and the Rope'）となっている。Part One は方法論、Part Two は文体がどの領域でどのような形で実現しているかを論じたものである。この本の著者の1人である Mick Short も後に *Exploring the Language of Poems, Plays and Prose*（Longman, 1996）という詩、劇そして散文の文学テクストの主領域をカバーする入門書を出している。内容は 1 Who is stylistics, 2 More on foregrounding, deviation and parallelism, 3 Style variation in texts, 4 Sound, meaning and effect, 5 Rhythm and metre in the reading of poetry, 6 Drama: the conversational genre, 7 The meaning of speech acts, turn-taking and politeness, 8 Assumptions, presuppositions and the inferring of meaning, 9 Fictional prose and point of view, 10 Speech and thought presentation, 11 Prose style, 12 Bringing in all together となっており、それぞれの領域が持つ言語特徴を最新の言語理論を用いて分析例を示している。例えば第6章では 'Normal non-fluency does not occur in drama dialogue, precisely because that dialogue is written'（177）（通常の非流暢的特徴はドラマでは生じないが、それはそこでのやりとりは書かれたものだからである）とある。この指摘は重要で、劇の言語では、この自然言語の話し言葉の特徴からの分析には制限があるということを示している。3冊目は Birmingham 大学の Michael Toolan（著）*Language in Literature: An Introduction to Sytlistics*（Arnold, 1996）で、著者は前書きで

'The goal of this book is to sharpen your awareness of how language works in texts—particularly, here, in literary texts'. (iix)（本書の目的はテクスト——特にここでは文学テクスト——の中で，言語がどのような働きをするかについての読者の気づきを高めることである）と述べているように，この書物も特定の理論に偏らず，様々な言語学的分析手段を用いて文学テクストを分析して見せている。内容は次のようになっている: 1 Getting started, 2 Cohesion: making text, 3 Modality and attitude, 4 Processes and participants, 5 Recording speech and thought, 6 Narrative structure, 7 A few well-chosen words, 8 Talking: acts of give and take, 9 Presupposition。一例をあげると第3章で '"Van der Graaf's Folly" is a dead cert for the 3:30 at Ascot'.（「ヴァン・ダー・グラーフ・フォリー」はアスコット競馬場での3:30のレースで，100%勝ち馬だ。）という表現は '"Van der Graff's Folly" will certainly win the 3:30 at Ascto'. の意味であるが，'a dead cert' というのは '"metaphorized" modality'（「メタファー化された」法性）と呼べるものであるとする。

　2014年には文体論関連のハンドブックが2冊相次いで出た。ひとつは Peter Stockwell and Sara Whiteley（編）*The Cambridge Handbook of Stylistics* (Cambridge University Press, 2014) で，Part I は The discipline of stylistics の題で，文体論の概略を述べている。例えば，その Section 2 では Michael Toolan が 'The theory and philosophy of stylistics' を，Section 7 では Geoff Hall が 'Stylistics and literary criticism' を書いている。Part II は Literary concepts and stylistics と題していて，文学上の諸概念と文体路の関わりを示している。その Section 11 では Dan McIntyre が 'Characterization' について書いている。Part III は Techniques of style で，その Section 16 では Manuel Jobert が 'Phonostylistics and the written text' を，Section 23 では Mick Short が 'Analysing dialogue' を書いている。全部で Part V，Section 39 まである。2つ目は Michael Burke（編）*The Routledge Handbook of Stylistics* (Routledge, 2014) で，こちらも同様の形式を取っている。Part I Section 1 は Historical perspective in stylistics と題していて編者の Michael Burke が 'Rhetoric and poetics: From classical rhetoric to cognitive neuroscience' を書いている。Part II は Core issues in stylistics の題で例えば Section 13 では Joe

Bray が 'Speech and thought presentation in stylistics' を書いている。全部で Part IV, Section 32 まである。用語の解説書としては，Katie Wales（著）*A Dictionary of Stylistics*（3rd edn）（Routledge, 2011）があり，これは初版は 1989 年で，この初版の訳である豊田昌倫（監訳）『英語文体論辞典』（三省堂，2000）が出ている。また研究社出版株式会社から出ている『英語年鑑』には「文体論研究」（豊田昌倫執筆担当）の章があり，ここに毎年，内外の文体論関係の主要な書籍や論文が紹介されている。

　文学テクストを語学的に論じる我が国における学会としては，英語を初めとする諸言語の文体を扱う老舗の「日本文体論学会」（1961 年に「日本文体論協会」として設立）がある。その他，「近代英語協会」（1983 年設立），「日本中世英語英文学会」（2007 年設立），および「日本英文学会」（1928 年に組織変更して発足），中でも「日本英文学会中国四国支部」（1947 年設立）では，多くの語学的な文学テクストの研究発表が行われている。学術誌を見ると，類似の学術誌では文学研究と言語学研究が分離する中，広島大学の『英語英文學研究』（1954–）と *ERA*（The English Research Association of Hiroshima）（1964–）では語学的な文学テクスト研究が継続的に行われている。

　イギリスにおいては文学言語を扱う 2 つの著名な学会がある。ひとつは Geoffrey Leech, Mick Short, Ronald Carter らを founding fathers とする The Poetics and Linguistics Association（PALA）で 1980 年に Nottingham で初の大会を開いている。会長は Paul Simpson（2015 年迄）で，この学会の学術誌としては Geoff Hall を編者とする *Language and Literature*（Sage Publications）が年 2 回発行されている。もうひとつは 1990 年に第 1 回の大会が開かれた Jeremy Scott を会長とする The International Association of Literary Semantics（IALS）で，この文学意味論の学会は，Trevor Eaton が 1972 年に初代の編者となり現在は Michael Toolan が編者をつとめる *Journal of Literary Semantics: An International Review*（Mouton）を年 2 回発行している。アメリカでは Northern Illinois University から出版されている，John V. Knapp を編者とする *Style* 誌があり，年 4 回発行されている。

参照文献

Abbott, HP (2002) *The Cambridge Introduction to Narrative*. Cambridge: Cambridge University Press.
上利学 (2003)「Malory における *Appeyche*」菅野正彦 (編)『"FUL OF HY SENTENCE" 英語語彙論集』英宝社, 35–40.
Adamson, S (2010) 'Questions of identity in Renaissance drama: New historicism meets old philology'. *Shakespeare Quarterly* 61 (1): 56–77.
Aristotle (1995) *Poetics* (Loeb Classical Library 199) (2nd edn) (trans. S Halliwell). Cambridge, Massachusetts: Harvard University Press.
Aristotle (2000) *Art of Rhetoric* (Loeb Classical Library 193) (trans. JH Freese). Cambridge, Massachusetts: Harvard University Press.
Aronstein, P (1926) *Englische Stilistik*. Berlin: B.G. Teubner.
Bakhtin, MM (1984 [1929]) *Problems of Dostoevsky's Poetics* (Theory and History of Literature Series 8) (ed. and trans. C Emerson). Minneapolis: University of Minnesota Press.
Bal, M (2009 [1985]) *Narratology: Introduction to the Theory of Narrative*. Toronto: University of Toronto Press.
Bally, C (1952 [1935]) *La Langage et la Vie* (Nouvelle Édition Revue et Augmentée; Ser. Linguistics 5). Zurich: Max Niehans. (小林英夫 (訳)『言語活動と生活』岩波文庫, 1941)
Bally, C (1963) *Traité de Stylistique Française*. Heidelberg: Carl Winters.
Barthes, R (1968) 'La mort de l'auteur'. *Manteia* 5: 12–17.
Barthes, R (1970) *S/Z: Essais*. Paris: Seuil. (沢崎浩平 (訳)『S/Z バルザック「サラジーヌ」の構造分析』みすず書房, 1973)
Benveniste, É (1966) *Problèmes de Linguistique Générale* (Bibliothèque des sciences humaines). Paris: Gallimard.
Bex, T (1996) *Variety in Written English — Texts in Society: Societies in Text* (Interface series). London: Routledge.
Boase-Beier, J (2003) 'Mind style translated'. *Style* 37 (3): 253–265.
Boase-Beier, J (2004a) 'Translation and style: A brief introduction'. *Language and Literature* 13 (1): 9–11.
Boase-Beier, J (2004b) 'Knowing and not knowing: Style, intention, and the translation of a holocaust poem'. *Language and Literature* 13 (1): 25–35.
Boase-Beier, J (2004c) 'Saying what someone else meant: Style, relevance and translation'. *International Journal of Applied Linguistics* 14 (2): 276–287.
Boase-Beier, J (2011) *A Critical Introduction to Translation Studies*. London: Continuum.
Booth, W (1961) *The Rhetoric of Fiction* (2nd edn). Chicago: University of Chicago Press.
Bremond, C (1964) 'Le message narratif'. *Communications* 4: 4–32.

Bremond, C (1966) 'La logique des possibles narratifs'. *Communications* 8: 60–76.
Burke, M (ed.) (2014) *The Routledge Handbook of Stylistics*. London: Roudlege.
Carston, R and Uchida, S (eds) (1998) *Relevance Theory: Applications and Implications*. Amsterdam: John Benjamins.
Carter, R (2004) *Language and Creativity: The Art of Common Talk*. London: Routledge.
Chatman, S (1978) *Story and Discourse: Narrative Structure in Fiction and Film*. Ithaca: Cornell University Press.
Chloupek, J (1993) 'Publicist style'. In: Chloupek, J and Nekvapil, J (eds) *Studies in Functional Stylistics* (Linguistic and literary studies in Eastern Europe 36). Amsterdam: John Benjamins, 112–126.
Clark, B (2014) 'Stylistics and relevance theory'. In: Burke, M (ed.) *The Routledge Handbook of Stylistics*. London: Roudlege, 155–174.
Cook, G (1989) *Discourse* (Language teaching series). Oxford: Oxford University Press.
Cook, G (1994) *Discourse and Literature* (Oxford applied linguistics series). Oxford: Oxford University Press.
Coulthard, M (1985) *An Introduction to Discourse Analysis* (Applied linguistics and language study series) (new edn). London: Longman.
Cressot, M (1947) *Le Style et Ses Techniques: Precis d'Analyse Stylistique*. Paris: Presses Universitaires de France.
Croce, B (2006 [1902]) *Aesthetic: As Science of Expression and General Linguistic*. (Trans. from the Italian by D Ainslie and SC Charleston) Charleston, South Carolina: BiblioBazaar.
Crystal, D and Davy, D (1969) *Investigating English Style* (English language series 1). London: Longman.
Culler, J (1975) *Structuralist Poetics: Structuralism, Linguistics, and the Study of Literature*. Ithaca, N.Y.: Cornell University Press.
de Beaugrande, R and Dressler, WU (1981) *Introduction to Text Linguistics*. Greenwich, CT: Ablex.
de Buffon, G-LL (1922 [1753]) *Discours sur le Style* (7th edn). Paris: Hachette.
de Saussure, F (1966 [1916]) *Course in General Linguistics* (ed. C Bally and A Sechehaye; trans. W Baskin). New York: McGraw-Hill.
Deutschbein, M (1932) *Neuenglische Stilistik*. Leipzig: Quelle and Meyer.
道木一弘 (2009)『物・語りの『ユリシーズ』ナラトロジカル・アプローチ』南雲堂.
Eagleton, T (1983) *Literary Theory*. Oxford: Blackwell.
Enkvist, NE (1964) 'On defining style: An essay in applied linguistics'. In: Spencer, J (ed.) *Linguistics and Style* (Language and language learning series). London: Oxford University Press, 1–56.
Fairclough, N (2000) *New Labour, New Language?* London: Routledge.

Fairclough, N (2001 [1989]) *Language and Power* (2nd edn). London: Longman.
Fish, S (1980) *Is There a Text in this Class?: The Authority of Interpretive Communities*. Cambridge, Mass.: Harvard University Press.
Fludernik, M (1993) *The Fictions of Language and the Languages of Fiction*. London: Routledge.
Fludernik, M (2009) *An Introduction to Narratology*. London and New York: Routledge. Also available at: http://elsru.ir/wp-content/uploads/2013/09/Monika-Fludernik-An-Introduction-to-Narratology-2009.pdf (accessed 6 February 2015)
Fónagy, I (1991) 'Paralinguistic uiversals and preconceptual thinking in language'. In: Waugh, LR and Rudy, S (eds) *New Vistas in Grammar: Invariance and Variation*. Amsterdam: John Benjamins, 495–516.
Fowler, R (1977) *Linguistics and the Novel* (New accents series). London: Methuen.
Fowler, R et al. (1979) *Language and Control*. London: Routledge and Kegan Paul.
Fowler, R (1981) *Literature as Social Discourse: The Practice of Linguistic Criticism*. London: Batsford Academic and Educational.
Fowler, R (ed.) (1987) *A Dictionary of Modern Critical Terms* (revised and enlarged edn). London: Routledge and Kegan Paul.
Fowler, R (1991) *Language in the News: Discourse and Ideology in the Press*. London: Routledge.
Fowler, R (1995) *The Language of George Orwell* (The language of literature). Basingstoke: Macmillan.
Fowler, R (1996 [1986]) *Linguistic Criticism* (2nd edn). Oxford: Oxford University Press.
Freud, S (1990 [1907]) 'Delusions and dreams in Jensen's *Gradiva*'. In: Freud, S *Art and Literature: Jensen's Gradiva, Leonardo da Vinci and other works* (The Penguin Freud library 14). Harmondsworth: Penguin, 27–118.
Fuami, K (2003) 'The subjective/objective case distinction, with special reference to Eighteenth-century fictional prose'.『甲南女子大学研究紀要』39: 23–32.
福元広二 (2010)「Shakespeareにおける命令文主語と文法化」吉波弘・中澤和夫・竹内信一・外池滋生・川端朋広・野村忠央・山本史歩子 (編)『英語研究の次世代に向けて』(秋元実治教授定年退職記念論文集) ひつじ書房, 361–372.
Gavins, J (2007) *Text World Theory: An Introduction*. Edinburgh: Edinburgh University Press.
Genette, G (1980 [1972]) *Narrative Discourse: An Essay in Method* (trans. JE Lewin). Ithaca, N.Y.: Cornell University Press.
Genette, G (1988 [1983]) *Narrative Discourse Revisited* (trans. JE Lewin). Ithaca, N.Y.: Cornell University Press.
Greimas, AJ (1983 [1966]) *Structural Semantics: An Attempt at a Method* (trans. D McDowell, R Schleifer, and A Velie). Lincoln: University of Nebraska Press.
Grice, HP (1975) 'Logic and conversation'. In: Cole, P and Morgan, JL (eds) *Syntax*

and Semantics, Vol. 3: Speech acts. New York: Academic Press, 43–58.

Guiraud, P (1955) *La Stylistique* (Que sais-je? 646) (9th edn). Paris: Presses Universitaires de France.

Gumperz, JJ (1972) 'Sociolinguistic and communication in small groups'. In: Pride, JB and Holmes, J (eds) *Sociolinguistics: Selected Readings*. Harmondsworth: Penguin, 203–224.

Hall, G (2014) 'Pedagogical stylistics'. In: Burke, M (ed.) *The Routledge Handbook of Stylistics*. London: Roudlege, 239–252.

Halliday, MAK (1971) 'Linguistic function and literary style: An inquiry into the language of William Golding's *The Inheritors*'. In: Chatman, S (ed.) *Literary Style: A Symposium*. London: Oxford University Press, 330–368.

Halliday, MAK and Hasan, R (1976) *Cohesion in English*. London: Longman.

Halliday, MAK and Martin, JR (1993) *Writing Science*. London: Falmer Press.

浜田秀（2007）「カテゴリーとしての詩―余白の生み出す民族詩学」『認知言語学論考』7：169–212.

花輪光（編）（1985）『詩の記号学のために：シャルル・ボードレールの詩篇「猫たち」を巡って』書肆風の薔薇.

橋本功（2010）「聖書のメタファと翻訳」吉波弘・中澤和夫・竹内信一・外池滋生・川端朋広・野村忠央・山本史歩子（編）『英語研究の次世代に向けて』（秋元実治教授定年退職記念論文集）ひつじ書房，145–156.

橋本功・八木橋宏勇（共著）（2011）『聖書と比喩―メタファで旧約聖書の世界を知る』慶應義塾大学出版会.

Hendricks, WO (1976) *Grammars of Style and Styles of Grammar*. Amsterdam: North-Holland.

Herman, D (ed.) (1999) *Narratologies: New Perspectives on Narrative Analysis*. Columbus: Ohio State University Press.

Herman, D, Manfred, J and Ryan, M-L (2007) *Routledge Encyclopedia of Narrative Theory*. London: Routledge.

Hausenblas, K (1993) 'The position of style in verbal communication'. In: Chloupek, J and Nekvapil, J (eds) *Studies in Functional Stylistics* (Linguistics and literary studies in Eastern Europe, 36). Philadelphia and Amsterdam: Academia, J. Benjamins, 51–67.

東森勲・吉村あき子（2003）『関連性理論の新展開―認知とコミュニケーション』研究社.

平山直樹（2012）「『パストン家書簡集』における ME THINKS」『尾道市立大学日本文学論叢』8：1–18.

Hori, M (2004) *Investigating Dickens' Style: A Collocational Analysis*. Basingstoke: Palgrave Macmillan.

Hughes, R (1996) *English in Speech and Writing: Investigating Language and Literature*. London: Routledge.

Hymes, D (1968) 'The ethnography of speaking'. In: Fishman, JA (ed.) *The Sociology of Language*. The Hague: Mouton, 99–138.

Ihwe, J (1973) 'On the validation of text-grammars in the "study of literature"'. In: Petöfi, JS and Rieser, H (eds) *Studies in Text Grammar*. Dordrecht: Reidel, 300–348.

池上嘉彦（1975）『意味論』大修館書店.

池上嘉彦（2012）「話者による〈事態把握〉（construal）の営みの相対性と翻訳―日本語話者好みの〈主観的把握〉をめぐって」『文体論研究』58: 91–104.

池上嘉彦（2011）「日本語話者における〈好まれる言い回し〉としての〈主観的把握〉」『人工知能学会誌』26（4）: 317–322.

Iser, W (1974 [1972]) *The Implied Reader*. Baltimore: John Hopkins University Press.

石川慎一郎（2014）「コーパス文体論の可能性―ブロンテ姉妹の文体的位相を例に」『文体論研究』60: 121–143.

Jakobson, R (1960) 'Linguistics and poetics'. In: Sebeok, TA (ed.) *Style in Language*. Cambridge, MA: MIT Press, 350–377.

ヤーコブソン，R（著），川本茂雄（監）（1973）『一般言語学』みすず書房.

Jakobson, R (1973) *Questions de Poétique*. Paris: Seuil.

Jakobson, R (1981) *Selected Writings III: Poetry of Grammar and Grammar of Poetry*. The Hague: Mouton.

ヤーコブソン，R（著），川本茂雄（編）（1985）『ロマーン・ヤーコブソン選集 3』大修館.

Jakobson, R (1987) *Language in Literature* (eds K Pomorska and S Rudy). Cambridge, MA: Belknap.

Jakobson, R and Jones, LG (1970) *Shakespeare's Verbal Art in Th'Expense of Spirit* (Series practica 35). The Hague: Mouton.

Jakobson, R and Lévi-Strauss, C (1962) '"Les Chats" de Charles Baudelaire'. *L'Homme: Revue Française d'Anthropologie* 2（1）: 5–21.

Jacobs, PS and Rosenbaum, RA (1971) *Transformations, Style, and Meaning*. Waltham, Mass: Xerox College Publishing.

Jimura, A, Nakao, Y, Matsuo, M, Blake, NF, and Stubbs, E (eds) (2002) *A Comprehensive Collocation of the Hengwrt and Ellesmere Manuscripts of The Canterbury Tales: General Prologue* (The Hiroshima University Studies, Graduate School of Letters（『広島大学大学院文学研究科論集』）62, Special Issue 3): 1–63.

Jobert, M (2014) 'Phonostylistics and the written text'. In: Stockwell, P and Whiteley, S (eds) *The Cambridge Handbook of Stylistics*. Cambridge: Cambridge University Press, 231–248.

片見彰夫（2011）「中英語から近代英語における説得の技法―反復表現とワードペアの観点から」『近代英語研究』27: 49–73.

河井迪男（1984）「小説における会話の言語と文体」『近代英語研究』1: 62–69.

Kikuchi, S (2010) 'Unveiling the dramatic secret of 'Ghost' in *Hamlet*'. *Journal of Literary Semantics* (Mouton de Gruyter, Germany) 39 (2): 103–117.

Koguchi, K (2014) 'Stylistic use of personal pronouns in *A Tale of Two Cities*'. In: Nakagawa, K (ed.) *Studies in Modern English* (The thirtieth anniversary publication of the Modern English Association). Tokyo: Eihosha, 385–400.

小迫勝他（編）（2010）『英語教育への新たな挑戦—英語教師の視点から』英宝社.

Labov, W and Waletzky, J (1967) 'Narrative analysis and oral versions of personal experience'. In: Helm, J (ed.) *Essays on the Verbal and Visual Arts: Proceedings of the 1966 Annual Spring Meeting of the American Ethnological Society*. Seattle: University of Washington Press, 12–44.

Lakoff, G and Turner, M (1989) *More Than Cool Reason: A Field Guide to Poetic Metaphor*. Chicago: University of Chicago Press.

Lakoff, R (1975) *Language and Woman's Place*. New York: Harper and Row.

Lanser, SS (1981) *The Narrative Act: Point of View in Narrative Fiction*. New Jersey: Princeton University Press.

Leech, GN (1969) *A Linguistic Guide to English Poetry* (English language series 4). London: Longman.

Leech, GN and Short, MH (1981) *Style in Fiction: A Linguistic Introduction to English Fictional Prose* (English language series 13). London: Longman.

Leech, GN and Short MH (2007) *Style in Fiction: A Linguistic Introduction to English Fictional Prose* (English language series 13) (2nd edn). London: Longman.

Lévi-Strauss, C (1963 [1958]) 'The structural study of myth'. In: Jacobson, C (trans.) *Structural Anthropology*. Harmondsworth: Penguine Books, 206–231.

MacMahon, B (1996) 'Indirectness, rhetoric and interpretative use: Communicative strategies in Browning's My Last Duchess'. *Language and Literature* 5(3): 209–223.

Marouzeau, J (1941) *Précis de Stylistique Française*. Paris: Masson et Cie.

Masui, M (1964) *The Structure of Chaucer's Rime Words: An Exploration into the Poetic Language of Chaucer*. Tokyo: Kenkyusha.

松井信義（2010）「I mean の機能—The Cather in the Rye を中心に」『現代英語談話会論集』5: 53–66.

Matutani, M (2001) 'Language expressing modality in Jane Austen's novels: With special reference to auxiliaries and adverbs'. In: Nakao, Y and Jimura, A (eds) *Originality and Adventure: Essays on English Language and Literature* (In Honour of Masahiko Kanno). Tokyo: Eihosha, 145–158.

Matsuura, K (2009) 'Negatives in Sir Philip Sydney'. *ERA* 26 (1&2): 9–24.

Mills, S (1995) *Feminist Stylistics*. London: Routledge.

水野和穂（2006）「コーパスと後期近代英語研究」『英語コーパス研究』13: 209–226.

村上彩実（2014）「KWL 法を活用した英語リーディング教授法のすすめ」『言語文化学会論集』43: 205–209.

村上彩実（2015）「大学英語教育における Project-Based Learning（実践報告）」『言語文化学会論集』44: 331–337.

Nakagawa, K (ed.) *Studies in Modern English* (The thirtieth anniversary publication of the Modern English Association). Tokyo: Eihosha.

Nakao, M (2012) 'Subjective truth in Barry's narrative'. *Studies in Modern English* (『近代英語研究』) 28: 71–76.

Nakao, Y and Iyeiri, Y (eds) (2013) *Chaucer's Language: Cognitive Perspectives* (Stuides in the history of the English language). Osaka: Osaka Yosho.

Nash, W (1997) 'Tabloid rhetoric: or sentences that say it all'. Lecture delivered at the 1997 PALA conference entitled 'The New Rhetoric' held in July 1997 in Nottingham, organised by the University of Central England and the University of Wolverhampton.

Nishio, M (2010) 'The development of idiomatic expressions in Dickens'. PALA 2010 Proceedings Online. Available at: http://www.pala.ac.uk/2010.html (accessed 25 March 2014).

西岡啓治（2004）『フランシス・ベイコン著「エッセイ」の文体研究』ふくろう出版.

西原貴之（2013）「大学英語教育に文学教材を使用する際の留意点：文学テストのスコアと授業成績及び TOEIC のスコアとの相関分析からの示唆」『日本英文学会第 85 回大会プロシーディングス（Proceedings: The 85th General Meeting of The English Literary Society of Japan）』, 25–26 May 2013. 215–216.

西村秀夫（1999）「Chaucer の強意副詞再考」稲田俊明他（編）『言語研究の潮流―山本和之教授退官記念論文集』開拓社, 247–260.

Ohno, H (2010) 'Impersonal and personal construction in the language of Chaucer'. In: Imahayashi, O, Nakao, Y, and Ogura, M (eds) *Aspects of the History of English Language and Literature: Selected Papers Read at SHELL 2009*, Hiroshima. Frankfurt am Main: Peter Lang, 115–129.

Ohno, H (2015) *Variation between Personal and Impersonal Constructions in Geoffrey Chaucer: A Stylistic Approach*. Okayama: University Education Press.

大堀壽夫（2004）「物語の構造と発達」大堀壽夫（編），池上嘉彦・河上誓作・山梨正明（監）『認知コミュニケーション論』大修館書店, 243–278.

奥聡一郎（2012）「教育的文体論から考える文学テクストの教材化―英詩による言葉への気づきと小説コーパスの活用」『科学／人間』41: 83–102.

Pagnini, M (1987) *The Pragmatics of Literature* (Advances in semiotics) (trans. N Jones-Henry). Bloomington: Indiana University Press.

Pearsall, D (1992) *The Life of Geoffrey Chaucer*. Oxford: Blackwell.

Petöfi, JS (1973) 'Towards an empirically motivated grammatical theory of verbal texts'. In: Petöfi, JS and Rieser, H (eds) *Studies in Text Grammar*. Dordrecht: Reidel, 205–275.

Pilkington, A (1994) *Poetic Thoughts and Poetic Effects: A Relevance Theory Account of the Literary Use of Rhetorical Tropes and Schemes*. PhD dissertation. University of London.

Pilkington, A (2000) *Poetic Effects: A Relevance Theory Perspective*. Amsterdam: John Benjamins.

Prince, G (1982) *A Grammar of Stories: An Introduction*. Berlin, New York and Amsterdam: Mouton.

Propp, V (1968 [1928]) *Morphology of the folktale* (trans. L Scot) (2nd edn). Austin: University of Texas Press.

Quirk, R (1982) *Style and Communication in the English Language*. London: Arnold.

Quirk, R, et al. (1985) *A Comprehensive Grammar of the English Language*. London: Longman.

Richards, IA (1926) *Principles of Literary Criticism* (2nd edn). London: Kegan Paul.

Rieser, H (1973) 'Sentence grammar, text grammar, and the evaluation problem'. In: Petöfi, JS and Rieser, H (eds) *Studies in Text Grammar*. Dordrecht: Reidel, 276–299.

Ross, JR (1970) 'On declarative sentence'. In: Jacobs, RA and Rosenbaum, PS (eds) *Readings in English transformational grammar*. Waltham, Mass: Blaisdell-Ginn, 222–272.

Sacks, H (1972) 'An initial investigation of the usability of conversational data for doing sociology'. In: Sudnow, D (ed.) *Studies in social interaction*. New York: The Free Press, 31–74.

Saito, Y (1993–1994) 'Towards a theory of creative stylistics—A study of some applications of stylistic theory to creative writing'. *Language, Information, Text* 1.1. April 1993–1994: 91–100.

Saito, Y (1997) *Style and Creativity: Towards a Theory of Creative Stylistics*. Nottingham: University of Nottingham Press.

Saito, Y (2001) 'Fiction as historical discourse: Diachronic analysis of the narrative structures of English fiction'. *POETICA* 58: 21–31.

Sakauchi, H (2004) 'Critical linguistic approaches to the British press reports on a criminal trial'. In: Imahayashi, O and Kouji, F (eds) *English Philology and Stylistics: A Festschrift for Professor Toshiro Tanaka*. Hiroshima: Keisuisha, 207–220.

Sakemi, K (1997) 'Notes on Chaucer's *wente*'. *Research Bulletin of the Hiroshima Institute of Technology* 31: 7–14.

Sando, M (2002) 'Repetition and emphasis in *The Catcher in the Rye*—With special reference to Holden's speech and narration'. *Kwansai Review* 21: 195–207.

Searle, JR (1969) *Speech Acts: An Essay in the Philosophy of Language*. Cambridge: Cambridge University Press.

Sebeok, TA (ed.) (1960) *Style in Language*. Cambridge, MA: MIT Press.

Sell, RD (ed.) (1991) *Literary Pragmatics*. London: Routledge.

Semino, E (2009) 'Text worlds'. In: Brone, G and Vandaele, J (eds) *Cognitive Po-

etics: Goals, Gains and Gaps. Berlin: Mouton de Gruyter, 33–71.

Semino, E and Culpeper, J (eds) (2002) *Cognitive Stylistics: Language and Cognition in Text Analysis*. Amsterdam: John Benjamins.

Semino, E and Short, M (2004) *Corpus Stylistics: Speech, Writing and Thought Presentation in a Corpus of English Writing* (Routledge advances in corpus linguistics). London: Routledge.

Semino, E and Swindlehurst, K (1996) 'Metaphor and mind style in Ken Kesey's *One Flew Over the Cuckoo's Nest*'. *Style* 30(1): 143–166.

瀬良晴子(2014)「*Snow Country* における感情表現の描写」『人文論集』(兵庫県立大学) 49: 71–85.

瀬戸賢一(1995)『メタファー思考』講談社.

瀬戸賢一(2003)(編著)『ことばは味を超える』海鳴社.

瀬戸賢一(2005)(共著)『味ことばの世界』海鳴社.

Shiina, M (2005) 'How playwrights construct their dramatic worlds: A corpus-based study of vocatives in Early Modern English comedies'. In: Caldas-Coulthard, CR and Toolan, M (eds) *The Writer's Craft, the Culture's Technology*. Amsterdam and New York: Rodopi, 209–224.

篠田義博(1977)「*Cursor Mundi* の Adverbials の位置について」『広島女学院大学論集』27: 77–86.

Shklovsky, VB (1990 [1925]) *Theory of Prose* (trans. B Sher). Elmwood Park, IL: Dalkey Archive Press.

Short, M (1996) *Exploring the Language of Poems, Plays and Prose*. London: Longman.

Sinclair, JMcH, Forsyth, IJ, Coulthard, RM and Ashby, MC (1972) 'The English Use of Teachers and Pupils'. Final report to SSRC. University of Birmingham.

Sperber, D and Wilson, D (1995) *Relevance: Communication and Cognition* (2nd edn). Oxford: Blackwell. (内田聖二他(訳)『関連性理論―伝達と認知』研究社, 1999)

Spitzer, L (1961 [1928]) *Stilstudien II*. Munich: Max Hueber.

Spitzer, L (1962 [1948]) *Linguistics and Literary History: Essays in Stylistics*. Princeton, New Jersey: Princeton University Press.

Stanzel, FK (1984 [1979]) *A Theory of Narrative*. Cambridge: Cambridge University Press.

Staten, H (1997) 'The decomposing form of Joyce's *Ulysses*'. *PMLA* 112(3): 380–392.

Steinthal, H (1881) *Einleitung in die Psychologie und Sprachwissenschaft*. Berlin: Dummler.

Stockwell, P (2002) *Cognitive Poetics: An Introduction*. London: Routledge.

Stockwell, P and Whiteley, S (eds) (2014) *The Cambridge Handbook of Stylistics*. Cambridge: Cambridge University Press.

Strohmeyer, F (1924) *Der Stil der franzosischen Sprache*. Berlin: Weidmannsche Buchh.

田畑智司 (2003)「Dickens における -ly 副詞の分布―計量分析序説」大森文子 (編)『レトリック研究の方法と射程』言語文化共同研究プロジェクト 2002 (大阪大学言語文化部・大阪大学大学院言語文化研究科),27–32.

田淵博文 (2010)「短編小説の読み方―Roald Dahl の短編を用いて」小迫勝他 (編)『英語教育への新たな挑戦―英語教師の視点から』英宝社,130–144.

Tanaka, T (1991) 'Notes on grammar and usage in *Evelina*'. *Hiroshima Studies in English Language and Literature* (『英語英文學研究』) 36: 27–37.

Tani, A (2010) 'Word pairs in Chaucer's *Melibee* and their variant readings'. In: Imahayashi, O, Nakao, Y and Ogura, M (eds) *Aspects of History of English Language and Literature*. Frankfurt am Main: Peter Lang, 101–113.

Tannen, D (1990) *You Just Don't Understand: Women and Men in Conversation*. New York: William Morrow.

Tannen, D (1994) *Gender and Discourse*. New York: Oxford University Press.

Taylor, JT and Toolan, M (1996) 'Recent trends in stylistics'. In: Weber, JJ (ed.) *The Stylistics Reader: From Roman Jakobson to the Present*. London: Arnold, 87–91.

Teranishi, M, Saito, A and Sakamoto, K (2012) 'The role of stylistics in Japan: A pedagogical perspective'. *Language and Literature* 21 (2): 226–244.

Thomas, M (ed.) (2014) *Roman Jakobson:Critical Assessments of Leading Linguists* (4 volumes). London: Routledge.

Thorne, JP (1970) 'Generative grammar and stylistic analysis'. In: Lyons, J (ed.) *New Horizons in Linguistics*. Harmondsworth: Penguin Books, 185–197.

Todorov, T (1969) *Grammaire du Décaméron* (Approaches to semiotics 3). The Hague: Mouton.

Toolan, M (1988) *Narrative: A Critical Introduction*. London: Routledge.

Toolan, M (1996) *Language in Literature: An Introduction to Stylistics*. London: Arnold.

Toolan, M (1997) 'What is critical discourse analysis and why are people saying such terrible things about it?'. *Language and Literature* (6)2: 83–103.

Toolan, M (1998) 'A reply to Pilkington, MacMahon and Clark'. *Language and Literature* 7(1): 65–69.

Toolan, M (1999) 'Notes and Discussion: Integrational linguistics, relevance theory and stylistic explanation: a reply to MacMahon'. *Language and Literature* 8(3): 255–260.

Toolan, M (2008) 'Verbal art: Through repetition to immersion'. Second International Stylistics Conference, China (SISCC). Shanghai International Studies University, Shanghai. October 22–25, 2008. Available at: http://professormichaeltoolan.wordpress.com/publications/ (accessed 11 December 2014)

豊田昌倫 (1981)『英語のスタイル』研究社.

豊田昌倫（1991）「言語学と文体論」日本文体論学会（編）『文体論の世界』三省堂, 52–66.
Toyota, M（2001）'Stylistics revisited in Japan'. *Poetica* 58: 1–6.
豊田昌倫（2012）「Phonostylistics への試み—Auden と Owen の詩を中心に」『文体論研究』58: 105–111.
豊田昌倫（2013a）「英語の好音調—頭韻を中心に」『現代英語談話会論集』8: 1–24.
豊田昌倫（2013b）「『収斂』から『拡散』へ—Wilfred Owen, 'Futility' の音を読む」*Albion* 59: 1–23.
豊田昌倫（2014）「『緊張』から『解放』へ—Robert Brwoning, 'Porphyria's Lover' の音を読む」『現代英語談話会論集』9: 1–24.
Uchida, S（1998）'Text and relevance'. In: Carston, R and Uchida, S（eds）*Relevance Theory: Applications and Implications*. Amsterdam: John Benjamins, 161–178.
魚住香子（2009）「Graded Readers で読む『フランケンシュタイン』—読み物としての簡約版」『現代英語談話会論集』4: 1–27.
van Dijk, TA（1972）*Some Aspects of Text Grammars: A Study in Theoretical Poetics and Linguistics*. The Hague: Mouton.
van Dijk, TA（1976）'Pragmatics and poetics'. In: van Dijk, TA（ed.）*Pragmatics of Language and Literature*. Amsterdam: North-Holland, 23–57.
van Dijk, TA（1977）*Text and Context*. London: Longman.
van Dijk, TA（1984）*Prejudice in Discourse*. Amsterdam: Benjamins.
van Dijk, TA（1987）*Communicating Racism*. Newbury Park, CA: Sage.
van Dijk, TA（2005）*Racism and Discourse in Spain and Latin America*. Amsterdam: John Benjamins.
Verdonk, P（1984）'Poetic artifice and literary stylistics'. *Dutch Quarterly Review of Anglo-American Letters* 3: 215–228.
Verdonk, P（2002）*Stylistics*. Oxford: Oxford University Press.
Verdonk, P（2010）'A cognitive stylistic reading of rhetorical patterns in Ted Hughes's "Hawk Roosting": A possible role for stylistics in literary critical controversy'. In: McIntypre, D and Busse, B（eds）*Language and Style in Honour of Mick Short*. Basingstoke: Palgrave, 84–94.
von Humboldt, W（1876）*Über die Verschiedenheit des menschlichen Sprachbaues: Und ihren Einfluss auf die geistige Entwickelung des Menschengeschlechts*.（1. Bd; 2. Bd）. Berlin: S. Calvary.
von Lerch, E（1930）*Hauptprobleme der Franzosischen Sprache: Allgemeineres*. Brauschweig: G. Westermann.
Vossler, K（1904）*Positivismus und Idealismus in der Sprachwissenschaft: Eine Sprach-philosophische Untersuchung*. Heidelberg: Carl Winter.
Vossler, K（1925）Neue Denkformen im Vulgarlatein. In: *Geist und Kultur in der Sprache*. Heidergerg: C. Winter, 56–83.
脇本恭子（2001）「Goldsmith の *The Vicar of Wakefield* における会話部の考察—自

由間接話法を中心として」『菅野正彦教授退官記念　独創と冒険―英語文学論集』英宝社, 297–311.
Wales, K（2001）*A Dictionary of Stylistics*（2nd edn）. London: Pearson Education.
Wales, K（2011）*A Dictionary of Stylistics*（3rd edn）. London: Routledge.（豊田昌倫（監訳）『英語文体論辞典』三省堂, 2000（初版の訳））
Weber, JJ（1996）*The Stylistics Reader: From Roman Jakobson to the Present*. London: Arnold.
Werth, P（1976）'Roman Jakobson's verbal analysis of poetry'. *JL* 12: 21–73.
Werth, P（1999）*Text Worlds: Representing Conceptual Space in Discourse*（Textual explorations）. Harlow: Pearson Education.
Widdowson, HG（1975）*Stylistics and the Teaching of Literature*（Applied linguistics and language study series）. London: Longman.
Widdowson, HG（1995）'Discourse analysis: A critical view'. *Language and Literature* 4(3): 157–172.
Wilson, E（1962 [1938]）*The Triple Thinkers: Twelve Essays on Literary Subjects*. Harmondsworth: Penguin.
Wundt, W（1901）*Sprachgeschichte und Sprachpsychologie: mit Rücksicht auf B. Delbrücks 'Grundfragen der Sprachforschung'*. Leipzig: Engelmann.
八木克正（編）（2007）『新英語学概論』英宝社.
山崎のぞみ（2014）「会話における *because* 節の相互好意的機能」『現代英語談話会論集』9: 25–47.
山本忠雄（1938）『文體論研究』三省堂.
山本忠雄（1940）『文體論』賢文館.
Yamamoto, T（2003 [1952]）*Growth and System of the Language of Dickens: An Introduction to A Dickens Lexicon*（3rd edn）. Hiroshima: Keisuisha.
山梨正明（2012）「認知言語学から見た文体論の展望―認知文体論へのアプローチ」『文体論研究』58: 121–152.

第 2 部

文学テクストを語学的に読む：論文解題

イギリスの 3 人の学者による論文解題について

菊 池 繁 夫

このセクションでは Geoffrey Leech 教授 (University of Lancaster, Department of Linguistics and English Language), Michael Toolan 教授 (University of Birmingham, Department of English), そして Jean Boase-Beier 教授 (University of East Anglia, School of Literature, Drama and Creative Writing) に語学的観点から文学テクストを論じた論文の解題をしていただいた。各タイトルに stylistics とあるが, 本書で用いている「語学」という概念に近い。したがって, それらには言語学的 (linguisitc) なものや文学的 (literary) なアプローチをとる論文も含まれている。文学テクストに関して学術論文を書こうとする研究者達にとっては, これらの論文は, 先行研究としても, またどのように論文でオリジナリティーを発揮するかという点においても参考となる, 必読の諸文献である。

The University of Lancaster の名誉教授である Geoffrey Leech 教授は, この 'The best of the bunch: Ten articles on literary stylistics' で述べておられるように, 文学言語への強い志向性から出発し, 途中 Pragmatics (語用論) と Corpus Linguistics (コーパス言語学) という新分野に惹かれて行ったとある。2008 年に *Language in Literature: Style and Foregrounding* という文体論関係の論文集を出されてはいるが, これは主に新分野に惹かれ始める前に書かれたものを集めたものである。教授が大学を卒業されたのが 1959 年で, これは Indiana University での有名な文体論関連の学会が開かれた年である。この学会の発表をまとめたものが Thomas A. Sebeok (編) の *Style in Language*

(1960)で，Leech 教授はこの中で最も重要な論文が Roman Jakobson の closing statement として掲載されている 'Linguistics and Poetics' であるとする。この論文は文体論における 'a combination of functionalism and formalism' の方向性を示し，このことは 'which remains, for me, central to stylistics' であるとしている。これが第1の論文である。2つ目の論文としては Jakobson と同じく Prague 学派の Jan Mukařovský の 'Standard language and poetic language' (1964) があげられ，中心的概念として 'foregrounding' (前景化) が論じられている。Roger Fowler らの言語学的な精緻な分析は F. W. Bateson ら批評家の反発を招いたが，それを収めた Roger Fowler and F. W. Bateson の 'Argument II: Literature and Linguistics' (1967, 1968) が3つ目の論文としてあがっている。第4の Paul Werth の 'Roman Jakobson's verbal analysis of poetry' (1976) は，Roman Jakobson の精緻な分析が新聞の記事や文学的価値の高くない詩作品にも適用され得ることを示しながら，形式的な分析の限界を論じている。ここで Leech 教授は，形式のみならず 'meaning and interpretation' も文体論分析の中心でなければならないとしている。5番目の Ronald Carter and Walter Nash (著) 'Language and literariness' (1983) では，literary と non-literary を明確に分けることはできず，そこには 'a cline of literariness' (文学性の連続) があるとする著者達の主張を紹介している。また 'autonomy of the text' (テクストの自律性) に異を唱える第6の Peter Verdonk の論文は，'context' (文脈) の重要性を '"We have art that we may not perish from the truth" The universe of discourse in Auden's "Musée des beaux arts"' (1987) で主張しているとする。7番目の論文は，Leech 教授がコーパス研究に忙しく文体論に手を染めることができないでいた時期に出た 'corpus stylistics' (コーパス文体論) という文体論の領域を切り開いた Mick Short, Elena Semino and Jonathan Culpeper (著) 'Using a corpus in stylistic research: speech and thought representation' (1996) である。この論文で新しい文体論の道が開けたとする。8番目に論じられるのは Willie van Peer (著) 'Introduction to foregrounding: a state of the art' (2007) で，ここでは 'foregrounding' (前景化) の理論がさらなる 'reader's response' (読者反応) 理論への橋渡しが行われている。Katie Wales (著) 'The stylistics of poetry: Walter de la Mare's "The

Listeners"'（2010）が 9 番目の論文である。Wales は，読者が，なぜこの詩を好ましいと思うかを，文体的な証拠をあげながら徹底的に説明している。最後の 10 番目の論文には，Michael Toolan（著）'Is style in short fiction different from style in long fiction?'（2013）が来る。この論文では Toolan の，短編は短いゆえに一気に読まれ，したがって最後に 'a High Emotional Involvement passage' と呼ばれる 'a particular "emotively immersive" passage（a kind of climax）' が来るという主張を高く評価している。

次のセクションの 'A sample of memorable articles on stylistics and text analysis from the past fifty years: A personal selection and commentary' は The University of Birmingham の Michael Toolan 教授によるものである。Toolan 教授は出版されるに値する文体論やテクスト分析の論文としては，読み手がそこで論じられた手法を自分に身近なテクストに応用してみたく思う，あるいは論じられた作者や作品についてもっと知りたく思うような論文のことであり，この基準に合致する論文として 11 編を選んだとある。 教授はまず John Sinclair（著）'Taking a poem to pieces'（1966）を第 1 の論文としている。この論文では Sinclair は Philip Larkin の詩 'First Sight' における 'bound and free clauses' などの文法的パターンを細かく分析し記述する。そして文法的な面を越えた解釈的な要素は徹底的に排除している。第 2 の論文は生成文法に基づく文体論で，James Peter Thorne（著）'Generative grammar and stylistic analysis'（1970）である。Thorne は，ある詩なり散文なりの解釈上の印象を，それを生成した文法に遡って説明しようとしている。3 つ目は Ronald Carter（著）'Style and Interpretation in Hemingway's "Cat in the Rain"'（1982）である。Leech and Short（著）*Style in Fiction*（1981）がこの論文の 1 年前に出ているが，この本で示された分析例を，さらにひとつの作品に限って詳細に分析して見せてくれているのがこの Carter 論文であると，Toolan 教授は述べる。4 つ目は Deirdre Burton（著）'Through glass darkly: Through dark glasses'（1982）で，Burton は Halliday の意味システムを Sylvia Plath の *Bell Jar* 中の節に現れた行為の種類を 3 つの基本的な Actor-Goal のパターンに分類する。5 番目は Michael Hoey（著）'The discourse colony: A preliminary study of a neglected discourse type' (1986) で，この論文では，斬新な考えである 'text of texts'（いくつかのテクストから成るテクスト），Hoey の言葉を借りれば 'discourse colony'（談話のコロニー）が論じられている。6番目は Roger Fowler（著）'Meaning and world view' (1986) である。Fowler は M. A. K. Halliday の機能言語学に拠って文学テクストの分析を試みているが，その際に語句の 'choice'（選択）から，その人物が 'overtly'（明示的に）伝えるものではなく，'reveal'（開陳する）ことになるその人物の 'meanings, values, or attitude'（意味，価値観，態度）を見ようとする。7つ目の論文として Toolan があげるのは，Kate Clark（著）'The linguistics of blame: Representations of women in *The Sun*'s reporting of crimes of sexual violence' (1992) である。この論文は後の批評的談話分析（Critical Discourse Analysis）(CDA) に通じるもので，Clark は *The Sun* 誌に掲載された男女の暴力問題を8週間にわたって収集し，記事のヘッドラインや冒頭が男性の側の犯罪性を隠ぺいし，被害者の女性に責任ありとする形になっていることを示した。8番目は William Louw（著）'Irony in the text or insincerity in the writer? The diagnostic potential of semantic prosodies' (1993) で，この論文の中心概念は 'semantic prosody' というもので，それは言語形式がコロケーションによって持つようになった意味のオーラのようなもののことである。したがって，この 'semantic prosody' は直感的よりは言語コーパスを 'intertextual' にコンピュータ処理して初めて理解できる現象であるとする。9番目は Paul Simpson（著）'Point of view in narrative fiction: A modal grammar' (1993) で，Simpson はナラティブにおいて 'point of view'（視点）を形成する上で modal 化した命題の重要性を指摘している。10番目は Malcolm Coulthard（著）'Author identification, idiolect and linguistic uniqueness' (2004) である。ここでは書き手の特徴を探ることで，その書かれた文章の authorship を論じている。最後の11番目の論文は評者の Michael Toolan（著）'Poem, reader, response: Making sense with "Skunk Hour"' (1984) で，この論文はアメリカの詩人 Robert Lowell の 'Skunk Hour' を分析したもので，中では例えば 'voiceless affricate [tʃ] a kind of prominence in this stanza'（スタンザの中でプロミネンスを与えられている無声破擦音である [tʃ]）と 'voiced affricate [dʒ]'（有声破擦音 [dʒ]）の対立をはじめ，きめの細かい語

学的分析がなされる。しかし Toolan 教授は 'literary reading'（文学的読み）は 'a method' に収斂されず，それは詩のみならず通常の言語も同じで，'indeterminacies' に開かれたものであるとしている。

　Jean Boase-Beier 教授の 'Articles relating to stylistics and translation' では翻訳学と文体論が歴史的にどのように互いに関連しあいながら発展していったかという観点から論文が選ばれている。最初の論文は Donald Freeman（著）'The strategy of fusion: Dylan Thomas's syntax'（1975）で，この論文は，各詩人には特有の 'poetic design'（詩的デザイン）を有しており，そこから 'stylistic choice'（文体的選択）が行われるとする。逆に言えば 'stylistic choice' を研究すれば 'poetic design' に迫ることができるとして，それを実践して Dylan Thomas を分析している。2つ目の Michael Riffaterre（著）'Transposing presuppositions on the semiotics of literary translation'（1992）は，翻訳学に貢献する論文と見ることができる。Riffaterre は，文学テクストの各部は互いにリンクしあって内部完結しているので，文学の翻訳はこれらの特性を反映すべきであるとする。この意味では Freeman の 'poetic design' に近いものを見ることができる。Francis Jones（著）'On aboriginal sufferance: A process model of poetic translating'（1989）が3番目の論文である。Jones によると翻訳の過程とは Jakobson が述べたように 'recreative'（再創造的）な過程である。第4の論文は Kirsten Malmkjaer（著）'Translational stylistics: Dulcken's translation of Hans Christian Andersen'（2004）で，ここでは Malmkjaer が 'translational stylistics'（翻訳的文体論）と呼ぶ視点を示している。ここでの主張は，文体というものを書き手による 'the result of choices'（（言語単位の）選択の結果）とすると，翻訳されたテクストの書き手は，その書き手が語句の選択をしているわけであるので，翻訳家ということになるというものである。著者である Boase-Beier 教授の論文 'Translating Celan's poetics of silence'（2011）が次の5番目にあがっている。これまであげられた論文は文体論的概念が翻訳を論じるのに如何に有益であるかを語っていたが，この論文を含めて，これ以降，テクストを越える認知的なものと社会的なものの必要性が視野に入ってくる。6番目の論文は J. Boase-Beier, A. Fawcett and P. Wilson

（共編）*Literary Translation: Re-Drawing the Boundaries*. London: Palgrave Macmillan（2015）に所収の Jean Boase-Beier（著）'Using translation to read a poem' である。第4の Malmkjaer の論文は，そこでの 'translational stylistics' というものは文体論のひとつの分野であるのに対し，Boase-Beier 教授の2つの第5と第6の論文は，文体論はもともと本質的に 'translational' であるというものである。

The best of the bunch: Ten articles on literary stylistics

Geoffrey Leech

I had been invited to select my ten 'best' papers or articles on stylistics, and to write about them. For me, this task became a historical (and to some extent autobiographical) reconstruction of the history of stylistics. In the English-speaking world, stylistics—understood as the study of literary texts informed by linguistics—began in the later 1950s. The choice was also very parochial: I tried to deal only with the UK and with English language and literature.

I have adopted this historical, quasi-autobiographical approach because my academic career more or less began with the birth of stylistics. As an undergraduate, I studied for a B. A. in 'English Language and Literature' at University College London—where, despite the ordering of words in this title, the greater emphasis (as in all British universities at that time) was on literature. I chose, as far as possible, a syllabus weighted towards language, and so, when I started my academic career as a junior lecturer, I found the building of bridges between language and literature the most congenial and fruitful way to develop my research interests. I was asked to teach a course on 'Rhetoric' to first year students, and in those laissez-faire days, I was allowed to teach more or less what I wanted—which, in this case, was a linguistic perspective on literature.

So I began my teaching and research with stylistics—and this remained one of my main interests for the next twenty years. But later in my career I was distracted from literature by newer developments—particularly in pragmatics and corpus linguistics—which then meant that I rather neglected stylistics for the next twenty years. I published only the occasional article on the language of literature—until I produced a book (*Language in Literature: Style and Foregrounding*, 2008) which, although largely based on earlier publications, was a more substantial re-entry into the stylistics world. I have mentioned this to explain why my familiarity with published work in stylistics was strongest in the earlier period—say, up to c. 1980—and why many of my 'favourites' belong to that period.

The year when I graduated, 1959, happened to coincide roughly with the start of stylistics in the English-speaking world. That beginning is often associated with a conference on Style and Language at Indiana University in 1958, and the subsequent publication of its proceedings in Style in Language, edited by Thomas A. Sebeok (1960). The conference covered a strange mixture of topics, and the dominant paradigms of linguistics, particularly in the US, were post-Bloomfieldian structuralism and early Chomskyan generative grammar—neither of which was particularly hospitable to literature and the study of meaning. By far the most influential paper in that volume was the (1) **'Closing statement' by Roman Jakobson (1960)**, whose brilliant mind and erudition schooled in Russian formalism and Czech functional structuralism brought a more humanistic outlook to join the brash rigour typical of North American linguistics at that time. Jakobson's paper, which as a 'closing statement' was no doubt meant to reflect back on the proceedings of the conference, was in practice a new beginning—pointing the way to a combination of functionalism and formalism which remains, for me, central to stylistics.

I have already mentioned the Prague School of functional structuralism, and my next choice is a paper from that school, (2) **'Standard language and poetic language' by Jan Mukařovský (1964)**. Originally published in Czech in the 1930s, this article did not become known in the English-speaking world until translated by Paul Garvin in 1964. Garvin's choice of the term foregrounding to translate the Prague School term *aktualisace* was not particularly accurate, I gather, but provided a key that unlocked, for me, the special nature of literary language: that by using language in extraordinary ways, literary writers 'foreground' or give psychological prominence to their special linguistic effects, which then lead to extraordinary interpretations. But for Mukařovský, the quantity of foregrounding was not the key to poetry: the key was in the 'consistency and systematic character of foregrounding'. This was how, to my mind, the more diffuse, liberal tradition of poetics in Continental Europe brought a deeper grasp of literature to join with the formalistic English-language linguistics that was catching on in my own country.

The 'new stylistics' (as it was called by its chief champion in the UK, Roger Fowler) was embraced by linguists who have since become famous for their wider ground-breaking contributions to linguistics: for example, M. A. K. (Michael) Halliday and John Sinclair. But tackling literary texts with the tools of linguistics all too often met with incomprehension from literary critics. Sinclair (1966) wrote a paper 'Taking a poem to pieces' which did just that— much to the amused disdain of the Oxbridge literary establishment, as represented by the Oxford don F. W. Bateson. In the journal he edited—*Essays in Criticism*—Bateson published a damning review, and averred that he would not let his daughter marry a linguist. Fowler replied to Bateson's raillery with a measured and reasoned defence of stylistics which I choose for my third sample: (3) **'Argument II: Literature and Linguistics' by Roger Fowler and F. W. Bateson (1967, 1968)**. It apparently had a mollifying effect, for Bateson responded with a semi-retraction: 'Would I allow my daughter to marry a linguist? It is a good question. And I suppose, if I am honest, I would much prefer *not* to have a linguist in the family. But at least I would not forbid the banns...' (*ibid*, 1968: 176).

One triumph that stylistics pioneers achieved was the conversion of the revered literary critic, I. A. Richards, to the merits of linguistic analysis by Jakobson—who, with his co-author Jones, had produced a microscopically detailed analysis of the intricate multi-faceted binary parallelistic patterning of Shakespeare's 129th sonnet, as a testimony to the Bard's greatness (Jakobson and Jones 1970). However, the formalistic brilliance of Jakobson's meticulous analysis did not impress everyone. (4) **'Roman Jakobson's verbal analysis of poetry' by Paul Werth (1976)** made a big impression because it demonstrated that Jakobson's techniques could be applied, with equal intricacy and painstaking detail, to the parallelistic patterning in a newspaper article, or in a bad poem by the well-known Victorian poetaster William McGonagall. Purely formal analysis, however clever, could not establish the quality of a work of literary art. Not just form but also meaning and interpretation (as I had argued in my first stylistic publication, Leech 1965) had to be at the basis of stylistic analysis.

With its focus on formalistic methods, stylistics in the early days was taking its cue from the New Criticism movement of scholars like Wimsatt and Beardsley, with its insistence on the text as the only reality to study in literary criticism. Extraneous matters of context, such as the author's intentions, the reader's interpretation, and the biographical background, were excluded from serious consideration. Let us call this the 'autonomy of the text' thesis. Another fetish of early stylistics was the need to pin down the concept of 'literariness'. According to what Pratt (1977) called 'the poetic language fallacy', it was theorized that some magic formula or other—for example some litmus test applied to the formal qualities of a text—could determine whether it was literature or not. The article that, to my mind, put paid to this vain theorizing was (5) **'Language and literariness' by Ronald Carter and Walter Nash (1983)**. The authors carefully analysed the literariness of prose style and demonstrated, by a number of different characteristics and sample texts, that the difference between literary texts is wrongly portrayed as a barbed-wire fence dividing literary sheep from non-literary goats—instead, it is better to think of a cline of literariness—a continuum of multiple criteria are in play.

In refutation of the thesis of the 'autonomy of the text', which was popular in the early days of stylistics, I need to recall the admirable work of another leading stylistician—Peter Verdonk. He has shown, by his sensitive and painstaking analysis of style over many years, that a poem cannot be properly understood without the fullest exploration of its context. Nothing known to or felt by the author (in so far as we can reconstruct it) can be excluded *a priori* from the interpretation of a literary text. The article which, for me, best shows this is (6) **'"We have art that we may not perish from the truth": The universe of discourse in Auden's "Musée des beaux arts"' by Peter Verdonk (1987)**. Auden's iconic poem philosophises on the art of the Flemish artist Pieter Brueghel, and particularly on the well-known painting, *Landscape with the Fall of Icarus* (the classical story of how a young Greek attempted to fly with artificial wings, plunged into the sea and died). This tragic event is depicted as a small detail in the background of the painting, whereas in the foreground we see peasants and their animals—the whole panorama taking in both the tragic and the humdrum of the everyday world. As Verdonk shows, Auden's poem builds on the paradox of the painting and applies to art generally. Verdonk's sympathetic insight interweaves poetry and painting—and without our imaginative comprehension of the context, we could not appreciate the poem.

I have mentioned that I was distracted away from stylistics, especially in the 1980s and 1990s, when I was very busy with non-literary areas of research—for example, with the building of the British National Corpus in 1991-5. I would have liked to bring together my favourite research fields of stylistics and corpus linguistics—and the possibilities of this have now been well demonstrated. But at that time I was unable to see the potential of this apparently ill-matched marriage of the humanistic and the computational. I was delighted, however, when three of my colleagues engaged in perhaps the earliest project in corpus stylistics. This was a project in which the characteristics of discourse representation (direct speech, indirect speech, free indirect thought, and so on) were compared by means of a corpus of literary texts and a parallel corpus of press writing. The first fruits of this project in publication were found in the paper (7) **'Using a corpus in stylistic research: speech and thought representation' by Mick Short, Elena Semino and Jonathan Culpeper (1996)**, showing how the annotation and analysis of a corpus can help to test stylistic classification schemes and hypotheses. A new window on stylistic possibilities had opened.

The concept of foregrounding, which I had borrowed from the Prague School in the 1960s, had been sporadically useful not only to myself, but to other stylistic authors such as Roger Fowler, Peter Verdonk and Mick Short. But it lacked a certain credibility, because needed empirical research had not been done. The first successful attempt to fill this gap was a book (van Peer 1986) on the psychological testing of foregrounding, and twenty years later the same author edited a special issue of Language and Literature, from which I choose my next article: (8) **'Introduction to foregrounding: a state of the art' by Willie van Peer (2007)**. This introduction, and the whole issue that followed, brought up to date the research done on foregrounding, and showed how, over a range of approaches, the linguist's identification of foregrounded features of language coincided with what is striking, important and worthy of further discussion in the reader's response. Foregrounding had 'come of age' and was no longer just an appealing idea.

There is a habit, within stylistics, of mingling subjective preference with scientific rigour. This is (in my view) a danger only if we fail to separate the two, and consequently let our likes and dislikes interfere with our analysis. I have always maintained that the stylistician should have no prejudices except a prejudice *in favour of* the work being examined. We choose texts for analysis because we feel they are interesting and challenging, but also because we love them. The last two places in my list of ten favourite articles are reserved for two authors whose work in stylistics I particularly admire, and which have a tendency to help me to love and understand (*to appreciate*) the literature better. First, I choose (9) **'The stylistics of poetry: Walter de la Mare's "The Listeners"' by Katie Wales (2010)**. Wales takes as her theme a poem which has been very popular among English-speaking people (Number 3 on the 1995 top poem list), and has hence been endlessly anthologized, though deeply despised by serious critics. She shows us the reasons (in the language and the implications of context) why the poem has had a strange hold over the popular imagination. She makes us, in a fresh spirit, love the poem that has been looked down upon. In (10) **'Is style in short fiction different from style in long fiction?' by Michael Toolan (2013)**, another leading stylistician seizes on an interesting idea which, as far as I know, nobody has tackled before. We feel that the style of short stories is somewhat different, in a nebulous way, from the style of long fiction—of novels. Is this just a vague feeling, or does stylistics have tools subtle enough to investigate the puzzle and answer this question? Toolan points out that the distinctiveness of short stories is that they are short enough to be read at one sitting, and consequently, towards the end one tends to find a particular 'emotively immersive' passage (a kind of climax) which he calls a High Emotional Involvement passage. Analysing the characteristics of such passages—including the likelihood of such linguistic features as private verbs, free indirect thought, and non-sentence grammar—Toolan takes an important step towards defining the characteristic stylistics of short fiction. A very worthwhile theme to investigate.

I was invited to include discussion of one or two articles of my own in the ten top articles. But I find I have no room for them, which is just as well: it would be invidious, I feel, to include them. I have mentioned, in passing, the earliest and almost the latest of my stylistic publications: this is enough. I can hazard a guess that the earlier ones will be longer-lasting than the later one.

References

Carter, R and Nash, W (1983) 'Language and literariness'. *Prose Studies* 6(2): 123–141.

Fowler, R and Bateson, FW (1967) 'Argument II: Literature and linguistics'. *Essays in Criticism* 17: 322–347.

Fowler, R and Bateson, FW (1968) 'Argument II (contd.): Language and literature'. *Essays in Criticism* 18: 164–182.

Jakobson, R (1960) 'Closing statement'. In: Sebeok, TA (ed.) (1960) *Style in Language: Proceedings of the Conference on Style held at Indiana University 1958*. Cambridge, MA: MIT Press, 350–377.

Jakobson, R and Jones, L (1970) *Shakespeare's Verbal Art in 'Th'Expense of Spirit'*. The Hague: Mouton.

Leech, G (1965) '"This bread I break"—Language and interpretation'. *A Review of English Literature* 6: 66–75.

Leech, G (2008) *Language in Literature: Style and Foregrounding*. Harlow, UK: Pearson/Longman.

Mukařovský, J (1964) 'Standard language and poetic language'. In: Garvin, PL (tr.) *A Prague School Reader on Esthetics, Literary Structure and Style*. Washington DC: Georgetown University Press, 40–56.

Pratt, ML (1977) *Towards a Speech Act Theory of Literary Discourse*. Bloomington, In: Indiana University Press.

Richards, IA (1970) 'Jakobson's Shakespeare: The subliminal structure of a sonnet'. *Times Literary Supplement* 28.5.70: 589–90.

Sebeok, TA (ed.) (1960) *Style in Language: Proceedings of the Conference on Style held at Indiana University 1958*. Cambridge, MA: MIT Press; New York: John Wiley and Son.

Short, M, Semino, E and Culpeper, J (1996) 'Using a corpus for stylistic research: Speech and thought representation'. In: Thomas, J and Short, M (eds) *Using Corpora for Language Research: Studies in Honour of Geoffrey Leech*. London: Longman, 110–131.

Sinclair, JMcH (1966) 'Taking a poem to pieces'. In: Fowler, R (ed.) *Essays on Style and Language*. London: Routledge and Kegan Paul, 68–81.

Toolan, M (2013) 'Is style in short fiction different from style in long fiction?'. *Études de Stylistique Anglaise* 4: 95–106.

van Peer, W (2007) 'Introduction to foregrounding: A state of the art'. *Language and Literature* 16 (2): 99–104.

van Peer, W (1986) *Stylistics and Psychology: Investigations of Foregrounding*. Beckenham, Kent: Croom Helm.

Verdonk, P (1987) '"We have art that we may not perish from the truth": The universe of discourse in Auden's "Musée des Beaux Arts"'. *DQR: Dutch Quarterly Review of Anglo-American Letters* 17 (2): 78–96.

Wales, K (2010) 'The stylistics of poetry: Walter de la Mare's "The Listeners"'. In: McIntyre, D and Busse, B (eds) *Language and Style. In Honour of Mick Short*. Basingstoke: Palgrave Macmillan, 71–83.

Werth, P (1976) 'Roman Jakobson's verbal analysis of poetry'. *Journal of Linguistics* 12 (1): 21–74.

A sample of memorable articles on stylistics and text analysis from the past fifty years: A personal selection and commentary

Michael Toolan

Introduction

I am happy to write a commentary on a selection of articles on stylistics and written text analysis which seem to me in one way or another to be exemplary, and a model for any young scholar. To these, at the request of the editor of this volume, I have added one article of my own, selecting it because I still remember, these many years later, that it was satisfying to write, and because it can be seen to be in dialogue with several of the other articles I will be discussing. I should not speak for my own, but all the other articles I think demonstrate the kinds of things that make a paper worth publishing — from the point of view of the journal as well as that of the author. They take a substantial topic, and make a distinct contribution. If the topic is a well-recognised one (most are), they show they understand what others have said on the matter, but still offer a fresh view of their own, sometimes enabled by new texts, new methods, or a new technology. If the topic is not a familiar and established one, they introduce the reader to the new question in an accommodating way, making what might have been alien accessible. Either way, thoughtful analysis is combined with clarity of expression. One proof of a highly publishable (and highly readable) stylistic or text-analytic article is that the reader finishes it wanting to apply the proposed method on other suitable texts familiar to them, or wanting to read more of the poet or author whose work has been discussed. These articles I believe pass that test.

1 Sinclair, John (1966) 'Taking a poem to pieces'. In: Fowler, Roger (ed.) *Essays on Style and Language*. London: Routledge, 68–81.

Sinclair's was possibly the first stylistic study of a poem by Philip Larkin, a true contemporary (Sinclair's first footnote mentions other papers with similar objectives to his own, a fuller linguistic description of a poem than had been customary, but they are of older poets, no longer living: Yeats, Hopkins, Thomas, cummings). The selected Larkin poem, "First Sight", describes the shock a lamb must experience at birth (possibly in the Yorkshire dales, though this isn't specified), the 'vast unwelcome' of snow and glare, and the incomprehensible otherness of being outside the ewe. Larkin was a fine choice as he combined brevity, accessibility and lexicogrammatical ingenuity in all his poems. The Sinclair study focusses on grammatical description, and on factors like the patterning of bound and free clauses, points of surprising grammatical arrest (a postponing of the material required for the sentence to be complete) or grammatical release (where there are no further grammatically required elements) and their sometimes unsettling effects. He eschews any kind of interpretive speculations, beyond the grammatical facts. So the most he offers in the way of synthesizing remarks are sentences like: "[So] the free clauses have complements but not adjuncts, and the bound ones adjuncts but not complements" (77). Still he uses his grammatical analysis to further some selectivity, advising that we pause to consider "the four complements involving adjectives" (79). Here he departs from his initial declaration that he would consider grammar only and not lexis — since as yet "we have no proper description of English vocabulary patterns" (68) — to observe that these four complements "also contain most of the unusual vocabulary juxtapositions" in the poem. The four complements in question, underlined here but with their preceding Subjects and verbs also recorded, are:

> *[lambs] meet <u>a vast unwelcome</u>;*
> *[lambs] find <u>a wretched width of cold</u>;*
> *[lambs] know <u>nothing but a sunless glare</u>;* and
> *[there] lies <u>earth's immeasurable surprise</u>*

In effect Sinclair treats these complements as foregrounded or marked by virtue of the highly unexpected word-class shifts involved (treating the normally adjectival *unwelcome* as a noun; collocating *cold* with *width*). He also notes all the 'reversing affixes' at work in these phrases — *un*welcome, *sun*less, etc. — surely calculatedly avoiding the term 'negation', but describing the effects of these reversing affixes much as others subsequently talked of the comparative evaluative effect of negation. This feature of reversal (as he calls it) is what he concludes his brief analysis with, persuasively seeing it at work in the poem's final sentence: *They [the lambs] could not grasp it if they knew, / What so soon will wake and grow / Utterly unlike the snow*. Nowhere in the poem (or Sinclair's commentary) is there mention of the abattoir and the butcher's shop (or, today, the supermarket), where most of these lambs will soon be headed; perhaps rightly so, that being part of the utterly unknowable that will emerge soon enough. One reviewer at the time commented on the Sinclair article as follows:

> Sinclair's study of Philip Larkin's short poem, 'First Sight', is fourteen pages long and includes five charts of such features as clause- and nominal group-structure, but in the last paragraph reaches the conclusion that "the exercise shows how some aspects of the meaning of the poem can be described quite independently of evaluation." In the context of descriptive linguistics this is a sensible conclusion, but as literary criticism it is awfully trivial. (Melia, 1974: 592)

If the above were Sinclair's only conclusion, this would indeed be a muted achievement, but it isn't: Sinclair's ideas about arrest and release in clause structuring and the expectations that these different options meet or frustrate were an important contribution to a more systematic understanding of sentence and verse rhythm and the effects (sometimes iconic) of so-called 'loose' sentences and periodic sentences. A more insightful review came from Freeman, who admired Sinclair's thorough analysis of the frequent congruence but local non-congruences of grammar and metrical form; Sinclair showed how "poetry strains syntactical as well as lexical rules in a strategic way" (Freeman, 1968: 111). The other thing to say about the Sinclair remark quoted by Melia is that it takes a position that later writers have increasingly questioned: few stylisticians today would accept that neutral or non-evaluative description of text language is really possible (so they would not share Professor Melia's own evaluation that this was 'a sensible conclusion').

2 Thorne, James Peter (1970) 'Generative grammar and stylistic analysis'. In: Lyons, John (ed.) *New Horizons in linguistics*. Harmondsworth: Penguin, 185–197. Reprinted in Freeman, Donald (ed.) (1981) *Essays in Modern Stylistics*. London: Methuen and Company, 42–52.

Thorne's essay of nearly 50 years ago was aimed in part at showing the relevance of stylistics and literature to grammatical theory, as its title suggests. The main steps in Thorne's argument are still found in stylistic studies today, despite the huge changes in theory and technology in the intervening years. He attempts to trace interpretive impressions of a poem or prose passage back to sources in the grammar that 'generated' the relevant text, declaring "What the impressionistic terms of stylistics are impressions of are types of grammatical structures". Thorne was a generative linguist, and he sees an affinity between stylistics and generative grammar since both are essentially mentalistic, and build upon language-users' grammatical intuitions. Description of surface patterns was not enough: as Chomsky implied, a 'surface' description will not capture the deep meaning- and structure-differences between *John is eager to please* and *John is easy to please*. Thus a clear 'mission' for stylistics was identified: that of raising to awareness and analytic scrutiny the deep structure facts that account for a text having its particular style.

Thorne's most fully discussed example in the article is a grammatical analysis of a passage from Raymond Chandler's crime novel, *The Lady in the Lake* (1943), narrated in the first person by Philip Marlowe, the 'hard-boiled' private detective who, we infer, has been in something of a temper and is shown becoming calm and peaceful. Thorne postulates an array of grammatical *indices* of the initial angry restlessness, and the subsequent quiet (or torpor, even). He suggests that for much of the passage the underlying grammatical structure is highly repetitive, with in rough terms a *I VP-ed and I VP-ed* pattern. Thus, repeatedly there are two conjoined clauses each with *I* as their Subject and the following Verb Phrase in the past tense: *I pushed it to one side and (I) had another drink* (the pattern is slightly masked by the deletion of the repeated first person pronoun in the second conjunct). Thorne claims the 'highly repetitive style' is instrumental in creating 'the mood of aimless, nervous agitation the passage conveys' (191); in contrast, the final sentence stands apart, he says, announcing a change of mood in part by being grammatically different. The grammatical exceptionality he highlights (and implies contributes to the mood change) is the fact that only the final sentence has initial *And,* followed shortly by overt first person Subject pronoun.

Thorne's grammatical description is not above criticism or amendment (but stylisticians now more regularly realise that most grammatical descriptions are open to contrasting re-description), and the final sentence of his selected passage can be contrasted stylistically with those preceding it in other ways than he notes (see discussion in Toolan, 2014). But that is as much a strength as a difficulty: Thorne encourages the reader to look at the grammar of the text in a rigorous way, and inspires with his enthusiasm and his claims about the flexibility of grammar, its adaptability to the needs of individual literary works. And he incorporates his grammatical description into a large provocative claim: given the 'deviant' rules of composition in individual poems, Thorne speculates that every poem has its own distinct dialect, so "the task that faces the reader [of a poem] is in some ways like that of learning a new language (or dialect)" (Thorne 1970: 194). At around the same time, in a celebrated study of the grammar(s) of William Golding's novel, *The Inheritors*, and despite using a quite different grammatical system, Halliday (1971) adopted a somewhat similar strategy.

3 Carter, Ronald (1982) 'Style and Interpretation in Hemingway's "Cat in the Rain"'. In: Carter, Ronald (ed.) *Language and Literature: An Introductory Reader in Stylistics*. London: Allen & Unwin, 65–82.

Ron Carter's article on 'Cat in the Rain' can lay some claim to be the single most read and taught stylistics article in the UK. For those reasons alone it deserves the attention of anyone who wants to publish an article that 'makes an impression'. Like Clark's (see below), it is arguable that Carter's does not contain anything exceptionally original in its grammar or argument; but it is admirable in its lucidity, in its deft use and accompanying explanation of the steps in a stylistic analysis, and in its choice of text for discussion. At the time of publication, relatively few stylistics papers had ventured beyond the short poem, so discussing a short story was comparatively ambitious and innovative (not that Carter undertook to 'say everything relevant, stylistically, about 'Cat in the Rain'; but he did implicitly promise to make some 'key' stylistic points and, I believe, succeeded). Leech & Short's celebrated survey of *Style in Fiction* had appeared the year before (1981), but offered innumerable samples, rather than a study of a single prose fiction work. So Carter arguably 'caught the zeitgeist' especially well, and perhaps the best articles mostly do just that. Having said that, a chapter from Leech and Short (1981) could certainly figure among the most important and effective publications in stylistics over the past forty years — perhaps especially their influential chapter 10, on Speech and Thought Presentation, a rich discussion of the topic. Inter alia they were the first systematically to develop the argument that with Indirect Thought and Direct Speech as 'default' presentation options (since, 'normally', a reporter can capture others' direct speech but can only relay indirectly a wording of their thoughts), Free Indirect Thought is a narrowing of the teller-character separation (implying empathy?), while Free Indirect Speech is a widening of it (implying irony or criticism?). Only because that chapter is really part of an integrated book-length study do I exclude it from the items discussed here.

Much like Thorne, Carter argues that his (our) interpretive intuitions about the opening paragraphs of a literary text such as the Hemingway story "are to a large extent conditioned by linguistic patterning" — patternings that the linguist or stylistician is well-placed to identify and describe. But how do we know which patterns to select? How do we know which patterns are the crucial ones doing the conditioning of interpretive intuitions or responses, and not minor ones? Carter's answer is 'those that are most striking', meaning here 'striking to the analyst'. The conventional metaphor of 'strikingness' is very prominent in this phase of the stylistic analysis; it is a variant of more abstract formulations in terms of 'foregroundedness' or 'prominence' or 'markedness'. He proceeds methodically: there are various linguistic patterns in the text, these patterns foster our intuitions and impressions (e.g., of alienation and restlessness in 'the American wife' and even in the depicted setting at the opening of Hemingway's story), and these are the basis of extended critical discussions. As Carter shows, at the story's opening there is a high frequency of definite noun phrases with minimal modification ('bare head' NPs), denoting quasi-generic items (*the couple, the hotel, the garden, the square*), and very few indefinite noun phrases. The bare, stereotypic noun phrases, he argues, help create a sparse and stereotypic scene and situation, something so familiar and typical and uninteresting (the narrator, here aligned with the bored and frustrated American woman, implies) that it simply does not merit fuller description. Furthermore, if the 'sparse NP' is a strong pattern, it is also arguably a local or text-internal norm. Against that norm, a copiously-modified indefinite NP becomes itself a striking exception. And there is indeed one maximally contrasting NP, late in the story, and as is well-recognised, itself an interpretive crux that has generated many stylistic analyses (see, e.g., Kikuchi 2007):

> *a big tortoise-shell cat pressed tight against her and swung down against her body*

Similarly, if modals and auxiliaries are in general sparse or non-existent, the brief passage where the woman thinks about going into the square and finding the cat is marked or contrastive. *The cat would be around... perhaps she could go ...* Again, the stylistician's hunch is that this switch or modulation is not merely formal (and arbitrary), but that the formal modulation signals and is motivated by a narratological change, to the intermittent disclosure of the woman's own thoughts, in Free Indirect Thought.

4 Burton, Deirdre (1982) 'Through glass darkly: Through dark glasses'. In: Carter, Ronald (ed.) *Language and Literature: An Introductory Reader in Stylistics*. London: Allen & Unwin, 195–214.

Burton begins her article by noting that Stylistics articles (rather as Labov and others had observed with regard to personal narratives), once they have put their 'victim' poem or passage through the slicing and dicing, labelling, counting and tabulating of findings, really ought to be able to address the "So what?" question. What was the point of a linguistic analysis of a text, literary or otherwise, Burton asked, unless you could connect it up with some sort of personal, social or political consequence—preferably of an ameliorative or progressive kind? (There is a fairly direct line linking Burton's article and Clark's, fifteen years later.) Accordingly there is a strong flavour of engagement and protest in the broad trajectory of Burton's article, which could be read in part as an articulation of how, in selected passages of her autobiographical *The Bell Jar* (1963), Sylvia Plath powerfully represented the mind style of a subjugated and even harmed psychiatric patient (herself), upon whom the horrors of electro-convulsive therapy (ECT) were imposed. Other literature of the 1950s and 1960s (e.g. Ken Kesey's *One Flew Over the Cuckoo's Nest* 1962) similarly characterized ECT as pernicious and akin to the ghastlier forms of scientific experimentation upon non-consenting humans. With the benefit of hindsight, we should not that, although ECT doses in earlier years were dangerously large, the treatment itself has proven safe and beneficial.

Burton's article explains a method of semantic analysis of sentences (Hallidayan transitivity), argues that this is an invaluable means of drawing up an 'impartial' and systematic map of the 'Who does what to whom?' of a narrative, and then backs up that claim by demonstrating the descriptive system at work on passages of *The Bell Jar*. The connections with Sapir and Whorf's thinking, to the effect that our habitual ways of representing the world in language reflect and maintain our habitual ways of thinking about the world and its contents, are direct. But whereas Whorf tended to assume the habits were 'in' the language (or even a whole cluster of languages, such as those he lumped together under the label Standard Average European), later critical linguist writers such as Fowler and Burton argued that there were dialects and varieties *within a language* where some of the most contentious habits of patterning were entrenched. If men habitually refer to women at their workplace as *the girls in the office*, while equally habitually referring to males as *the men in the office* (not *the boys*), a host of male cognitive subordinatings of women become 'natural'—and male treatment of women as equals becomes awkward and difficult. Or a profession, such as the medical profession, might develop such a sophisticated way of talking about cases and treatments that compassionate attention to the individual identity of the patient is neglected. All of this is complex and multi-faceted, but Burton adopted Halliday's simple semantic parsing system, to sort the kinds of actions reported in the clauses of *The Bell Jar* passages into 3 basic Actor-Goal patterns: intentional human actions (*Mary kissed John*); unintended (superventional) human actions (*John accidentally broke the vase*); and non-human events (*The bomb exploded;* or *The explosion deafened John*).

Burton argues that in the passage Plath "writes herself into a concept of helpless victim", in part by resorting to a pattern of "disenabling metaphors, disenabling lexis, and disenabling syntactic structures". Some of Burton's analytical decisions (e.g. concerning which clauses are events, which are intentional, and which are superventions) may be questioned, and certainly the Halliday transitivity system is somewhat revised today. Nevertheless, her conclusion holds, that in the selected passages depicting application of ECT to the narrator-patient, those that are represented as Actor and agentive are the nurse, the doctor, and the electricity itself, and almost never the patient. Again, we might argue that the electricity should be classified as Instrument, not Actor, used by the doctor, the covert or implicit Actor; and it might be felt to be expected that an anaesthetised person will inevitably be the grammatical as well as literal patient, the 'done to', in a medical intervention of this kind. Still, it remains noteworthy in Burton's view that, overwhelmingly, it is the patient or her body that is affected, by others, while she herself affects little, and certainly affects nothing that extends beyond her own body: her most dynamic or transitive action here is *I shut my eyes*.

5   Hoey, Michael (1986) 'The discourse colony: A preliminary study of a neglected discourse type'. In: Coulthard, Malcolm (ed.) *Talking about Text: Studies Presented to David Brazil on his Retirement*. Birmingham: English Language Research, University of Birmingham, 1–26.

Michael Hoey has been for many years one of the most original and stimulating commentators on the structure of English text. His more recent book on his theory of lexical priming—his own reinterpretation of the idea of collocation that shows it operating by way of norms of patterning or selection at multiple levels of text organisation—has rightly attracted much attention. But his 1991 *Patterns of Lexis in Text* is a classic, built around a brilliant shaping idea concerning the importance of cohesion by means of cross-sentential lexical repetition. His articles are equally inspiring, and well worth retrieving from their sometimes obscure places of publication. His paper outlining his notion of the 'discourse colony' appeared in a festschrift for another deeply original Birmingham-associated linguist whose work is still relevant today, David Brazil.

Hoey's starting-point is the observation that distinct text-types have distinct and characterizing internal structure; each text-type has its own 'grammar'—in the sense of having its own pattern of textual or linguistic 'ingredients'. This has long been recognized, with the result that many kinds of written text have had their text and generic structure copiously analysed: narratives, for example, but also essays, newspaper editorials, personal letters, business reports, print advertisements, political speeches, classroom interaction, and so on.

Other kinds of texts, however, were more of a 'Cinderella' kind, Hoey argues—being too easily overlooked by analysts, despite being important in our everyday dealings and having interesting characteristics. One such, a kind of 'text of texts', Hoey called the *discourse colony* (using the word 'colony' in the sense of a structure built by aggregation, as in a bee-hive or an ant-hill). A mundane discourse colony is the humble shopping list: this comprises a variety of items that contribute to the whole rather as individual bees help build a hive (and not as the individual limbs or organs combine in a human body). As with the removal or death of individual ants or bees, removal of specific items from a shopping list do not render what remains a dysfunctional or incomplete shopping list. Further discourse colonies include: phone books; the newspaper, and the various sections within the newspaper; trade directories; legal statutes; dictionaries and encyclopedias; classified ads; and so on. In truth, for many people their chief use of written texts is with discourse colonies rather than any of the more admired kinds of text. Best of all, Hoey went on to identify nine main characteristics of discourse colonies. Not all nine characteristics will apply in every discourse colony, but a preponderance will:

Characteristics of Discourse Colonies:
1. Meaning is not derived from sequence (just as bees enter the hive in any order).
Adjacent units do not form continuous prose (fellow bees do not mate)
2. There is a framing context (there is a larger text framing this text) (bees need a hive) 'The framing context of a colony is usually essential for its interpretation in a way that is not normally the case for 'mainstream' discourses' (Hoey, 9). Colony titles may help identify just what the colony is, or they may help explain the contents.
3. There is no single author and/or it is anon: no strong sense of an authorial persona.

4. One component may be used by the addressee without referring to the other components.
5. Components can be reprinted or reused in subsequent works.
6. Components may be added, removed or altered.
7. Many of the components serve the same function.
8. Alphabetic, numeric or temporal sequencing.

The 'texts' that make up a discourse colony may be one word long (e.g., the items in a shopping list), or many thousands of words long (e.g., essay-length articles in an encyclopedia), in which case they will usually have their own kind of internal structure. The implications of Hoey's study of the list, and a pragmatic (rather than semantic) basis for text-sequencing, reach wide and are especially relevant to web-based digital information dissemination.

6 Fowler, Roger (1986) 'Meaning and world view'. In: Fowler, Roger *Linguistic Criticism*. Oxford: Oxford University Press, 147–167.

After a number of years of enthusiasm for generative linguistics, Fowler adopted Hallidayan linguistic description and a Bakhtinian, socially-embedded theory of language (Whorf and Orwell, throughout, were intellectual influences on him also). The Hallidayan approach is to the fore in this final substantive chapter of Fowler's 1986 introduction to stylistics. Where his chapter title uses the word 'meaning' he could have alternatively used the Hallidayan 'ideation', or representation. Fowler's purpose was to show how a close attention to the kind of language and language choices in a passage of textual representation could reveal the meanings, values, or attitude of the person understood to be the text's source, *quite apart from whatever declarations of values and attitudes that speaker might state overtly* (we are well aware that people can say one thing but mean another). To encapsulate this idea that a speaker's or teller's style could even unwittingly disclose their true mind, Fowler coined the phrase *mind-style*. He first introduced the phrase in a slim Methuen volume called *Linguistics and the Novel* in 1977 (by way of abridging and rendering more pithy a wording he had derived from Uspensky: 'point of view on the ideological plane'), but the exemplification is fuller in the 1986 chapter. The phrase's great strength was and is its brevity combined with its suggestiveness. Despite various re-interpretations by subsequent scholars, Fowler's simple idea remains compelling: that the reader is often steered to postulate specific and out-of-the-ordinary psychological or ideological characteristics in a narrator on the basis of a cluster of style features in their narration. If *le style c'est l'homme même*, then we are often willing to entertain the idea that an overt narrator's language tendencies may be indicative of their mind-set, their preoccupations, their fields of knowledge and ignorance, their temperament, judgement, and values.

What does Fowler concentrate on, in uncovering the ideational implications of style choices? He looks at three linguistic areas: vocabulary, transitivity, and syntax. Under the first of these he succinctly (he was always admirably succinct in his demonstrations) explains what underlexicalisation and overlexicalisation are, and diagnoses them in a Wallace Stevens poem and at the opening of Keats's "Ode to Autumn", respectively. Under transitivity he advocates use of much the same semantic classification of roles (Agent, Affected, Instrument, etc.) and processes (material action, mental reaction, verbal process, etc.) as Burton had; and under clause syntax he focuses on the basics, such as the kind and frequency of departures from SVO order in simple clauses. He brings the three areas together in rapid but incisive and detailed observations on the styles of passages from a gothic novel, a Hemingway story, and a Hammett detective novel; and having described something of their distinct styles, he draws plausible conclusions about the minds that adopted those styles. This short chapter ends with some observations about the seeming stylistic links between textual reporting of 'alienated sex' in Lawrence's *Sons and Lovers*, and depictions of violence, and of mere body parts (not people) as semantic roles, in the Hammett passage. All these Fowler speculatively links up in relation to pornographic narration—a speculation that could easily be the basis of a whole doctoral thesis, and is typical of the buzz of fresh ideas that accompanied all Fowler's best writing.

7 Clark, Kate (1992) 'The linguistics of blame: Representations of women in *The Sun*'s reporting of crimes of sexual violence'. In: Toolan, Michael (ed.) *Language, Text and Context*. London: Routledge, 208–224.

Kate Clark was the least academically qualified of the contributors to the volume of twelve essays on 'contextualised stylistics' that I solicited and edited in the early 1990s. And yet her article has been by far the most cited and, I suspect, most used in undergraduate teaching, in the two decades since. Doctorates and tenure are only one kind of qualification, of course, and Clark had others: after an English Language and Literature degree at the University of Liverpool completed in 1987 she had worked in Palestine, and at the time her article was published she was back in London, active in the Women's Movement and enlarging her understanding of the Middle East by learning Arabic. And she came to my notice via Deborah Cameron (whom I had also invited to contribute to the volume). Other qualifications surely included Clark's youth and gender, and her excellent writing style. The latter has been confirmed by her subsequent distinguished career in journalism: from 1999-2002, for example, she was the BBC's Kabul correspondent, and she is now freelance, reporting for various media on Afghanistan, Pakistan, and the Middle East.

Clark's article was a 'critical linguistic' analysis (written before the advent of CDA) of one British tabloid newspaper's reporting of sex-related crimes against women (especially, the crime of rape). It was also an early form of corpus-based study: she collected all the news stories about male/female violence printed in *The Sun* newspaper in an 8-week period. She showed how the wording of story headlines and opening paragraphs obscured the criminality and responsibility of the male perpetrator, and insinuated that some of the responsibility could be laid at the door of the female victim. She relatedly showed how *The Sun* sexualised these crimes, thus casting them in terms that would again mitigate the perpetrator's culpability, whereas to report the crimes in the terms that would make sense of the victims' experience would have involved much fuller report of the violence, the physical harm, and the often long-term psychological damage. The frequent naming of the male perpetrators by [-HUMAN] dead metaphors (*fiend, monster, beast,* etc.) tended to obscure their personal human responsibility. The naming of the women victims equally depersonalised them, tending to reduce them to a role (and, often, a role that is interpretable relative to a male other): *wife, unmarried, vice-girl*. Hallidayan transitivity was used to highlight how the agency of the rapist or murderer is often obscured (by passivisation with agent-deletion, or use of middle-voice verbs). A headline and opening sentence from one 1986 story is sobering exemplification:

> Girl 7 murdered while Mum drank at the pub.
> Little Nicola Spencer was strangled in her bedsit home—while her Mum was out drinking and playing pool in local pubs.

Clark's article was also timely—especially for British readers—coming early in the Thatcher era (before the Falklands war and the repression of the miners's strike revived that prime minister's declining political capital), when there were still hopes of progressive reform of some of the more objectionable sexist and racist attitudes detectable in Britain's tabloid press.

Why has Clark's article been such a success with students and academics? Not, I believe, because it said sharply original things about the sexist and sensationalist representation of women (especially young and attractive women), and of sexual or violent crimes against women; rather, because it told a story about news media sexism really well, and clearly, and persuasively, even movingly. It used relatively familiar linguistic descriptive methods to demonstrate bias and asymmetry in *The Sun*'s naming of the perpetrators and victims of these violent crimes, and in that newspaper's representation of the events and states involved.

8   Louw, William (1993) 'Irony in the text or insincerity in the writer? The diagnostic potential of semantic prosodies'. In: Baker, Mona, Francis, Gill and Tognini-Bonelli, Elena (eds) *Text and Technology: In Honour of John Sinclair*. Philadelphia/Amsterdam: John Benjamins, 157–176.

The idea of a prosodic meaning extending from a node word to one or even several words before or after it was perhaps first raised by Sinclair in relation to verbs like *happen*, *cause*, and *set in*, which normally collocate with references to unpleasant or undesirable rather than positive or welcome outcomes. But

Louw's article of 1993 really put the idea on the map. Semantic prosody as described by Louw extends the definition to focus on a consistent series of collocates; for him, the semantic coherence of a word's collocates taken as a whole is what generates the semantic prosody attached to that word. And this also makes semantic prosody more difficult to identify automatically, on the one hand, or intuitively, on the other. This latter point is why, along with other corpus linguists who have championed the slightly-controversial process of 'looking at a lot of language', Louw has argued (1993: 159) that semantic prosody is "a phenomenon that has been only revealed computationally, and whose extent and development can only be properly traced by computational methods". (The implied contrast between corpus linguists looking at a lot of language and other linguists not doing so is open to question. No linguist can 'look at' more than about five words at a time; but with digital and computational resources corpus linguists can sort language, find patterns, and count phrases, much faster than hitherto.)

Just as a phonological prosody can span a whole phrase or line, a semantic prosody is not confined to a single word, its notional source, but enters into the meaning of adjacent words; it is a "consistent aura of meaning with which a form is imbued by its collocates" (Louw 1993: 157). Now part of the importance of Louw's 1993 article is that it has become a kind of authoritative source on the notion (even if, as Louw himself has emphasized, Sinclair had previously used the phrase): the numerous articles on the topic since, many giving only qualified assent to Louw's claims, have clearly felt it important to engage with his article. Again there is a 'zeitgeist' factor here: if you can identify a coming topic, and write about it with insight and ambition, preferably finding a phrase that sums up a whole constellation of ideas—*semantic prosody, mind style, discourse colony, blaming the victim*—then you can add to the perceived importance of your contribution.

Part of the attraction of the phrase Louw championed was the use of the word 'prosody', such an entrenched term in the study of suprasegmental phonology—it analogised a locally prevailing meaning or evaluation to something syntagmatically extended, like an intonation contour: one of the rival terms, semantic preference, carries none of these associations and also seems to turn the focus back on the speaker (preferring this meaning to that) rather than implying that the meaning is simply 'in' the syntagmatically-enchained wording. Louw relates the term to Firth's ideas about phonological prosody, where

Firth was describing forms of assimilation—the effects of the pronunciation of one phone on that of an adjacent phone. The analogy is inexact, with all elements in the semantic case being altered, something nor apparent in phonological assimilation. But another of the valuable aspects of the Louw article is the way he builds on the semantic prosody idea, as his subtitle indicates. If a variety of words (*cause, happen, bent on, utterly*, etc.) normally keep company in which they in concert convey a particular evaluative colouring, then situations where they seem not to be so used should trigger an implicature of 'falsity'. And the falsity cannot but be either conscious and intentional speaker irony, or a kind of mistake, an unconscious slip, and therefore indicative of the speaker's insincerity 'showing through' (in western discourses, salespeople and politicians have proven good sources of semantic prosody reversals of the unintended and thus insincerity-disclosing kind, for some reason). Now when I write *for some reason* there, I am certainly being ironical, pretending to an unknowing surprise where in fact I don't find it at all surprising that those bent on getting your money or your vote almost at any cost should be caught out sometimes. Whether *for some reason* has a semantic prosody, I leave to others to explore.

Irony is often deliberate: the author intends to create the effect produced by the reversal of the semantic prosody. Analysis of the uses of the adjective *fine* in texts shows that it normally expresses a positive semantic prosody, as in the example *a fine actress*. This prosody can then be reversed, in which case it becomes ironic, as in the almost fossilized ironic idiom *fine mess*—frequently occurring in the longer sequence *another fine mess* (X has got X or Y into).

9 Simpson, Paul (1993) 'Point of view in narrative fiction: A modal grammar'. In: Simpson, Paul *Language, Ideology, and Point of View*. London: Routledge, 46–65.

Paul Simpson's chapter, too, has a buzz about it, the thrum of a linguist conveying the richness of effects that writers secure by judicious choice of tone or stance. His chapter on point of view in narrative fiction is 'in dialogue' with Fowler, and with Uspensky in the further distance. He tactfully but firmly explains his dissatisfactions with received schemas of types of narration, which in the 1980s still leaned quite heavily on the basic 'first person/third person' contrast (and showing vs. telling), albeit recognising as everyone since Lubbock has, that distinct from the neutral or narratorial reporting of characters who are pronominalized in the third person, we have often since Henry James encountered a version of third-person narrative which is specifically aligned with one of the main characters (sometimes shifting among several characters), so that we are largely told just what that character sees, hears and know, rather than what any detached observer could report. But in addition to a three-way distinction among standard voices (of course there are others besides, including so-called *you*-narration, but his focus is on the main types), Simpson argues that we can use modality and other grammatical devices disclosing speaker stance and evaluation to distinguish three 'shadings' of the events and states reported: positive, negative, and neutral. Events are positively shaded where the narration includes mental process verbs and *verba sentiendi* disclosing characters' mental reactions, boulomaic and deontic modality indicating what various characters wish for or judge to be needed, and generic sentences encapsulating what the narrator again confidently asserts to be invariably the case. Of course the emphatically positively-shaded narration may reflect a deluded and unreliable narrator, full of false confidence, but that is a separate issue. Negatively-shaded narration is that intriguing situation where boulomaics and deontics and mental reaction verbs are scarce but epistemic uncertainty is prominent, as if the narrator isn't quite sure what happened; as a corollary, perception verbs and words of estrangement (*it seemed that x, as if y*), Simpson suggests, are typical. Here is a narrator partly excluded or alienated from a deeper inside knowledge about the story they have undertaken to tell. Neutral, unshaded narration is detached but not excluded/alienated (it has made no claims to have insider knowledge), and is similar to old-style 'objective' journalism (more honoured in the breach than the observance, of course): the narrator reports just the observable facts, in so-called 'minimalist' style, without any judgemental slant added (Hemingway and Carver are standard exemplars).

One of the considerable strengths of Simpson's chapter is that it builds, by stages, to its conclusion that this 9-cell typology (3 types of narrator, in positive, negative, and neutral versions) can informatively capture many of the distinctions among kinds of narratorial perspective and engagement that will be relevant. The chapter also has a pleasing rhythm in the way it introduces complications, ideas for further testing of the system, and speculations about which of the 9 types are most conducive to devices like free indirect thought. What about re-writing: can we take a first person positively-shaded story opening and re-write it third person 'unaligned' negatively-shaded mode? What are the difficulties in doing so, and what are the different effects achieved? The best stylistics papers give the reader room to take and creatively redeploy whatever bits of grammar have been under discussion, and the Simpson essay is outstanding at this. Finally, the literary passages selected as test-bed of the revised model are palpably different from each other (so we can see that there are contrasts for a system to capture), and richly entertaining in their own right. None more so than the bizarre but hilarious Beckett passage, the first to be given extensive analysis:

> Your mother, said the sergeant, is your mother's—Let me think! I cried. At least I imagine that's how it was. Take your time, said the sergeant. Was mother's name Molloy? Very likely. Her name must be Molloy too, I said. They took me away, to the guardroom I suppose, and there I was told to sit down. I must have tried to explain. I won't go into it. I obtained permission, if not to lie down on a bench, at least to remain standing, propped against the wall.

10   Coulthard, Malcolm (2004) 'Author identification, idiolect and linguistic uniqueness'. *Applied Linguistics* 25(4): 431–447.

This article explores how far idiolect and the uniqueness of individual utterances can be used to answer certain questions about the authorship of written documents—e.g. concerning how similar two essays need to be to justify a charge of plagiarism. Coulthard presents and discusses two ways of measuring textual similarity: the proportion of shared vocabulary (clearly, quite a gross measure, but still a revealing one); and the number and length of shared phrases. It is a major strength of the article that these diagnostic tests are illustrated with examples drawn from both actual criminal court cases and genuine incidents of student plagiarism. The examples—because they are so apposite—advance the presentation, remind the reader of why these issues are important, and make the questions feel 'real'. Plagiarism and collusion are forms of theft or cheating with large consequences for perpetrators and victims.

This article is admirable for the quiet authority with which it makes a number of important points, issues on which Coulthard's many years of thinking and researching underwrite his conclusions. One of these concerns the superficially attractive idea that a speaker's or writer's speaking or writing style amounts to a kind of 'linguistic fingerprint', by which, as the analogy implies, we might be able to identify uniquely the author of a particular contentious text. Can X, whose 'linguistic fingerprints' linguists have on record, be confidently identified as the author, or not the author, of this text? Against this naïve optimism Coulthard cautions: "The value of the physical fingerprint is that every sample is both identical and exhaustive, that is, it contains all the necessary information for identification of an individual, whereas, by contrast, any linguistic sample, even a very large one, provides only very partial information about its creator's idiolect."

In the reality of forensic linguistic analysis—and the huge attraction of research like Coulthard's is that it can make a real contribution to crime-detection or the correction of unjust convictions—the 'search space' can be much narrower than this. So Coulthard goes on to show how a kind of style-matching was after all invaluable in the tracking down of the 'Unabomber', notorious for sending one parcel bomb per year through the mail to various US universities and airlines, until his 35,000-word diatribe about industrial society was published. He goes on to report other studies on plagiarism and collusion, which again enrich our understanding of the process by looking a little more closely at the degree of lexical sharing between two or more texts. In the case of students essays, for example, Johnson found that where three students had colluded on their essays, the first 500 words of their essays shared 72 different lexical types; by contrast the first 500 words of the essays of three non-colluding students shared only 13 lexical types. A further level of certainty is established by the fact that among the far more frequent shared types in the colluding students' essays, many of the types occur just once, i.e. in just one token. So for each of the three essays, these items are hapax legomena, and yet they appear also in the two other essays.

Thus a major theme of Coulthard's essay is that there is often something suspicious about high levels of identical wording between text A and text B (e.g., one essay or witness statement and another), where the person who has prepared the surprisingly similar text B insists (may even swear on oath) that they have had no sight of text A and were in no way guided by it. For example,

Coulthard and others have presented plentiful evidence that even very attentive listeners manage a word-for-word reproduction of less than half the sentences that have been presented to them orally a short while earlier. So the claims of police officers who had not taken notes when interviewing a suspect, but 'wrote up' a transcript of the interview at a later point and insisted that it was reliable, strained credulity. (In more recent years, all UK police interviews are mandatorily audio-recorded, so the conditions have changed.)

The article also encourages us to think about 'linguistics in the world', in that like any forensic linguist Coulthard does not want to see his research confined to the seminar room and the academic conference, but rather carrying some weight in the courtroom and the police station. The criminal courtroom, for example, is already a confrontation of the distinct and sometimes conflicting power and authority of the judiciary, the jury, the police and prosecuting counsel, and the defendant with their legal representative (intent on maintaining the defendant's innocence until such time as they are proven guilty). These contending forces are predictably wary about accepting linguistic experts anywhere near the scales of justice, lobbing in a stone or two of unknown weight. Coulthard's discussions of how the forensic linguist must think hard about how best to present their arguments first to persuade their own side, even to be allowed by them to enter the witness box, are instructive. And he is not afraid to tell an example against himself: of having prepared quite a telling demonstration of the prevalence of 'uniqueness of utterance', using a newspaper report of an Appeal Court ruling as exemplification. Before the trial in which he hoped to present this 'proof', Coulthard rehearsed the demonstration to the barrister who had retained him for the case; but he simply "smiled indulgently and described my intended presentation as whimsical and decided not to use it". The instance can be generalised: there are many situations involving other professionals sensitive about their own positions, or simply the lay public who feel with good reason that they 'own' the language and can have views about it with as much justification as the expert, where a good deal of tact and guile in the deployment of linguists' knowledge, without ethical compromise, is needed. Otherwise our linguistic 'insights' can become the Wittgensteinian wheel that turns but engages with no other part of the machinery.

11 Toolan, Michael (1984) 'Poem, reader, response: Making sense with "Skunk Hour"'. In: Nicholson, Colin E. and Chatterjee, Ranjit (eds) *Tropic Crucible*. Singapore: Singapore University Press, 121–140. (Shortened version reprinted in Ronald Carter and Peter Stockwell (eds) *The Language and Literature Reader*. London: Routledge, 85–95.)

I have no enthusiasm for promoting one of my own articles, but at least if I discuss this one it might draw a few readers back to the wonderful poetry (and criticism) of the mid-twentieth century American poet, Robert Lowell. When I was a student, Lowell's star shone as brightly as his near-contemporary Sylvia Plath, but in the decades since, his has waned while hers (rightly) waxes. The 'main course' of this article is a relatively straightforward application of a range of 'standard stylistic procedures' circa 1980 to Lowell's poem 'Skunk Hour'; but this was made more interesting (I hope) by being flanked by starter and pudding courses in which I tried to situate stylistic analysis in relation to then-current debates about the roles of self and theory in the humanistic disciplines (the theme of the book to which this was an invited contribution), systematicity and subjective interpretation. The essay was written in 1983: deconstructionism and critical theory, and a general antagonism towards the grand narratives of structuralism were strong, although renewed attention to context was only gradually emerging (contexts of gender, race, class, nationality, and so on). In relation to all that, I still think the Lowell poem was a suitable choice: it certainly dramatizes the provisional and fractured accommodation of self (especially a deeply unhappy self) and the normative theories of 'reasonable behaviour', the community censor, of ambient society.

One thing I aimed to do in the outer sections of the essay (parts 1 and 3, as it were), was to manage some kind of dialogue with the editors of the collection, both of whom were antipathetic towards 'grand theory' and, even more so, the totalitarian tendencies of structuralism—where the assertion that 'everything has its place' (Meillet) could easily modulate into the coercive-sounding 'a place for everything and everything in its place'. If *that* were how languages and poems worked, what place for the self, for change, for difference and differing? There we all were, we contributors to *Tropic Crucible*: as expatriate academics in Singapore, we ourselves were translations from elsewhere. Living in the tropics, we felt we should welcome change, being troped or turned. By virtue of this book, the editors perhaps wished us to say, we have turned; and they probably had no objection if we had turned "every one to his own way", as the sheep-like chorus in Isaiah confesses (also heard in the *Messiah* libretto). That would fit with their commitment to the self. Not that the changing or re-thinking was all 'from within': in part, we had turned or been changed by Singapore itself, and the nexus of circumstances that threw us together there, as colleagues (thank you, Margaret Thatcher).

So the introductory and closing parts of my essay warned about the 'over-determinations' of meaning, and the over-reliance on the names and classifications of linguistics, that stylistics can engender (and had, I believe, in the 1960s and early 1970s: Stanley Fish's criticisms had some justification). Stylistics tries to be methodical and can in local topics be methodical, but literary reading cannot finally be reduced to a method, I argued. It is a way, a chosen journey through the text or reception, among a multiplicity of possible ways: someone of a different time and place, or a different class or gender or ethnicity, may choose a different way through. The most we could hope for were kinds of convergence: reconciliation but not 'truth'. I was coming to terms with integrational linguistic thinking at the time. So my argument was not that the diversity of subjective readings and analyses of poems arises because poems are 'different'. Rather the argument was that all language use was like poetry-reading, equally open to indeterminacies as to meaning and form, only constrained and closed-down by the exigencies of interactants wishing to coordinate their activities and goals. Determinacies were speaker- and situation-specific, rather than an imperfect compliance with a fixed autonomous system encoded in the dictionary and the grammar ('the English language').

I still believe those things, but they are dry abstractions, and hard for reader-interactants to engage with. Much more pleasure I find in talking about my reading of a poem like 'Skunk Hour' and the stuttering, mordant, distracted, frustrated, aimless mind of its speaker. Clever and allusive too. Well, he starts out pretty aimless, with his triple of paradoxes or absurdities: the heiress who pointlessly lives on the ultra-cheap, and buys up eyesore properties to ensure they decay, the plaything that is converted back to a work tool (the summer millionaire's yawl sold off to lobstermen), the gay shopkeeper whose business, the speaker says, is doing so badly he'd rather marry (meaning, given the times and the law, take a heterosexual partner for purposes of economic survival). In sum, all service 'industry' and no manufacturing, no creativity, no adapting and evolving, no real presence, no purposeful engagement. Five stanzas obliquely describe orders of dysfunctionality, absence, voyeurism, where the half-rhymes *hill*, *hull*, *hell*, *ill* dominate. Then comes stanza 6, the penultimate, and the only one structurally and semantically adjoined to its predecessor. The speaker has just declared "I myself am hell; // nobody's here" but now continues:

> only skunks, that search
> in the moonlight for a bite to eat.
> They march on their soles up Main Street:
> white stripes, moonstruck eyes' red fire
> under the chalk-dry and spar spire
> of the Trinitarian Church.

There are so many kinds of syntactic, semantic, and phonological cleverness here, making this brief picture exceptionally wrought, multi-layered, allusive but integrated. Very little of this did I draw attention to in my stylistic paper, but it is not difficult to show the multiplicity of kinds of patterning in this stanza, far beyond anything found in the previous five. There is, for example, the sequence of rhymes and half-rhymes that takes us from *search* to *march* to *chalk* to *Church*. (If inter alia these give the voiceless affricate [tʃ] a kind of prominence in this stanza, these are nicely contrasted with the voiced affricate [dʒ] that is prominent in the final stanza, in *garbage, jabs*, and *wedge-head*.) The skunks march up Main Street like human soldiers, obviously, but on their soles—which licenses whimsical thought of the homophonous souls, and this along with the picture of them walking in the shadow of the Trinitarian church spire might make us imagine them as a shadow or a mocking mimickry of Christian soldiers, "marching as to war". But the skunks have been anthropomorphised even before this picture develops, in line 2's describing them as in search of *a bite to eat*—a strictly human-reference synecdoche, and suggestive of leisured informality, or a tourist's disposition. But the church and environment here is parched in its dryness, arid or combustible perhaps (how many of us read *spar spire* and 'automatically' add a fused third, *spare*?). With their white stripes, the skunks are at one with the chalk-coloured church spire. And the speaker is untroubled by the repetition, two lines apart, in mention of the *moonlight* setting and the skunks' *moonstruck* eyes' red fire. If this stanza projects aridity, the next and final one is altogether more damp and fertile, and is the skunks' destination (Main Street is just their access route): here the air is rich, and there's garbage to swill. Incidentally, while the skunks are the only animal to be anthropomorphized in the poem (and by implication putting the speaker and other drifting, self-absorbed humans to shame), they are not the only animal to feature: we've also met *sheep, lobster, fox*, and *ostrich*.

We've had first person plural pronouns earlier in the poem, but rather inclusive ones, denoting 'all of us living on Nautilus Island'. But now in the final stanza there is a much more personal 'we', presumably comprising only the speaker and his family or co-residents: "I stand on top/ of *our* back steps and breathe the rich air—" (italics added). A small marker, but it quietly projects a parallel between the mother skunk and her kittens, on the one hand, and the speaker and those few using these back steps, on the other.

Great poems are, for the reader, the texts that keep on giving; and that the stylistician can come back to a poem some years later and say a number of *different* things about the poem than before, albeit congruent with what they discussed before, is a proof of this. That is the spirit in which the foregoing couple of paragraphs were written. And I will not rehearse here my 1984 argument that by a multiplicity of means (including clause structuring and, transitivity) the poem advances to the full, purposive instrumentality of the mother skunk, the cat that gets the cream, intent on fight rather than flight, and a corrective for the slant-minded human observer. Yet there is hope in the bi-directional *and will not scare* with which the poem ends: the speaker will not scare the skunk, the skunk will not scare the speaker.

'Skunk Hour' is just one of many memorable poems, quite able to stand alone and be the basis of wide-ranging analysis, from Lowell's *Life Studies* and other collections. Some of Lowell's lines once learned are never forgotten. E.g., the portrait of his 'Grandparents', recently deceased at the time of his writing, with its perfect opening: *they're altogether otherworldly now*. Or the inspired innocence and fun of these lines, addressed to his infant daughter, evidently wanting to play with him in the bathroom one morning: 'Dearest I cannot loiter here/ in lather like a polar bear.' All the more poignant for coming in the middle of the poem 'Home After Three Months Away'—*three months away* here being a euphemism for the time Lowell had recently completed in psychiatric hospital, struggling with the manic depression that dogged him all his adult life.

References

Burton, D (1982) 'Through glass darkly: Through dark glasses'. In: Carter, R (ed.) *Language and Literature: An Introductory Reader in Stylistics*. London, Allen & Unwin, 195–214. (Reprinted in Weber, J-J (ed.) (1996) *The Stylistics Reader: From Roman Jakobson to the Present*. London: Edward Arnold, 224–240.)

Carter, R (1982) 'Style and interpretation in Hemingway's "Cat in the Rain"'. In: Carter, R (ed.) *Language and Literature: An Introductory Reader in Stylistics*. London: Allen & Unwin, 65–82.

Fowler, R (1986) *Linguistic Criticism*. Oxford: Oxford University Press.

Freeman, DC (1968) '"Review" of Fowler, R (ed.) (1966) *Essays on Style and Language*. London: Routledge'. *Journal of Linguistics* 4(1): 109–115.

Halliday, MAK (1971) 'Linguistic function and literary style: An enquiry into the language of William Golding's "The Inheritors"'. In: Chatman, S (ed.) *Literary Style: A Symposium*. New York: Oxford University Press, 330–368. (Reprinted in J-J Weber (ed.) (1996) *The Stylistics Reader: From Roman Jakobson to the Present*. London: Arnold, 56–86.

Kikuchi, S (2007) 'When you look away: "Reality" and Hemingway's verbal imagination. *Journal of the Short Story in English* 49: 149–155.

Leech, G and Short, M (1981 [2007]) *Style in Fiction*. London: Longman.

Melia, D (1974) '"Review" of Fowler, R (ed.) (1966) *Essays on Style and Language*. London: Routledge' *Foundations of Language* 11(4): 591–594.

Thorne, JP (1965) 'Stylistics and generative grammars'. *Journal of Linguistics* 1(1): 49–59.

Thorne, JP (1970) 'Generative grammar and stylistic analysis'. In: Lyons, J (ed.) *New Horizons in linguistics*. Harmondsworth: Penguin, 185–197. (Reprinted in Freeman, D (ed.) (1981) *Essays in Modern Stylistics*. London: Methuen and Company, 42–52.)

Toolan, M (2014) 'The theory and philosophy of stylistics'. In: Stockwell, P and Whiteley, S (eds) *The Handbook of Stylistics*. Cambridge: Cambridge University Press, 13–31.

Articles relating to stylistics and translation

Jean Boase-Beier

Introduction

In general it could be said that style is the most important aspect of translation, especially literary translation, and that therefore stylistics as a discipline is indispensable in the discussion of translation, and stylistic analysis a prerequisite for analysis of texts, either before they are translated or after they have been translated. It was this insight that led a very early study of the stylistics-translation link, first written in 1958 (Vinay and Darbelnet 1995), to posit that translation was a practical application of "comparative stylistics" (1995: 4).

Yet until relatively recently works which deal explicitly with the link between style and translation have been few and far between. Nevertheless, style and stylistics were frequently (or perhaps always) implicit in translation studies, and it was for this reason that I wrote *Stylistic Approaches to Translation* (2006). However, the converse does not apply: it has not always been implicit in studies of English stylistics (or the stylistics of any language, for that matter) that we need to consider the place of translation. And yet we do, for many of our basic texts have come to us through translation, and the question of translation hovers behind almost everything written by those early forerunners of modern stylistics, the Russian Formalists and Prague Structuralists. In discussing how translation and stylistics interact, then, we need to be aware of two possible ways that interaction might happen:

(1) We need to analyse the style of the source text and the target text comparatively to have any sense of what translation means.
(2) When we discuss an English text, examining what translators have done

with it will always shed light on the stylistic nuances of the text.

The first interaction concerns what stylistics tells us about translation and the second what translation tells us about stylistics.

There are many reasons why the above two interactions come about. Firstly, and in relation to (1), we know from anecdotal statements by translators (such as those in Biguenet and Schulte 1989) that style, with or without a definition based in stylistics, is the basis of the translator's art. Secondly we know, also in relation to (1), that scholars of translation studies often, if not always, discuss the style of the text (see, for example, Holmes 1988 and Munday 2008). That this usually happens in a somewhat haphazard and terminologically loose way has to do with the lack of training in stylistics that was, until recently[1], common among translation scholars. And, furthermore, it has to do with the rejection, among some modern translation theorists, of a view of translation that they fear might be overly linguistic, systematic, even pseudo-scientific, and too little concerned with questions of ethics, allegiance, power and context (cf. Venuti 1998: 21). And thirdly, in relation to (2), the roots of modern English stylistics, as suggested above, are to be found outside the English-speaking countries, and therefore have themselves entered the English language through translation. Moreover, and crucially, they come from a more multi-lingual tradition than ours. If we think back to Jakobson's work in the early 1960s (see, for example, Jakobson 1960) or Mukařovský's (see 1964) or Riffaterre's (as in the 1985 article discussed here), the notion that the finely-nuanced study of any text could be undertaken while blocking out one's own multilingual background would have been ridiculous.

The mindset of English stylistics is thus in its origins not the anglo-centric discipline it can seem today, but a study rich in concern for questions of universality and specificity, of the context of writing and its possibility for geographical and historical change, and of the sense that the big issues that haunt stylistics—Where do we locate meaning? How do meaning and style relate? How do different stylistic levels in the text relate to speaker's choice, attitude and background? What is the link between style and context?—are inseparable from the human ability to speak in, and represent, many voices and tongues.

---

1) In fact stylistics forms the basis for training translators at the University of East Anglia; this is in part the legacy of Roger Fowler, who taught there.

In explaining the close relationship between translation and style at the origins of modern English stylistics and the importance of that relationship to the above questions, we merely need to remember that the vast majority of the world's population is not monolingual. The dominance of English is not in itself a monolingual one, since most speakers of English world-wide are multilingual, and English stylistics as a monolingual enterprise is, to many scholars (myself included), a strange and unlikely thing.

Bringing together articles on stylistics and translation is not an easy task. In one sense, there are not many, or were not many, until recently, that explicitly made this link, as explained above. In another sense, such articles are unlimited in number, because of the implicit presence in each discipline of the other. I have chosen to discuss here six articles. The first of these (that by Freeman) does not mention translation at all. But it raises many questions of great importance to English stylistics in its multilingual context. The second (by Riffaterre) is an example of stylistics that shows, in its structuralist origins, the impossibility of leaving translation out of consideration. The third and fourth articles (by Jones and Malmkjaer) are by translation scholars whose work takes stylistics as a given. The last two essays are my own, and demonstrate the two types of interaction with which I began. The first illustrates how comparing style, and using stylistics as a basis, is necessary to understand what happens when we translate a poem. And the second illustrates how reading a poem from the point of view of translation leads to stylistic insights that might not otherwise be gained.

The six articles are also intended to illustrate another point that I wish to make about reading and analysing the works of others. This is that academic studies, as much as literary texts (and perhaps, indeed, more so) are located in a particular historical time. They are reacting to thinking that is current at the time of their writing. To ignore this when engaging with them in one's own work is just as grave an error as it would be to pretend that Shakespeare was writing yesterday, or that the class system with which Lawrence engages has not changed since he wrote his works. The historical grounding of academic articles is essential to understanding them and thus to their integration into the current discussion of which one's own scholarship forms a part.

1 Freeman, Donald (1975) 'The strategy of fusion: Dylan Thomas's syntax'. In: Fowler, Roger (ed.) *Style and Structure in Literature: Essays in the New Stylistics*. Oxford: Blackwell, 19–39.

The title of the volume in which Donald Freeman's article appears gives a clue to the importance of history and context in reading, discussing and using the work of the leading scholars of the past. The 'New Stylistics' of 1975 is the old stylistics of 2016. Indeed, it was recently referred to at a PALA[2] conference as "steam stylistics", in analogy to the much-loved steam trains of England, now only kept alive for short journeys by enthusiasts but seen by many to embody ideals of industrialisation, freedom of movement, and a sense of adventure that today's trains (and today's stylistics) must be careful to preserve and to revivify if necessary.

Freeman, in this article, was responding to the rise in studies based on "linguistic aspects of literature" that Fowler discusses in his Introduction to the volume in which it appears (1975: vii). In order to understand what Freeman is saying, one needs to know the context, and the work of the two scholars—Ohmann and Chomsky—with whom his article opens.

Freeman begins by saying that he agrees with Richard Ohmann (a stylistician writing in the 1960s and 70s; see Ohmann 1962) that stylistic choices reflect a particular state of mind or way of thinking. This was a view also, incidentally, held by Roger Fowler, the book's editor, who, a little later, famously coined the term "mind style" (see Fowler 1977). Freeman refers also to the generative grammar of Noam Chomsky, which was the linguistic framework within which all the articles in this book are formulated (see e.g. Chomsky 1957).

The article argues that principles of "poetic design" (p. 20) peculiar to a particular poet are reflected in the style of the text. For the writer, the "poetic design" drives stylistic choice—in this case syntactic choice. For the scholar, analysing the syntax gives access to the poetic design. Because what we need in stylistics is not a complete description but an analysis of those points that are important, we can use foregrounding (here Freeman refers to Mukařovský's 1964 article) to discover which aspects are important.

Freeman shows how Dylan Thomas uses syntax to create fusion, between

---

2) Poetics and Linguistics Association; the conference in question was the July 2013 conference, in Heidelberg.

natural processes and humans, and between individual life and "cosmic history", and illustrates three such strategies of fusion in three poems. The first is the strategy of contradiction in 'Light breaks where no sun shines', which leads us to a metaphorical interpretation of "light". The second is the syntactic linking of propositions so that humans and nature become fused; he illustrates this with 'The force that through the green fuse drives the flower'. And the third is the paradox of mourning and refusing to do so, played out in the syntax of 'A Refusal to Mourn'. Here the fronted syntax, and the suspension of resolution while reading which it causes, make the reader see that death is not only death but new life, embedded in its "cosmic context". Dylan Thomas's syntax, then, reflects his poetics.

In this article, as in everything Freeman has written, the link between the linguistic and the poetic is demonstrated. There is an emphasis on the linearity of reading and the mental processes that are occasioned by the syntax. The article is clearly structured, in that Freeman first sets out his linguistic and stylistic background and situates them in the then current debate: transformational grammar, the beginning of concern for what syntax actually reflects in terms of how the mind (the poet's and the reader's) works. Once the framework is clear, Freeman introduces the poet and immediately characterises him as a "poet of fusion" (21), so we know what is being argued. The poems are discussed in terms of the increasing force of their parallelism between syntax and the nature-human fusion it illustrates. The whole article thus has a rhetorically pleasing and argumentatively effective structure. Freeman sums up his argument at the end.

In terms of our own academic work, this perfectly-structured essay can teach us a lot. Freeman states his argument clearly, saying at the start what his main point is: that Thomas is a poet of fusion and that the syntax makes this poetic imperative clear. The reader is never left to guess what argument is being made. Freeman points to linguistic studies to provide evidence for his assertion that the syntactic structures he discusses are unusual, and foregrounded, and therefore central to Thomas's poetics. He also picks up central statements in stylistics, such as Jakobson's assertion that poetic language projects equivalence from selection to combination (i.e. to syntax; see Jakobson 1960) and shows how his arguments relate to them. He provides many examples and diagrams to make his points clearer.

Some things have changed since Freeman was writing. Though his use of

128   第2部　文学テクストを語学的に読む：論文解題

"he" for the poet can often be justified in that he was speaking of a male poet, he also uses "he" generically, something that is completely unacceptable in academic discourse today. He is also able to quote complete poems. Though copyright law does in fact allow this, even today, as "fair dealing", most publishers are nervous of allowing such long passages to be quoted and the writer must seek permission from the original publisher, and sometimes pay a fee. It is worth knowing which publishers will not require a fee, and how much it is acceptable to quote.

Though Freeman does not mention translation, his assumption that style reflects poetics is central to all current thinking on stylistics and translation, and is behind the notion that the translation of a literary text is the translation of its poetics (see Boase-Beier 2011, discussed below) and not merely a translation of the text on a superficial level.

2   Riffaterre, Michael (1992) 'Transposing presuppositions on the semiotics of literary translation'. In: Schulte, Rainer and Biguenet, John (eds) *Theories of Translation: An Anthology of Essays from Dryden to Derrida*. Chicago: University of Chicago Press, 204–217.

Michael Riffaterre's article, first published in 1985, illustrates another important point about academic context: the book in which the article appears provides its own context, which supplements the historical, geographical and academic context in which it arose. This article appears in a book on translation theories, aimed specifically at translation scholars. Whereas, in a volume of Riffaterre's work, this article might be seen as a contribution to stylistics, it will be read here as a contribution to the discipline of Translation Studies which, in 1992, after its establishment in the 1970s (see Holmes 1988) was still finding a direction between the linguistic studies of the 1970s (e.g. Catford 1965) and the later, more culturally-based theories of the late 1980s and early 1990s (e.g. Venuti 1998).

Riffaterre's article illustrates well the importance of reading the work of other scholars in its historical context, the necessity of criticism (especially when viewed in the context of current thinking) and, above all, the importance for translation and stylistics of textual detail and of a consideration of its implications.

Riffaterre begins by stating that literary language differs from non-literary language in its focus on the style of the text itself. This is a view that derives from Prague Structuralism (see e.g. Mukařovský's 'Standard language and poetic language', 1964) but it has been disputed by many stylisticians (e.g. Fowler 1975), especially in this extreme form. Riffaterre's reasons, besides the focus on style, are the indirect way meaning is expressed in literary language, and intertextuality.

He notes, interestingly, that a literary text always presupposes what he refers to as the "traces left by its production". His view is that these must be made explicit by the translator or the target language reader will not understand the text. It is exactly this "domesticating" view of translation which was called into question by Venuti in 1995 (see Venuti 2008) and has generally been rejected as a way of translating since then.

Riffaterre, in a manner reminiscent of Freeman, says that what we need to get at are the presuppositions that drove the text; these amount to something very close to Freeman's "poetic design". Translation scholars now would not dispute this, but many would dispute that such presuppositions should be made explicit in the translation, as this reduces the reader's possibility of engagement with the text.

Much of the article focuses on intertextuality: Milton's translation of Horace suggests (or presupposes) a poem by Catullus, and Riffaterre examines several translations of this poem, pointing out that the various ways of rendering the bare-breasted nymphs in the poem all fail to capture the connotations of the original: that one nymph in particular will be a mother of heroes. He links this presupposition to foregrounded lexical choice and calls the foregrounding "the locus of originality" (211). His solution is to translate periphrastically and make explicit what is implicit in the original. As a strategy, this would no longer be deemed acceptable (see e.g. Venuti 2008: 14), and this fact demonstrates very clearly the need to locate writing within its contemporary context.

In terms of structure, the reader will notice how much more difficult Riffaterre's article is to read than Freeman's. This is largely because its structure is far less clear. It does not say what it is going to argue, but plunges straight into its topic. It also makes a number of sweeping statements such as "Western sociolects [...] tend to separate sex from motherhood" (210) and "translation must reflect or imitate these differences" (204). In the second decade of the twenty-first century, the first can seem unacademic and the second quaint. Riffaterre, who emigrated from France to the United States in the late 1940s, is not writing in his native language or tradition, and this might partially explain the tendency to unsubstantiated statements. But he was also writing at a time when the freedom we would today expect translation theory to accord its object was not generally acceptable.

For one's own academic writing, this article suggests both that clear structure would improve readability and also that unclear structure does not invalidate otherwise interesting points. Above all, it shows, though, the importance of historical awareness. If a translator working today were to fail to see Riffaterre's argument in its historical context, any discussion that scholar presented would appear irrelevant.

3 Jones, Francis (1989) 'On aboriginal sufferance: A process model of poetic translating'. *Target* 1(2): 183–199.

Francis Jones was writing in 1989 from the position of an award-winning poetry translator with a background in applied linguistics. Though not explicitly discussing stylistics (though he does in later works, e.g. Jones 2011), because writing at a time when 'Stylistics and Translation' was not as common a topic for academic study as it is now becoming, he shows how the sensibility of close-reading of a text, combined with a background in linguistics and the use of linguistic models, produces a useful interaction for translation studies, just as it had done in early stylistic work such as the two previous articles.

Jones discusses the process of translation in this article, and his argument is that it is essentially what he calls a "recreative" (184) process. In using this term he echoes Jakobson, who famously, in 1959, spoke of literary translation as "creative transposition" (2012: 131). Most writers on translation, maintains Jones, focus on the relationship between target text and source text in a prescriptive way. Instead, he wants to examine what actually happens and at the same time develop strategies for the translation of poetry. In part, he reconstructs strategies from different existing translations of the same source text, but, aware of the uncertainty of this as an empirical procedure, he here outlines a basis for research he was later (e.g. 2011) to take further, which takes into account his own experience as a practising translator.

He begins by demonstrating the potential pitfalls of attempting textual equivalence without detailed stylistic analysis of the source text and also, and in particular, a concern for the stylistics of the target text one is writing. His model has stages of reading, including stylistic analysis, and of target text creation, but the intermediate stage, which he calls "interpretation" is concerned with equivalences between the original and its potential translation. He points to the importance of words or even morphemes here, a point taken up by later studies such as the three discussed below. For this stage he has five strategies: one-to-one transference, divergent or convergent inference, improvisation, abandonment and estrangement. Abandonment depends upon an assessment of the relative weight of poetic devices, and is thus a strategy reminiscent of Levý (1969). Estrangement is a particular type of what Venuti (2008) has called foreignisation, and depends upon leaving elements untranslated to indicate the communication of the foreign. The final stage, of recreating the target text, depends upon the creative freedom of the translator to fashion a stylistically coherent text.

The structure of this article is extremely clear, and recalls that of the Freeman article discussed at the outset. It states that it will present a model, gives a diagram, discusses each stage in turn, with examples, and has a concluding section where a brief summary of the main argument is given.

What the reader can take away from a reading of this article for his or her own work are both the ideas and the structure. If you present a model, a diagram is helpful, and numbers—three stages, five strategies—help to add signposts to the text. Jones is innovative in stating clearly that one has better access to one's own strategies than to other people's, and that one's own introspection is thus a perfectly valid source of data, especially when based upon practice from which the model is abstracted.

4 Malmkjaer, Kirsten (2004) 'Translational stylistics: Dulcken's translation of Hans Christian Andersen'. *Language and Literature* 13(1): 13–24.

Malmkjaer's article is written from within a growing trend in translation studies to integrate stylistics, as the latter began to shed its reputation (which persisted in translation studies and literary theory far longer than it did in stylistics itself) for formality at the expense of context. As stylistics became more contextualised (see e.g. Bex, Burke and Stockwell 2000) from the late 1990s on, it also became both more interested in the cultural and linguistic transfer implicit in translation, and more useful in providing tools and explanation for it. Malmkjaer's article suggests that we should speak of a particular type of stylistics, "translational stylistics", which is comparative in nature.

In terms of the interactions between stylistics and translation mentioned at the beginning of this chapter, this article represents the first type: the need to perform stylistic analysis of source and target and compare the two, if we are to describe what translation does.

Malmkjaer's point is that, taking the notion of stylistics as the result of choices made by a writer, one needs to be aware that the writer of the translated text was a translator. We can therefore only analyse the style of a target text in relation to its author if we also consider its relation to its source text. Malmkjaer shows that, whereas much recent stylistics takes the text as given, concentrating on how we read it, and analysing that reading, it is also possible to link such effects to the writer's choices, as suggested by Fowler (e.g. 1996) and many other stylisticians, especially those working in critical linguistics or critical discourse analysis.

Seeing choice as the key problem for stylistics, Malmkjaer contrasts the freedom of the source text writer with the additional constraints imposed upon the translator by the source text itself. She refers to the type of stylistics which takes this relationship into account as "translational stylistics" (15). Translational stylistics is not just comparative, as in Vinay and Darbelnet's 1958 study, mentioned earlier (Vinay and Darbelnet 1995), but it also takes into account the purposes of the target text, its audience, and the translator's aims and interpretation of the original.

In the comparison of target text with its source, which she illustrates with Dulcken's translation of a Hans Christian Andersen story, differences in approach between Andersen and Dulcken can be found, and can help to explain Dulcken's choices. In particular, recurrent patterns in those differences, especially taking into account other work by the original author and a number of translations, can shed light on the style of the translation as a set of choices by a translator.

Malmkjaer's article sets out at the start what it will discuss, contrasting her "translational stylistics" with stylistics of translation which does not take the comparison into account. She summarises at the end a number of factors which can be seen to affect the translator's choices.

This article was important in the development of stylistics and translation, as a particular area of study located at the cross-over of the two disciplines, because it sets out clearly what a stylistics of this type needs to do. It was also important because it was included in a special edition of the journal Language and Literature which was dedicated to 'Translation and Style' and which helped establish the parameters for the interaction of the two disciplines.

5 Boase-Beier, Jean (2011) 'Translating Celan's poetics of silence'. *Target* 23(1): 165–177.

With this article we are now in a period in which translation and stylistics are more commonly written about together. While many studies (e.g. Jones and Malmkjaer, just discussed) focus on the helpfulness of stylistic notions and terminology in discussing translation, others, like this article, examine stylistics as something which also describes what is beyond the text, and tries to demonstrate that what is beyond the text, in its context, now understood as both a mental and a non-mental entity, is crucial to understanding the text. Context, in today's stylistics, integrates what Freeman, in the article discussed here, called "poetic design". But it is only accessible through an understanding of style and stylistics and it is only with their help that the transfer of what is beyond the text, as the central part of translation, can be understood and explained.

This article considers a poem by the Holocaust poet, Paul Celan. Holocaust poetry, because it was triggered by real events, raises particular issues for the translator: in addition to the constraints imposed by the source text (as the article by Malmkjaer discussed) and the need to create a target poem that works poetically (as Jones pointed out), there is an added constraint that the poem must not appear to misrepresent events. The article discusses the poet, Celan, and his particular use, in common with many Holocaust poets, of silences and gaps in the text that demand particular engagement by the reader.

Using cognitive poetics as a basis, the effects of the original poem can be described as making the reader attempt conceptual blending in order to close gaps in the text, but, because these blends fail, the effect upon the reader is one of loss. Celan's poem 'Espenbaum' is analysed as presenting a series of couplets in which the mother of the narrator is compared to a natural object, but the comparison does not work. The mother cannot echo nature, and remains separate: the sort of human-nature blend which informs pathetic fallacy, and might also bring comfort, is denied. And the failure to blend is foregrounded by stylistic parallelisms between the lines, which suggest it might have been possible. The translation needs to retain both clues that lead the reader to perform blends and stylistic devices that make them impossible, if it is to have a similar effect on the mind of the reader. What this article illustrates is that it is not possible, when talking about translation, to ignore the cognitive effects of style. Early stylisticians such as Jakobson and Riffaterre (as above) did in fact speak at length about the effects of textual features. For translators, the need to find equivalences that are not merely linguistic will inevitably lead to considerations of both the state of mind embodied in the source text (discussed by Fowler as mind style; 1977) and the effects upon the reader of the target text. Cognitive stylistics allows a more precise way of describing the effects a translator aims to re-create (which Riffaterre calls "literariness-inducing presuppositions" (1992: 205)) in terms of such mental operations as blending.

The article thus demonstrates, as do those of Jones and Malmjkaer, how stylistics for translation is influenced and shaped by the need to think cross-linguistically, just as it was for the earliest stylisticians such as Mukařovský or Jakobson.

6 Boase-Beier, Jean (2015) 'Using translation to read a poem'. In: Boase-Beier, Jean, Fawcett, Antoinette and Wilson, Philip (eds) *Literary Translation: Re-Drawing the Boundaries*. London: Palgrave Macmillan.

Again it is useful here, as indeed with all the articles I have discussed, to consider the forum in which they appear. This article, like the previous four, appears in the context of translation studies. In this and the previous article, stylistics is the discipline that helps explain translation, that is itself more adequately explained with the help of translation, and that is by nature translational. The difference between these two final articles and that by Malmkjaer is that, whereas Malmkjaer suggests a category of stylistics she calls 'translational stylistics', these two final articles presuppose that stylistics is inherently (and not merely historically) translational.

My 2015 article on the translation of R. S. Thomas explains that we can better understand R. S. Thomas's work when we consider how to translate it. That is, it addresses the second type of interaction with which the present chapter began, and suggests that a translational view of phenomena that might also be studied using only the methods of English stylistics in fact enhances their analysis and understanding. This seems especially appropriate in the case of a poet like R. S. Thomas, who was in fact not English but Welsh, whose English poetry was thus written in the context of a bilingual environment, and a correspondingly enhanced understanding of the power and poeticity of words. The article begins by asking how translation can be helpful in performing a stylistic analysis of a text, especially when the stylistics is broadly cognitive in orientation in that it takes pragmatic, contextual, mental and emotional aspects into account. Whereas some studies of translation with a view to its relevance for style are aimed at finding differences between target and source texts in order to pinpoint passages and devices of particular stylistic interest in the original (e.g. Parks 2007), this article looks at how reading target and source comparatively can lead to an enhanced reading of the original. The article then examines two poems by R. S. Thomas, 'A Life' and 'Remembering'. In both cases, a reading of the German translation by Kevin Perryman, which has not kept the ambiguity of the original, serves to draw attention to that ambiguity. This leads the reader to consider it in greater depth. The second case is particularly interesting because the ambiguity in the original revolves around the reference of "it" in a way typical of Thomas. The disambiguation of "it" in the German produces such a different effect that the reader is forced to re-read the original to see what is happening there. The three possible interpretations can then be seen not to be mutually exclusive. They all obtain at once, thus causing the reader to engage in a great deal of mental processing, echoing the difficulty of the poem's narrator, but also leading the reader to see other elements in the poem as similarly ambiguous. A poem which appeared simple (as indeed Thomas's work has appeared to many of his critics) is now seen to be extremely complex, and its reading to involve a number of complex mental processes.

The article is structured so that, although the issues to be examined are set out at the start, they are framed as questions such as: how will comparison with the translation change the way we read the original?

The article is thus organised around a set of discoveries, and follows in its structure the linear nature of reading in several stages, with the more complex readings, involving revisiting of earlier readings, coming later. The concluding section notes how a reading that starts from gaps (caused by ambiguities) in the text can be related to Thomas' philosophy. In this sense the stylistic analysis that takes translation into account is better able to reconstruct what Freeman, in the article discussed earlier, referred to as "poetic design".

Summary

Overall, the articles discussed in this chapter illustrate a number of things:

(i) The historical development of a discipline (such as stylistics) or sub-discipline (such as stylistics and translation) will inform what a work says and how it says it, and so every article must be read against the background of its appropriate context.

(ii) There are different ways of structuring essays: they can set out their argument at the start, or present a descriptive model, or discover new readings, and in each case the structure will echo the methodology.

(iii) Clearly-written and clearly-structured articles are more pleasing to read, and easier to process.

(iv) When stylistics overlaps with other disciplines (in this case translation studies), such overlap can affect either the way we think of translation (point (1) in my Introduction to this chapter) or the way we do stylistics (point (2) in my Introduction).

(v) If we remember how stylistics developed, we will be less inclined to perform it monolingually.

The articles discussed can serve as various models for one's own academic writing. They also suggest which elements are outdated (e.g. use of the generic "he") and which elements are less likely to work in a less experienced writer (e.g. Riffaterre's somewhat chaotic style is perhaps not one to imitate). In the overall context of English studies, they demonstrate the particular importance of interdisciplinary and multi-disciplinary work.

Bibliography

Bex, T, Burke, M and Stockwell, P (eds) (2000) *Contextualised Stylistics: In Honour of Peter Verdonk*. Amsterdam: Rodopi.

Biguenet, J and Schulte, R (eds) (1989) *The Craft of Translation*. Chicago: University of Chicago Press.

Boase-Beier, J (2006) *Stylistic Approaches to Translation*. Manchester: St. Jerome Publishing.

Boase-Beier, J (2011) 'Translating Celan's poetics of silence'. *Target* 23(1): 165–177.

Boase-Beier, J (2015) 'Using translation to read a poem'. In: Boase-Beier, J, Fawcett, A and Wilson, P (eds) *Literary Translation: Re-Drawing the Boundaries*. London: Palgrave Macmillan.

Catford, J (1965) *A Linguistic Theory of Translation*. Oxford: Oxford University Press.

Chomsky, N (1957) *Syntactic Structures*. The Hague: Mouton.

Fowler, R (ed.) (1975) *Style and Structure in Literature: Essays in the New Stylistics*. Oxford: Blackwell.

Fowler, R (1977) *Linguistics and the Novel*. London: Methuen.

Fowler, R (1996) *Linguistic Criticism*. Oxford: Oxford University Press.

Freeman, D (1975) 'The strategy of fusion: Dylan Thomas's syntax'. In: Fowler, R (ed.) *Style and Structure in Literature: Essays in the New Stylistics*. Oxford: Blackwell, 19–39.

Holmes, J (1988) *Translated! Papers on Literary Translation and Translation Studies*. Amsterdam: Rodopi.

Jakobson, R (1960) 'Closing statement: Linguistics and poetics'. In: Sebeok, T (ed.) *Style in Language*. Cambridge, Massachusetts: MIT Press, 353–358.

Jakobson, R (2012) 'On linguistic aspects of translation'. In: Venuti, L (ed.) *The Translation Studies Reader* (3rd edn). London: Routledge, 126–131.

Jones, F (1989) 'On aboriginal sufferance: A process model of poetic translating'. *Target* 1(2): 183–199.

Jones, F (2011) *Poetry Translation as Expert Action*. Amsterdam: John Benjamins.

Levý, J (1969) *Die literarische Übersetzung: Theorie einer Kunstgattung*. Frankfurt: Athenäum.

Malmkjaer, K (2004) 'Translational stylistics: Dulcken's translation of Hans Christian Andersen'. *Language and Literature* 13(1): 13–24.

Mukařovský, J (1964) 'Standard language and poetic language'. In: Garvin, P (ed.) *A Prague School Reader on Esthetics, Literary Structure, and Style*. Washington: Georgetown University Press, 17–30.

Munday, J (2008) *Style and Ideology in Translation: Latin American Writing in English*. New York: Routledge.

Ohmann, R (1962) *Shaw: The Style and the Man*. Middletown, Connecticut: Wesleyan University Press.

Parks, T (2007) *Translating Style* (2nd edn). Manchester: St. Jerome Publishing.

Riffaterre, M (1992) 'Transposing presuppositions on the semiotics of literary translation'. In: Schulte, R and Biguenet, J (eds) *Theories of Translation: An Anthology of Essays from Dryden to Derrida*. Chicago: University of Chicago Press, 204–217.

Venuti, L (1998) *The Scandals of Translation*. London: Routledge.

Venuti, L (2008) *The Translator's Invisibility: A History of Translation* (2nd edn). London: Routledge.

Vinay, J-P and Darbelnet, J (1995) *Comparative Stylistics of French and English: A Methodology for Translation* (trans. Sager, JC and Hamel, M-J). Amsterdam: Benjamins.

日本の論文でテクストを読む

菊池繁夫

はじめに

先に，イギリスの三者によって日本以外での文体論（Stylistics）を中心とする語学的な文学テクスト研究に関する論文の解題をしていただいたので，ここでは日本人による比較的最近の代表的な関連論文を，その優れた点を取り上げながら紹介を試みたい。これらは先の三者の取り上げた論文と同じく，語学的文学テクスト研究には必読のものである。各セクションの末尾に，論評で引用した文献があげてあるが，さらに詳しい文献については，各論文を参照されたい。なお，各論文中に示されていない訳は脚注に付けておいた。

1 Masui, Michio (1974) '*The Prioress's Prologue and Tale*: A structural and semantic approach'. 『東田千秋教授還暦記念論文集―言語と文体』大阪教育図書, 9–18.

この 'The Prioress's Prologue and Tale' はユダヤ人に殺された子供の話で，子供は信仰心が篤く，死んでからも聖母マリアを称える賛歌 'O Alma Redemptoris mater'（おお救世主のうるわしき母よ）を歌い続けたために捨てられた場所から発見されたというものである。この作品を論じる切り口として，著者は 'structure, theme and meaning' の観点から分析を試みている。

「英詩の父」と称される中世のロンドンに生きた Geoffrey Chaucer（1343–

1400）は，他の同時代の作品群と同じく，その多くの作品において 'prayer' を含むと著者は述べる。そして，その形式は The Knight's Tale を除き，大半はスタンザ形式であるため Chaucer は prayer を用いる際に，この形式を適当と考えたのであろうとする。それはスタンザが 'move spirally' (11) であるのに対し，カプレットは直線的であるからである。この論文で扱われる The Prioress's Prologue and Tale も詩形式において例外ではなく，スタンザの進行様式が敬虔な心が祈りを込めるリズムに合っているのであろうとする。

The Prioress's Prologue は 7 行より成る 5 つのスタンザでできているが，ナレーターである Prioress（尼僧院長）は聖母マリアを称えていて，Tale の前置き的な働きをすると共に宗教的な雰囲気を盛り上げる働きをしている。

Tale の方は，各 7 行から成る 29 のスタンザで構成されている。賛歌 'O Alma Redemptoris mater'（おお救世主のうるわしき母よ）はここで 5 回歌われる。4 回は部分的に，1 回は完全な形で歌われる。それらの場面を，もう少し詳しく見ると以下の如くである：

(1) 子供が他の子供が子の参加を歌うのを聞く場面
(2) 子供がユダヤ人街を通って学校に通う場面
(3) 子供が喉を切られ棄てられた場所で歌う場面
(4) 棺台の上の子供に修道僧達が聖なる水を注いだ場面
(5) 子供が，なぜ自分は喉を切られているのに歌うことができるのかを説明する場面

このように賛歌が反復され，それによって聴衆もしくは読者に，自分達が常に聖母の御前にいることを思わせる。これが，Chaucer が構造的に設定した物語の効果である。

意味論的には，キーワードとなる語が，その形を変えながらも，反復して異なる文脈で現れ，それがこの物語の主題と関連している点が重要であると著者は主張する。その第 1 は 'sweetness' という語である：

The swetnesse has his [the child's] herte perced so
Of Cristes mooder that, to hire to preye,
He kan nat stynte of syngyng by the weye. (555–557)（原著者による [ ]）[1]

著者は 'the sweetness of the Mother of Christ has pierced his heart' (15) が，この子供の殉教の物語の中心的主題であると述べる。そして，この語は子供が奇跡を説明する箇所で再び現れる：

'This welle of mercy, Cristes mooder sweete,
　I loved alwey, ...'　　　　　　　　　　　　　　　(656–657)[2]

これは先行する 'The swetnesse ... Of Cristes mooder'（キリストのお母様の優しさ）のエコーであり，ナレーターである尼僧院長による地の文と，彼女の語る物語内の登場人物である子供の言葉が，密接にリンクしていることを示すと著者は述べる。そして，'This usage of the same word in different contexts is a recurrent practice in Chaucer's art.' (15) と述べる。

　著者の指摘する，もうひとつのキーワードは 'enclosen' という語である。これはまず子供の母親が彼を探しに行く場面で用いられている：

With moodres pitee in hir brest *enclosed*　　　　　　　　(594)
　　　　（以下，断りのない限り引用文のイタリクスは著者）[3]

ここでは，この語は母親について比喩的な用い方がされている。同じ語は別の文脈で再び現れる。この例では，子供について物理的なものを示している：

And in a tombe of marbul stones cleere
Enclosen they his litel body sweete.　　　　　　　　(681–682)[4]

---

1) キリストのお母様の優しさが彼の心に突き刺すように深くふれたので，彼女にお祈りするために，少年は道すがら歌うことを止めることができないのです。（桝井迪夫（訳）『完訳 カンタベリー物語』（中）岩波書店，1995）
2) 「この慈悲の泉，キリスト様の美わしのお母様を，わたしは…いつも愛しておりました。」（同訳）
3) 胸のうちに母親のいとおしさの心を秘めて（同訳）
4) そして輝くばかりの大理石の墓の中に，この少年の美しい小さい体を埋めました。（同訳）

この語は母親と子供を結びつける働きをしていて、この埋葬の部分を書く際に Chaucer は、先の549行目の 'With moodres pitee in hir brest enclosed' を意識していたであろうと著者は述べる。

さらに興味深い点として、上の引用は 'his litel body sweete' の形式で 'the sweetness of Christ's Mother'（キリストのお母様の優しさ）が、この Tale で最後に響く箇所でもある。

もうひとつ反復する語としては、控え目な 'litel' があげられている：'a litel clergeoun, hir litel sone, this litel child, my litel child, his litel body' (16) などである。この語は詩全体に漂う 'pervasive mood of innocence and pathos' (16) を高める働きをしていると著者は主張する。

さらに最も重要な語は 'greyn'（= grain「種子の粒」）であろう。この語は3度現れる。物語の初めに1度は文中で、残りは文末で脚韻として現れている：

> ... and whan that I hadde songe,
> Me thoughte she leyde a greyn upon my tonge.　　　(661–662)[5]

> Wherfore I synge, and synge moot certeyn,
> In honour of that blisful Mayden free
> Til fro my tonge of taken is the greyn;　　　(663–665)[6]

> This hooly monk, ...
> His tonge out caughte, and took awey the greyn,　　　(670–671)[7]

この種子の粒は、小さな殉教者と聖母マリアの間の the Holy Communion（正

---

5) そしてわたしが歌うと、彼女はわたしの舌の上に種子の一部を置かれたように思われました。（同訳）
6) そのゆえにわたしは歌います。必ず歌わなければなりません。かの聖なる気高い処女を崇めるために、わたしの舌からその粒がとり払われるまで。（同訳）
7) さて、この聖なる修道僧、…その彼が、少年の舌をとり出してその上の粒を取り去りました。（同訳）

饗）のシンボルと言えると，Madeleva（1951）を引用しながら，著者は主張している。

　この論文は，まず物語を構造的な枠組みから分析し，その中で反復される賛歌 'O Alma Redemptoris mater'（おお救世主のうるわしき母よ）が聴衆もしくは読者に，自分達が常に聖母の前にいることを思わせる働きをするとしている。そして，その後，場面ごとに散りばめられた，いくつかのキーワードを意味論および主題的連関のうちにとらえて，作品の宗教的な効果を説明している。Chaucer の本作品が持っている宗教的な教えを，反復の効果という形で説明しようとする本論文は，音楽理論を思わせる，大変優れた文体論の論文となっている。また，著者の流麗な英文を改めて認識させてくれる論文でもある。

参考文献

Gray, D（1972）*Themes and Images in the Medieval English Religious Lyric*. London, Boston, Routledge and K. Paul.

Madeleva, SM（1951）*A Lost Language and Other Essays on Chaucer*. New York: Sheed and Ward.

Muscatine, C（1972）*Poetry and Crisis in the Age of Chaucer*. Notre Dame, IN: University of Notre Dame Press.

2 Nakagawa, Ken（2005）'"Through" in *The Prelude*'. In: Japan Association of English Romanticism（ed.）*Voyage of Conception: Essays in English Romanticism*. Tokyo: Kirihara-shoten, 118–133.

この Wordsworth の *The Prelude* は，自然（nature）との交流を通して詩人の精神が成長していく過程を描いており，その成長がキーワードとしての前置詞 'through' に反映されているというのが論文の趣旨である。この論文が優れているのは，作品の特定の語の計量的な分析から，その作品の解釈の問題へと進んでいる点である。逆に言えば，キーワードと想定される語に計量的な裏付けを取っていると言えよう。

機能語・内容語を問わず，The Prelude における語の出現頻度を見ると，なんと 36 位に 203 回出現の 'through' が来る。The Lancaster-Oslo/Bergen Corpus[8] によると，'through' は頻度としては 120 位に位置づけられている。Brown Corpus では 102 位，Leech et al. (2001) では 192 位である。このように The Prelude において 'through' がランクリスト上位にある，すなわち多く使われているのは，この作品において 'the frequent interrelations between the poet's inner world and the outer world of Nature'. (119)（詩人の内面世界と自然という外界の間に多くの相互作用の関係）があるからである。言い換えると，前置詞 'through' の出現順位が通常のコーパスにおける数値より異様に高いのは，詩人の内界と外界の自然の頻繁な交流の語彙面での表れと断言できると著者は言う。

　次に Kadokawa's New Dictionary of Synonyms（『角川類語新辞典』，1981）の語彙分類にしたがって 'through' に後続する名詞を見ると，'time' や 'through' などの抽象名詞の方が 137 例と，'field' や 'world' などの具象名詞 101 例より多く，一般的に信じられている Wordsworth は自然を描く詩人なので具象名詞の方が多いであろうという予測に反している。

　The Prelude の BOOK 1 の中のボートを盗むエピソードでは，わずか 20 数行のうちに 4 度も 'through' が現れる：

　　　... through the water　　　　　　　　　　　　　　　(1.403)
　　　... through the silent water　　　　　　　　　　　　(1.413)
　　　... through the meadows　　　　　　　　　　　　　(1.416)
　　　... through my mind　　　　　　　　　　　　　　　(1.426)

そのうち初めの 3 例は外界を 'through' の目的語としており，最後の 1 例は詩人の内面を目的語としている。この 'through' とその目的語の変化に，全

---

8)　The Lancaster-Oslo/Bergen Corpus は LOB Corpus と呼ばれる。この章でも執筆されているランカスター大学の Geoffrey Leech 他によって 1970 年から始められた英語コーパスで，アメリカの The Brown Corpus のイギリス版。1961 年以降の 100 万語が 15 のテキストカテゴリー別に集められている。以下 LOB と略。

体としてこの詩人の意識の動きがすでに現れているのだが，その点を論じる前に著者はさらに 'through' の持つ動きの意味に注目する。

この 'through' の例を他に探してみると，例えば

  stalking through the fog   (8.401)
  through Paris   (9.40)

などとあり，それぞれ *in* the fog や *in* Paris となっていないことからも，Wordsworth は 'through' に特別の感情を込めていたことが分かる。これらの例に代表されるように 'through' は定点としての場所というよりは動きとしての 'motion' に焦点を当てており，それも外界を通して徐々に内面世界に到る，その両者をつなぐ働きをしている（'The abundant use of 'through' can be said to result from the frequent interrelations between the poet's inner world and the outer world of Nature'.（119））と主張する。

最後に，著者は最も重要な部分として下を引用している。

 1   [...] and from the shore
 2 At distance not the third part of a mile
 3 Was a blue <u>chasm</u>; a <u>fracture</u> in the vapour,
 4 A deep and gloomy <u>breathing-place</u>, ***through*** which
 5 Mounted the roar of waters, torrents, streams
 6 Innumerable, roaring with one voice.
 7 The universal spectacle ***through***out
 8 Was shaped for admiration and delight,
 9 Grand in itself alone, but in that <u>breach</u>
10 ***Through*** which the homeless voice of waters rose,
11 That dark deep ***thorough***fare, had Nature lodg'd
12 The Soul, the Imagination of the whole.   (13.54–65)

スノードン山（Mt Snowdon）の頂から下の雲海を見て詩人が，その情景を描写する箇所だが，内容はこうである：「岸の向こうに青色の割れ目（chasm）があったが，それは霧が裂けた所（a fracture），呼吸をする深くて暗い場所（A ...

breathing-place) で, そこから (through which) 無数の流れの轟 (roar) がひとつの声 (one voice) となって立ち昇って来た。この光景全体 (throughout) は称賛と喜びに値する雄大なものなのだが, あのどこからとも知れない水の声 (voice of waters) が立ち上がる (Through which) 裂け目 (breach), あの暗くて深い通り道 (thoroughfare) に, 大自然 (Nature) は全てを見通す想像力そのものである魂 (The Soul) を住まわせて来ていたのだ。」

この短い 12 行の中に, 詩全体では 4 例しかない through ＋関係代名詞のうち 2 例がここに集中している。さらに, 7 行目の副詞の '*throughout*' (全体), 11 行目の本来は 'through' と 'fare' の合成語である '*thorough*fare' (通り道) も加えると 'through' および, その関連語が 4 例もこの箇所に集中して現れていると著者は述べる。そして, この 'through' で動きを形容される, 立ち昇る轟 (roar, roaring) が声 (voice) に昇華される様を活写する外面描写は, 実は詩人の内面で想像力が湧き上がる様と並行していると説く。

コーパスを用いた分析は, そのままでは, あるキーワードに現れた作者の内面的な感情の動きに迫れないという問題があるが, 著者は, このコーパスを用いた計量的な分析と, 深い読みを中心とした伝統的な文体分析を見事に融合して見せてくれる。伝統的な Jakobson (1960) 流の詩の分析を発展させた, 最新の知見の融合した論文として, この分野を志す者には必読の論考である。William Empson の名論文 'Sense in *The Prelude*' を彷彿させる刺激的な好論と言える。

参照文献

Empson, W (1967) *The Structure of Complex Words*. Michigan: Michigan University Press.

Jakobson, R (1960) 'Closing statement: Linguistics and poetics'. In: Sebeok, TA (ed.) *Style in Language*. Cambridge, Mass: MIT Press, 350–377.

Leech, G, Rayson, P and Wilson, A (2001) *Word Frequencies in Written and Spoken English*. London: Pearson Education.

Ono, S and Hamanishi, M (eds) (1981) *Kadokawa's New Dictionary of Synonyms*. Tokyo: Kadokawa Shoten. (大野晋・浜西正人『角川類語新辞典』角川書店, 1981)

3 Nakao, Yoshiyuki (1995) 'A semantic note on the Middle English phrase *As he / she that*'. *North-Western European Language Evolution* (*NOWELE*) (Odense University Press) 25: 25–48.

この論文は，古フランス語 (OF) com cil / ele qui の ME 期における観念借入語であると考えられる as he / she that 句の意味論的変遷を考察したものである。類似の ME 期の観念借入語には，例えば *by aventure* < *par aventure*, to *have compassioun of* < *avoir compassioun de* などがある。

この as he / she that 句は 1066 年の Norman Conquest 以降，その使用が増え始めるので，この句はフランス語起源と考えることができると著者は仮説を立てる。したがって，Sir John Gower (1330?–1408) は *Confessio Amantis* (『恋人の告白』) (1393) で，この as he / she that 句を用い，*Mirour de l'Omme* (『夢想者の鏡』) (1376–1379) では com cil / ele qui 句を用いているのは偶然ではないとする。

この古フランス語の com cil / ele qui 句には 3 つの働きが認められている：

> sense 1: 'a generic in function ... exhibiting similarity to the referent'
> sense 2: 'exhibiting identity with the referent'
> sense 3: 'expression employée pour indique une cause'

下の *Le Roman de la Rose* (『薔薇物語』) (?1237–) で用いられたこの句の意味は sense 2 で '[she had not been slow to ...] as is natural of one who was very angry' か，あるいは，もっと高い可能性としては sense 3 の 'as / since / [disjunct] for she was very angry' で用いられている：

> N'el n'auoit sa robe chiere
> En maint leu l'auoit desciree,
> *Con cele qui* mout fu iree.   (*Le Roman de la Rose* 311–318)[9]

---

9) そしてドレスをあちこち破いてしまった／そして，喉をかきむしった，／怒りに満ちた女ならするであろうように [怒りに満ちていたので]

もちろん Chaucer のこの箇所の訳は，並行的に元の2つの意味を含んでいるが，sense 3 の「原因・理由」の意味が強いことは同じである：

> And for to rent in many place
> Hir clothis, and for to tere hir swire,
> *As she that* was fulfilled of ire.　　(*The Romaunt of the Rose* 320–326)[10]

　著者は次に，なぜこの句が英語に借入語として入って来たかを論じる。英語がフランス語と接触し始めた時期には，英語には「原因・理由」を示す接続詞が発達していなかった。縦続接続か等位接続かで for は曖昧であったし，because はまだ用いられていなかった。
　「原因・理由」を示す as は形成途上であり，もともと時間的な意味を示す sith / sithen / sin ('since') も「原因・理由」の意味を形成しつつある段階だった。このことから com cil / ele qui 句が as he / she that として借入された初期中英語期は「原因・理由」を示す接続語句を必要としたのであろうと著者は推論する。そういう理由があって，以下の *V and V* で，この句が sense 3 で使われているのだろうとは著者は考える：

> Đus us halede ure halend Iesu Crist, þus us aliesde ure aliesend, and seððen aros of deaðe, *alswo he þe was soð lif*, and bar up to heuene ure loac ...
> 　　(*V and V* II. 25–27)[11]

この句が sense 3 の「原因・結果」を示すのは，次の例からも分かる。それは，*Le Roman de la Rose* の Chaucer 訳で，「原因・理由」を示すフランス語の que の訳として，この as she that 句が用いられていることである。

> *Qu*'el les auoit tretoz deroz

---

10)　ドレスを何か所も破り，喉を引き裂いた，怒りまくっている女の人によくあるように［怒りまくっていたので］

11)　かくして救世主イエス・キリストは我々を救ってくれた，かくして救い人は我々が罪を犯すのを防いでくれたのだ，そうして死から蘇った，真理の生を貫く人ですから

De mautalant e de corroz.　　　　　　(*Le Roman de la Rose* 321–322)[12]

As she that hadde it al torent
For angre and for maltalent.　　　　(*The Romaunt of the Rose* 329–330)[13]

　そして著者は，この as he /she that 句は，元のフランス語の句よりも，その「原因・理由」の意味を示す機能としては，同じMEのforに比べて弱かったとする．例えば，Whi ...? に対する答えとしては as he /she that 句は用いられない．それに対して，*for* は用いられる．したがって as he /she that 句は sin / sith / sithen もしくは，縦続接続詞としての for ではない離接詞（disjunct）の for に近いと言える．

　この英語の観念借入語句は，初めは元のOFの意味である sense 3 を色濃く保っていたが，英語の中で使われることにより，英語の構造から来る意味合いを強く持つようになる．例えば，対象との類似性を示す sense 1 の意味で用いられている例がME West Midland のテクストで既に多く見られる．13世紀の *Ancrene Wisse* がそうである：

Þe bacbitere cheoweð ofte monnes flesch I fridei & bea keð wið his blake bile o cwike charoínes *as þe þ is þes deofles corbin of helle*.
　　　　　　　　　　　　　　　　　　(*Ancrene Wisse* 45. Ll. 8–11)[14]

この sense 1 を発達させる傾向は，次の Chaucer の *Troilus and Criseide* の例のように，後期ME期には更に進んだと見られる：

As ȝe haue herd; *swich* lif right gan he lede,
As he that stood bitwixen hope and drede.
　　　　　　　　　　　　　　　　　　(*Troilus and Criseide* V 629–630)[15]

---

12) 彼女はそれ（＝髪）をばらばらにしていたので／激情と怒りから
13) 彼女はそれ（＝髪）をばらばらにしていたので／嘆きと恨みから
14) 陰口をきく人は，金曜日に人々の肉体に歯を立て，彼の黒い嘴で生あるにも拘らずまるで死肉のようにつつくのだ．地獄から来た悪魔のごときカラスのように
15) おききのみなさま，彼はまさにこのような生き様でした，希望と恐怖の間で葛藤している人のような

そして，この句が adjunct でなく complement として使われた時には sense 1（下の例では 'a mous'（二十日ねずみ））との類似性を示し，sense 3「原因・理由」の意味は不可能となる：

"We faren *as he that dronke is as a mous.*"　　（Knight's Tale I (A) 1261）[16]

接続詞の as は *MED* によると中世の頃には manner / role / causal の3つの意味を発達させていた。この as の持つ多義性が，as he /she that 句を，元のフランス語と合体した意味から遠ざける大きな貢献をしたと言えよう。

さらに関係節内の法（mood）と相（aspect）の制約を受ける動詞もこの動きに大きく関わったと言える：

And sche [i.e. Diana] was wonder wroth withal,
And him [i.e. Acteon], *as sche which was godesse*,
　　　　　　　　　　　　　　　　　（*Conf Am* i 368–369）[17]

To themperour and he goth straight,
And in his fader half besoghte,
As he which his [i.e. the emperor's] *lordschipe soghte*,
　　　　　　　　　　　　　　　　　（*Conf Am* ii 1482–1484）[18]

このような stative aspect（状態相）や高度に記述的な動詞の場合，意味は事実に基づいたものとなり，仮定法でのように想像的なものとはならないところから，これらの動詞は sense 2（対象との同一性）と sense 3（原因・理由）を持つのが特徴である。ただ，この特徴は sense 1（対象との類似性）を示す as

---

16)　「われわれは二十日ねずみみたいに，酔っぱらいのような生活をしているんだ。」（桝井迪夫（訳）『カンタベリー物語』（上）岩波文庫，1973）
17)　彼女ダイアナは，怒りの眼差しを向けて，／彼女は女神だったので（注：理由の意味（sense 3）＋同一（sense 2）），彼アクテオンを…
18)　皇帝のところへまっすぐ行き，／そして父のために嘆願し，／皇帝にこう求めたので…

の持つ比較の働きによって弱められ，この句が対象との同一性や対象の典型例を示すようになる。そのことからこの句の持つ sense 3 の背後には sense 2 が潜んでいることは十分に考えられる。この句の代わりに，as や sin や for などが使われると，この二重性は無くなるわけである。

そして著者は，com cil / ele qui 句が sense 3 の「原因・理由」の意味にまとまって行き，一方，英語の as he / she that 句が，元のフランス語の句の意味を保持しながら，徐々に sense 1 の意味を発達させて行った過程を下のように図式化してまとめている：

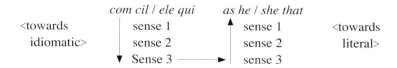

この論文はフランス語からの観念借用語句の意味的変遷について，きわめて論理的に，多くの文献を渉猟しながら論じたものである。文学テクストを読む際に，ある語句が歴史的にどの位置にあるのかを知ることができれば，Spitzer 的な視点から，その表現が持つ微妙な変化の相を味わうことができる。その意味でも，この論文は，文学テクストを読むひとつの優れた姿勢を示していると言えよう。最後に付け加えると，この as he / she that 句と Chaucer の作品における曖昧性の問題は著者の *The Structure of Chaucer's Ambiguity* (Peter Lang, 2014) および『Chaucer の曖昧性の構造』（松柏社，2004）で詳しく論じられている。

参照文献

Donaldson, ET (1970) *Speaking of Chaucer*. London: The Athlone Press.
Prins, AA (1952) *French Influence in English Phrasing*. Leiden: Universitaire Pers Leiden.
Sutherland, R (ed.) (1968) *The Romaunt of the Rose and Le Roman de la Rose: A Parallel-Text Edition*. Oxford: Basil Blackwell.

4 Jimura, Akiyuki (1998) 'An approach to the language of Criseyde in Chaucer's *Troilus and Criseyde*'. In: Fisiak, Jacek and Oizumi, Akio (eds) *English Historical Linguistics and Philology in Japan*. Berlin and New York: Mouton de Gruyter, 91–110.

著者は中英語文学の最高峰である Geoffrey Chaucer の長編 *Troilus and Criseyde* のヒロイン Criseyde の言語の特性を論じようとする。この物語は，トロイ戦争におけるトロイ側の神官の娘 Criseyde とトロイの王子 Troilus の悲恋物語であるが，Criseyde の英語には，もちろんこの物語が描かれた 14 世紀英国のロンドンの上流階級の婦人の英語が反映されていると考えられる。それを探ろうとするのが本論文である。

　この論文の優れた点は，中世における宮廷夫人の言語が反映されていると考えられる Criseyde の英語の特徴を，現代英語における女性の言語の特徴から推論の梯子を慎重に伸ばしながら，復元していることである。Spoken の言語データの少ない，あるいは手に入らない時代の，ある言語特徴を推論するという困難な作業の手本となる論文と言ってよい。

　焦点が当てられている言語面は発音，文法，語彙，誓言 (swearing) およびタブー表現，読み書きの力 (literacy)，冗長 (verbosity) の 6 つである。これらのうち，いくつかを紹介してみたい。

　文法であるが，Coates (1985: 24) によると男性の方が女性よりも formal な言語を使う傾向があるが，これは男性の方がより高い教育を受けるからである。ただし Criseyde の場合は，その courtly speech から判断すると十分な教養を身につけていると考えられる。それは，例えば，

　　　"What! Bet than swyche fyve? I! Nay, ywys!" 　　　(2.128)[19]

のように文を短く切る ellipsis (省略) を行う表現方法や，

---

[19] 「え！ 5 倍よりもっといい事なの？ まあ，なんてこと！」

"And whi so, uncle myn? Whi so?" (2.136)[20]

などのように，語句の repetition（反復）に見られる。また，判断を常に相手にゆだねて，控え目でいることを表す interrogative sentence（疑問文）などにも，その教養ある courtly speech は現れている：

"Sey ye me nevere er now? What sey ye, no?" (2.277)[21]

"Now em," quod she, "what wolde ye devise?
What is youre reed I sholde don of this?" (2.388–89)[22]

また Coates（1985: 26）によると，男性の言語は if や which から成る従属文を用いる hypotaxis なものであるのに対し，女性の表現は and や but や or などの等位接続詞を使う parataxis な文になる傾向を持つ。その中でも and に焦点を当ててみると，Troilus の方は Book IV 958–1978 の 121 行の中で and を 19 回用いており，それに対して Criseyde は Book IV 1254–1414 の 161 行中で 45 回用いている。この and の使用が Troilus よりも多いことから，Criseyde は Coates（1985）の言う女性特有の paratactic な言語を用いる傾向があると言えよう。

語彙を見てみると，Lakoff（1975: 54–55）のいう女性に特有な強意副詞（intensive adverbs）の多用が Criseyde にも見られる。iwis / iwys / ywis / ywys 'certainly, truly' と表記される副詞は Book III では，Troilus はこの副詞を 2 度用いているのに対し Criseyde は 100 度程用いている。Troilus も確かに，この語を用いているが，それは例えば Book IV の場合，下の例のように自分で自分に言い聞かせる場面で用いられている：

---

20) 「なぜ，そうなんですの，おじ様。なぜ，そうなの」
21) 「私を今までしっかりとご覧になったことはありませんでしたの？ どうなの，ありませんでしたの？」
22) 「おじ様」と彼女は言った。「どのようなご忠告をいただけますの？／私は，この事で，どうすればいいとお考えなのでしょう？」

> "For in hym, need of sittynge is, *ywys*,
> And in the, need of soth; and thus, forsothe,"　　　　　(4.1034–35)[23]

それに対して，Criseyde の場合は，上の Troilus でのように説得的トーンが必要な場面でなく，その友達に対して気軽に用いている:

> "*Iwis*, so wolde I, and I wiste how,
> Ful fayn," quod she, "Alas, that I was born!"
> 　　　　⋮
> "*Iwys*, my deere herte, I am nought wroth,
> Have here my trouthe!"...　　　　　(3.1102–11)[24]

著者は，控え目に，この表現は確かに Criseyde 特有のものとは言えないかも知れないが，当時の上流階級の婦人達が用いていた表現と考えてよいであろうとしている。これは健全な考え方で，14 世紀のロンドンの上流階級の婦人の言語という言語使用域は，当然いくつかの言語特徴の束から成っているわけで，Criseyde は，その束と多くを共有しているわけである。その重なりの部分は，当時の上流階級の婦人の言語であり，かつ Criseyde の言語でもあるわけである。

　語彙の中でも estat は Tyalor (1969: 163–65) が，honour, name は Shirley (1978: 50–55) が指摘しているように，Criseyde の関心が社会的地位や富にあるということが分かり興味深いと著者は言う。また著者は 'Criseyde's use of "honour" diminishes with the development of the story'. (101) と述べるが，このような巧みな物語展開の中で用いられた honour は，中世ロンドンの上流社会の女性も，同様の思いを込めて使った語であったことは十分に推測さ

---

23)「というのが，その（座っている）人においては，彼は必ず座っているという必然があり，そう，／そして君においては，その（座っている人のことを座っているという）判断をしているという必然があるのだ; したがって，もちろん」
24)「わかりました，そういたします。どうすればいいか分かりさえすれば，／とても喜んで」と彼女は言った。「ああ，生まれなければよかったのに！」…「ああ，私の大切な方，私は怒ってはいません，／誓って！」

れる。

　以上，Criseyde の言語は当時のロンドンの上流社会の婦人の言葉を反映するものであったろうという推論のもとに，著者は現代の社会言語学的観点を応用して，虚構の存在である Criseyde の言語を立体的に浮かび上がらせている。この論文は，社会言語学的なデータが十分でない時代の文学言語を扱う際には，現代の言語学的観点から推論の梯子を伸ばすという方法を示してくれている点で，大変有益な論文である。

参考文献
Chaucer, G（1987）*The Riverside Chaucer*（ed. LD Benson）. Boston: Houghton Mifflin Company.
Coates, J（1985）*Women, Men and Language*（2nd edn）. London: Longman.
Lakoff, R（1975）*Language and Women's Place*. New York: Harper & Row.
Tyalor, D（1969）*Style and character in Chaucer's* Troilus. PhD Thesis, Yale University, USA.

5　Imahayashi, Osamu（2007）'A stylistic approach to Pip's class-consciousness in *Great Expectations*'.『近代英語研究』（*Studies in Modern English*）23: 1–21.

　この論文は，英国の 19 世紀を代表する作家 Charles Dickens の *Great Expectations*（1860–1861）において主人公 Pip の階級意識がどのように変化して行くかを，いくつかのキーワードに焦点を当てながら論じている。

　Pip は両親を亡くし親戚の Joe Gargery で鍛冶屋の見習いとして，つまり労働者階級として人生を歩むよう運命づけられていたが，ある日おじの Pumblechook に連れられて Satis House と呼ばれる屋敷に行き，老未亡人 Miss Havisham と，Estella という美貌の少女に出会う。彼女は Pip の労働者階級の服装と言語を冷笑する。

　著者は，Pip の姉の夫の鍛冶屋 Joe Gargery と同じ階級に属することを示すために，Joe と同じく，労働者階級の方言に特有の *h*-dropping を行わせている。Slate に書く文章では 'I hope' を 'i opE' と書かせており，Joe の発話

では 'health' を elth, 'a dwelling-house' を a dwelling-ouse と発音させている。後段になるが，この h-dropping は Pip が Joe と住んでいた時には，このように普通に使用されていたが，London に出てからは，彼はその労働者の階級の方言とは縁遠い存在になっている。Joe の語る Miss A について Pip は次のように /h/-full で問い返す：

"Miss A., Joe? Miss Havisham?" (224)

次に，著者は the meshes (*The English Dialect Dictionary* によると 'marsh' の意味で Norfolk, Suffolk, west Hampshire および Devon の方言) という表現に注目し，この語の定冠詞を明確に発音しているのは Pip のみであり，この語を発する Mrs. Gargery (Pip の姉で鍛冶屋 Joe の妻) と Joe においては音脱落 (elision) が生じているとする：

a. " ... Hulks are prison-ships, right 'cross *th' meshes*." (Mrs. Gargery, 15)
b. " ... I'm wrong out of the forge, the kitchen, or off *th'meshes* ..." (Joe, 225)
c. "You've been lying out on *the meshes*,..." (Pip, 19)

このことから分かることは，Dickens は Pip に Joe 夫妻と同じく地域方言としての meshes は使わせているが，Joe 夫妻のように階級方言としての音脱落のある th'meshes は使わせていない。Pip と Joe 夫妻は Kent に住んでいるのであるから，この地域方言を使うのは当然だが，それに加えて，Dickens は Pip と階級方言の関係を意識していることが分かる。Dickens は Pip に単に Joe 夫妻と同じ階級方言を語らせているのではないことが分かる。

Pip は未亡人 Miss Havisham の住む Satis House と呼ばれる屋敷で美貌の少女 Estella から，彼の言葉と服装を冷笑されるが，これも Pip における言語と服装における階級意識の目覚めのきっかけを Dickens が示したものである：

"He *calls the knaves, jacks*, this boy! ... And what coarse hands he has. And what *thick boots*!" (61)

この Estella の言葉が Pip の階級上昇志向を刺激する形になっているということは，上の3つの Estella の言葉（the knaves, Jacks, coarse hands, thick boots）が Satis House での回想として Pip によって反復されている（63, 66, 71）ことや，ここでの思い出を 'a memorable day' (73) と Dickens が言わしめていることからも分かる。

著者は次に Joe の idiolect である *larks* 'merriments' に焦点を当てる。この語は鍛冶屋の Joe のみが使用することから，この Joe の階級を象徴的に示す Joe の idiolect となっている：

> "You know, Pip," replied Joe, "as you and me were ever friends, and it were look'd for'ard to betwixt us, as being calc'lated to lead to *larks* ..."
> (100)

この語は，Pip の幼な馴染で Estella とは対照的な Biddy の Pip への手紙の中で，Joe が what larks という句を 2 度 Pip に伝えてくれと述べたというくだりからも分かる。

以上見て来たように，この論文は主人公 Pip の階級意識が，Pip 自身，あるいは彼を取り巻く人達の言語と対比されながら，どのように言語的に変化して行ったかを，いくつかのキーワードに焦点を当てながら示し，この作品の中での文体的意義を提示して見せる。その文体論的視点が，単なる社会言語学的現象を扱う視点とは異なるわけである。例えば /h/-less の発音は，通常の社会言語学的な問題としては，ある社会階層グループの特徴として論じられるところから，Pip や Joe の階級方言をある時代における特定の地域，ここでは Kent, の方言を反映したものとして見ることはできる。文体論の場合，そういう視点に留まらず，その目的として，文学テクスト上のある人物の特定の言語使用に焦点を当て，言語を通してその人物を見るところにあるとすると，この論文は，その模範的な方法論を示していると言える。

参考文献

Adamson, S (1998) 'Literary language'. In: Romaine, S (ed.) *The Cambridge History of the English Language Vol. IV, 1776–1997*. Cambridge: Cambridge University

Press, 589–692.
Blake, NF (1981) *Non-standard Language in English Literature*. London: André Deutsch.
Brook, GL (1970) *The Language of Dickens*. London: André Deutsch.
Dickens, C (1993 [1860–1861]) *Great Expectations* (The Clarendon Dickens) (ed. M Cardwell). Oxford: The Clarendon Press.
田中逸郎（1972）「Joe Gargery の方言と職業語」桝井迪夫・田辺昌美（編）『ディケンズの文学と言語―ディケンズ没後百年記念論文集』三省堂，153–187.
Yamamoto, T (2003 [1950]) *Growth and System of the Language of Dickens: An Introduction to A Dickens Lexicon* (3rd edn). Hiroshima: Keisuisha.

6 福元広二（2010）「Shakespeare における命令文主語と文法化」吉波弘・武内信一・外池滋生・中澤和夫・野村忠央・川端朋広・山本史歩子（共編）『英語研究の次世代に向けて―秋元実治教授定年退職記念論文集』ひつじ書房，361–372.

初期近代英語の命令文は，下の（1）のように2人称代名詞主語を伴うことが多いところから（Rissanen 1999），著者は「Shakespeare の4つの知覚動詞を取り上げて，命令文主語としての代名詞のコロケーションについて文法化の観点から考察し」（370）ている：

（1） *Capulet*: Go thou to Juliet.　　（Shakespeare *Romeo and Juliet* 4.2.41）[25]

ここで論じられている知覚動詞とは look, hark, hear, mark の4つである。そのうち look が人称代名詞と共起する例，その中でも look you の例が圧倒的に多いことが著者のあげている下の表で分かる：

Look you	83	*Hark you*	22	*Hear you*	17	*Mark you*	11
Look ye	4	*Hark ye*	9	*Hear ye*	2	*Mark ye*	1
Look thou	1	*Hark thou*	0	*Hear thou*	1	*Mark thou*	1
Look thee	6	*Hark thee*	6	*Hear thee*	1	*Mark thee*	1

[25]　キャピュレット「お前はジュリエットのところへ行って，…」（中野好夫（訳）「ロミオとジュリエット」『世界文学大系75　シェイクスピア2』筑摩書房，1960）

議論の都合上,この表の左上の句から見て行く。

Look you については以下の表のように談話標識としての用法が多数である:

| 知覚的意味 | 23 (27.7%) |
| 談話標識 | 60 (72.3%) |

知覚的用法の場合は,「聞き手の視線をどこかに向けさせることが目的であるので」「look you の後に there や here といった場所を表す副詞を伴うことが多い。」(366) と著者は述べている:

(2) *Hamlet*: Why, look you there, look how it steals away! (*Hamlet* 3.4.134)[26]

これに対して談話標識としての look you は「聞き手の注意を引くために使われている。」(366) この用法は圧倒的に散文において多く用いられている (55例 (91.7%)) が,Shakespeare では,「ある特定の下層階級の人物の特徴として使われている。」(367) としている。次の,Shakespeare の時代の典型的なウェールズ人を代表する Fluellen は *Henry 5* の中で,この用法を 22 回も使っている:

(3) *Fluellen*: Tell you the Duke, it is not so good to come to the mines; for look you, the mines is not according to the disciplines of the war; the concavities of it is not sufficient. For look you, th' athversary—you may discuss unto the Duke, look you—is digt himself four yard under the counter-mines. (*Henry* 5 3.2.57–63)[27]

---

26) ハムレット「ほら,あそこを! 御覧なさい,すごすごと消えてゆく!」(野島秀勝 (訳)『ハムレット』岩波書店,2002)

27) フルーエリン「坑道へ行くのはそんないいことじゃないと公爵に言って欲しいんじゃ。ちゅうのは,いいかな,ここの坑道は作戦要務令の定むる通りになっとらんのじゃ。凹状面の掘り下げ方が十分でないんじゃ。ちゅうのは,いいかな,当面の敵しゃんは,公爵に論じて欲しいんじゃが,いいかな,対敵坑道下四ヤードをくっさくしおったんじゃ。」(大山俊一 (訳)「ヘンリー五世」『世界文学大系75 シェイクスピア2』筑摩書房,1960)

4例の look ye は「複数の人物に対してしばしば用いられ」るが「『見る』という知覚的な意味であり，完全な談話標識の例はない。また，look ye の場合は，聞き手が単数，複数に関わらず，聞き手に対して敬意を表している場合が多い。」(365) としている。

 Look thou の例は下の 1 例のみであるが，これは Romeo と Juliet の 2 人が thou を使っているので you には成り得ないことと，副詞が後続しているという理由による (Rissanen 1999: 279):

(4)　*Romeo*: ... Look thou but sweet,
　　　　 And I am proof against their enmity. (*Romeo and Juliet* 2.2.72–73)[28]

またこの例では「look は『見る』という知覚的な意味を持っており，談話標識にはなっていないことも重要である。」(363)

 6例ある look thee の例では Brook (1976: 72) を引用しながら，著者は再帰動詞の影響としながら ('This usage may be due to the influence of reflexive verbs as in: Hast thee for thy life'. (*Lear* V.3.251).「オルバ　急いで，命懸けで！」(坪内逍遥訳))，characterization の一環として，この用法は下層階級の登場人物に用いさせているとする。6 例のうち 3 例は Shepherd によって用いられている：

(5)　*Shepherd*: But look thee here, boy. Now bless thyself: thou met'st with
　　　　 things dying, I with things new-born. Here's a sight for thee; look
　　　　 thee, a bearing-cloth for a squire's child! Look thee here, take up,
　　　　 take up, boy; open't.　　　　　(*The Winter's Tale* 3.3.114–6)[29]

---

28)　ロミオ「…やさしいあなたのまなざし。それさえあれば，なんの奴らの憎しみなど。僕は不死身だ。」(中野好夫 (訳))「ロミオとジュリエット」『世界文学大系 75　シェイクスピア 2』筑摩書房，1960)

29)　羊飼い「だがな，俺，これを見ろ。ありがたいこった，おまえは死にかけてるもんに出会ったが，おれは生まれたばかりのもんに出会ったぞ。ほら，ようく見ろ，どうだ，りっぱな産着（うぶぎ）だろう，えらい人の子供にちがいない！　おや，なんだ，こりゃ？　拾って，蓋を開けてみろ。」(小田島雄志 (訳))『冬物語』白水社，1983)

Hark you は look you と同じく最も例が多く 22 例ある。Hark ye は「目上に向かって使われており，look you と同様に，話し手の敬意を表している」(368)。Hark thee は「look thee と同様に，下層階級の人物の台詞によく見られる。」(368)

Hear に関しても上の表が示すように，you を取る形の hear you が最も多く，look you と同様に呼びかけ語が続くことが多いとしている。Hear ye でも，呼びかけ語がしばしば続く。Hear thou は 1 例しかなく，Rissanen (1999: 279) は look thou と同じく後続副詞のためであるとする。Hear thee は 1 例しかないが，その例では Bassanio が you から thee に変えており，「彼の感情の高まり」故に親称形に変えられたとする:

(6) *Bassanio*: Why then you must. But hear thee,
    (*Merchant of Venice* 2.2.180)[30]

Mark も you を取る形が一番多く他は 1 例ずつしかない。Shakespeare では mark you は指示詞の this や that を伴い，他動詞として使われており，談話標識としての例はなく，したがって，この時代にはまだ「文法化していないことがわかる。」(371):

(7) *Antonio*: Mark you this, Bassanio.   (*Merchant of Venice* 1.3.97)[31]

また，それ以外の人称代名詞との組み合わせでも，全て目的語を伴っている。

結論として著者は，look you の場合はほとんどが談話標識として用いられているが，他の代名詞では知覚的な意味を残している。その他の動詞では命題的な意味を保持しているとしている。

この論文は 4 つの知覚動詞の命令文という，語学的な訓練を受けていない者ならば見過ごすであろう用法の研究である。我々が Shakespeare の作品を

---

30) バッサーニオウ「じゃ，行くさ。だがね，…」(菅泰男 (訳)「ヴェニスの商人」『世界文学大系 75　シェイクスピア 2』筑摩書房，1960)
31) アントウニオウ「聞いたか，バサーニオウ。」(同訳)

論じる際に，その命令文を知覚動詞的な意味を残したものとして理解するべきか，談話標識として理解すべきなのかに関して，優れた指針を提供してくれる。

参考文献

Brook, GL (1976) *The Language of Shakespeare*. London: André Deutsch.
Nevalainen, T (2006) *An Introduction to Early Modern English*. Edinburgh: Edinburgh University Press.
Rissanen, M (1999) 'Syntax'. In: Lass, R (ed.) *The Cambridge History of the English Language*. *Vol. III 1476–1776*. Cambridge: Cambridge University Press. 187–331.

7　浮網茂信（1992）「シェイクスピアの強調表現と女性―フォールスタッフ劇を中心に」『英語青年』138 (4): 2–6.

本論文は『英語青年』第 138 巻第 4 号（1992）に巻頭論文として掲載されたものである。先にあげた Jimura (1998) 論文では Geoffrey Chaucer の作り出した Criseyde という人物に焦点を当てて，その言語の特徴を論じている。その論点のひとつが強調表現であるが，この論文も Shakespeare，特に Falstaff 劇における女性の言語を，同じく強調表現の観点から見ようとする。それは「『一般的に言って，性別による言葉使いの違いは少な』」（Trudgill 1974: 90）いが「『強調表現』には性別による差が比較的現れやすい」からであるとする。

　Jimura (1998) 論文でも述べたが，文学作品での会話表現は社会言語学で扱われる対象としての言語とは異なりあくまでも作家の頭の中で作られたフィクションとしての言語現象である。このことは著者もよく心得ていて，

> 文学作品の話し言葉に見られる男女差は，作家の創造力を通して作り上げられた一種の speech-stereotypes と考えられる。文学作品の話し言葉は実社会の言語そのものではないにしても，それを反映したものになっているはずである。(2)

と述べる。

　著者は，まず男性の表現との対比において女性の言語を見ようとする。そのひとつとして「'God's blood' などの『God's＋その属性名詞』型の誓詞表現がつづまった形」をフォールスタッフ劇の中に見ようとする。この形式は Falstaff や Hotspur によっては多く使われているが——Falstaff は 11 回，Hotspur は 4 回——Prince Hal においては 1 度も現れない。そしてもちろん女性は 1 度も用いていない。このことから，この表現は社会階層と性別に関係してくる表現と言えよう。

　次に著者は 1 Henry 4 からの次の一節を取り上げる。Hotspur 伯爵（本名は Henry Percy）とその伯爵夫人：

> HOTSPUR Come, Kate, I'll have your song too.
> LADY PERCY Not mine, in good sooth.
> HOTSPUR Not yours, in good sooth! *Heart*, you swear like a comfit maker's wife—"Not you, in *good sooth*!", and "*As God shall mend me*!", and "*As sure as day*!"—　　　　　（1 Henry 4 3.1.239ff）[32]

Hotspur 伯爵の用いる 'by God's heart' の短縮形である 'Heart' は「直接的で，強く，粗野な表現」であるのに対して，女性の誓言とされる他の 3 つは，より「間接的で軟らかい（mild な）表現と言える」とする。

　男性的表現との対比では，次のような例もあげられている。代表的なものと思われるものを拾ってみる：

> ［命令形＋I say］ Empty the basket, *I say* (Ford; *The Merry Wives of Windsor* 4.2.131) / Peace, *I say* (Host; *Ibid.* 3.1.89, 92) / Away, *I say* (Falstaff;

32）　ホッパー「さあ，ケート，お前も一つやれ。」
　　ホッパー夫人「絶対いやですわ，わたし。」
　　ホッパー「絶対，いやか！　まったく，お前という女は，菓子屋の内儀(かみ)さんそっくりの誓言をやる——『絶対にいや！』だの，『正真正銘，掛値なし！』だの，やれ，『首が飛んでも』だの，『天地が逆さまになっても』だのと，——…」（中野好夫（訳）「ヘンリー四世第一部」『世界文学大系 75　シェイクスピア 2』筑摩書房，1960）

　　　　Ibid. 5.1.7）
　　［do (or, do but) ＋命令形］do but mark the countenance that he［Henry
　　　　V］will give me.（Falstaff; *2 Henry 4* 5.5.7）
　　［What *a plague* 型］"What *a plague* have I to do with a buff jerking?"
　　　　"Why, what *a pox* have I to do with my hostess of the tavern?"
　　　　（Falstaff & Prince; *1 Henry 4* 1.2.44–47）

　これらは男性の表現であるが，「フォールスタッフ劇の中では各表現とも劇中での役割を持っている。『命令形＋I say』は *Wives* 中で多用され，劇の雰囲気作りに利用される。『do＋命令形』はフォールスタッフ劇では少ない。'What a plague' の形式は 1 Henry 4 のフォールスタッフとハル王子の間で用いられ，2 人の仲間関係を印象づけるのに役立っていると考えられる」が，男性にのみ許された表現ではなく，ただ男性に多いということで，逆に言えば，女性はあまり用いない表現である。ただし，「フォールスタッフ劇の中の女性は『命令形＋I say』の表現は決して用いない。」（160）したがって，次の例では男装した Rosalind がこの表現を用いている：

　　TOUCHSTONE　Your betters sir.
　　ROSALIND　　Peace, *I say*.　　　　　　　　（*As You Like It* 2.4.67）[33]

　ここでは「自分が男性であることを宣言しておくことが，劇的に必要であったと考えられる」から，Rosalind はこの男性に多く用いられる表現を用いたとする。女性が用いるのは次のような召し使いに対する呼びかけの定型表現においてのみである」としている：

　　... what, John, *I say*!（Mistress Quickly; *The Merry Wives of Windsor* 1.4.37）／
　　What, Robin, I say!（Mistress Ford; *Ibid*. 3.3.3）

---

33)　タッチストウン「目上の人だぞ。」
　　　ロザリンド「まあ静かに。…」（阿部知二（訳）『お気に召すまま』岩波書店，1974）

このように,「少なくとも協調表現に限って見るかぎり,シェイクスピアにおける女性はこのようにかなり制約を与えられ,stereotype 化されている,と言える。」

最後に著者は,この論文では男性の言語に照らした形で女性の言語を見て来たが,「女性の言語を論じる場合,厳密には他の社会的要因も考慮に入れる必要があろう」として,「世代・年齢」「社会階層」による要因をあげている。

虚構として存在する Shakespeare における女性の言語を,Shakespeare によりステレオタイプ化されたものとして,男性の言語との対比のうちに,その輪郭を読者に示してくれる,大変優れた論文である。

参考文献
中谷喜一郎 (1979)「Shakespeare の言語に対する社会言語的な関わり方」『広島大学学校教育学部紀要』2-1: 59–64.
中谷喜一郎 (1990)「Shakespeare の英語とスタイルの問題点」『近代英語研究』6: 63–67.
Trudgill, P (1974) *Sociolinguistics: An Introduction*. Harmondsworth: Penguin.

8 Hori, Masahiro (1999) 'Collocational patterns of intensive adverbs in Dickens: A tentative approach'. *English Corpus Studie* 6: 51–65.

本論文はコロケーション (collocation) 研究の第一人者による Dickens 論である。

副詞の 'infinitely' は *OED^2 on CD-ROM* の 1413 年の例 'passeth infynytely' に見られるように,本来は動詞と共起していた。17 世紀の初めまではこのように動詞と共起しているが,中頃から動詞よりも形容詞や副詞と共起する傾向を示すようになる。これにはもうひとつ傾向があって,'infinitely' は 19 世紀から 20 世紀にかけて比較の形容詞や副詞と共起する傾向を示し始め,その共起率は約 50% にも達するようになる。

Dickens の 8 作品における 'infinitely' の使用例を調べると,全部で 41 例あり,形容詞・副詞と共起している例は 32 例 (78%),動詞との共起は 9 例

(22%) あり，この78％という数字は19世紀全体の共起率と合致する。しかし，この形容詞と副詞の32例は全て比較級であり，この点で見ると，上に述べたように19世紀では全体で約50％の割合でしか比較の副詞や形容詞と共起していないので，大きく異なる様相を呈している。この 'infinitely' の比較の副詞や形容詞との共起の多さが Dickens のひとつの文体的特徴と言えようと，著者は述べる。

次に 'considerably' を見ると，この語が比較の副詞・形容詞と共起する率は18世紀後半から増加する。しかし 'infinitely' と異なり，この 'considerably' が比較級と共起するのは Dickens の作品中では，39例中ただ1例のみである。また，この語は Dickens の作品では39例中27例の70％が動詞や動詞から派生した過去分詞の 'astonished' や 'startled' など驚きや戸惑いを示す語と共起している。

また著者は 'a habitual collocation or an idiomatic collocation' を破る用法が Dickens では見られると主張する。それは登場人物なり状況なりに合わせるための新しいコロケーションであり，ここも Dickens の文体的特徴が示されるとする：

  'Why, Lord love you,' returned the Captain, with something of compassion for Mr. Toots's innocence. 'When she warn't no higher than that, they were as fond of one another as two young doves.'
  'Were they though!' said Mr. Toots, with *a considerably lengthened face*. (*Dombey and Son*, 464 (Chapter 32))（イタリックスは原著者）[34]

この 'lengthened face' は Dikens では1例しか用いられていないが，悲しみや厳かな気持ちを表す通常のコロケーションである 'long face' の long を過去分詞化した特殊な用法である。その特別なコロケーションである上に，さ

---

34) 「ああ，よくぞ申された」と船長はトゥーツ氏の純情が何やら不憫になって返して。「譲さんがまだほんのそんくらいの時分から，あいつと譲さんはまるで二羽の小鳩のように仲ようしてござっての」
  「け，けどマジで？！」とトゥーツ氏はいたく浮かぬ顔をして。（田辺洋子（訳）『ドンビー父子』（下）こびあん書房，2000）

らに，'considerably' と共起している 'anomalous collocation' を形成している。もうひとつの例は Judy Smallweed の老齢を示す，'a perfectly geological age' (*Bleak House*, 293) の 'perfectly geological' である。この 'perfectly' は通常は程度の大小を表す 'gradable adjective' と共起するが，ここでは，それとは異なる非段階的形容詞の 'geological' を修飾していると著者は述べる。

　他の高い程度を表す 'perfectly'，'highly' そして 'greatly' は価値を表す語と共起するが，その場合 Dickens では 'ironically' な使われ方をして，その人物を特殊化していると著者は述べる：

> It would have been next to impossible to suspect him of anything wrong, he was so *thoroughly respectable*. Nobody could have thought of putting him in a livery, he was so *highly respectable*.... Peter might have been hanged, or Tom transported; but Littimer was *perfectly respectable*.
> (*David Copperfield*, 299 (Chapter 21))

Steerforth の召使である Littimer が強意副詞と共起しかつ反復する 'respectable' という語で導入される時，そこには，その人物の 'respectability' は表面的なもので，実際は道徳的価値を疑われるべきものだという含意が生じるとする。

　以上，本論文で論じられた強意の副詞のうち，いくつかを紹介してみた。本論文は，Ito (1993) 等の伝統を継ぐものであり，その線上で著者はコロケーションという言葉のひとつの現象を通して Dickens の文体に迫ろうとしており，文体研究にこの方法を用いようとする者にとっては必須の文献である。

参考文献

Firth, JR (1951) 'Modes of meaning'. In: Firth, JR (1957) *Papers in Linguistics: 1934–51*. London: Oxford University Press, 190–215.

Hori, M (1993) 'Some collocations of the word "Eye" in Dickens: A preliminary sketch'. *Aspects of Modern English*. Tokyo: Eichosha, 509–527.

Ito, H (1993) 'Some collocations of Adverbs in Richardson's Clarissa Harlowe'. *Aspects of Modern English*. Tokyo: Eichosha, 528–547.

Sinclair, J (1991) *Corpus, Concordance, Collocation*. Oxford: Oxford University Press.

Yamamoto, T (1950) *Growth and System of the Language of Dickens*. Osaka: Kansai

University Press.

9　山口美知代（1992）「総称代名詞 one と自由間接話法—ヴァージニア・ウルフへの文体論的アプローチ」*Zephyr* 6: 69–80.

この論文は，Virginia Woolf（1882–1941）の小説の自由間接話法／思考（Free Indirect Speech/Thought）における総称代名詞 one の用法の文体論的特徴を，この自由間接発話／思考の確立期の Jane Austen（1775–1817）の使用法と比較しながら論じている。そして，ひとつの仮説が提示でき，それは「Woolf では総称代名詞 one の総称性が低くなり，1 人称的になったことが，one が間接話法，自由間接話法に自由に現れるようになったひとつの要因だ，というものである」(76)，そして純粋に総称的な one では現在時制が基本であるので，「この，時制の一致と総称的現在の問題点が，Austen が総称性の強い種類の one を直接話法のみで使うのにとどまらせた一因である」(76)，とする。

　以下，著者の議論を見てみたい。なお，この論文では発話（Speech）と思考（Thought）は統語論的には同じ変化をするので共に「話法」ということで論じられている。

　まず著者は Leech and Short（1981）で論じられた思考の描出モードの枠組みとして，思考（Thought）は次のような形を取るとする。この論文の議論の中心となる自由間接話法は太字で示してある：

Does she still love me?	自由直接思考（Free Direct Thought（FDT））
He wondered, "Does she still love me?"	直接思考（Direct Thought（DT））
Did she still love him?	自由間接思考（**Free Indirect Thought**（**FIT**））
He wondered if she still loved him.	間接思考（Indirect Thought（IT））
He wondered about her love for him.	思考行為の物語的報告（Narrative Report of a Thought Act（NRTA））

　著者は Wales（1981）に基づいて one を以下のように分類する。ここでは少し簡略化して示す：

	USE	MODALITY	TENSE
one 1 =	'indefinite'	generic, hypothetical, gnomic	present
one 2 =	'generic/egocentric' includes speaker	representative generic, reflective gnomic	present, past
one 3 =	'advanced egocentric' (a direct equivalent of I)	cognitive, factive	present, past, future

One 3 は 1 人称代名詞と同じ意味で使われるので，認知に関する動詞や事実を述べる動詞が使われる。Woolf の *Mrs Dalloway* では 111 例のうち 63 例 (57%) という高い比率で，この 1 人称的な one 3 が主語として用いられている。その中でも自由間接話法や間接話法で使われている例は 39 例 (64%) も使われている。したがって，one に続く述語動詞が時制の一致の結果として過去時制あるいは過去完了時制を取っている。次の (1) が，そのひとつの例である：

(1) I can't keep up with them, Peter Walsh thought, as they marched up Whitehall,... *One* had to respect it; *one* might laugh; but *one* had to respect it, he thought. (57–58)（イタリクスは評者。元の論文では下線。以下の引用でも同じ）

この文章の 'I can't keep up with them, Peter Walsh thought'. は直接思考であるが，後半の 'One had to respect it; one might laugh; but one had to respect it, he thought'. の部分は自由間接思考である。これら 3 つの one は形式的には総称代名詞だけれども，意味的には I に近くなっている。

このように Woolf の文体では自由間接話法中で I に近い総称的 one 3 が現れるが，Austen の *Emma* (1816) では 1 人称的な one 3 は 41 例中 10 例 (24%) 現れていて，これらは全て直接話法の中で現れている。直接話法の中で現れるので，当然のことながら時制の一致の法則を受けない：

(2) 'Very true,' said Harriet. 'Poor creatures! One can think of nothing else.' (111)

このことは Woolf の *one* と Austen の *one* が性質的に異なることを反映しているとする。

一般に自由間接話法は，先の Leech and Short (1981) に見られるように，人称代名詞と時制を間接話法に移行して，語順などは直接話法のままにとどめるわけであるが，この *one* を用いた構文では *one* は *one* のままで，人称代名詞としての移行はなく，時制のみ変化することになる。したがって，one 3 を用いた場合，直接話法とは時制のみ異なる，「直接話法に近い（自由）間接話法，という文体上の効果を持」ち，「より『間接性の少ない』間接モードが得られることになる」(78) と著者は述べる。つまり Leech and Short (1981) の思考 (Thought) と発話 (Speech) の枠組み上に位置づけると以下のようになるとする：

one 3 を用いた自由間接話法

上の図は，左端が最もナレーターの関与が強く，右端が最も低いことを示すが，Woolf の one 3 を用いた自由間接話法は，one 3 を用いない自由間接話法と直接話法の中間のような文体であると著者は結論づけている。

この論文は，Woolf の文体のひとつである自由間接話法に新しい光を当てているのみならず，Austen から続く自由間接話法の歴史的発展の研究という新しい研究の地平を切り開く好論文である。

参考論文

Leech, G and Short, MH (1981) *Style in Fiction*. London: Longman.
Wales, KM (1980) '"Personal" and "indefinite" reference: The users of the pronoun one in present day English'. *Nottingham Linguistics Circular* 9: 93–112.

10 池上嘉彦（2012）「話者による〈事態把握〉(construal) の営みの相対性と翻訳—日本語話者好みの〈主観的把握〉をめぐって」『文体論研究』58: 91–104；池上嘉彦（2011）「日本語話者における〈好まれる言い回し〉としての〈主観的把握〉」『人工知能学会誌』26 (4): 317–322.

「言語の〈話者〉としての〈ひと〉が〈文〉を発話する前には，〈認知〉(cognition) レベルでの大変な営みがその〈ひと〉によって〈主体的に〉行われている…」(91) という言葉で池上 (2012) は始まっている。続けて，著者は次のように言う。「〈話者〉は〈発話の主体〉(speaking subject, sujet parlant) として振る舞う前に，〈認知の主体〉(cognizing subject) として振る舞うという過程があるわけで，この過程のことを認知言語学では〈事態把握〉(construal) と呼んでいる。」(92)

この〈事態把握〉には〈主観的把握〉と〈客観的把握〉の 2 つの類型があり，前者は「話者は自らの〈事態把握〉の対象とする事態の中に身を置き，自らにとっての事態の〈見え〉を輪状的・体験的なスタンスで言語化する。」後者の〈客観的把握〉では「話者は自らの〈事態把握〉の対象とする事態の外に身を置き，自らにとっての事態の〈見え〉を観察者的・傍観者的なスタンスで言語化する。」(95)

著者の例としてあげる，道に迷った時の慣用表現で見てみると次のようになる：

a) 'Where am I?'
b) 「ここはどこですか？」

a) では，「迷い込んだ本人が事故の分身を場に残したまま自らは場の外に身を置き，そういうスタンスで自らの〈見え〉を言語化」している。それに対し，b) では「話者は発話の場に埋もれており，自分自身は〈見え〉に含まれず，言語化されていない。」

次に著者は川端康成『雪国』の翻訳の問題に目を向ける：

（1）　国境の長いトンネルを抜けると雪国であった。
（2）　The train came out of the long tunnel into the snow country.
（E. Seidensticker 1957）

これらを比べると（1）の原文では〈主観的事態把握〉をしており，「日本語で言語化している原作者は，自らの視座を列車の中の主人公に合わせ…知覚できるのは，もっぱら座っている席から窓を通して外に見える景色で…言語化は事態の中に身を置く当事者の視点」(99) であるとしている。(2) は〈客観的事態把握〉で「列車の中の主人公の分身が事態の外へ出て，主人公のもう一つの分身を乗せたまま移動する汽車を外から知覚の対象として捉え，傍観者の視点で…捉え，言語化するという形になっている。」(99) 池上 (2011: 319) の次の例では「芭蕉の原文では見えた情景だけが言語化され，視る主体（芭蕉と共の曾良）は表現されていない。英語訳では見た情景だけでなく，視る主体も視るという行為も言語化されている。」：

（3）　まず高舘に登れば北上川，南部より流るる大河なり。
（芭蕉『奥の細道』）
（4）　We first climbed up to Palace-on-the-Heights, from where we could see the Kitagami, a big river tha flows down from Nambu. (D. Keene 訳)

以上は発信者の視点であるが，次に著者は受信者の立場から事態把握の違いを論じている。例えば次の場合

　　海は広いな，大きいな
　　月が昇るし，日が沈む

このような表現に向かう時「日本語話者は…状況の中に自らの身を置く…状況を頭に描いてみる…のではなかろうか。…読み手の側からの積極的な参与

なしには…従って，そのようなスタンスへの傾斜を有しない読者にとっては」(101) 理解は難しいと思われるとする。

最後に著者は「ある言語の話者の好んで採る〈事態把握〉における特徴的な振舞い方は，その言語を素材として成立しうる…作品の特徴に何らかの制約を加えるものであろうか。」(102) と結んでいる。

このような認知的な視点の導入によって客観化されることで，特に，作者の自然に対する感情を歌う詩の研究で大いに本領を発揮するのではなかろうか。なお，この主観的／客観的事態把握の問題は次の山梨論文でも取り上げられている。

参考文献
Langacker, RW (1990) 'Subjectification'. *Cognitive Linguistics* 1: 5–38.
Ikegami, Y (2005) 'Indices of a subjectivity-prominent language: Between cognitive linguistics and linguistic typology'. *Annual Review of Cognitive Linguistics* 3: 132–164.
Ikegami, Y (2007) 'Subjectivity, ego-orientation and subject-object merger: A cognitive account of the zero encoding of the grammatical subject in Japanese'. In: Ikegami, Y, Eschbach-Szabo, V and Wlodarczyk, A (eds) *Selected Papers on Semantic and Cognitive Japanese Linguistics*. Tokyo: Kuroshio, 15–29.
Ikegami, Y (2008) 'Subjective construal as a "fashion of speaking" in Japanese'. In: González, M de los ÁG, Mackenzie, JL, González-Álvarez, EM (eds) *Current Trends in Contrastive Linguistics: Functional and Cognitive Perspectives*. Amsterdam and Philadelphia: John Benjamins, 227–250.

11 山梨正明（2012）「認知言語学から見た文体論の展望―認知文体論へのアプローチ」『文体論研究』58: 121–152.

本論文は認知言語学の観点からスタイルの概念を3つにまとめ，それぞれにどのようなスタイル論が可能かを論じ，文学作品に関わるスタイルは，この三者のうちのひとつであるとする。その3つのスタイル概念とは，次のA～Cの3つである：

〈言語的自立レベルの変異性〉に関わるスタイル

「パラフレーズの関係にある言語表現のパターンの違い」(122)に関係するスタイルで，このスタイルを変える能力は「母語話者に共通する基本的な能力である。」(131) ここでは「図・地の文化と反転」「プロセス的認知とモノ的認知」「イメージスキーマ変換」「イコン的認知と言語化のモード」「空間移動と主観的知覚」「言語行為の前景化と背景化」が論じられているが，このうち2つを取り上げてみる：

(1) 「図・地の文化と反転」という観点からは full と half のどちらに焦点を置くかによって次のスタイルの返還が可能である：
  a. The bottle is half full.
  b. The bottle is half empty.
(2) 「イメージスキーマ変換」の観点からは，
  a. デモ隊が会場に流れ込んで行った。
  b. 泥水がプールに流れ込んで行った。
のように，非連続的な個体の集合 (a) は「(b) のような不可算的な連続体として把握され」(127) ている，つまり「イメージスキーマ変換」という「外部世界を把握していく言語主体の主観的な認知プロセス」(127) を経たスタイルと，とらえることができる。

〈話者／作者の表現レベルの変異性〉に関わるスタイル

文学作品などにおいて話者／作者が「意識的ないしは無意識的に操作する個別的なスタイル」(123)，「作者の個別的な表現形式」(131) はこのスタイルである。認知的な視点としては「プロ・ドロップの認知モード」「焦点シフトとオヴァーラップ」「メトニミーの認知プロセス」「視覚の認知プロセスと修辞性」「焦点化と身体部位のメトニミー」の5点が論じられているが，ここでは2つを取り上げる：

(1) 「メトニミーの認知プロセス」の点からは次のような例が説明可能である：

a. When Miss Emily Grierson died, our whole town went to her funeral.
(William Faulkner, 'A Rose for Emily', 217)

b. Aren't you going to answer the door? He'll wake the whole hotel.
(Arthur Miller, *Death of a Salesman*, 90–91)

c. You're the first human face I've seen for ages.
(Iris Murdoch, *Under the Net*, 173)

上の our whole town と the whole hotel はそれぞれ 'all the people in {the town / the hotel}' の意味だが、これは次の左の (a) のようなメトニミーの認知プロセスにより「人々」の意味となっている：

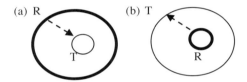

つまり、この (a) 図が示しているように、「ある認知のドメインの全体が参照点 (R) となり、この参照点からその一部のドメインをターゲット (T) として認知していくプロセス」(135) が作用している。右の (b) はその逆であり、face から人物全体をターゲット (T) として認知して行くプロセスである。

(2) 「焦点化と身体部位のメトニミー」の観点からは次のような例が説明可能である：

a. ... my infant tongue could make of both names nothing longer or more explicit than Pip. So I called myself Pip, and came to be called Pip.
(Charles Dickens, *Great Expectations*, 9)

b. "You do love me!" she whispered, assertive. And his hands stroked her softly, as if she were a flower without the quiver of desire, but with delicate nearness. (D. H. Lawrence, *Lady Chatterley's Lovers*, 164)

「この種の表現法は…行為者の行為が直接的に関わるアクティヴ・ゾーン (active zone) を焦点化し，その部分を言語化した表現スタイルの一種と言える。」(138) と著者は述べる。上では身体のうち推論で復元できるため潜在的に留まる形でよいはずの 'my infant tongue' と 'his hands' の部分が，焦点化し言語化されているスタイルというわけである。

〈異なる言語レベルの変異性〉に関わるスタイル
「作者の母語を特徴づける，その言語に独特の表現の仕方に関係している」(123) スタイルを指す。Langacker (1985) は「主観性の視点構成を標準視点構成 (canonical viewing arrangement) と自己中心的視点構成 (ego-centric viewing arrangement) に区分している。この区分は，以上の〈状況外的認知〉と〈状況内的認知〉の区分に相当する。」(142) として，著者は次の例をあげる：

 a. 国境の長いトンネルを抜けると雪国であった。　　　（川端康成『雪国』5）
 b. The train came out of the long tunnel into the snow country.
（Yasunari Kawabata, *Snow Country*, 3）

a は〈状況内的認知〉の方で「主体が問題の事態 (i.e. 列車に乗っている事態) の中に臨場的に身をおいて…雪国に入っていく状況を主観的に表現していて…〈主客融合の視点的な構図〉が認められる。これに対して」，b では「主体と主体が語る事態は区別され，主体が問題の事態を外から客観的に見て表現していて…〈主客分離の視点的な構図〉が認められる。」(143) と著者は述べる。こういった，その言語特有の，表現主体の事態解釈に関わる認知プロセスの違いは，日英両者に独特の表現スタイルをもたらす。

　以上，著者はスタイルには A〜C の全てが関連するとしながらも，文学のスタイルでは B が問題となるとする。A はパラフレーズの問題であり，C は「各言語の担い手に共有される表現性の問題である」(147) とする。従来の分析は直感的で「主体の表現力の基礎となる認知能力の観点から明示的な形で体系的に分析していく研究はなされていない」(147) ため，このような認知科学的な観点より見た，より客観的な形の認知文体論の可能性がある，と著

者は結んでいる。

　認知言語学によるスタイルの概念の明確化と，その分析装置を用いたより客観的な文体論の可能性を示している点において，文体論学者が一度は目を通しておくべき優れた論文と言えよう。

参考文献

Faulkner, W (1963) 'A rose for Emily'. In: Angus, D (ed.) *The Best Short Stories of the Modern Age*. Greenwich, Conn.: Fawcett.

Dickens, C (1963) *Great Expectations*. New York: Signet.

池上嘉彦（2003）「言語における〈主観性〉と〈主観性〉の言語的指標（1）」『認知言語学論考』3: 1–49.

Kawabata, Y (1957) *Snow Country* (trans. EG Seidenstikcer). Tokyo: Charles E. Tuttle.

川端康成（1967）『雪国』（改版）新潮文庫.

Langacker, RW (1985) 'Observations and speculations on subjectivity'. In: Haiman, J (ed.) *Iconicity in Syntax*. Amsterdam: John Benjamins. 109–150.

Lawrence, DH (1962) *Lady Chatterley's Lovers*. New York: Signet.

Miller, A (1949) *Death of a Salesman*. Harmondsworth, Middlesex: Penguin.

豊田昌倫（1981）『英語のスタイル』研究社.

Yamanashi, M (2010) 'Metaphorical modes of perception and scanning'. In: Burkhardt, A and Nerlich, B (eds) *Tropical Truth(s): The Epistemology of Metaphor and Other Tropes*. Berlin / New York: Walter de Gruyter. 157–175.

12 Saito, Yoshifumi (2001) 'Fiction as historical discourse: Diachronic analysis of the narrative structures of English fiction'. *POETICA* 58: 21–31.

この論文は著者が冒頭で述べているように 'the organic dynamics of narrative discourse'（ナラティブの談話が持つ有機的なダイナミズム）を明らかにし，同時に 'a new diachronic dimension of stylistic study'（文体研究の新しい次元）(22) を探ることを目的としている。ナラティブの持ついくつかの特性の中でも，特にナレーターの歴史的変化に焦点を当てながら作品の持つ特徴を論じている好論文である。

プロローグを提供するものとしてのナレーター (Narrator as Prologist)

1人称ナレーターに対して3人称ナレーターという言葉があるが，これは1人称が姿を隠した 'the potential I-narrator' (22) であると著者は述べる。

　例えば，次の編者は全て潜在的な1人称ナレーターであると言える。Daniel Defoe の *Robinson Crusoe* (1719) では編集者の Preface が物語の外側に置かれていて，その Prologue がいわば 'let me tell you a story' の句に相当する機能を果たしている。Samuel Richardson の *Pamela* (1740–1741) では Pamela の手紙の編者による前書きで始まっている。それは，この時代にあっては，そのまま手紙の内容が始まるのではなく，手紙を公にする人間が介在する方が適切だったことによるのだろう，と著者は述べる。これらの例にあるように，1人称ナレーターが，当時適切と考えられた編者の姿を借りて物語を語り始めるのである。

　このような「前書き」の役割は，の3人称の姿を借りたナレーターとナレーティー (narratee と綴られる，ナレーターが語る理論上，想像上の相手で，reader である読者とは理論的には異なる) の関係を作り出すところにあり，基本的には現在もしくは未来時制で語られる。それに対して物語の本文は過去時制となる。例えば Henry Fielding の *Joseph Andrews* (1742) は 'The authentic history with which I now present the public, is an instance of...' のように現在時制での書き出しで始まり，第2章では 'Mr Joseph Andrews, the hero of our ensuing history, *was esteemed* to be the only son of Gaffar and Gammer Andrews...' (イタリクスは原著者) と過去時制へと変化している。*Tom Jones* (1749) も同様であるとする。また Lawrence Sterne の *The Life and Opinions of Tristram Shandy, Gentleman* (1759–1767) について著者は，この小説の真に innovative なところは，伝統的な物語構造と19世紀的な 'authoritative narrative voice' (24) を合体させたことであるとする。18世紀のナレーターは物語の初めに現れて物語への導入を行う伝統的な story teller であるが，Tristram はそれ以上に物語全体を支配しようとする (24)，と著者は述べ，物語の冒頭の部分を引用している。スペースの関係上，短くして引用する:

　　I wish either my father or my mother, or indeed both of them, as they were in duty both equally bound to it, had minded what they were about when they begot me; had they duly considered how much depended upon what they were then doing; ...[35]

この部分はフィクションの慣習である過去時制で始まり，外側の大きな枠組みを構成している。しかし，次の3点で，その形から離れる：（1）主人公に関して「事実」を述べるのではなく，彼の人生と異なるものを仮定している；（2）主人公の誕生の時点から始まらず，その前の彼が「しこまれた」時点から物語が始まっている；（3）この部分は，次のようにナレーターとしてのTristram は読者である Madam に「章全体を読み返す」ように要求する：

... turn back, that is as soon as you get to the next full stop, and read the whole chapter over again.　　　　　　　　　　　　　　（Vol. 1, Ch. 20）[36]

このように *Tristram Shandy* ではナレーターが大きな物語全体をコントロールする力を持っており，そのことで 18 世紀特有のナレーターの振る舞いを越えて，19 世紀のビクトリア朝の全知のナレーターに近くなっている。

全能者としてのナレーター（**Narrator as God**）
19 世紀では全知のナレーター（omniscient narrator）が登場するが，次の Dickens の *David Copperfield* は，全知のナレーターが語りを行った *Tristram Shandy* の冒頭に大変よく似ている：

CHAPTER 1

I am born

WHETHER I shall turn out to be the hero of my own life, or whether

---

35）　私めの切な願いは，今さらかなわぬことながら，私の父か母かどちらかが，と申すよりもこの場合は両方とも等しくそういう義務があったはずですから，なろうことなら父と母の双方が，この私というものをしこむときに，もっと自分たちのしていることに気を配ってくれたらなあ，ということなのです。（朱牟田夏雄（訳）『トリストラム・シャンディ』（上）岩波文庫，1969）

36）　この次の文章の切れ目のところに辿り着き次第，もう一度前の章にもどって，十九章全体を読み返していただきます。（同訳）

that station will be held by anybody else, these pages must show. To begin my life with the beginning of my life, I record that I was born (as I have been informed and believe) on a Friday, at twelve o'clock at night. It was remarked that the clock began to strike, and I began to cry, simultaneously.[37]

ここでもナレーターは冒頭で未来および現在時制を用いて，読み手との基本的な関係を打ち立て，その後，語りのモードに入って過去時制を用いている。このような意味において，全知の語り手が物語を展開する他のビクトリア朝の作品と大きく変わるところはないと言えるとする。

脱特権化されたナレーター（De-authorized Narrator）

19世紀から現代に至る過程はナレーターを脱特権化する過程と言えると著者は述べる。脱特権化のひとつは，Virginia Woolfの *To the Lighthouse* (1927) に見られるように意識の流れの手法などがその脱特権化の代表的なものである。中心部分のみ著者の引用から載せておく：

And it was not true, Lily thought; it was one of those misjudgments of hers that seemed to be instinctive and to arise from some need of her own rather than of other people's. He is not in the least pitiable. He has his work, Lily said to herself.[38]

---

37) 第一章
　　　出　生
　私自身の伝記ともいうべきこの物語で，果たして私が主人公ということになるか，それともその位置は，誰かほかの人間によって取って代られるか，それは以下を読んでもらえればわかるはずだ。ところで，まず出生というところから始めるに当り，ここではただ私は（といっても，勿論他人から聞いて信じているにすぎないが），ある金曜日の夜中十二時に生れた，ということだけを記しておく。つまり，時計が十二時を打ち始めると同時に，私は産声をあげたのだそうである。（中野好夫（訳）『デイヴィッド・コパフィールド』(1)新潮文庫，1967)

38) でもそれは間違っている，とリリーは思う。夫人特有の勘違いの一つと言ってもいい。たぶんその気持ちの動きは夫人の心の中に本能的に根ざしたもので，他人のためというよりむしろ自分自身の必要に駆られて生じているのだろう。バンクスさんをあわれむ必要なんてまったくない。ちゃんとご自分の仕事をお持ちなのだから，とリリーは考えた。（御輿哲也（訳）『灯台へ』岩波文庫，2004)

脱特権化の2つ目は，Kazuo Ishiguro の *The Remains of the Day* に見られるような信頼できないナレーター (unreliable narrator) である：

> I proceed to serve port to some other of the guests. There was a loud burst of laughter behind me and I heard the Belgian clergyman exclaim: 'That is really heretical! Positively heretical!' Then laugh loudly himself. I felt something touch my elbow and turned to find Lord Darlington.
> 'Stevens, are you all right?'
> 'Yes, sir. Perfectly.'
> 'You look as though you're crying.'[39)]

結局ここでのナレーターは自分の内面には気づかず，別の登場人物による外面から見た内面の状態の指摘で，それに気づくという，19世紀的な全知のナレーター (omniscient narrator) とは異なった存在である，と著者は指摘する。

Robert Cooper（著）*Pinocchio in Venice*（1991）では，異なる時間連鎖が現在時制のもとに用いられており，従来の現在時制 → 過去時制への転換にとらわれない豊かな表現環境が現在時制のもとで作り出されている。

脱特権化のもうひとつの例は James Kelman（著）*How Late it was, How Late*（1994）で，ここでは，ナレーターがグラスゴーの労働者階級のアクセントで語ることにより，読み手に「人間的な視点」と「全知の視点」という2つの視点からテクストを読むことを強いており，そのことによって主人公が経験をして行く中で，主人公と同じ不安な感情を抱くように工夫されている：

> "Ye wake in a corner and stay there hoping yer body will disappear, the thoughts smothering ye;..."[40)]

---

39) 私はほかのお客様にワインを注いで回りました。私の後ろでどっと笑い声が起こり，ベルギーの牧師様が「これは異端だ。異端の説と言うしかない」と大声で叫ぶと，ご自分でも笑いだされました。肘に触れるものがあり，振り返ると，そこにダーリントン卿が立っておられました。
「スティーブンス，どうした？ 大丈夫か？」
「はい，なんともございません」
「なんだか，泣いているように見えたぞ」（土屋正雄訳『日の名残り』中央公論社，1990）
40) 「片隅で目を覚まして，消えっちまいたいと思いながらそこにいて，そんな考えで息が詰まる気がして」

この論文では以上のようにナレーターと読者の関係が歴史的にどのように変化して来たかを，著者の優れた読みと洞察力で展開して見せてくれる。先には著者についての論考が多く，現代では読み手の理論に関する者が多い中，このようなナレーターに焦点を当てたものは貴重で，文学テクストを研究する上で必須の文献と言えよう。

参考文献

Auerbach, E (1953) *Mimesis: The Representation of Reality in Western Literature*. Princeton: Princeton University Press. (Translated from the German by Willard R Trask. First published in Berne, Switzerland by A Francke Ltd. Co., 1946)

Leech, GN and Short, MH (1981) *Style in Fiction: A Linguistic Introduction to English Fictional Prose*. London: Longman.

Lodge, D (1992) *The Art of Fiction*. London: Penguin.

Spitzer, L (1948) *Linguistics and Literary History: Essays in Stylistics*. Princeton: Princeton University Press.

Stephens, J and Waterhouse, R (1990) *Literature, Language and Change: From Chaucer to the Present*. London: Routledge.

Wales, K (1989) *A Dictionary of Stylistics*. London: Longman.

Watt, I (1989) 'The comic syntax of *Tristram Shandy*'. In: H Bloom (ed.), *Modern Critical Interpretations: Laurence Sterne's* Tristram Shandy. New York: Chelsea House Publishers, 43–57.

13 豊田昌倫 (2013)「『収斂』から『拡散』へ―Wilfred Owen, 'Futility' の音を読む」*Albion* 59: 1–23.

この論文は音声文体論 (Phonostylistics) と呼ばれる，文体論の1分野を代表するものである。Roman Jakobson の詩の分析は，彼の音韻論的弁別素性の研究に見られるように，静的な音韻的特徴，およびそれより上位の言語単位の分布を詩の中に見ようとするものであるが，それと比べて，本論文はテクストの中の動的な音声の振る舞いにも分析の光を当てている点で，ユニークで優れた論文となっている。

この 'Futility' は 1918 年 5 月に Yorkshire の Ripon で書かれ，1918 年 6

月発行の The Nation 誌に掲載されたものである。2連から成るこの詩は以下のようになっている：

$_1$Move him into the sun—
$_2$Gently its touch awoke him once,
$_3$At home, whispering of fields unsown.
$_4$Always it woke him, even in France,
$_5$Until this morning and this snow.
$_6$If anything might rouse him now
$_7$The kind old sun will know.

$_1$Think how it wakes the seeds, —
$_2$Woke, once, the clays of a cold star.
$_3$Are limbs, so dear-achieved, are sides
$_4$Full-nerved—still warm—too hard to sitr?
$_5$Was it for this the clay grew tall?
$_6$—O what made fatuous sunbeams toil
$_7$To break earth's sleep at all?[41]

著者は第1連においては，子音は鼻音を，母音は前舌母音を避けて後舌母

---

41) 彼を太陽の下に移そう——
かつてその日差しは優しく彼を目覚めさせた，
故郷で，種が半分撒かれた畑のことをささやきながら。
いつも太陽が彼を起こした，フランスでも，
今朝，この雪の朝まで。
今彼を起こすものがあるのか
あの懐かしい優しい太陽ならわかるだろう。

太陽が諸々の種をどのように目覚めさせるか思ってごらん——
かって冷たい一つの星の土塊たちを目覚めさせたことを。
これほど見事に作られた手足が，強健な肉体が，
まだ温かいのに身動き一つできないのか。
あの土塊たちが大きく成長したのはこのためだったのか。
——一体何が愚かな日光に
わざわざ大地の眠りを破らせたのだ。

（中元初美（訳）『ウィルフレッド・オウェン戦争詩集』英宝社，2009）

音へと「収斂」する傾向を，その特徴としてあげることができるとする。

子音については，その主要語（名詞，形容詞，動詞，助動詞，副詞）の特徴を次のような表にしている：

鼻音	*M*ove, hi*m*, su*n*, Ge*n*tly, o*n*ce, ho*m*e, whisperi*ng*, u*n*sow*n*, eve*n*, Fra*n*ce, *m*orni*ng*, s*n*ow, a*n*ythi*ng*, *n*ow, *k*i*n*d, *m*ight, *kn*ow
側音	Gent*l*y, A*l*ways, fie*l*ds, o*l*d, wi*ll*
無声破裂音	Gen*t*ly, awo*k*e, whis*p*ering, *t*ouch, wo*k*e, *k*ind
破擦音	Gently, tou*ch*

これら主要語は鼻音と側音を持ち，/n/ ... /l/ ... /n/ ... /l/ ... /n/ という「なめらかな横糸を形成する」(6) とする。これは English Faculty Library (Oxford) 所収の草稿でも変わらない。

著者はさらに，この詩の第1連の主要語における強勢を持つ25の母音を基本母音図上にプロットして，その分布を論じている。二重母音の /eʊ/ に関しては，現代の容認発音 (RP) ではなく20世紀初頭の標準音としての /oʊ/ を採用している：

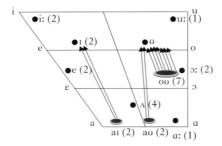

この図の中の「矢印は二重母音の移動方向，括弧内の数は頻度数を示す。また，二重母音の分類は第2音 (target quality) による。」(8) この基本母音図上にプロットされた母音の分布が示すように，第1連で使われた母音は，図の右側，「すなわち，後舌母音が圧倒的に多いのが分かる。…読者にとってもっ

とも印象価値の高い脚韻語についても，sun, once, unsown, France, snow, now, know のうちで前舌母音は 0，後舌母音が sun, once 以外の 5 語という分布を示す。」(9) さらに著者は「後舌母音を『暗く』('darker')，前舌母音は『明るく』('lighter') 感じる」(9) とする Jakobson and Waugh (1979: 188) を引用しながら，「'Futility' 第 1 連の母音が軌を一にして /ʊ/ に向かうのは，詩人の意識下に潜む『暗い』思い，戦場で倒れた若き兵士を前にしての胸を打つ憐憫および愛惜の情，その発露ではなかったか」(10) と説く。この詩の草稿では，3 行目と 5 行目は以下のように変更されている：

In *Wales*, whispering of fields unsown. → At *home*...
It *broke* his sleep, today in France. → Until this morning ... *snow*.

3 行目では 'home' の持つ /oʊ/ の後舌母音が選択されており，5 行目でも，この後舌母音がより効果的な脚韻で使用されている。「6 行目の *rouse* は草稿の段階から一貫して使用されている。第 1 連では woke, awoke，第 2 連 1 行では wakes が用いられているところから，語彙の結束生の観点からここでは wake が選ばれる可能性が高いとはいえ，詩人の耳には前舌母音を持つ wake よりも後舌母音を持つ rouse の方が，この文脈では好ましいと感じられたのであろう。」(10) として，この連における詩人の後舌母音に対するこだわりを論じている。

　第 2 連では，結論から言えば，子音も母音も特定の音への偏りが無く，第 1 連の「収斂」に対して，ほぼ全ての音域で母音が使用され均等に音が広がる「拡散」と呼べる傾向があるとする。

　主要語の子音については，第 1 連では鼻音への偏りがあったのと異なり，それぞれ均等に用いられている：

鼻音	Thi*n*k, o*n*ce, li*m*bs, Full-*n*erved, war*m*, *m*ade, su*n*beams
側音	c*l*ays, co*l*d, *l*imbs, Fu*ll*-nerved, sti*ll*, c*l*ay, ta*ll*, toi*l*, s*l*eep, a*ll*
無声破裂音	Thin*k*, wa*k*es, Wo*k*e, *c*lays, *c*old, s*t*ar, s*t*ill, *t*oo, s*t*ir, *c*lay, *t*all, *t*oil
破擦音	Dear-a*ch*ieved, fa*tu*ous

しかし，局地的な特徴は認められ，「1–2 行の命令文については，第 1 連を特徴づける『優しく』『快い』鼻音の使用は減少し，代わって『硬く』『激しい』/k/ が浮上する。」1 行目と 2 行目の前半部では /k/ 音が子音韻を構成するが，それは「2 行目の後半では clays, cold の頭韻となって詩行を支配し，さらに clays の子音束 /kl/ は cold (/k...l/) に「拡張」されてゆく」:

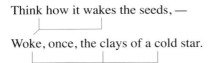

次の第 2 連の基本母音図は，第 1 連の基本母音図の母音の動きと異なり，ほぼ均等に使用されることを示している:

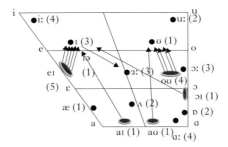

Carter and Long (1987: 113) は，この第 2 連の stir に至る 3, 4 行を読みにくいと評し，その読みにくさから，どのような感情が読み取れるのか考察する必要があると問うているとする。その理由であるが，「予測される自然な音韻の流れ，リズムおよび構造とこの 2 行の乖離が読みにくさの原因」(18) ではなかろうかと著者は考える。

まず第 3 行の 'Are limbs' (/ˈɑː lˈɪmz/) が読みにくいが，その理由として，予測される自然な音韻の流れに反しているからである。下図のように /ɑː/ という後舌低母音が /ɪ/ という前舌高母音 (次ページの①の方向) に移動するが，この流れが不自然と言える。同行の後半に置かれた 'are sides' (/ɑ/ → /aɪ/) も，

また第 4 行の 'hard'(/hɑːd/) 'to stir'(/stɜː/) も同じく発音が容易でない。逆の /ˈlɪmz ˈɑː/（②の方向）だと発音が容易になる。この容易な方の方向性は tick-tack や this and that のように慣用句に多く見られる。

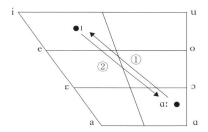

「4 行の *stir* は 2 行の *star* と脚韻語の関係にあり，名詞の *star* と動詞の *stir* が Owen 独特の不完全韻（pararhyme）を踏む … *star* と *stir* および *hard* と *stir* の不完全韻は *stir* でその終結点に至り，前途有為な青年兵士の将来を奪った戦争に向けられる悲嘆の念が *stir* で極点に達する。」(16)

著者はさらにこの前半の 1 行と 2 行は弱強 3 歩格を持つが，この 3, 4 行は 4 歩格となり，3 行目の 'Are limbs' や 'are sides' は「弱強」のリズムが予測されるが，「強弱格への変換」も可能ではなかろうかとする。「『冷静で規則的な弱強格』によるよりも，戦争の犠牲となった兵士を前にして悲しみと怒りの念を明示するために，あえて変速の強弱格を取りたく」なると著者は考える。

これらが，この箇所を読みにくくし，それによって「悲嘆」の感情を際立たせている理由である。

感情の嵐の後に続く最後の 3 つの行では，冷静さが戻ってくる。まず著者は唯一 /æ/ の音価を持つ 'fatuous' という外来語に注目する。この詩で使われている外来語のうち 'move'，'Gently'，'touch' は中英語期に借用して同化されており，最後の 2 語の 'achieved' と 'nerved' は複合語で［本来語＋借用語］の後半を占めているので，純粋な外来語は 'fatuous' のみとなり，この「愚かな」という語を前景化しているとする。

音韻論学者の Roman Jakobson の有名な数々の詩の分析と比べて，音韻論

的にはより多角的な側面から切り込みを見せている本論文は，誠に音声文体論 (Phonostylistics) と呼ぶにふさわしい優れた論文である．

参考文献

Carter, R and Long, M (1987) *The Web of Words: Exploring Literature Through Language*. Cambridge: Cambridge University Press.

Jakobson, R and Waugh, LR (1979) *Sound shape of language*. Bloomington, Ind: Indiana University Press.

14 豊田昌倫 (1997)「現代英語のスタイル」(1)–(12)『英語青年』143 (7): 14–16; 143 (8): 62–64; 143 (9): 33–35; 143 (10): 34–36; 143 (11): 18–20; 143 (12): 32–34; 144 (1): 45–47; 144 (2): 32–34; 144 (3): 34–36; 144 (4): 18–20; 144 (5): 39–41; 144 (6): 18–20.

本論文は『英語青年』に 1997 年 10 月 (Vol. 143, No. 7) より，翌年の 1998 年 9 月 (Vol. 144, No. 6) まで連載された現代英語について論じられたものである．この章では，中英語および近代英語の社会言語学的視点を取り入れたいくつかの考察を取り上げているが，本論文は，それの現代語版と言えよう．現代英語で書かれた作品の，言語実態に基づいた文体論的考察を行う際には必須の論考であるので，ここで取り上げた．ここでの議論は 20 世紀後半のものであり，21 世紀ではさらなる変化が予測されるが，真の意味での社会言語学的研究に基づいた，広義の「文体論」研究，著者の言葉では「スタイル」の研究をする上で，その視点を教えてくれている文献として有意義である点は不動である．

(1)「変わりゆく King's English」(143 (7): 14–16) では，Kingsley Amis の *King's English* (Harper Collins, 1997) の 'Pronunciation as they broadcast it' の項目が取り上げられる．この箇所で Amis は「今や単母音 e はかつての単母音 a に近い．放送では 'lass attantion in the Prass' [less attention in the

Press] と発音しているようだ」(14) と述べている。つまり Amis は /e/ → /a/ となっていると述べているわけである。

　Amis があげているもうひとつの特徴は /æ/ → /ʌ/ で，'the imp*u*ct [=impact] of bl*u*cks [=blacks]' att*u*cks [=attacks] on other bl*u*cks' のような放送英語で見られ，この変化は彼の作品 *Girl, 20* (1971) の 17 歳のヒッピーとして登場する Sylvia のアクセントに反映されている：

> 'What a terribly nice fl*u*ht [=flat],' she said, using the then fashionable throaty vowel. Her voice was think and clear, with the sort of accent that Roy tried to suppress in his own speech.

Wells (1982) などではイングランドでの /æ/ → /a/ の変化が述べられているし，Jones (1997¹⁵) の改訂版である 15 版の基本母音図では /æ/ は 14 版でよりも /a/ 近くに位置づけられているが，Gimson (1994⁵) では「RP の多くの若い話者は [a] 周辺のより広い音を用いている。/ʌ/ が近年前方に移行して /a/ に近づいてきたので，ときには /æ/ と /ʌ/ の中和という結果をもたらすことがある」(15) と説明されている。Kingsley Amis が聞きとるのはまさに「/æ/ と /ʌ/ の中和」された音にほかならないと著者は述べる。

　上に述べた 2 つの音の変化は「一連の音韻変化と考えるべきで」(15) あり，「/æ/ → /a/ の移行にともない，/æ/ の位置を埋めるべく一段上の /e/ が下降したと考える」とし，「20 世紀後半の音のスタイルを概観して気づくのは…よりくだけた多様性と大衆性へと向かう」(16) 変化であると著者は結論づけている。

　この「変わりゆく King's English」では Amis を中心に，その作品に反映された特異な音が，現代イギリス社会の音変化を反映したものであるとしている。

　(2)　「浮上する『河口域英語』」(143 (8) : 62–64) では，Rosewarne (1984) の 'Estuary English'「イングランドの東南部で話される新しいタイプの英語」(62) が「RP とコックニー…の中間領域に位置づけられ」(62) る英語として，

現れてきているが,「下層中産」階級の英語という色合いが濃く,「『新しい標準英語』ないしは『明日のRP』となるかどうかは予断を許さない」(64) としている。

　(3)　「'outsider' の声—Diana 妃の英語」(143 (9): 33-35) では,「ロンドンの Sloane Square を中心として見うけられた上流階級の若者をさす用語として」(33) の Sloane Ranger の英語が論じられる。その中で Diana 皇太子妃は代表格である。特に女王陛下との対比のうちに [a] と [ʔ] の音が論じられる。著者は Wells (1982) が述べる RP の上流階級における変種としての U-RP (upper-crust RP) と,Gimson (1989⁴) の用いた RP の下位区分としての conservative RP, general RP, そして advanced RP と Wells (1982) の区分に基づいて,新しい下のような区分を提案する。そこでの /æ/ の音の違いは右端の音声記号に現れている:

　　conservative U-RP　（女王陛下の RP）　family [fɛ́æmlɪ] [féæmlɪ]
　　advanced U-RP　　（Diana 妃の RP）　family [fámlɪ]

Sue Townsend の *The Queen and I* (Methuen, 1992) という小説では女王陛下の ax の母音を [ɪx] と発音させ,それに基づいて Wales (1994) で女王の発音は /æ/ を /ɪ/ とすると述べているが,これは小説中で誇張されたものであって,そのまま実際の発音とするわけにはいかないとする。もうひとつの声門閉鎖音 [ʔ] の方は,'There's a loʔ ov iʔ abouʔ' は Diana 妃の音ではあるが女王陛下は決して,そして Charles 皇太子も発しないであろう音である。これらに見られるように,Diana 妃の悲劇の背後に,U-RP の中で 2 つの声の対立があったとする。

　(4)　「報道英語の二重性」(143 (10): 34–36) では,いくつかの新聞の例をあげて,*Times* のような高級紙では「参加者,特に動作主を表出することなく出来事を抽象的に表現する傾向がある」のに対し,*Sun* や *Daily Mirror* などの「大衆紙では事件ないし出来事の参加者を具体的に描写する」(36) とし

ている。前者は「動作主を表出することなく出来事を抽象的に表現する傾向があ」り，語彙，統語法共に透明度が低いとしながらも，「香港の返還」の見出しとしての 'Hong Gone' (*Daily Star*) に見られるように，大衆紙には独自のひねりがあるとする。

(5) 「大衆紙のレトリック」(143 (11): 18–20) は大衆紙の独特の表現が取り上げられる。例えば，以下の文は2つの点で通常の文の形に反する:

Princess Diana's hiss-and-tell friend James Hewitt was named Turkey of the Year yesterday.　　　　　　　　　　　　(*Daily Express*, 7 December 1994)

ひとつは，「文末重点」(end-weight) の原理に反して，「〈James Hewitt is Princess Diana's kiss-and-tell friend〉のように文で表される概念を移行して凝縮した」(18) ものが文頭で用いられており，そこが重くなっている例。2つ目は，Quirk et al. (1985) の言う核強勢の問題である。「新聞では前日の朝刊以降の24時間に起きた出来事を報道するために，報道英語における yesterday はむしろ旧情報となる。」(19) そのため，上記の 'yesterday' は「新情報を示す核音調を持たないことになる。このように2つの原理に反して，文頭を重く文末を軽くするところに，タブロイドの際立った特徴が認められる」(19) と著者は述べる。また固有名詞も「*Mum* Joanne Rowling, *Teenager* Christ Dennett, さらには *Shopper* Sarah Jameson のように」「固有名詞に冠」(19) がつき句の頭を重くする。また談話にもこの「重」から「軽」への原理は認められるという。そして，大衆紙には，OED^2 の tabloid 誌の定義に見られる「集中的でわかりやすい形式」があるのだとされる。

(6) 「ジャンルを越えて—放送の英語と報道の英語」(143 (12): 32–34) では，例えばテニスの試合を報じる放送英語では有力選手は固有名詞が主に用いられ，非有力選手には様々な変奏が用いられる点が論じられる。Gabriela Sabatini には，姓名が3回，Sabatini が6回，Gabriela が8回，変奏としての the giant が1回用いられるのに対し，非有力選手の日本人である Rika

Hiraki には姓名が 8 回,Rika が 2 回,the Japanese girl 2 回,the young Japanese girl, the young Japanese player, her opponent, her qualified opponent, the baseliner などが各 1 回用いられている。その際に her (= Sabatini) opponent のように,多くは有力選手からの視点で放送が行われるとしている。それに対して,新聞英語では有力選手にも非有力選手にも等しく変奏が用いられているとする。この先,さらにジャンルの下位区分による分析が必要となると結んである。

(7) 「文語と口語」(144 (1): 45–47) は主に Quirk 教授が関係したコーパスにおける言語分類の話が展開し,その分類範疇がイギリス英語の発話媒体の進歩と並行している点が紹介される。

　著者は 'Survey of English Usage' (SEU) (Svartvik and Quirk 1979) での分類を下のようにまとめる。ここでは script (原稿) があるかないかが文語と口語を分ける基準となる:

議会の発言は用意された原稿に基づくものが多いのでこの区分では Writing の方に入っているが,Biber (1988) は 'Spontaneous speeches' に含め,Greenbaum 構想の「英語の国際コーパス」(Nelson 1990) では 'Dialogue の 'public' に入れている。見直された図式 (Quirk 1986) では口語は script があるかどうかではなく face-to-face か unseen かが基準となり，以下のようになっている：

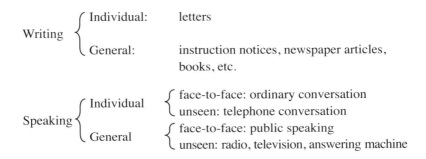

ここに留守番電話のメッセージが含まれているのは，イギリスでの普及率の高さを反映しているという。またここに含まれない重要な口語の範疇にインタビューがある。

(8)「'relaxation' の指標—日常会話の言語」(144 (2): 32–34) では会話の非流暢性 (non-fluency もしくは disfluency) の特徴が論じられる。これには 'I mean' などの談話標識 (discourse marker) や出だしの誤りであるフライング (false start) などが含まれる。これらは無いと「聞き手にとっても息苦しい」ので，「今自分は肩のこらない会話を楽しんでいるという標識と考えてはどうか」(34) と著者は提案する。Hughes (1996) は，非流暢的特徴 (non-fluency features) はもっといい表現を探して会話をよくするために協力している特徴ととらえたが，この「relaxation の標識」というとらえ方は斬新である。「台本に依存する戯曲や映画は基本的には文語に分類されて」(34)，つまり (7) の分類で「書かれた言葉」である Writing とされているが，自然言語の特徴を持つ台本無しの映画が紹介されていて，それは Mike Leigh 監督・脚本 *Secrets and Lies* (1996) で，地下鉄の Holborn 駅で実母と娘が出会うシーンでは，この 2 人の女優は本当に初対面だったとのこと。

(9)「虚構としての会話」(144 (3): 34-36) では，Kingsley Amis の作品にふんだんに用いられている，優れた観察眼に基づく自然言語の会話の特徴に触れた後，著者は Hughes (1996) を引用しながら，これらの自然言語の会話の特徴は「小説の中に移されると別の役割を果たし…ときには緊張や情緒の不安定を暗示する『困難な会話』の標識と受け取られかねない」(36) と述べる：

　　'Would you mind very much...' Buckmaster said to Bowen *with evident difficulty.*' I have something urgent business to discuss with Dr Lopes here... 　　　　　　　　　　　　　　　（Kingsley Amis *I Like It Here*, 1958）

この「前半部の '…' は自然な躊躇というよりも，『困難な』発話を示す」(36) と著者は述べていて，こういった点は，文学の会話を考える際に大変参考になる。文学の会話は単なる自然な会話の特徴を反映しているわけではないのである。

　(10)「定型への回帰―ロマンスの世界」(144 (4): 18-20) は，*Time Out* の恋人募集の欄 'Lonely Hearts' で使われている英語には，'*S*mart, *s*lim, *s*treet-wise, *s*ophisticated, *s*ocial, *s*olvent and *s*olo' などのように頭韻が用いられたりしていて読者を楽しませてくれるという著者の言葉で始まる。続いて，著者はハーレークインの文体を分析し，例えば次の例では

　　Heart beating over-fast, eyes wide, frightened, she ran.

Nash (1990) では前置されている分詞節は読者の注意をそこに集中させるとあるが，意識が集中するのは，むしろ「核強勢（nuclear stress）をになう動詞の ran …とは考えられないだろうか。」(19) と著者は提案する。また全体の構造としては3つの特徴があるとする。まず，伝達部に関してはロマンスでは
　① 'Q' SV [Adv]（Q は非伝達部で右辺への移行が可能）
　② 'Q' VS [Adv]

のうち①が圧倒的とする。例えば,

　　'Oh,' Githa murmured absently as she continued to watch him from the corner of her eye.　　（Emma Richmond *His Temporary Mistress*, 1997）

のごとくである。これに対して,通常の現代小説では主語が代名詞以外であれば (2) のような倒置は普通に行われている。2つ目に,ロマンスでは伝達動詞は「'whispered' や 'murmured' などの様態記述動詞 (manner-descriptive verb) が好んで用いられる」(19) とする。「これは基本動詞 say からの一種の変奏と考えられ,それが多用されれば特定の文体標識となる。」(19) と述べる。第3には副詞に特徴があり,-ly の形を取るものが圧倒的に多く①を書き換えた以下の形だと言えるとする：
　①′　'Q' AV ly-Adv
例えば無意味な副詞をつけた murmur quietly などでは,このパターンが作用したものと著者は述べる。そして lonely heart の持ち主であるポップフィクションの読者にとっては「反復する形式こそが望ましく心地よい」(20) と結んでいる。

　(11)「非人称から代名詞へ—Plain English への道」(144: 5, 39–41) は British Library での書物の予約の仕方を指示する文書の歴史的変遷を追い,そこでは 'officialese' と呼ばれる受動態や無生物主語が減少し,それと並行して読み手に向けての you / your,さらには we / our が登場し,イギリスで1979年に始まった Plain English 運動が達成されつつあるとする。

　(12)「普遍性と個性—Agatha Christie」(144: 6, 18–20) で,著者はこよなく愛してやまないミステリーの女王 Agatha Christie のスタイルを論じて,このシリーズを終える。Christie の人物描写では抽象性の高い形容詞を用い,「類型描写」(19) と呼んでいい手法が用いられている：

　①　She was an attractive young woman, he thought,...

(Ordeal by Innocence)

② She was a good-looking young woman of perhaps nearer thirty than twenty,...
(The Body in the Library)

Christie の描く町や村についてもありふれた「イギリスの田園風景」(19) が描かれ「細部描写」(19) が避けられる。著者はこのことを称して Christies の描写対象は「『全体としての様子』('a general air')」を持つと述べている。そして，Barnard (1980) の言葉を借りて，こういった文体こそ彼女の普遍性の原因だとする。

個性的な言葉のスタイルを持つ人物も，もちろん，Christie には登場し，著者は Hercule Poirot と Miss Marple をあげる。前者は例えば

'I hope I do not *derange* you, Madame.'
(Third Girl)

フランス語の 'deranger' は「仕事を中断する」の意味から，ここでは「おじゃまではございませんか」のフランス語の意味で用いた語が，現代英語の「混乱させる」の意味を同時に持ち，そこで生じた「意図と効果のずれ」(20) が興味深いとする。後者の Miss Marple の英語は

'Well, of course, I am rather older now. And one has so many ailments ... Oh, dear, one shouldn't talk about these things. *What a very nice house you have*!'
(Nemesis)

に見られるように上流ないし上層中産階級のものである。例えば 'one' は「上位の階層との連想」(20) を持ち，最後の文の 'a very nice house' は Ross (1956) の言う U であり，non-U の 'a lovely home' と対照的である。

著者は 12 回にわたって，contemporary なイギリス社会における英語のスタイルを論じ（つまり広い意味での文体論，もしくは study of style)，それとの距離において文学のスタイル（狭い意味での文体論，もしくは Stylistics）に言及する。例えば Shakespeare など，十分な社会言語学的データの揃わな

い時代の文学テクストの文体を論じる際には，望むべくもないアプローチであるが，原点として，この著者のような視点で文学テクストを分析すべきであろう。

参考文献

Amis, K（1958）*I Like it Here*. London: Gollancz.
Amis, K（1997）*King's English: A Guide to Modern Usage*. London: Harper Collins.
Amis, K（1971）*Girl, 20*. London: Jonathan Cape.
Barnard, R（1980）*A Talent to Deceive: An Appreciation of Agatha Christie*. London: Collins.
Biber, D（1988）*Variation across Speech and Writing*. Cambridge: Cambridge University Press.
Gimson, AC（1989）*An Introduction to the Pronunciation of English*（4th edn）. London: Edward Arnold.
Gimson, AC and Cruttenden, A（1994）*Gimson's Pronunciation of English*（5th edn）. London: Edward Arnold.
Jones, D（1997［1909］）*English Pronouncing Dictionary*（15th edn）. Cambridge: Cambridge University Press.
Leigh, M（dir.）（1996）*Secrets and Lies*. Distributed by Film Four Distributors.
Nash, W（1990）*Language in Popular Fiction*. London: Routledge.
Nelson, G（1990）'The design of the corpus'. In: Greenbaum, S（ed.）*Comparing English Worldwide: The International Corpus of English*. Oxford: Clarendon.
Hughes, R（1996）*English in Speech and Writing: Investigating Language and Literature*. Routledge.
Quirk, R, et al.（1985）*A Comprehensive Grammar of the English Language*. London: Longman.
Quirk, R（1986）*Words at Work: Lectures on Textual Structure*. Singapore: Singapore University Press.
Richmond, E（1997）*His Temporary Mistress*. Richmond, Surrey: Mills & Boon.
Rosewarne, D（1984）'Estuary English'. *Times Educational Supplement*, 19（October 1984）.
Ross, ASC（1956）'U and non-U: An essay in sociological linguistics'. In: Mitford, N（ed.）*Noblesse Oblige*. London: Hamish Hamilton.
Svartvik, J and Qurik, R（eds）（1979）*A Corpus of English Conversation*. Lund: CWK Gleenrup.
Townsend, S（1992）*The Queen and I*. London: Methuen.
Wells, JC（1982）*Accents of English 1: An Introduction*. Cambridge: Cambridge University Press.

15 Kikuchi, Shigeo (2010) 'Unveiling the dramatic secret of "Ghost" in *Hamlet*'. *Journal of Literary Semantics* (Mouton de Gruyter, Germany) 39 (2) 103–117.

最後になるが，拙論も論じてみたい。この論文では Shakespeare の *Hamlet* における 'Ghost' の役割を理解することを通して Shakespeare の制作意図 (author's intent) に迫ろうとするものである。その際に，より構造的に単純な作品（ここでは *Othello*）から論じ，そこから推論の梯子を，*Othello* と相似的構造を持つと思われるより複雑な作品に伸ばしていくことで，その複雑な作品に迫っている。方法論的には機能主義的構文論のテクスト構成機能に着目して，それを文学テクストレベルに応用するという形を取っている。

まず *Othello* の荒筋から述べる。Venice 公国の Othello 将軍はムーア人でありながら将軍の地位にまで上り詰めた男である。この Othello に対して妻の Desdemona が部下の Cassio と浮気をしたと，同じく部下の Iago が思い込ませ，Othello に妻を殺させるという話である。この作品では，この Iago という人物が Shakespeare が造形した人物の中でも最も魅力的な人物であるとされて来た。

Iago に関して，イギリスのミステリーの女王と呼ばれた Agatha Christie は彼女の Hercule Poirot シリーズの最後の作品 *The Curtain* で大変鋭い観察を見せている。Poirot に Iago は 'the perfect murder' であると言わせているのである：

> The play of *Othello*. For there, magnificently delineated, we have the original of X. Iago is the perfect murderer. The deaths of Desdemona, of Cassio—indeed of Othello himself—are all Iago's crimes, planned by him, carried out by him. And he remains outside the circle, untouched by suspicion—or could have done so. For your great Shakespeare, my friend, had to deal with the dilemma that his own art had brought about. To unmask Iago, he had to resort to the clumsiest of devices—the handkerchief—a piece of work not at all in keeping with Iago's general technique and a

blunder of which one feels certain he would not have been guilty.
(Christie *Curtain*, 254)

『オセロ』だ。この戯曲には X の原型がみごとに描かれている。イアーゴは完全殺人者だ。デズデモーナの死も，キャシオーの死も——じつにオセロ自身の死さえも——みなイアーゴによって計画され，実行された犯罪だ。しかも，彼はあくまで局外者であり，疑惑を受けるおそれもない——はずだった。ところがきみの国の偉大なシェイクスピアは，おのれの才能ゆえのジレンマと闘わなければならなかった。イアーゴの仮面を剥ぐために，彼はせっぱつまったすえなんとも稚拙な工夫——例のハンカチ——に頼ったのである。これはイアーゴの全体的な狡智とは相容れない小細工であり，まさかイアーゴほどの切れ者がこんなヘマをしでかすはずはないと，だれしも思うに違いない。

(中村能三（訳）『カーテン—ポアロ最後の事件』ハヤカワ，1982)

Iago の最初の計略は，'What dost thou say?' と問いかける Othello とのやりとりで始まる。この後，いくつかの同種の場面があるが，ここでは，Iago が Othello の心の中に疑念を生じさせようとする第 1 の場面のみをあげる。Othello は 'say' を使っているので 1 次的な意味内容にしか興味を示していない:

IAGO	Ha, I like not that.
OTHELLO	What dost thou say?
IAGO	Nothing, my lord; or if—I know not what.
OTHELLO	Was not that Cassio parted from my wife?
IAGO	*Cassio, my lord?* no, sure, *I cannot think it That he would steal away so guilty-like Seeing you coming.*
OTHELLO	I do believe 'twas he.

(*Othello* 3.3.34–40)[42]

---

42) イアーゴウ「あ！ これはいかん。」
オセロウ「なんだ？」
イアーゴウ「あ，いや，なんでもございません。が，あるいは——いや，わかりません。」

Iago の返答の 'Cassio, my lord?' の部分は，情報量の点で，ここで必要とされている量よりも少ない。Othello が求めているのは，男が Cassio であるかどうかの確認を要求しているにもかかわらず，Iago は an echoing reply のみを与えていて，こういった反復的な返答は必要とされるより少ない情報しか提供しないので，聞き手は，話し手は開示をしたくない大切な情報を持っているのかも知れないと思わせ，聞き手にそれにふさわしい推論を行わせる。2つ目の 'I cannot think it / That he would steal away so guilty-like / Seeing you coming.' もまた，必要以上の量の情報を提供していることから量の公理に違反することになる。忠義の将軍 Othello は協調して談話の一貫性を保とうとしているために，存在しない含意を推論してしまうのである。この Othello が抱く疑念を Ghost Implicature（亡霊の含意）と呼ぶこともできよう。

次に Hamlet に進んでみよう。Hamlet の制作年代は 1600 年前後とされていて，制作年代は Hamlet よりも Othello の方が後というのが通説であるが，構造的には Othello の方が単純なので，それを手がかりに Hamlet に迫ることができるわけである。

荒筋を述べる。物語の舞台はデンマークで，父である King Hamlet がおじの Claudius に殺され，母の Gertrude はそのおじと結婚してしまうという悲劇的な状況の中で，ある夜，お城に King Hamlet と称する亡霊が現れ，息子の Hamlet 王子に自分は Claudius に殺されたのだと告げる。復讐について Hamlet は苦悶するが，最後には宰相の息子の Leataes との剣の試合の最中に Claudius を殺す。

Othello では，心の中で推測された不確かな「疑わしき世界」を作り出すのは Iago であった。だまされる方を（　）に入れると Iago (Othello) の形となる。それに対し，Hamlet では，この「疑わしき世界」に Hamlet 王子を導

　　オセロウ「今妻のところから別れて行ったのはキャシオウではなかったか？」
　　イアーゴウ「キャシオウ，でございますって？　いいえ，とんでもない，そんなはずはございません，あなたがおいでになったのを見て，あの男が，悪いことでもしたようにこそこそ出て行くなんて。」
　　オセロウ「いや，たしかにあの男だった。」
　　　　　　　　　　　　　　　　　　　　　　（菅泰男（訳）『オセロウ』岩波書店，1960）

き入れるのは，まず亡霊である．亡霊が *Othello* における Iago の役を果たし，Hamlet 王子が Othello 将軍の役を果たしている．次には，この Hamlet 自体が亡霊の役を担い，Claudius を不確定の疑いの世界へと導き入れる．次のように図式化できようか：Ghost（Hamlet（Claudius））．このように *Hamlet* という作品は，Hamlet が亡霊により「疑わしき世界」に引き込まれる世界と，Hamlet により Claudius が「疑わしき世界」に導き入れられる世界の二重構造になっている．

Hamlet においては，亡霊によって証明不可能な毒のある言葉を耳に流し込まれた Hamlet 王子は，その耳に Iago によって，同じく毒のある言葉を入れられた Othello 将軍と同じ土俵に立っている．そして，Hamlet 王子は，今度は，亡霊や Iago と同じ役割を演じて，Claudius に自分は Claudius の隠された犯罪を知っているという印象を与える．しかし，Hamlet が事実を知っているかどうかは Claudius には証明不可能である．ここに，Hamlet と Claudius が共に「見かけ通りの世界」から，「疑わしき世界」——亡霊が証明不可能な言葉をささやく「疑わしき世界」を Hamlet の前に示して見せた時，Hamlet は，あの有名な 'To be, or not to be' の言葉を吐く——を通して，疑わしき事柄は「そうに違いない」という世界に導き入れられるという構図が見て取れる[43]． Hamlet 王子が Horatio 達の制止を振り切って亡霊に 1 人でついて行き，1 人で亡霊の告白を聴く，1 人しか聴かない，という設定はこの構図を作り出すためである．

Claudius が，Hamlet が彼の犯罪を知っているのを知るためには，Claudius は Hamlet から Hamlet が知っているという証拠を引き出さねばならない．他方，Hamlet は，Claudius の犯罪に関する明らかな証拠は持っていない．したがって，Hamlet は Claudius の犯罪に関して何もはっきりとは述べることはできない．エリザベス朝の時代においても，Claudius 自身の自供がないのに，亡霊によってなされた告白だけは証拠として通用するものではなかった．しかし，Hamlet が彼の犯罪に関する明らかな証拠を持っていない限り，Clau-

---

43) この論文で用いた seeming という概念は，従来から言われて来た，例えば Iago は見かけは善良だが実際には悪人だったような appearance と reality の対立ではなく，reality そのものがそもそも不確かな世界を表しているという視点である．

dius は，その自供をする必要はない。そして，注意すべき点なのだが，劇中劇の後の Claudius の告白シーンで，Hamlet は Claudius が告白している場に登場するが，彼はその告白内容を聞いていない。したがって，Hamlet は Claudius の犯罪の証拠を得ていないのである。そのセリフは以下の通りである：

> HAMLET　Now might I do it pat, now a is a-praying.
> And now I'll do't. [*Draws his sword.*]
> 　　　　　　　　And so 'a goes to heaven;
> And so am I reveng'd. That would be scann'd:
> A villain kills my father, and for that
> I, his sole son, do this same villain send
> To heaven.
> Why, this is hire and salary, not revenge.
> 　　　　　　　　　　　　　　(*Hamlet* 3.3.52–79)[44]

Hamlet は Claudius が告白をしているのを「見る」だけで聞いてはいない。さらに，もっと重要なことだが，Hamlet は彼の告白に関心を示さない。つまり，この段階において，Hamlet は直接的な証拠を握っていないにもかかわらず既に Claudius の犯罪に確信を持っているかのように観客に見えるように振る舞っている。言い方を変えれば Shakespeare が Hamlet にそのように振る舞わせている。劇中劇のシーンで Hamlet は Claudius の犯罪を確信したと一般的には思われているが，劇中劇で確信を持ったとしても，それは告白に比べれば証拠性の乏しいものであり，ここで告白をしているのであるから，証拠を得ようとして通常ならその内容に大いに関心を示すはずである。つまり，Hamlet と Claudius は共に，互いに相手の知識に対して「～ではなかろうか」

44）ハムレット 「今ならやれる，きれいさっぱりと。奴は祈りの最中だ。さ，やろう。［剣を抜く］これで奴は天国行き，おれは見事，仇が討てる。いや，まて，ここは思案のしどころだ。悪党が父を殺した，それで一人息子のこのおれが，その悪党を送り込む，天国へ…なんだ，これでは盗っ人に追い銭だ，復讐にはならぬ。」

　　　　　　　　　　　　　　（野島秀勝（訳）『ハムレット』岩波書店，2002）

と推測する世界にいるのである。Hamlet が抱く「Claudius が父を殺したかも知れない」という「疑わしき世界」と Claudisu が抱く「Hamlet は自分が King Hamlet を殺したことを知っているかも知れない」という「疑わしき世界」が並行している。つまり，互いに相手を推測する状態，にいるのである。互いに相手からは直接的な証拠を引き出すことができず，そのまま最後の決闘のシーンへと続いて行く。

　この論文は文学テクストをひとつの説 (clause) ととらえて，Mathesius (1975) や Halliday (2004) で展開された機能主義的構文論のテクスト的な働きを，テクスト内に見出して論じている。この論文で用いられている図を簡略化して示すと下のようになる。Hamlet の世界に「疑わしき世界」としての亡霊が登場したように，劇の途中から，Claudius の世界に，真実を知っているように見える「疑わしき世界」としての Hamlet が登場する。理論的には，節 (clause) における主題―題術 (theme–rheme) 構造のように，前半の「疑いのない世界」が，この「疑わしき世界」に媒介されて，後半の「そうに違いない世界」に変貌する。その媒介者が，*Othello* においては Iago であったが，この *Hamlet* においては亡霊であり，Prince Hamlet である：

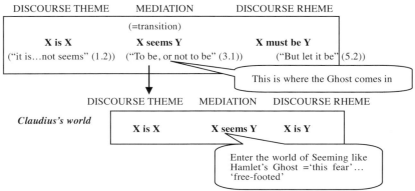

この劇の様々な要素は，観客に Hamlet が Claudius に対する復讐を成し遂げたと思わせるように配置されていると言えよう。繰り返すと，祈りのシー

ン（ACT 3, SCENE 3）では，ClaudiusはHamlet王の殺害を告白するが，Hamletはそれを聞いていない。しかしながら，このシーンまでの間に，観客は亡霊の告白によってClaudiusの犯罪を確信する心の準備ができている。さらにGonzago劇での類似の告白によっても，その心の準備が確かとなる。（この場面でHamletがClaudiusの犯罪を確信したと取ってしまう現代の読み手は，当時の観客と同じ状態になっているわけである。）そして，だれに対して復讐がなされるかについての心の準備ができている。さらに，『原Hamlet』の内容を知っていたり，当時の他の復讐劇を知っていたりする観客は，このHamletでも復讐がなされるだろうと期待しているわけである。Hamletが行う復讐への期待に加えて，劇中劇のシーンで観客はまた，HamletがClaudiusの犯罪を確信したと思ってしまうのである。そして，観客はHamletがClaudiusを殺す決闘のシーンで復讐を成し遂げたと思い込む。しかしながら，実際には，HamletはClaudiusがHamlet王を殺害したという明白な証拠無しに死んで行くし，Claudiusの方もHamletが，自分がHamlet王を殺したということを知っているという明らかな証拠無しに死んで行くのである。

　この論文では，「テクスト内に作られたグランド・デザインとしての物語世界を文脈とする発話」という観点から，'To be, or not to be' の句にShakespeareが持たせた意図に機能主義的に迫っている。フィクションとしての文学テクストにおいては，物語内の発話は物語世界内で発せられ，それを取り巻くように現実の「作者―読者」の世界がある。したがって，'To be, or not to be' の句の場合も作者のグランド・デザインとしての物語世界が意味するところと密接に結びついており，それを理解することで，この句に込めた，「そうである明瞭な世界」と「そうであるに違いない世界」を媒介する「疑わしき世界」という「作者の意図」（author's intent）に迫ることができるわけである。

参考文献

Coulthard, M (1977) *An Introduction to Discourse Analysis*. London: Longman.
Halliday MAK (2004) *An Introduction to Functional Grammar*. London: Arnold.
Kikuchi, S (2001) 'Lose heart, gain heaven: The false reciprocity of gain and loss in Chaucer's *Troilus and Criseyd*'. *Neuphilologische Mitteilungen* (Bulletin of the

Modern Language Society, Finland) CII (4): 427–434.

Kikuchi, S (2006) 'To Leave or to Settle?: Kazuo Ishiguro's Remains of the Summer in Nagasaki'. *Philología* (University of Belgrade, Serbia) 4: 129–138.

Kikuchi, S (2013) 'Poe's Name excavated: The mediating function and the transformation of discourse theme into discourse rheme'. *Language and Literature* (Sage, UK) 22 (1): 3–18.

Mathesius, V (1975) *A Functional Analysis of Present Day English on a General Linguistic Basis*. The Hague: Mouton.

第 3 部

文学テクストの語学的研究の試み

ジェイムズ・ジョイスの『ユリシーズ』と2人の歩くキャンドル[1]

菊 池 繁 夫

はじめに

ここでは，Kikuchi (2001, 2010, 2013) で論じた，フィクションの談話における「主題化」(thematization) の概念に従い，James Joyce の *Ulysses* における2人の主人公である Stephen Dedalus と Leopold Bloom が，いわば 'a dying Dublin' (死に行くダブリン) の枕元に置かれた2本のキャンドルに相当するということを論じたいと思う。

1 'The Sisters' に初めて現れる2本のキャンドル

Joyce の初期の短編集である *Dubliners* の冒頭に収められている 'The Sisters' は，彼の作品群における「作者の意図」(author's intent) を，グランド・デザインとして示しているものとして注目に値する。この作品は冒頭，2本のキャンドルの話で始まる。実際に2本のキャンドルが置かれる状況は物語の半ばで生じるが，作品の冒頭にこのキャンドルの話があるということは，いわば

---

[1] この章は2014年7月5日にイギリスの University of Kent で開かれた The 6th conference of the International Association of Literary Semantics: Literary Semantics: Past, Present, Future? (IALS 2014) での発表に基づいている。なお，この研究は，日本学術振興会の科学研究費助成事業 基盤研究 (C) (「James Joyce 作品における談話的主題化の問題」研究者番号: 70204831) の助成を受けている。

言語的に2本のキャンドルが，この作品の冒頭に置かれていると言えよう。そして，この 'The Sisters' は *Dubliners* の冒頭に収められているので，この *Dubliners* の頭に，2本のキャンドルが「言語的に」置かれていると言えよう。このグランド・デザインは，主人公の少年が亡くなった牧師の通夜の行われている彼の住まいを訪れる際に再び現れる。そこでは，その牧師の2人の姉妹がまるで2本のキャンドルのように通夜を取り仕切っている。

 'The Sisters' の冒頭の部分を見てみる：

> THERE was no hope for him this time: it was the third stroke. Night after night I had passed the house (it was vacation time) and studied the lighted square of window: and night after night I had found it lighted in the same way, faintly and evenly. If he was dead, I thought, I would see the reflection of candles on the darkened blind for I knew that *two candles must be set at the head of a corpse*.
>
> (*Dubliners*, 'The Sisters', 3)（イタリスクは筆者）

> 今度は助かる見込みはない。三度目の発作だったから。毎晩ぼくは家の前を通り（休暇中だった），明かりの灯った四角い窓を見つめた。そして毎晩，窓は同じように，ほのかに，また均等に，照らされていた。もしあの人が死んだら，と僕は考えてみた。暗く閉ざされたブラインドに蠟燭の明かりが照らし出されることだろう。
>
> （結城英雄（訳）『ダブリンの市民』岩波書店，1999）

この *Dubliners* の冒頭を飾る，2本のキャンドルは *Dubliners* の中の後に続く物語群に長い光を投げかけている。そして，その光は作品を越えて，さらに長く後続の作品にまで届いている。

　Joyce の後期の作品である *Ulysses* でも，主人公の Dedalus は Dublin の街をさまよい Bloom とすれ違いながら，最後には Bloom の家で，2人で並び立ちながら放尿をする。ちょうど，「この世」から「あの世」への「境」を越えて行った 'The Sisters' の牧師に捧げられた2本のキャンドルのように。そしてこの放尿の記述は最終章の Bloom の妻である Molly の，文の言語的「境」を越えて流れる「意識の流れ」(stream of consciousness) の文体へと続い

ている。DedalusとBloomが，2人で交わることなくDublinの街をさまよう段階を，作者Joyceが語ろうとする主題（theme）もしくはトピック（topic）とし，Mollyの文の境を越えて展開する意識の流れ，すなわち「境あるものの超越」（border crossing）の箇所を，作者が主題に対して与えた題述やコメント（rheme, comment）としてとらえることにより，Ulyssesにおける作者の意図（author's intent）に迫ることができよう。つまり2人がさまよう段階が，死者に捧げられる2本のキャンドルが並び立つまでの状態，2人が放尿するシーンが2本のキャンドルが死者の枕元に立つ段階で，その時点で，分別されている世界の境が越えられると見ることにより，'The Sisters'において用いられた同じグランド・デザインが，相似形としてUlyssesにおいても用いられているのが見て取れるのである。

　本章では，この2つのキャンドルという枠組みが，難解と言われるUlyssesを読み解く上でどのように役に立つかを，プラーグ学派およびM. A. K. Hallidayが唱えた節（clause）レベルでの主題化（thematization）の視点をテクストレベルに取り入れながら論じて行きたい。

2　文学テクストにおけるコミュニケーション上の枠組み

Austin (1975) によると平叙文は遂行部分（performative part）と命題を担う部分（proposition）に分かれる（図1）。どのナラティブ（narratives）においても，ナレーター（narrator）は話し手であり，ナレーティー（narratee）は聞き手である。アメリカの社会言語学者であるWilliam Labovの分析したナラティブは，この図1の表す構造を持っている。'The steering wheel hit this fellow in the heart'と語っているのはナレーターである。多くは，この図1の自然ナラティブの構造が文学テクストの構造と同じであると思っているが，実は異なっている。

　図1を文学テクストの枠組みを示していると取る人達は，文学テクストによって，それが事実を語っていると錯覚させられていると言えよう。文学を楽しむ時には，我々は通常，そこで語られる話を，現実の世界で実際のナレー

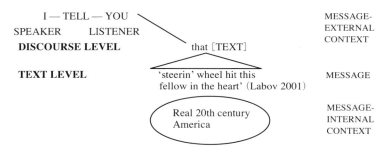

図1 自然ナラティブのコミュニケーション構造

ターによって語られている自然ナラティブだと信じ，あるいは信じるふりをして読む。文学を楽しむ際に，我々は，その話を語る（narrate）人物の背後に，実際の，その虚構の話を作り出した人物がいることをややもすると忘れがちである。自然ナラティブでは作者（author）とナレーター（narrator）は同一であるが，文学などの虚構ナラティブでは，この両者は理論上区別されている。下の図2に，この文学ナラティブの枠組みを，'The Sisters' の人物を組み込んで示してみた。この図を見れば，この錯覚の生じる理由がよく分かる。すなわち，点線内の世界が図1の表す世界と類似していることから，この点線の世界を自然ナラティブと読者は錯覚するわけである：

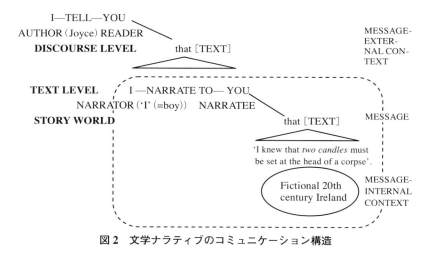

図2 文学ナラティブのコミュニケーション構造

図2の点線内の世界は Austin の命題を担う部分（proposition）に相当する。そして，我々の世界を把握する仕方が機能的観点から見て，節（clause）とテクストで同じとすると，テクストは節と同じ意味構造を持つことになる。節の意味構造を，文学である虚構テクストに拡大することで，次の図3を得ることができる：

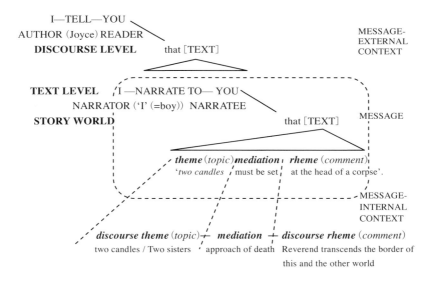

図3 節および文学ナラティブの相似形をなすテクスト的意味構造

Austin の枠組みの命題部分，つまりテクストレベルでの物語世界（図3の STORY WORLD）に，Halliday の機能言語学で言う，発話者（ここでは著者）のコミュニケーション意図を表す，主題（theme, topic），媒介（mediation, transition），そして題述（rheme, comment）から成るテクスト部門（textual component）をかぶせることができる。

3　*Dubliners*, *A Portrait of the Artist as a Young Man*, そして *Ulysses* の 3 作品におけるテクスト部門

　まず，*Dubliners* における物語の展開のグランド・デザインをもう少し詳しく見ておきたい。

　初めに述べたように，*Dubliners* の第 1 の物語である 'The Sisters' の冒頭では，危篤の Father Flynn の枕元には，まだ，死者を弔う実際のキャンドルは置かれていないが，ナレーターは 2 本のキャンドルのことに言及している。つまり，言語的にこのキャンドルが物語の冒頭に置かれている。Joyce はこの 2 本のキャンドルという概念を，この *Dubliners* の最初の物語 'The Sisters' の頭に置いていて，このことは *Dubliners* 全体の冒頭にキャンドルが言語的に置かれていることを意味する。

　死者のために置かれる，この 2 本のキャンドルのイメージはナレーターである少年が Great Britain Street にある，亡くなった Father Flynn 宅を訪れる際に再び現れる。2 人の女性と 1 人の少年が，その家の入口に掲げてある，Father Flynn の死亡の知らせを読んでいる：

> A crape bouquet was tied to the door-knocker with ribbon. Two poor women and a telegram boy were reading the card pinned on the crape. I also approached and read:
>
> July 1st, 1895
> The Rev. James Flynn (formerly of S. Catherine's Church,
> Meath Street), aged sixty-five years,
> *R. I. P.*
>
> ('The Sisters', 5)

黒絹の花束がリボンでドアのノッカーに結びつけられている。貧相な 2 人の女と電報配達の少年が黒絹にピンで留められたカードを読んでいた。ぼくも近づいて読んだ。

一八九五年七月一日
ジェイムズ・フリン師（ミーズ通り
聖カタリナ教会前司祭）
享年六十五歳
安らかにいこい給え　　　　　　　　　　（同訳）

この2本のキャンドルのイメージは司祭の棺の置かれている建物の中で，再び現れる。主人公の少年とおばは，お悔やみを述べるために亡くなった司祭の家を訪問し，そこで，まるで2本のキャンドルのように棺の近くに侍る，司祭の2人の姉妹であるElizaとNannieとに出会う。

このように，2本のキャンドルとその相似のイメージは 'The Sisters' において3度現れる。ここで3度現れる状況を図示してみると，次の図4のようになる：

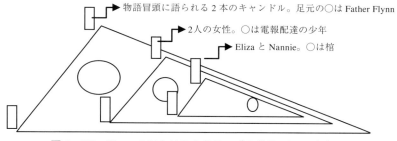

図4　'The Sisters' におけるナラティブのグランド・デザイン

この図4のグランド・デザインはJoyceの *A Portrait of the Artist as a Young Man* にも現れる。物語の第1章という早い段階で，主人公Stephenの父と母が彼に別れを告げるシーンは，何の意味もなくそこに置かれているわけではない：

> Then at the door of the castle the rector had shaken hands with his father and mother, his soutane fluttering in the breeze, and the car had driven off with his father and mother on it.

They had cried to him from the car, waving their hands:
　—Goodbye, Stephen, goodbye!
　—Goodbye, Stephen, goodbye!

(*A Portrait of the Artist as a Young Man*, 7)

　それからお城の玄関の出口で校長先生がおとうさんおかあさんと握手しているとそよ風が校長先生の僧衣をひらひらさせ，そして，馬車がおとうさんおかあさんをのせて走りだした。馬車から手をひらひらさせながらふたりは叫んでいた。
　—さようなら，スティーヴン，さようなら！
　—さようなら，スティーヴン，さようなら！

(大澤正佳（訳）『若い芸術家の肖像』岩波書店，2007)

　この状況を図4にならって示すと下図のようになろう。2本のキャンドルのように並べられた，父と母の2つの別れのセリフを受けて，Clongowes Wood College で新たに寄宿生活を始める「新生」Dedalus が生まれる構図となっている。この作品においても，父と母という2つのものが，いわば古い Stephen を越えて新生 Stephen を生み出しているわけである:

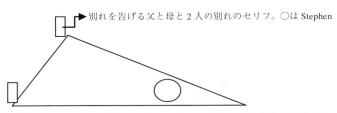

図5 ***A Portrait of the Artist as a Young Man*** **第1章に見られるナラティブのグランド・デザイン**

　これらの構造的にはより単純な枠組みから，より複雑な *Ulysses* へと推論の梯を伸ばして行くことが可能である。*Dubliners* では2本のキャンドルが，*A Portrait* では，父と母および彼らの2つの並び立つ別れのセリフであったものが，この *Ulysses* では Stephen Dedalus と Leopold Bloom となって再登場している。この2人を 'dying Dublin'，しかし新生するダブリンでもある

街に対して捧げられた2つの 'walking candles' ととらえることで，先行作品群と同一の主題的解釈を，この Ulysses に与えることができる。

　Ulysses では，ダブリンの街を，それぞれ独立してさまよいながら，Stephen Dedalus と Leopold Bloom は最後には，Bloom の家で2本のキャンドルのように並び立ちながら立小便をする：

> At Stephen's suggestion, at Bloom's instigation both, first Stephen, then Bloom, in penumbra urinated, their sides contiguous, their organs of micturition reciprocally rendered invisible by manual circumposition, their gazes, first Bloom's, then Stephen's, elevated to the projected luminous and semiluminous shadow.　　　　　(Ulysses, Episode 17, 655)
> スティーブンの提案で，またブルームの教唆により，初めはスティーブンが，続いてブルームが，暗闇に置いて放尿せり。並び立ちて，互いに放尿の器官を手で蔽い，彼らの眼差しを，初めブルームの，続いてスティーブンの眼差しを，映し出された明るい，また半ば明るい影に向けて上げたまま。

Hecimovich (2008: 26) は，ここの 'shadow' を「窓に映し出された妻の影」('the projected ... shadow' of his wife on the blond.) と解釈している。この窓の影に視線を向けるシーンは前に引用した Dubliners の 'The Sisters' (3) に出てくるシーンとパラレルである：'I ... studied the lighted square of window: and night after night I had found it lighted in the same way, faintly and evenly'. (ぼくは…明かりの灯った四角い窓を見つめた。そして毎晩，窓は同じように，ほのかに，また均等に，照らされていた。) この 'The Sisters' では窓の向こうでは Father Flynn が今まさに生から死へ越境をしようとしている。Ulysses でも，この放尿しながら見上げる窓とその影は同じ越境の意味合いを持っている。

　Ulysses では，この放尿のシーンに続いて，最終章にある，統語上の境界を越えて連綿と続く，Bloom の妻 Molly の「意識の流れ」(stream of consciousness) の文章が来る：

218　第3部　文学テクストの語学的研究の試み

　　Yes because he never did a thing like that before as ask to get his breakfast in bed with a couple of eggs since the City Arms hotel when he used to be pretending to be laid up with a sick voice doing his highness to make himself interesting to that old faggot Mrs Riordan...
　　　　　　　　　　　　　　　　　　　　　　(*Ulysses*, Episode 18, 690)

　そうだわ，彼が卵付の朝食をベッドまで運んで来てくれるなんてシティ・アームズホテル以来ないことだわ．その時には，彼は貴族ぶって病気みたいな声をして引きこもっていて，あの古い肉玉みたいなリオダン婦人に気に入られようと…

　Stephen Dedalus と Leopold Bloom が Dublin の街を別々に彷徨するシーンを，この作品の主題 (theme, topic) とし，のちに共に放尿し，続いて上に引用した最終章の Molly の連綿と続く「意識の流れ」の文章が来るシーン，つま

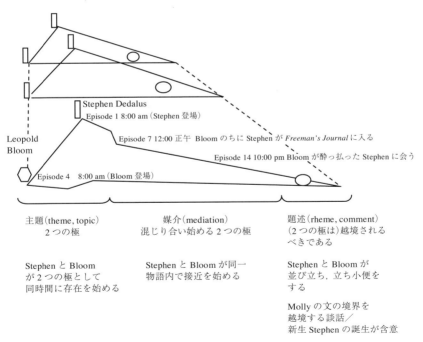

図6　*Ulysses* に見られるナラティブのグランド・デザイン

り，StephenとBloomという別々の存在が，死者に捧げられた2つのキャンドルのように並び立ち，文法的な境界が溶解する部分を，主題に対する「新生のために境界は交わり，越えなければならない」というコメント (rheme, comment) とすることで，先行する作品と同様の意味上のグランド・デザインを *Ulysses* に見ることができる。先に取り上げた3つの作品を重ね合わせると図6のような図ができる。

図6は *Ulysses* において Stephen Dedalus と Leopold Bloom が，いわば「死に行くダブリンの街」そして「再生すべきダブリンの街」に捧げられた2本のキャンドルの働きをしていることを示している。先行の2作品と相似形をなしているが，*Ulysses* では Stephen の物語が初めの3つの章で語られ，時間的に並行する形で Leopold Bloom の話が4章から6章にかけて展開しているので，この2人が後に並び立つ2本のキャンドルに相当するという構図が見えにくくなっている。

4　Joyce の越境への関心

このように，Joyce は2つの物を分け隔てる境界を越えることと，その結果の新生という点に関心があった。アイルランドとイギリスとの関係においてもそうである。

　Joyce はアイルランド独立と復興を願ったという説が根強い。果たしてそうであろうか。彼はアイルランドの側に立ったのか，それともイギリス側に立っていたのか。*Ulysses* の第2章にひとつのヒントがある：

> For Haines's chapbook. No-one here to hear. Tonight deftly amid wild drink and talk, to pierce the polished mail of his mind. What then? *A jester at the court of his master, indulged and disesteemed, winning a clement master's praise.* Why had they chosen all that part? Not wholly for the smooth caress. For them too history was a tale like any other too often heard, their land a pawnshop.
>
> (*Ulysses*, Episode 1, 25)（イタリクスは筆者）

ヘインズの物語本のためだ。ここにいる生徒達は誰一人私の話に耳を貸そうとしない。今夜，巧みに，酒と話の騒ぎの中で，彼の心の磨き上げられた鎧を貫くためだ。それからどうなる？

ここでの 'a jester' とはアイルランド系の作家を指している。Joyce が 1909 年に Trieste の新聞である *Il Piccolo della Sera* (24 March 1909) にイタリア語で書いた 1909 年のエッセイで，Joyce は Oscar Wilde について次のように述べている：

> In the tradition of the Irish writers of comedy that runs from the days of Sheridan and Goldsmith to Bernard Shaw, Wilde became, like them, court jester to the English.
> (James Joyce 'Oscar Wilde: il poeta di "Salomé"')
> (Mason and Ellmann 1964: 204–205)

　Sheridan と Goldsmith の時代から Bernard Shaw に至るアイルランド系のコメディの伝統の中で，Wilde は彼らのようにイギリス人に対する宮廷の道化のようになってしまった。

　Joyce の目には，上記の作家たちは全てイギリス人という宮廷に奉仕する道化師なのである。もしアイルランドとイギリスを２つのキャンドルとみなすならば，Wilde，Sheridan，Goldsmith そして Shaw 達は皆，イギリスという片方のキャンドルに奉仕していることになる。そのように Joyce の目には映ったのである。

　また Joyce は William Butler Yeats の側にも立っていない。Yeats は，その詩作品を通してアイルランドの神話や民話の復活を試みていた。Yeats は，Goldsmith や Wilde とは異なる，アイルランドというもう片方のキャンドルに仕える者と Joyce には思えたのである。

　Joyce の最終的な芸術上の目標は，今までの議論から分かる通り，アイルランドやイギリスという枠を越えたものを創造するところにあった。Joyce は Oscar Wilde の側にも W. B. Yeats の側にも立っていないのである。

　Ulysses の第２章にもうひとつ，この辺りをうかがわせる箇所がある。そ

の箇所は Stephen がパリの図書館を回想するシーンである：

 Across the page the symbols moved in grave morrice, in the mummery of their letters, wearing quaint caps of squares and cubes. Give hands, traverse, bow to partner: so: imps of fancy of the Moors. Gone too from the world, *Averroes* and *Moses Maimonides*, dark men in mien and movement, flashing in their mocking mirrors the obscure soul of the world, a darkness shining in brightness which brightness could not comprehend.
(Ulysses, Episode 2, 28)（イタリクスは筆者）

ページの上を記号達が厳かなムーア人のダンスを踊っている。文字の無言劇を踊っている，正方形や立方体の変わった帽子をかぶって。手を差し出せ，動き回れ，パートナーに頭を下げろ。ということで，まるでムーア人達の創造した小悪魔だ。この世からいなくなってしまったのだ。アヴェロウズもモーゼズ・マイモニデスという2人のアリストテレス学者達も。顔の表情や物腰の点で，色黒の男達。嘲笑的な鏡の中に，世界の隠れた根本原理をちらりと映す。それは，光が理解することのない，光の中で輝くひとつの闇。

Elizabeth B. Cullingford は，これら Aristotle を研究している2人の学者を名指しすることで Joyce は 'assert the Irish claim to intellect and civility'（アイルランドが知的で文明的であることを主張）しようとしたと述べる：

Stephen's meditation on the Moorish origins of mathematics reverses the Christian image of the Redeemer as a 'light shining in darkness' to affirm to 'dark men': the Jewish philosopher Moses Maimonides and his Islamic contemporary Averroes, who both worked in Spain. … Joyce revalued both the Spanish and the African associations of the word 'Moor' in order to assert the Irish claim to intellect and civility against the pejorative "barbaric" stereotype promulgated by the English press'.
(Cullingford 2000: 234–235)

数学はムーア人起源であるという黙想は，「黒い人達」を肯定しようとして「闇における光」がイエスであるというキリスト教的イメージをひっくり返している。ここで「黒い人達」というのは，共にスペインで活躍

したユダヤ人の哲学者である Moses Maimonides と，彼に対するイスラム教徒の同時代人 Averroes のことである。…Joyce はこの 'Moor' という語の持つスペイン的およびアフリカ的な連想を再評価しようとした。それはイギリスの新聞によって広められた軽蔑的な「野蛮な」というステレオタイプ的イメージに対抗して，アイルランドは知的で文明的だということを言わんがためである。

Cullingford の主張は正しいであろうか。この箇所で，Joyce は本当にアイルランドの文化的対等性を主張しようとしたのであろうか。Oxford 版の *Ulysses* にある，この箇所の註がこの問題に関するヒントを与えてくれる：

> Averroës (1126–98), Spanish-Arabian philosopher, commentator on Aristotle, attempted to *reconcile Aristotelian philosophy with Muslim orthodoxy*; similarly, Moses Maimonides (1135–1204), Jewish rabbi and philosopher, attempted to *reconcile Aristotelian thought with orthodox Judaism*. Both strongly influenced medieval Christian Scholasticism.
> (note from the Oxford *Ulysses*)（イタリクスは筆者）

Averroës (1126–98) はスペイン系アラビア人の哲学者で Aristotle に関する注釈者である。彼は Aristotle の哲学とイスラムの教えを調和させようとした。同様に，ユダヤ人の宗教上の指導者であり哲学者の Moses Maimonides (1135–1204) は Aristotle の思想と正統的ユダヤ教を調和させようとした。共に中世のキリスト教的スコラ哲学に強い影響を与えた。

Averroës と Moses Maimonides は共に2つの領域を「調和」(reconcile) させようとした。この「調和」という点が，Joyce が，今まで論じてきた彼の作品を通して描こうとして来た事柄である。もう少し本論文の趣旨に沿って言えば「境界の越境と新生」ということである。この「調和」(reconciliation) という注釈は，それに近い意味合いをよくとらえている。したがって，このパリの図書館での回想シーンは Cullingford が主張するような，アイルランドの文化的復権を願ったものではない。Joyce は2つのキャンドルのどちら側にも与せず，むしろその境を溶解し，新しいものの誕生を試みたのである。

もうひとつ加えておくと，この2人の学者の箇所は，言及されているのが2人である点が重要である．2人という数字そのものが越境されるべき「調和」の前兆なのである．

以上のことから，Joyce はイギリスに取り入って身を立てる点にも関心はなく，またアイルランド復興にも興味はなく，その両者を越えた新しい境地を切り開こうとしていたのである．

Ulysses には小エピソードとして，この2つのものの越境と新生を思わせる箇所にあふれている．もうひとつ例をあげておくと，Stephen が教えている学校の校長 Mr Deasy から給金を受け取るシーンがそれにあたる．ここでは，2枚の紙幣が並び置かれ，それに加えて真新しい金貨が1枚置かれる：

> He brought out of his coat a pocketbook bound by a leather thong. It slapped open and he took from it two notes, one of joined halves, and laid them carefully on the table.
> —Two, he said, strapping and stowing his pocketbook away.
> And now his strongroom for the gold....
> A sovereign fell, bright and new, on the soft pile of the tablecloth.
> —Three, Mr Deasy said, turning his little savingsbox about in his hand.
> 　　　　　　　　　　　　　　　　　　　　　（*Ulysses*, Episode 2, 29–30）

彼は上着から皮ひもで綴じた財布を取り出した．それをすばやく開いて，中から2つの紙幣を取り出した．そのうちの1枚は半分に破けたものをとじ合わせたもので，それら2枚を慎重にテーブルの上に置いた．

「まず2ポンド」と彼は言った．財布にひもをかけ上着にしまいながら．…

ソヴリン金貨が1枚，柔らかなテーブルクロスの上に落ちた．新しい金貨でキラキラ輝いていた．

「これで3ポンド」とディージー校長は言った，その硬貨入れを手の中で回しながら．

以上の議論から，Joyce は2つの明確に分かれた実体を主題 (theme) にあたるエピソードとして配置し，それに対するコメントにあたる，2つのもの

の融合，続く新生を題術 (rheme, comment) にあたるエピソードとして物語の中に配置したのだということが分かる。

5 その他の越境の文体
――ページの上で他者の言葉の中に流れ込む「思考」――

「意識の流れ」以外の文体上の工夫の中に，以上見て来たような「越境」へのこだわりを示す場面がある。

　Ulysses の Episode 2 は Stephen が学校で歴史を教えているシーンから始まる。Asculum での King Pyrrhus とローマ軍との戦いの場面で，Stephen は Armstrong という名前の生徒に Pyrrhus の死について尋ねる。それに対し，その学生は答えクラス中が大笑いをする：

　　—Pyrrhus, sir? Pyrrhus, a pier.
　　All laughed. Mirthless high malicious laughter. Armstrong looked round at his classmates, silly glee in profile.　　(*Ulysses*, Episode 2, 24–25)
　　「ピラスですか，先生？　ピラスは，'a pier'（桟橋）です。」
　　クラス中が笑った。情け容赦ない悪意のある高笑いだ。アームストロングはクラスメイト達を見まわした。愚かな喜びを浮かべた横顔。

注意すべきは，ここでの 'a pier'（桟橋）という語句は Armstrong の頭に生じたものである。'Pyrrhus' と 'a pier' の間には何の意味論的なつながりもないので，Armstrong のクラスメイト達は，この 'a pier' の音を聞き，彼らの頭の中に /ə pɪə/ という音声を構成しただけのはずである。Armstrong のクラスメイト達と Stephen に伝達されたのは，ただの /ə pɪə/ という音の連鎖，もしくはアイルランド英語に特有の rhotic r を発音する /ə pɪər/ という音の連鎖のはずであって，'a pier' という概念ではないはずである。'Pyrrhus' と 'a pier' を結び付ける者があるとすれば，それは語頭の /pɪ/ という音のみである。したがって，このページ上に表記された 'a pier' という語句は Armstrong

の心の中に生じた概念を作者がページ上に移したものに過ぎない。

　上記のやりとりのあと，この見方を裏付けるように Stephen は Armstrong に 'pier' とは一体何だねと尋ねる：

　　　—Tell me now, Stephen said, poking the boy's shoulder with the book, what is a pier?
　　　—A pier, sir, Armstrong said. A thing out in the waves. A kind of bridge. Kingstown pier, sir. 　　　　　　　　　　　　（*Ulysses*, Episode 2, 25）
　　「教えてくれ」とスティーブンは，その生徒の方を本でつつきながら言った。「'a pier' とは何だい？」
　　「'A pier' です」とアームストロングは言った。「海の中に突き出ている物です。橋の一種です。キングストン桟橋などです。」

Stephen の 'what is a pier?' という質問の中の 'pier' もまた Armstrong の頭の中にある概念の音声化を反映したものである。Armstrong の考えている概念が音声化したものが Stephen の考えの中に現れている。もし Stephen が，Armstrong が放った言葉を「船が離着する海の中に突き出た構造物」，つまり「桟橋」と理解していたのであれば，彼は 'what is a pier?' などとは訊かなかったであろう。ページ上では Stephen の質問が 'what is a pier?' と書き表されているが，これは 'what is /ə pɪə/' となるべきところである。Stephen は「桟橋とは何か？」と訊いたのではなく，/ə pɪə/ という音連鎖の意味するものは何かと訊いたのである。Stephen の台詞で 'a pier' とスペルアウトされている語句は Armstrong の頭の中にある概念を Joyce が言語化して見せているのであって，Stephen に伝達され，彼の頭の中で形成された概念が言語化しているわけではない。ここでもまた，生徒の頭の中の概念が Stephen の台詞の中に侵入して来ている。

　Armstrong は自分が言ったことが理解されていないと分かったからこそ，彼は急いで，その表現の説明を 'A thing out in the waves. A kind of bridge. Kingstown pier, sir'. と付け加えたのである。このシーンでも何人かの生徒が Armstrong の答えを聞いて笑う。最初の笑いでは 'Pyrrhus' と 'a pier' の間には何の意味的なつながりがないので，生徒みんなが笑い，この2度目では，

恋人達の出会いの場所であった 'Kingstown pier' のことを知っていた何人かの生徒達だけが笑ったのである：

> Some laughed again: mirthless but with meaning. Two in the back bench whispered. Yes. They knew: had never learned nor ever been innocent.
> (*Ulysses*, Episode 2, 25)
> 何人かが再び笑った。同じく情け容赦ない笑いだが，今度は意味ありげだった。後ろの席の2人が囁き合った。そうだ，彼らは知っているのだ。どこからかで学んだわけでもないし，また全く純粋というわけでもないのだ。

同様に，ある人物Aの考えが，別の人物Bという境界を越えて，その人物Bの頭の中に流れ込む様がKeller (1980) によって指摘さている。しかしながら，この場合は，Bという人物の思考の中に流れ込んでいるAという人物の思考とその表現は，Bによって意識されている：

> 　A wavering line along the path. They will walk on it tonight, coming here in the dark. He wants that key. *It is mine. I paid the rent.* Now I eat his salt bread. Give him the key too. All. He will ask for it. That was in his eyes. 　　　　　　（*Ulysses*, Episode 1, 20）（イタリクスは筆者）
> 道に沿って曲がりくねった筋がついている。彼らは今夜この上を歩くのだろう。この暗闇の中にやって来て。彼はその鍵が欲しいと思った。鍵は僕の物だ。僕が家賃を払ったのだ。今では僕は彼の塩パンを食べている。彼に鍵もくれてやれ。みんな。彼は鍵を要求するだろう。彼の顔にそう書いてある。

'It is mine. I paid the rent' は通常Stephenの「内的独白」(internal monologue) でMulliganの鍵が欲しいという願望を否定しているとされている。しかしながら，Stephenが学校で歴史を教えて得る給与では年間12ポンド ('Twelve quid' (17)) という家賃は払えないが，Mulliganは払える。Kenner (1980: 55n–56n) は，Mulliganが家賃を払ってきていて，上のイタリクスの部分は

Mulligan の声を反映したものと主張する：

> I owe to Arnold Goldman the suggestion that Stephen's unspoken words 'It is mine, I paid the rent' (26/20) are to be read in Mulligan's voice, between invisible quotation marks, as words Stephen can already hear Mulligan speaking when he demands the key. For it is unlike Stephen to assert ownership in consequence of payment—that is the way of the Mulligans and Deasys. Moreover, when Haines asks whether rent is paid for the tower, it is Mulligan who promptly answers with the exact amount, twelve quid. And this is a preposterous amount for us to think of Stephen getting together at any time. (Kenner 1980, 55n–56n)[2]
>
> アーノルド・ゴールドマンによるとスティーブンの言語化されない 'It is mine, I paid the rent' という言葉はマリガンの声と解釈されるべきである。つまり，目に見えない引用符に囲まれていて，マリガンが鍵を要求する時に語るのをスティーブンが聞くことができるであろう，そういった言葉として解釈されるべきである。なぜならば，スティーブンが払っているのなら鍵の所有権を主張することは考えられないからである。そういった主張をするのは社会の多くのマリガン達やディージー校長達である。さらに，ヘインズが塔の家賃が払われているか問えば，12ポンドと即座に答えるのはマリガンなのだ。そして，この法外な金額はスティーブンがいつでもかき集められるような金額ではない。

Kenner によると，もし Stephen が家賃を払えず，Mulligan が払えるとすると，この2つのイタリクスの部分は実際は Mulligan の言葉である。言いかえると，Mulligan の言葉が Stephen の思考の流れの中に挿入されているのである。これは Stephen の頭の中で生起する思考であるので，明示的な引用符なしに挿入されているのである。

自由間接話法などは Joyce の意識の流れの例としてよく議論されるが，'a pier' なども，1人の人物の思考を越えて越境する言葉の例とすることができ

---

[2] 川口 (1994: 22–24) は，この Keller の解釈を肯定的に紹介しており，一方，結城 (1999: 32–36) は否定的である。

よう．こういったところにも，Joyce の関心が，2 つのものを隔てる境を越えて新しいものが生み出る瞬間にあり，そのことは機能主義的に言いかえると，「2 つのもの」という主題 (theme, topic) に対して「越えて新しいものが生まれなければならない」という題術 (rheme, comment) という大きなグランド・デザインと相似的にパラレルになっていることが見て取れるのである．

6 まとめ——新生が繰り返し表現される——

Dubliners で描かれた，新生へと続く死者の枕元に添えられる 2 本のキャンドルを，キャンドルがまだ並び立っていない主題 (theme, topic) に対して提示された「越境と新生」を示す題術 (rheme, comment) ととらえると，そのテクストレベルでの枠組みが，相似的に反復して *A Portrait of the Artist as a Young Man* において，そしてさらには *Ulysses* で再び反復して現れている．

　Joyce の人生にも，主題としての並び立つべき 2 つのものと，それに続く題術としての新生の追求を見ることができる．Penguin 版の *A Portrait* により，その人生を辿ってみる．Joyce は 1880 年代の 2 番目の年である 1882 年の，2 番目の月である 2 月，そしてその月の第 2 の日である 2 日にダブリンで生まれた．University College Dublin を 1900 年代の 2 番目の年，つまり 1902 年に卒業し，その後 Joyce は医学を勉強するためにパリへ向かう．同年アイルランドに戻り，22 歳の誕生日には，*A Portrait* の初期版を *Stephen Hero* という題のものへと改訂する決心をする．同じく 22 歳の時に後に妻となる Nora Barnacle と出会う．その 2 年後には，彼女を伴ってパリへ向けて再びアイルランドを後にする．2 度目のアイルランド脱出である．1920 年には Ezra Pound の招きで Joyce はパリへ引っ越しをし，そこで 20 年を過ごす．1922 年には *Ulysses* の初版の 2 冊 ('First two copies of *Ulysses*') がフランスのディジョン (Dijon) から急行列車で Joyce のもとに届けられた ('delivered by express train from Dijon')．

　このように彼の人生の軌跡も示しているように，Joyce は *Ulysses* において，Stephen Dedalus と Leopold Bloom という 2 人の人物を「滅びゆくダブ

リン／新生ダブリン（新生 Stephen）」に捧げられた 2 本の歩くキャンドルとして創造したのである。

　この枠組みは *Ulysses* に続く *Finnegans Wake* にも引き継がれているであろうことは容易に想像できる。'wake' とは *OED On-line* によると，名詞ではアイルランドの慣習として「通夜」(**3.** The watching (esp. by night) of relatives and friends beside the body of a dead person from death to burial, or during a part of that time; ... Now chiefly Anglo-Irish or with reference to Irish custom.) であり，動詞としては「目覚める」(**II.** To become awake. **7. a.** intr. To come out of the state of sleep or unconsciousness; to be roused from sleep, cease to sleep.) とある。このタイトルからも分かるように，*Finnegans Wake* は，今まで論じて来たグランド・デザインを通して示された作者の題述（rheme, comment）である「新生」と一致していると言えるのである。

参考文献

Austin, JL (1975) *How to do Things with Words* (2nd edn). Oxford: Oxford University Press.

Cullingford, EB (2000) 'Phoenician genealogies and oriental geographies: Joyce, language and race'. In: Attridge, D and Howes, M (eds) *Semicolonial Joyce*. Cambridge: Cambridge University Press, 219–239.

道木一弘 (2009)『物・語りの『ユリシーズ』ナラトロジカル・アプローチ』南雲堂.

Hecimovich, G (2008) *Puzzling the Reader: Riddles in Nineteenth-Century British Literature*. New York: Peter Lang.

Joyce, J (2000 [1914]) *Dubliners*. Oxford: Oxford University Press.

Joyce, J (2000 [1916]) *A portrait of the artist as a young man*. Oxford: Oxford University Press.

Joyce, J (1998 [1922]) *Ulysses*. Oxford: Oxford University Press.

Joyce, J (2012 [1939]) *Finnegans Wake*. Oxford: Oxford University Press.

川口喬一 (1994)『「ユリシーズ」演義』研究社.

Kenner, H (1980) *Ulysses*. London: George Allen and Unwinl.

Kikuchi, S (2001) 'Lose heart, gain heaven: The false reciprocity of gain and loss in Chaucer's *Troilus and Criseyde*'. *Neuphilologische Mitteilungen* (Bulletin of the Modern Language Society, Finland) CII (4): 427–434.

Kikuchi, S (2006) 'To leave or to settle?: Kazuo Ishiguro's remains of the summer in Nagasaki'. *Philología* (The University of Belgrade, Serbia) 4: 129–138.

Kikuchi, S (2010) 'Unveiling the dramatic secret of "Ghost" in *Hamlet*'. *Journal of

Literary Semantics（Mouton de Gruyter, Germany）39（2）: 103–117.

Kikuchi, S（2012）'O I just want to leave this place: Auden's discourse of thematized self-alienation'. *Philologia*（The University of Belgrade, Serbia）10: 61–72.

Kikuchi, S（2013）'Poe's name excavated: The mediating function and the transformation of discourse theme into discourse rheme'. *Language and Literature*（Sage, UK）22（1）: 3–8.

Labov, W（2001）'Uncovering the event structure of narrative'.（A paper given at the Georgetown Round Table in March of 2001）Available at: http://www.ling.upenn.edu/~wlabov/home.html（accessed 26 July 2014）.

Leech, GN and Short, MH（1981）*Style in Fiction: A Linguistic Introduction to English Fictional Prose*. A Harlow: Pearson Education.

Mason, E and Ellmann, R（eds）（1964）*The Critical Writings of James Joyce*. New York: The Viking Press.

結城英雄（1999）『「ユリシーズ」の謎を歩く』集英社．

詩語の継承と排除[1]
―― マロリーの用語に関して ――

上 利 政 彦

はじめに

初期近代英語期 1557 年に OE 詩語がグリモールド (Nicolas Grimald) とワイアット (Sir Thomas Wyatt) によって一時的に用いられた。また，指摘されているように，近代期直前マロリー (Sir Thomas Malory) はこれらを一時的に使用したがすぐに排除した。そして 1485 年にキャクストン (William Caxton) はマロリーが一時的に用いた OE 詩語を彼の編纂した *Le Morte Darthur* では排除した。以下，これら詩と散文に見られる OE 詩語の継承と排除に関わる問題を英語史の視点から一歩進めて考えてみたい。

1　詩の場合

人文主義運動のなか，英国最初の秀歌集 *Songes and Sonettes*『歌とソネット』，通常 *Tottel's Miscellany*『トテル詩選集』(1557) (*SS*) の詩人たちはチョーサー (Geoffrey Chaucer) をはじめとする先輩詩人に珠玉の詩語を求めた。その結果，主として ME 詩に由来する古語が用いられることとなった (Agari, Introduction 参照)。そのなかでグリモールドとワイアットが例外的に OE 詩語

---

[1]　日本中世英語英文学会第 28 回大会（広島大学：2012 年 12 月 1 日）で発表した「異質性の排除――詩語の継承に関して」に基く。

でME頭韻詩に受け継がれた伝統的な頭韻語を用いている。それは「ひと，戦士，仲間」を表す6語である（詩語の規定はスウィート（Henry Sweet）による）：

資料1　*Songes and Sonettes* の OE 詩語
　　（見出し語，頻度，OE 形，OED 記載年，意味，使用詩人，例文（作品番号・行数）と続く）

1. beurn (1): *beorn* ...1515–1528: a warrior, hero, used by Nicolas Grimald (c1520–c1562):
   1. The boldest *beurn*, and worthiest in the feeld: (165.54, on Zoroas, Egyptian astronomer)
2. freke (1): *freca* ...15..–1555–1605: a warrior, man, used by Grimald:
   2. ...prayse Haddington thy lord, / From thee that held both Scots, and *frekes* of Fraunce: (156.13)
3. gadling (1): *gædeling* ...13..: a companion. Wyatt (c1503–1542), but in the sense 'wayfarer' (OED: 以後 1565 (poetry) の例のみ):
   3. The wandring *gadling*, in the sommer tyde, / That findes the Adder with his rechlesse foote / Startes not dismaid so sodeinly aside, / As iealous despite did, ... (55.1)
4. goom (1): *guma* ...1515: a man, hero. Grimald:
   4. No wastefull wight, no greedy *goom* is prayzd. (150.17)
5. renk (2): *rinc* ...1515–1535–1557: a man, warrior. Grimald:
   5. With semely gesture doth Polymnie stere: / Whose wordes holle routes of *renkes* doo rule in place, (133.16)
   6. One, Meleager, could not bear this sight: / But ran vpon the sayd Egyptian *renk*: (165.95, on Zoroas)
6. secg (1): *secg* ...1508–15..–1557–1567–1567: a man, warrior. Grimald:
   7. Wherwith a hole route came of souldiours stern, / And all in peeces hewed the silly *seg*. (165.98, on Zoroas)

近代期 1500 年代に入り *SS* 出版 1557 年までの状況を見ると，OED では，gadling 以外のすべてがスコットランド詩からの引用である。gadling 本来の意味 'companion' は短命で，OED は ME 期の例として 1300 年代のものを最後とする 3 例を挙げ，MED は 1460 年以前を最後とする 6 例を挙げてい

るに過ぎない。新たに 'scoundrel' という堕落した意味を得て ME 期を生き
延び (MED: a1300–a1500)，近代に入ってワイアット (1542) は更に新しい意味
'wayfarer' を与えた。この意味では OED は 1565 年の 1 例 (poetry) のみを
挙げる。これら古語の使用は実質的に SS の中でもグリモールドが最後と言っ
てよく，のちに生き延びることは殆どない (例外は二つ: freke, 1605 Sc.
poetry; seg, 1567 poetry)。スペンサー (Edmund Spenser) はこれらのいずれの
語も使用しない。

　ワイアットは当時の古語志向の機運の中でチョーサーからこの語を得たと
思われる (*The Romaunce of the Rose*, 938, in Thynne's edition of *The Works*, 1532)。
学者詩人グリモールドが OE 詩語を何処に求めたのか, seg [seg] は ME segge
[sedʒ] から得たと思われ，直接 OE *secg* に拠ったとは思われない。ダンバー
(William Dunbar) その他のスコットランド詩人から得たのか，そうだとすれば
SS の他の詩人たちは何故用いないのか？ OE 語法の復活を主張したチーク
(Sir John Cheke) の影響があったのか，不明である (この点について Agari, 69–70,
101 [note 11] を参照)。また，ワイアットは頭韻に無関心であるのに対し，グ
リモールドは OE 詩，ME 詩の頭韻法を維持する (上記資料 1.5.6. では ran-
renk と頭韻を踏む)。

　これら近代の SS における OE 詩語の再生は，共通の詩言語として北方か
ら発した真の回帰現象ではなく，一過性の個人的使用であったと思われる。

　では，近代に入ってスコットランド詩に残った OE 同意語群はそれ以前に
はどんな状況であったか。ME 詩とそれを遡る OE 詩を観察して，詩の言語
の継承のありようを垣間見たい。

　Beowulf に OE 詩学に関する言及がある。そこでこの詩を OE 詩のモデル
として取り上げたい。

資料 2　*Beowulf* と OE 詩学

1.　　　　　　　hwīlum cyninges þegn,
　　　guma gilp-hlæden, gidda gemyndig,
　　　sē ðe eal-fela eald-gesegena
　　　worn gemunde, word ōþer fand
　　　sōðe gebunden. Secg eft ongan

      sīð Bēowulfes snyttrum styrian
      ond on spēd wrecan spel gerāde,
      wordum wrixlan.（867b–874a）
Wrenn's translation: "from time to time one of the king's retainers, a man filled with poetic eloquence who remembered lays, who could call to mind a multitude of all kinds of ancient traditions, improvised (**fand**) new recitations (**word ōþer**) correctly linked in metre (**sōðe gebunden**): the man afterwards began skilfully to treat of Bēowulf's exploit and effectively to recite an aptly made tale, varying his words (**wordum wrixlan**)."（Wrenn's ed., 200）

「一方では，王の家臣の一人，詩的表現に富み古謡心得し者，ありとあらゆる古の申し伝えを吟じうる者が，正しい調べで連ねられし新たなることばを見出した。そのご歌いびとはベーオウルフの偉業を巧みに吟詠し，ことばを変えながら相応しい挿話を効果的に語った。」

2. 「ひと，武人」の同意語：æþeling, beorn, cempa, ceorl, eorl, freca, gædeling, gesīð, hæle, hæleð, leod, man, mon, ōretta, rinc, wer, wiga, wīgend; 複合語の一部：scearp scyld-wiga (288), sǣ-manna searo (329), gūð-rinc (838), etc.

3. ベーオウルフ（Bēowulf）を表す guma (1476), hæleð (3142), rinc (747), secg (1759) がグレンデル（Grendel）一族に使われる：グレンデルに guma (973, 1682), rinc (720), また hilde-rinc (986) がグレンデルに，そしてその母親にも secg (1379) が使われる。またベーオウルフとグレンデルは共に hæleð (pl. 2072) と呼ばれ，石塚を守る龍は戦士 gūð-freca (2414) と呼ばれる。

4. Ǣr hī þǣr gesēgan syllīcran *wiht*, / wyrm on wonge wiðer-ræhtes þǣr, / lāðne licgean:（3038–3040a: 斜体付加）

資料 2.1. について編者レン（C.L. Wrenn）は **wordum wrixlan**「ことばに変化を与える」が "the poetic technique of 'variation'"，即ち，同意語の使用を含む「変奏」の技法だと考え，**sōðe gebunden**「正しくつらねられた」は alliteration のことだと考えて，この数行が貴重な 'the technique of the Anglo-Saxon versification' に関する発言だと言っている。引用中，þegn と呼ばれる歌いびと scop は，以下 guma, secg に置き換えられる。*Beowulf* では同意語群は殆どの場合，頭韻を踏みながら表現に変化を与える。この他に，自らは頭韻を失うが複合語を構成する場合も見られる：scearp scyld-wiga (288) 等。

　頭韻は同意語の豊かさを生む反面，資料 2.3. に示したように「価値の両面性」とでも言うべき「矛盾」を生む。グレンデル一族はいずれも勇者ベーオウルフを相手に「戦うもの」と位置づけられていて，この点で両者は共通するが，他の点で両者は正反対である。ベーオウルフは真の「武人」にあるべき「力と精神の叡智」（mægen mid mōdes snyttrum 1706a）を持つ。しかもグレンデル一族は罪にまみれ，やがて最後の審判の日に神の裁きを受けることになる身だ (974–979)。

　異なる思考・指示 thought/reference が，異なる指示対象 referent を意図する場合，異なる記号 symbol を用いるのが通常の言語行為であるが (Ogden-Richards)，この場合そうではない。そうすれば，言葉の生命 spirit が失われることになるのではないだろうか。作者は「頭韻と変化」の詩学に内在するこの矛盾を意識し解決していると思われる箇所がある。資料 2.4.「まずもって彼らは［主君の亡骸に比べ］ぞっとするモノが其処に，反対側の地面に，忌むべきおろちが横たわるのを見た。」OED によると，wiht=wight は 'creature' の意味であり，'man' の意味で用いられるのは 1200 年以降である。グレンデルは最初に 'Wiht unhælo, / grim ond grædig' (120b–121a) と呼ばれたが，ここで同じ wiht によって詩人は偉大な武人主君と区別した。戦う怪物は今や単なるおろちである。ベーオウルフは死して 'wundur' (3032) であり，その死は 'wundor-dēaðe' (3037) であったのに，相手は 'syllīcran wiht' (=strange creature)，'wyrm...lāðne'「忌むべきおろち」と呼ばれる。彼我の対照を闡明にしたと言うべきか。だから secg などの両者共通の語を避けたのであろう。しかし，この箇所を除いて詩人は「戦うもの」のレベルに止まり，道徳的視点を排除している。「戦い」と「道徳」の二つのレベルが相交わることがない。OED は guma 以下の語におけるこれら対照的な意味の分化については指摘しない。'Contextual' という判断を下しているのであろう。「人，武人」を表す OE 詩語は ME 期の頭韻詩に伝えられるが (厨川 151)，ME 期におい

て意味の分化，特に下降が見られるのは，この double reference「矛盾指示」と関係があり，自らの消滅を早める一つの言語的原因となったのではないだろうか。

以上，OE 詩の同意語に見られる double reference による語の生命の危うさ，即ち生命の衰退を指摘した。この傾向は ME 期に受け継がれる。

語の消滅は一般語による代置によって示される場合がある。そのことを MED の引用例文から観察したい。

ME 期に入り，OE 詩語が時の経過とともに異語によって代替される。

資料 3　MED の引用例における異語 variants の記録

1. bern: *man, cnihtes, kempes, bar[o]un, baronage, erles*.
   1.(a) A man
      c1275 (?a1200) Lay. *Brut* (Clg) 7645 bern [Otho: man] [Otho=c1300]
   2.(a) A soldier
      Lay. *Brut* (Clg) 5005 burnes [Otho: cnihtes]
      Lay. *Brut* (Clg) 8474 beornnen [Otho: kempes]
      Lay. *Brut* (Clg) 23408 beornen [Otho: cnihtes]
      (b) A nobleman
      Lay. *Brut* (Clg) 16922 beorne [Otho: barun]
      c1400 (?a1387) *PPl.C* (Hnt HM) 4.477 berne [B: baroun] [Various dates]
      a1500 *Wars Alex*. (Dub) 984 bernes [Ash: baronage] [Bodleian, Ashmole=c1450 (?a1400)]
      Wars Alex. (Dub) 2517 bernes [Ash: erles]
2. freke: ―
3. gadeling: *traitour*
   (b) A nobleman
   a1400 (a1325) *Cursor* (Vsp A) 4410 gedling [Frf: traitour] [Bodleian, Fairfax=a1400]
4. gome: *man, manne, king, cnihtes, knyghtes, grom*.
   1.(a) A man
      Lay. *Brut* (Clg) 8542 an gume [Otho: a man]
      Cursor (Vsp A) 12698 gom [Göt: man] [University Library, Göttingen=a1400 (a1325)]

　　　　c1400（c1378）*PPl.B*（Ld Misc581）18.216 gome［C: man］
　　1.（b）［set phrases］
　　　　Lay. *Brut*（Clg）15843 gumenene［Otho: manne］
　　　　Lay. *Brut*（Clg）17295 gomenen［Otho: king］
　　2.（a）A warrior
　　　　Lay. *Brut*（Clg）26406 gumen［Otho: cnihtes］
　　　　c1330（?c1300）*Amis*（Auch）1309 gomes［a1500: knyghtes］
　　4.（c）A person
　　　　c1390 *PPl.A*（Vrn）11.170 gome［vrr.: man, grom］
5.　rink: *knyʒtes, messagers, renges*（renge=a line of fighting men）, *freikis*.
　　（a）warrior
　　　?a1450（a1400）*Siege Jerus.*（1）（Ld Misc 656）954 renkes［vrr.: knyʒtes, messagers］
　　　a1500 *Awntyrs Arth.*（Dc 324）640 renke［vr.: rengthe, *error* – MED］
　　　［Bodleian, Douce］
　　（b）A man
　　　c1400（a1376）*PPl.A*（Trin-C R）4.134 renkis［vrr.: Reynkes, renges 'a line of fighting men' – MED］
　　　c1400（c1378）*PPl.B*（Ld Misc）18.275 renkes［vr.: freikis］
6.　segge: *gleomenne*（gleeman=minstrel）, *cniht, man, folke*.
　　A man
　　　Lay. *Brut*（Clg）2548 segge［Otho: gleomenne］
　　　... 3985 sæg［Otho: cniht］
　　　... 3997 seg［Otho: man］
　　　c1400（a1376）*PPl.A*（Trin-C R）3.52 segge［vrr.: segg; man, folke; ...］
　　cf. kemp: 一
　　　（*Beow* 1312. OED: a700...1470–85Malory...1818Scott...1893.）

　代替語を持たない自己充足的な詩語は freke のみである。参考に挙げた kemp が自立的であるのはそれが常用される散文語のせいであろう（その例が bern の異語に kemp が使われる資料 3.1.2. に見られる）。理解容易な代替語が現れるのは Layamon's *Brut* の BL, Cotton Otho MS で，およそ 1300 年からだ。その頃 OE 詩語の使用に排除への変化が見え始めたと推測される。一般語の中に新たなフランス語由来の ME 語が現れる。即ち bern に baroun が，rink に messager と renge が代置される。gome に代わる grom は語源不明だが

ME 語である。rink の代わりに freik が用いられるのは珍しい交替例で，これは 15 世紀直前（*Piers Plowman B*）になっても見られる freik の生命力の証であろう。gadeling が 'nobleman' の項で 'traitour' に代置されているが，この語に意味的に secret な雰囲気が感じられ traitour とされたのかも知れない。

　次に *Beowulf* の例から予想される意味の分化，特にその下降現象を MED に見よう。

資料 4　MED に見る意味の分化と特に下降（**in bold**）の例

1. bern
   1.a.　a man: c1275（?a1200）Lay. *Brut*, Clg...a1500（?a1400）*WarsAlex*, Dub=17 exx.
      b.　bern ne best, etc.: c1390*PPl*A...c1450（?a1400）*WarsAlex,* Ashm=8 exx.
      c.　mate, husband: c1440（?a1400）*MorteArth*-c1450（?a1400）*WarsAlex,* Ashm=2 exx.
      d.　servant: c1400（?a1380）*Cleanness*...a1425–a1500（?c1350）*Libeaus*=4 exx.
   2.a.　soldier, esp. knight: c1275（?a1200）Lay. *Brut*...c1600（c1500）*AlexMaced*=17 exx.
      b.　a nobleman: c1275（?a1200）Lay. *Brut*...a1500（?a1400）*WarsAlex*, Dub=12 exx.
   3.　in address: man, sir: c1400（?c1380）*Pearl*...c1450（?a1400）*WarsAlex,* Ashm=7 exx.
2. freke（26）
   a.　a brave man: a1375*WPal*...a1475（?a1400）*TournTott*=7 exx.
   b.　a man: c1225（?c1200）*StKath*...c1500*The shype ax*=10 exx.
   c.　a human being, a creature: a1375（*WPl*）...c1600（c1350）*AlexMaced*=9 exx.
3. gadeling（35）
   a.　a companion in arms, man: c1275（?a1200）Lay.*Brut*...a1500（a1460）*Towneley Pl*=6 exx.
   b.　a person of low birth, scoundrel: a1300*I-hereþ*...a1500（?a1400）*Torrent*=27 exx.
   c.　*adj.*, **base**: c1380*Firumb*（1）-c1450*PPl*A（1）=2 exx.
4. gome（76）

1. a. a man: c1275（?a1200）Lay. *Brut*...c1600（?c1395）*PPlCreed*=19 exx.
   b. (set phrases): c1275（?a1200）Lay. *Brut*...c1400（?a1387）*PPlC*=7 exx.
2. a. a warrior: c1275（?a1200）Lay. *Brut*...a1500（?c1450）*Merlin*=16 exx.
   b. (set phrases): c1275（?a1200）Lay. *Brut*...c1400（?a1300）*KAlex*=7 exx.
3. a. a husband: a1225（?c1200）*HMaid*=1 ex.
   b. a man servant: a1400（a1325）*Cursor*...c1450（?a1400）*WarsAlex*, Ashm=4 exx.
   c. God: c1390*CastleLove*（1）-a1500（a1460）*TowneleyPl*=2 exx.
4. a. a boy: c1300（?c1225）*Horn*...a1450*YkPl*=4 exx.
   b. ?a woman: c1325*In a fryht*=1 ex.
   c. a person: c1275（?a1200）Lay. *Brut*...c1600（c1350）*AlexMaced*=17 exx.
5. rink（25）
   a. a warrior: c1275（?a1200）Lay. *Brut*...c1540（?a1400）*DestrTroy*=13 exx.
   b. a man: a1375*WPal*...a1500*The mone in*=11 exx.
   c. in address to God: c1400（?c1380）*Patience*=1 ex.
6. segge（20）
   A man: c1275（?a1200）Lay. *Brut*...c1600（c1350）*AlexMaced*=20 exx.

*Beowulf*において一連の同意語が「人，戦うもの」を共通の指示対象としていた。これと同様の傾向が ME 期に継承されるが，「戦うもの」という枠組みが破られ，新たな指示対象として，gome 及び rink が少数ながら「神」を指示する。また bern が「夫」に，gome が「少年」に用いられることも *Beowulf* には見られなかった現象である。既に *Beowulf* が示していた意味の下降の例として bern と gome が 'servant' を指示する。また，gadeling は 1300 年以前に堕落して，以後この意味 (scoundrel) が支配的になったように見える。引用例数は，本来の意味では 6 例と圧倒的に少ない（対 27 例）。接尾語 –ling ('a person or thing') は文献学的にはいまだ縮小的な意味を持たないが

（初出 codling c1314—OED），gather + ling は容易に意味の堕落をきたすように思われる。

マロリーの典拠とした *Morte Arthure*（*MA*）（後述）の状況を Hamel's glossary によって見よう。*Beowulf* に見られるもの以外の意味は資料 5 の通りである：

資料 5　Hamel's glossary to *MA*
1. bern: husband, creature
2. freke: creature, monster
3. gadeling: rascals, scoundrels
4. gome: —
5. rink: Christ
6. segge: [monster giant（資料 8.6.）]
cf. kemp: —

freke は *Beowulf* では指示対象が安定していたが，*MA* ではアーサーが戦う相手，怪物巨人を指示することがある。gadeling は堕落した指示対象を持つのみで，本来の「仲間」では使われない。ハメルは指摘しないが，segge=monster という堕落例が見られる。kemp は「戦士」として 1 例のみ使用される。この散文語は詩語としては殆ど排除されていて，この使用は頭韻のため一時的に使用されたのであろう（Crispid-kombide-*kempis*-knawe: 1003）。この語はマロリーでは，*MA* とは関係なく，Bk VII（305.35）にのみ 1 例が見られ，キャクストンに受け継がれる特別な語である。

　結論的に，*Beowulf* に見られた意味の曖昧性と生命の危うさは，ME 頭韻詩に継承された語彙において増幅されたと言えよう。指示対象が神・キリストから少年，夫，召使，怪物へと極端に広がったことは一見語の進化と思われるが，（口頭発表時の寺澤　盾教授による示唆に沿って言えば）OE 詩語は時を経て意味の構造的弛緩を増し語の存立を危うくし，この点で OE 詩語は ME 期において退化し，消滅への道を辿ったと言うべきであろう。OE 詩語の spirit が失せ，形骸化した form が残ったと言えば過ぎるであろうか。中世後期にチョーサーはこれらの同意語を実質的に避けた状態で時代は近代前

夜を迎える。

2 散文の場合

　これら OE 詩語は ME 頭韻詩に継承され，15 世紀後半マロリーはその一部を，原典である *Morte Arthure*（c1440［?a1400, i.e., possibly after 1400］: MED, Plan and Bibliography）から採ることになる（厨川 151–152，また Vinaver への指摘がある）。依拠の状況は資料 6 の通りである：

資料 6　マロリー（**Book V: *The Noble Tale of King Arthur and the Emperor Lucius*）と頭韻詩 *Morte Arthure*（*MA*）**
　　（見出し語に続くカッコ内は，Book V と *MA*（Hamel's glossary による）における OE 詩語の頻度を比較したものである）
1. freke（5: over 19）
    1. (Vinaver 199.8) that *freyke* a furlonge way: *MA* thate *freke* a furlange of waye (873)
    2. (202.17) the fowlyste *freyke*: *MA* the fulsomeste *freke* (1061)
    3. (235.24) 'ye ar *fraykis* in this fryth nat paste seven hondred': *MA* 'ȝe are at the ferreste noghte passande five hundrethe' (2741)
    4. (236.19) '... founde never *frayke* that myght abyde hym a buffette': *MA* 'He fonde neuer no *freke* myghte feghte with hym one' (2775)
    5. (236.25) all the fylth of the *freyke*: *MA* all þe filthe of þe *freke* (2782)
2. gadling（1: 4）
    1. (238.15) yondir *gadlynges* [fellows: Vinaver] be gone: *MA* ȝone *gedlynges* [base fellows: Hamel] are gon (2884)
3. rink（6: over 17）
    1. (207.11) 'I have no joy of youre *renckys* thus to rebuke me and my lordys': *MA* 'þou sulde repent full rathe of þi ruyde wordez.../ Siche a *rebawde* as þowe rebuke any lordez' (1332) (rebawde = ribald, i.e. one who uses offensive language)
    2. (216.28) the noble *renckys* of the Rounde Table: *MA* þe *renkez* of þe Rounde Table (1882)
    3. (218.26) *renkys* of the Rounde Table: *MA renkkes* renowned of þe

Rounde Table' (1994)
4. (236.26) Than lyghtly rydis a *raynke* for to rescowe that barowne: *MA* Than rydes a *renke* to reschewe þat byerne (2784)
5. (236.29) But the *raynke* Rycharde of the Rounde Table: *MA* Bot thane a *renke*, sir Richere of þe Rounde Table (2790)
6. (238.11) many a *raynke* for that prouesse ran into the grevys: *MA* the *raskaille* was rade and rane to þe grefes (2881)

この Tale V はマロリーの第一作と言われる（Vinaver li–lvi, 1vii；厨川 757–761）。そこには彼の依拠と自立の両面が見られる。彼は原典を半分の「長さ」に縮める（Hamel 4）。散文形式をとるにもかかわらず原詩の頭韻の手法を部分的に取り入れている。頻出する OE 詩語を全面的に採用も排除もしないが，うち 3 語合計 12 例を散文の言語として用いている。アーサー王とルーキウス（Lucius）皇帝の戦いという主題を前にして，愛国心から英国側に立って自国の古語を使用したのかも知れない。その結果，例外的に原典の ME 語（< OF）を OE 詩語に変えることがある：renckys＜rebawde（資料 6.3.1.）；raynke＜raskaille, i.e., common soldiers（資料 6.3.6.）。これらの例は原典依拠の枠を越えて，まさに vernacularism を意識した例と思われる。なお，頭韻のためか，原典とは無関係に自ら OE 詩語を選んだ場合もある：fraykis/fryth（資料 6.1.3.）。一方，barowne＜byerne（資料 6.3.4.）のように，より一般的な ME 語（< OF）による置き換えも見られる。これはマロリーの時代的な言語感覚を示すと思われる。V 巻はこのように OE 詩語の継承と排除が共に見られるという点で特異である。

マロリーは第一作 Tale V にのみ OE 詩語を使用し，他の作品ではこれらを含め OE 詩語（資料 2.2.）を一切使用しないが，この点は Winchester 写本も同様である。しかしキャクストンは *Le Morte Darthur*（1485）でこれらマロリーの OE 詩語をすべて排除している。その状況は以下の通りである：

資料 7　マロリーとキャクストン（1485）の対比
1. （資料 6.3.1.）**Malory** 'I have no joy of youre renckys thus to rebuke me and my lordys': **Caxton** 'ye shalle retorne to your lord and saye ye to hym

that I shall subdue hym and alle his londes' (Vinaver 207.4–6)
2. （資料6.3.6）**Malory** Than the ryche men of the Rounde Table ran thorow the thykkeste with hir stronge sperys, that many a raynke for that prouesse ran into the grevys: **Caxton** Thenne threstyd in amonge them the knyghtes of the table round and smote doune to the erthe alle them that wythstode them in soo moche that they made them to recuyelle & flee (238.3–6)
3. （資料6.3.3）**Malory** Than the kyng commaunded sir Cadore to take hede to the rerewarde: 'And take *renkys* of the Rounde Table that the beste lykes': **Caxton** Thenne the kyng commaunded syr Cador to take the rereward & to take with hym certayne *knyghtes* of the round table (218.15–219.1)

Caxton: 'the comyn termes that be dayli vsed' rather than 'the olde and auncyent Englisshe' (*Eneydos*, Blake 80; R. F. Jones 116; 厨川 760).
OE *cempa*:
  Malory: And than the Grene Knyght voyded his horse delyverly and dressed hym on foote. That sawe Bewmaynes, and therewithall he alyght and they russhed togydyrs lyke two myghty *kempys* a longe whyle, and sore they bledde bothe. (Book VII: 305.32–36)
  Caxton: And thenne the grene knyghte auoyded his hors lightly and dressid hym upon foote / That sawe Beaumayns And there with al he alighte and they rasshed to gyders lyke two myghty *kempys* a longe whyle / and sore they bledde bothe / (m7ᵛ, 31–35)

マロリーの対応する箇所をキャクストンは全面的に削除するほか，上の三つの例のように表現を変える場合もある。第三の例は詩語 renkys を普通に見られる knyghtes に置き換えている点で注目すべきである。これはキャクストンが散文の英語として 'the olde and auncyent Englisshe' ではなく 'the comyn termes that be dayli used' (*Eneydos*) を用いるという原則に沿うものであろう。OE 系であるが詩語ではない kemp (*cempa* warrior) を参考に指摘しておきたい。これは V 巻ではなくフランス語原典に拠るとされる VII 巻に 1 例が見られ，キャクストンも踏襲する。

　マロリーは *MA* を基にしながらキャクストンの上の言語選択の基準を大いに実践している。つまり，キャクストンとマロリーの言語選択の同質性が注

目されるのである：

資料 8　マロリーが MA の OE 詩語を一般語に置き換えた例
　　（人称代名詞を含む）

MA（line）	Malory（page / line）
1. bern	
beryn（116）	messyngers（185.13）
burelyche beryn（304）	kyng（189.3）
beste beryns（630）	galyard knyghtes（195.24）
biernes（1183）	all the comyns（204.20）
his byerns（1391）	his felowys（209.1）
his hathell bierneas（1662）	his knyghtes（213.13）
his byernez（2022）	his knyghtes（219.14）
byerne［Kay］（2202）	him（221.32）
lordlyche byernez（2541）	they（229.17）
2. freke	
frekkes ynewe（1360）	the Romaynes（208.3）
a freke all in fine golde（1364）	a gay knyght...all floryshed in golde（208.7）
Frekes（2822）	freysh knyghtes（237.19）
þat freke（557）	hym（192.21）
freke（973）	he（201.2）
syche a freke（1174）	suche one（204.27-205.1）
freke（2709）	we（234.17）
3. gadling	
ʒone gadlyngez（2854）	yondir boyes（238.4）
Siche gadlynges（2443）	they（227.20）
4. gome	
no gome ellis（1209）	no man ellys（205.11）
gome（1373）	knyght（208.11）
5. rink	
renkes（2278）	noble knyghtes（224.24）
All þe realeste renkes（1410）	the Romaynes（209.8）
his renkes（1973）	his peple（218.20）
the ryalle renkkes（2902）	our knyghtes（238.21）
the rennkkez of þe Rounde	tho knyghtes of the Rounde Table

	(2135) Table (221.19)
the Renke that on the Rode dyede (3217)	His death that on the roode dyed (245.3)
6. segge	
some segge (134)	they (186.2)
þe segge [monster] (1043)	he (202.9)

　このように，詩語が排除され一般的な散文語に代替される現象がマロリーとキャクストンに共通する。この点は両者の言語の同質性を語ると同時に，従って，OE 詩語の排除と共に，マロリーの近代性を語る重要な証拠となろう。

　以上，初期近代グリモールドとワイアット，彼らを 80 年余り遡るマロリーにおいて OE 詩語の使用状況を観察した。OE 詩語は同意語使用に内在する不安定な指示 reference によって，指示対象 referent の，特に下降的意味分化を促し，語の自立を危うくすると指摘した。この脆弱性は ME 頭韻詩に継承拡大されるが，総じて消滅の兆しは早く，それは個別の同意語の一般語による代替に見られる。MED の記録から，bern, gome, segge が c1300 年と早く，rink は 1400 年代，gadeling 'companion' は a1400 年に消滅が始まったと考えられよう（資料 3）。

　チョーサーは指摘した通り OE 詩語（資料 2.2.）の何れをも用いない。例外的に用いるのは，ME 期に入って新しい意味を得て，実質的には ME 語と言える gadeling 'scoundrel' だけである：

　　These bowes two helde Swete Lokyng
　　That semed lyke no gadlyng
　　　　　　　(*The Romaunce of the Rose* 937–938: Thynne's 1532 ed.)

　これ以外は，ロンドン地域言の中で，宮廷を中心に使われる英語，そして詩の英語として，ふさわしい英語でないと判断したからであろう。

　　歴史という連続性の観点から，マロリーによる OE 詩語の使用はグリモー

ルドの場合と同様，一過性の現象と思われる．1400年代後半に未だロンドンを含むEast Midland地域言に残るとはいえ，北方とスコットランドへと衰退したOE詩語を一時的に借用したことは否定できない．しかし，排除の観点からすると，マロリーの言語的振る舞いは重要な意味を持っているようだ．チョーサーの没した1400年は英語の変化の指標と言ってよい．長母音の上昇と二重母音化 (Great Vowel Shift) は既に始まっていて (Roger Lass, "Phonology and Morphology," *CHEL* III, 80)，更におよそ1430年以降から英語のChancery Standard「法務行政府基準」と，1476年キャクストンによる活版印刷の導入とが，それまでの地域別英語から全国的標準英語への機運を加速させたと言われる (Manfred Görlach, "Regional and Social Variation," *CHEL* III, 459–460; Blake[2], Ch. 7)．

　このような状況の中で，マロリーは作品を書き終わった1469年までに ("concluded", Vinaver, xx)，最初は原本の影響を受けてOE詩語を数語使ったが，そのご一連の詩語をすべて排除した．キャクストンは1485年のマロリー版で，マロリーが残した*MA*の影響を完全に排除した．両者共にOE詩語が生命を失って既に共通語でないと考えたことと，従って散文の英語にふさわしくないとみなしたことがその理由であろう．上に言及した*Eneydos* (c1490) のPrologueでキャクストンは，英語に'dyversite and chaunge'がある現状において古語でも舶来 ('curyous') 語でもなく今日使用されている，理解できる一般的な共通の語 ('comyn termes') を翻訳の英語として使用する，と述べている (Blake 79–80)．「一般的」であるが故に，多様な違いを超えた「共通の」英語を意図したものであろう．キャクストンのこの原則は，以後*SS*出版の1557年までの散文においても守られたようだ．近代の散文作品，トマス・モア (Thomas More) の*The History of King Richard III* (1513)，トマス・エリオット (Thomas Elyot) の*The Book Named The Governour* (1531)，トマス・ウィルソン (Thomas Wilson) の*The Rule of Reason* (1551) と*The Art of Rhetorique* (1553)，そしてHelsinki Corpus 1500–1570 (1996)，これらにはOE詩語は見られない．詩語と散文語の区別，即ち詩語を排除した散文語が，初期近代英語の始まりに大きく関与していることはキャクストンの言語観のmodernityの証であろう．

英語史における「近代性」の視点から以上の考察をまとめてみると，既に 1400 年以前に Great Vowel Shift が始まっていて，更に 1430 年以降から英語の Chancery Standard が全国的標準英語への機運を加速させていた。その中で，キャクストンは翻訳の英語に 'comyn termes' を使うと宣言して (c1490)，マロリー版 (1485) でマロリーが残した原典の頭韻詩 Morte Arthure 中の OE 詩語（freyke, gadlyng, renk）を他の一般語に代えて完全に排除した。以後初期近代英語の散文に OE 詩語が姿を消したのは，c1490 年の宣言に先立つこの排除と機を一にする。詩では SS 即ち Tottel's Miscellany (1557) に 6 語が使われるが，その他は北方・スコットランドに現れるのみである。一方，マロリーは原典の OE 詩語を 3 語以外はキャクストン同様，一般語の代替により避け，以後の作品では完全に排除した。一般的な散文語である kemp はキャクストンも踏襲した。OE 詩語の扱いに関する限りマロリーとキャクストンを隔てるものは，1469 年マロリー原稿完成から 1476 年キャクストン印刷術導入を経て 1485 年 Le Morte Darthur 印刷，そして 1490 年頃刊行の Eneydos における散文語宣言に至るわずか 15 年から 20 年の年数と，手稿と印刷本の違いのみである。一方，両者を分かつ大きな，そして決定的な違いは比較にならないほど膨大な読者数である。そのことを考えると，近代は着々と準備されながらもその扉はキャクストンによって魔術のごとく一挙に開かれたと考えざるを得ない。

テクスト

Blake, N. F. (ed.) (1973) *Caxton's Own Prose*. London: Andre Deutsch.

Chaucer, Geoffrey (2008) *The Riverside Chaucer*, Third Edition (gen. ed. L. D. Benson). Oxford: Oxford University Press.

Hamel, Mary (ed.) (1984) *Morte Arthure. A Critical Edition*. NY and London: Garland Publishing.

Malory, Thomas (1973) *The Works of Sir Thomas Malory*, Second Edition, 3 vols. (ed. E. Vinaver). Oxford: Clarendon Press.

Malory, Thomas (1976) *Le Morte D'Arthur, Printed by William Caxton 1485* (a facsimile with an introduction by Paul Needham). London: Scolar Press.

Rollins, H. E. (ed.) (1966) *Tottel's Miscellany (1557–1587)*, Revised Edition, 2 vols. Cambridge, Mass.: Harvard University Press.

Songs and Sonnets: Tottel's Miscellany 1557 (A Scolar Press Facsimile). Menston

and London: Scolar Press.
The Romaunce of the Rose（rep. from William Thynne's 1532 edition of Chaucer's *Works*）. NY: Johnson Reprint.
Wrenn, C. L.（ed.）（1959）*Beowulf*, revised and enlarged edition. London: Harrap.

辞書他

Davis, Norman et al.（compiled）（1979）*A Chaucer Glossary*. Oxford: Clarendon Press.
Kato, Tomomi（ed.）（1974）*A Concordance to the Works of Sir Thomas Malory*. Tokyo: University of Tokyo Press.
Kurath, Hans et al.（eds.）（1952–2001）*The Middle English Dictionary*（MED）. Ann Arbor: The University of Michigan Press. Electric edition available at http://quod.lib.umich.edu/m/med/
Kurath, Hans et al.（1954）*Middle English Dictionary: Plan and Bibliography*. Ann Arbor: University of Michigan Press.
Mizobata, Kiyokazu（ed.）（2009）*A Concordance to Caxton's* Morte Darthur（1485）（with CD-ROM）. Osaka: Osaka Books.
Simpson, John（ed.）（2002）*The Oxford English Dictionary*, Second Edition on CD-ROM. Oxford: Oxford University Press.
Sweet, Henry（ed.）（2006 [1896]）*The Student's Dictionary of Anglo-Saxon*. Richmond: Tiger of the Stripe.

参考文献

Agari, Masahiko（2011）*Archaism in Tottel's Songes and Sonettes*. Hiroshima: Keisuisha.
Bennett, H. S.（1989）*English Books and Readers*, Vol. I, 1475–1557 Second Edition. Cambridge: Cambridge University Press.
Blake[2], N. F.（1996）*A History of the English Language*. Basingstoke and London: Macmillan.
Brewer, D. S.（ed.）（1978）*Chaucer: The Critical Heritage*, Vol. I. London: Routledge and Kegan Paul.
Görlach, Manfred（1999）'Regional and social variation'. In: Lass, Roger（ed.）*The Cambridge History of the English Language*, Vol. III 1476–1776（*CHEL*）. Cambridge: Cambridge University Press, 459–538.
Jones, R. F.（1953）*The Triumph of the English Language*. Stanford: Stanford University Press.
Lass, Roger（ed.）（1999）*The Cambridge History of the English Language*, Vol. III 1476–1776（*CHEL*）. Cambridge: Cambridge University Press.
安東伸介・岩崎春雄・高宮利行（編）（1981）『厨川文夫著作集』（上下）金星堂.

モデルとテクスト[1]
──『トテル詩選集』翻訳詩から──

上 利 政 彦

Songes and Sonettes『歌とソネット』,通常 *Tottel's Miscellany*『トテル詩選集』(1557)(*SS*)と呼ばれる英国最初の秀歌集は,1530–1550 年代までの代表的な詩を収めていると言われる(Berdan 343, 445)。これがエリザベス朝期に伝えられることになるが,同時に初期近代詩の最初の成果としての近代性 modernity の産声でもある。この秀歌集で優れている詩は原典を持つ詩であると言われるが,ここでは,中世と古典の詩を基とした翻訳詩とともに原典を持たない自立した詩も選び,近代の個人の「声」をきいてみたい。

最初にグリモールド(Nicolas Grimald ?1520–?1562)の母の死を悼む詩(No. 162)を取り上げたい。彼は,当時人文主義運動のリーダーでありケンブリッジ大学ギリシャ語教授チーク(Sir John Cheke 1514–1557)との何らかの形での接触があったと考えられている学者詩人である(Berdan 356)。初版では 40 篇の詩が掲載されたが,2 ヶ月を経ずして出た再版では 10 篇に減らされたためもあって,後世知られることの少ない詩人である。ケンブリッジ大学,ついでオックスフォード大学で学位をとったのち,オックスフォードの Christ Church College の修辞学講師を 1552 年まで務めた。彼が本秀歌集随一の人文主義詩人と言われる所以である。多くの著作の中で,1556 年,本秀歌集を印刷したトテル(Richard Tottel)が印刷・出版した *Ciceroes thre bokes of duties* は 16 世紀後半によく読まれたという(O'Gorman, Introduction)。

---

1) 第 56 回熊本大学英文学会(2012 年 11 月 20 日)における講演「『トテル詩選集』について──ヒューマニズムを中心に」に基く。

SS 中，彼の40篇の作品には，「称賛」の詩（対象とするもののうち，貴婦人9，恋人3，これにヴァージル賛歌1）が合計13篇ともっとも多い。「追悼」が貴人，貴婦人，武人，知人，各2，母 Agnes，キケロ，各1，合計10篇。その他，徳，中庸，結婚，友情，生き方，各2，Muses，Mirth，法，庭園，謎，キケロ，ゾローアス (Zoroas)，各1で合計17篇である。これらのうち30篇が再版以降姿を消す。「称賛」(13) では貴婦人を対象とする9篇のすべてが，「追悼」ではキケロを除くすべて (9) も姿を消す。宮廷人に関する詩が排除されていることが注目されよう。詩の形式に関して注目されるのは，ヴァージル の *Aeneid* を叙事詩文体で称賛するソネットが1篇あること，キケロとゾローアスの死を描く長詩2篇 (Nos. 165, 166) が無韻詩 Blank Verse で書かれていることである（サリーの *Aeneid* II, IV の無韻詩訳が，『トテル詩選集』出版後，すぐに出版される。しかし最初の無韻詩はサリーが書いたと言われる (Thomas Warton II.346)）。

　さて，ここで扱う母アグネスを弔う詩 (No. 162: 99行) は，他の多くの詩と違って原典を持たない。しかし古典からの引用が詩の主題と意味に深く関わっているという点で人文主義運動の影響を示している。そして注目すべきは，詩の効用が意識されていることであり，しかも一人の女性が不朽の名声を得るということ，その上自らが大詩人としてそれを可能にするという，恐らく近代の個人主義的主張が見られることである。

　詩はまず嘆きの原因から始まる。嘆くのは大切な人を亡くしたからだ (1-4)，それを責めるのは自然の理 'the mighty natures laws' (7) も，子が母を思う古の例 'touching elders deeds...old saws' (8) も知らないからだ (5-8)，と言って，母への孝養と乳母の称賛の事例を古典から引く (11-26)。この導入部のあと，出生とそのごの成長，変わらぬ母の深い慈愛が語られる。そしてオックスフォードに学ぶことになって，喜びも一人(ひとしお)の時に母は病の床に臥し，「御霊は上空に飛んで去りました」"into ayre your sprite departed fled" (75) と言う。このように自らの生誕から母の死にいたるまで受けた愛情を愛惜の念を込めて振り返る (27-76)。そしてこの詩は次のように終わる：

No. 162　A funeral song, vpon the deceas of Annes his Mother.
Haue, mother, monumentes of our sore smart:
No costly tomb, areard with curious art:
Nor Mausolean masse, hoong in the ayre: 85
Nor loftie steeples, that will once appayre:
But waylful verse, and doolfull song accept.
By verse, the names of auncient peres be kept:
By verse, liues Hercules: by verse, Achil:
Hector, Ene, by verse, be famous still. 90
Such former yeres, such death hath chaūced thee:
Closde, with good end, good life is woont to bee.
But now, my sacred parent, fare you well:
God shall cause vs agayn togither dwell,
What time this vniuersall globe shall hear 95
Of the last troomp the rynging voyce: great fear
To soom, to such as you a heauenly chear.
Til then, reposde rest you in gentle sleep:
While hee, whom to you are bequeathd, you keep.

　　84 *areard*　　to arear, i.e., to erect
　　85 Caria の王 Mausolus の死を嘆いて妃 Artemisia は精巧な彫刻を施した巨大な墳墓を築かせた。
　　86 *appayre*　　to deteriolate, decay
　　87 *waylful*　　wailful この語は 1540 年代から流行したようだ (OED)。
　　89–90 Homer と Virgil により。
　　91 *thee*　　ライムのためと思われるが，thou / ye の区別が緩んできている。
　　93 *sacred*　　consecrated, hallowed
　　94 The Judgement Day
　　95 *What time*　　when
　　　　vniuersall　　entire, whole
　　99 *whom to*　　to whom (OED)
　　　　keep　　三人称単数現在の無変化形。ライムのためと思われる。この時期，散文においても使用される。

「母アンの死にさいして，弔いの歌」から
母上，私達の痛切な嘆きの記念碑を受けられよ。
精巧な技で建立された高価な墓石ではなく，
空中に聳えるマウソールス王の巨塊でもなく， 85

いずれは朽ちる聳える尖塔でもなくて，
悲痛な叫びと悲嘆に満ちた詩歌を受け取られよ。
詩歌により古の貴人の名は伝えられます。
詩歌によりヘラクレスやアキレスは生き続け，
ヘクトル，アエネーアースはいまだ名を知られます。　　　　　90
そんな古と同じ死が今貴女に降りかかったのです。
見事な生涯は見事な結末で閉じるのが常です。
しかし暫くはお別れです，神に捧げられし母上。
この全世界が最後のラッパの高らかな響きを
聞く時，ある者には大きな恐怖，また　　　　　　　　　　　95
貴女のような方には天の喜びにも聞こえて，
神が再び私達を共に住まうようになさいます。
その時まで，穏やかに眠り，お休み下さい。
貴女が委ねたお方が守っていて下さいますから。

　グリモールドは悲しみを歌うこの詩歌を壮大な墓石に勝る記念碑として亡き母に献じる (83–87)。彼はホーマー，ヴァージルといった古典の大詩人に続き，我グリモールドが近代の大詩人として，ヘラクレス，アエネーアースなどの英雄たちと同様，母アグネスに今この詩によって永遠の生命を与えようと言っているのである。市井の一女性が英雄に伍することができるのも近代的自我の自覚によるものであろう。しかし，彼，人文主義者が抱く不朽の名声への確信は，キリスト教信仰の前に微妙にゆれ動くようだ。この詩は弔いの詩である。キリスト再臨による神の国の再現，その時に「私たち」(= us 94) 義なる人が再び共に住まう至福千年の歓びが，古典的名声観を凌駕する。しかし前者はそれなりに現世の人の営為として重要である…，という確信もあり，古典・キリスト教両世界観の比較による価値の相克は無いと思われる。キリスト教的人文主義と言われるが，上の引用は，前・後半部が各々二分されていて，存分に古典の素材を使いつつキリスト教信仰で締めくくられる。対比表現 ('But' 93) の使用は人文主義初期における両文化の相克を反映したものかも知れない。

モデルとテクスト

ペトラルカ (1304–1374) からワイアットとサリーが Rime sparse 140 を訳している。原文を示すと:

Amor, che nel penser mio vive et regna
e 'l suo seggio maggior nel mio cor tene,
talor armato ne la fronte vene;
ivi si loca et ivi pon sua insegna.

Quella ch' amare et sofferir ne 'nsegna　　　　　　　　　　5
e vol che 'l gran desio, l'accesa spene
ragion, vergogna, et reverenza affrene,
di nostro ardir fra se stessa si sdegna.

Onde Amor paventoso fugge al core,
lasciando ogni sua impresa, et piange et trema;　　　　　　10
ivi s'asconde et non appar più fore.

Che poss' io far, temendo il mio signore,
se non star seco infin a l'ora estrema?
ché bel fin fa chi ben amando more.

私の想いの中に住んで支配し，
私の心の中で主座を占めている愛の神は，
時々全身武具を纏って私の額に出陣し，
そこに陣を張り旗印を掲げる。

彼女は，私たちに愛して耐えるように教え，　　　　　　　　5
この激しい欲望，火のついた願望を
理性，羞恥心，そして畏怖の念により抑えよと命じ，
大胆にもそれを破ると密かにさげすむ。

すると愛の神は恐れてあらゆる作戦を放棄して
心に逃げ帰り，泣きながら震え上がる。　　　　　　　　　　10
そしてそこに隠れて二度と姿を見せない。

我が主君が怯えている時，最後の時まで

共に留まる以外に私に何ができようか？
よく愛して死ぬ者は見事な最期を遂げるのだ。

ペトラルカの主旨は，主君キューピッドに仕えて「愛の殉死」を遂げる，という男の決断である。キューピッドが勝利の余勢をかって女に勝負を挑むが，「さげすみ」の反撃を食らって憐れ敗北。しっかりせねばならぬは，この男「私」だけだ，と言う。敗者の生きる道は，女の気持ちはどうであれ愛しつづけることにあるというわけである。

これをモデルに，まずワイアットが 14 行詩（sonnet）をつくる：

　　No. 37　The louer for shamefastnesse hideth
　　　　　　　his desire within his faith=
　　　　　　　　full hart.
　　THe longe loue, that in my thought I harber,
　　And in my hart doth kepe his residence,
　　Into my face preaseth with bold pretence,
　　And there campeth, displaying his banner.
　　She that me learns to loue, and to suffer, 　　　　　　　　5
　　And willes that my trust, and lustes negligence
　　Be reined by reason, shame, and reuerence,
　　With his hardinesse takes displeasure.
　　Wherwith loue to the hartes forest he fleeth,
　　Leauyng his enterprise with paine and crye, 　　　　　　　10
　　And there him hideth and not appeareth.
　　What may I do? when my maister feareth,
　　But in the field with him to liue and dye,
　　For good is the life, endyng faithfully.
　　（Egerton MS では l (1) が doth。他に重要な変更は無い。）

　「男はたしなみをもって欲望を忠実な心の中に隠す」
私が想いの中に秘めていて，
長い間心の中に住みついてしまった愛が，
大胆にも主人面をして私の顔に押し出でて，

そこに陣を張り，彼の旗印を掲げる。
彼女はいつも私に愛すること苦しむことを教え， 5
私の自信と欲望の放縦を，理性，羞恥心，そして
畏敬の念でもって抑えるように命じている。
だから愛の厚かましさに腹を立てる。
それを知って愛は，悲鳴をあげながら
作戦を放棄して，心の森に逃走する。 10
そしてそこに隠れて姿を見せない。
主君が怯える時，私はどうしたらよいのか。
ただ戦場で主君と生死を共にするだけだ。
最後まで忠実な生き方も良いからだ。

　ワイアットは終わり2行でやや曖昧な表現をしている。「戦場」(13)で「主君」(12)と生死を共にすると男は言うが，これは戦いにおいて主従の忠節を尽くすということである。更に「心の森」(10)が戦いのイメージを補強する。詩の全体を支配する戦いのイメージから見ると，彼の出だしは原詩と違って「戦い」が無い。しかし3行以後愛が支配的になるにつれて，原詩には無い「森」を用いる。森は戦場(field)と対照的に「隠れる場所，休息する場所」である。我が心の中で主君，愛の神を守り，戦場で生命をともにしようと言う。ワイアットの視点が戦いにおける殉死へと広がっている点がこの詩の特徴であろう。主君ヘンリー8世に仕える武人ワイアットの色合いが出ているようだ。
　次にサリーの試みを見よう。

  No. 6 Complaint of a louer
       rebuked.
LOue, that liueth, and reigneth in my thought,
That built his seat within my captiue brest,
Clad in the armes, wherin with me he fought,
Oft in my face he doth his banner rest.
She, that me taught to loue, and suffer payne, 5
My doutfull hope, and eke my hote desyre,

With shamefast cloke to shadowe, and refraine,
Her smilyng grace conuerteth straight to yre.
And cowarde Loue then to the hart apace
Taketh his flight, whereas he lurkes, and plaines   10
His purpose lost, and dare not shewe his face.
For my lordes gilt thus faultlesse byde I paynes.
Yet from my lorde shall not my foote remoue.
Swete is his death, that takes his end by loue.
(MS では cloke (7) が looke。他に重要な変更は無い。)

「酷い仕打ちを受けた男の嘆きの歌」
虜にしたぼくの胸の中に居城を築き，
心の中に住みつき支配する愛の神は，
ぼくと戦った時の鎧を着て
よくぼくの顔面に出て旗印を立てる。
すると彼女の優しい笑みは直ちに怒りに変わる。   5
愛して苦しみに耐え，当てなき希望と
熱い欲望を控えめに外套で
被い隠すように教えたのに，と言うのだ。
すると臆病な愛の神はすぐに心の中に
撤退し，身を隠して作戦の失敗を嘆き，   10
顔を見せない。我が主君の失策のため
かくも無実のぼくが苦しみに耐えるのだ。
だがぼくは主君を見捨てることは決してしない。
愛の神に仕えて終わる者に死こそ本望なのだ。

　この詩は非常にドラマティックに描かれていて特異である。ペトラルカが示唆した戦いのイメジ（'regna'）を，サリーは，ワイアットと違って最初から明示する（'reigneth'）。愛の神はぼくに勝ち，更に女に対して連勝を狙おうという訳だ。しかし難攻不落，彼女の要求はペトラルカの原詩ともワイアットの訳詩とも異なる。つまり，それぞれ 'ragion', 'vergona', 'reverenza' つまり 'reason', 'shame', 'reuerence' をもって男に欲望を抑えるように命じていた。

が，ここでは（原文では shamfast looke 顔赤らめて，とあり，「外套 'cloke' (7) で被い隠す」のはこの詩集の読みである），心のありようを男の表情に転換する。それは宮廷で，あるいは彼の周辺でよく見られる態のものだ。最初の戦いで敗れたが，次の戦いは主君が仕掛けたもの。従って敗戦の責任はぼくには無い。にもかかわらず彼は戦いを放棄，前進も退却もかなわず，「虜」であるぼくの心の中に閉じこもる。永遠に苦しむのはぼくだ。サリーは男と愛の神の関係を一層戯曲化して，warrior-lover のイメジを鮮明にしているように思われる。最後にサリーは叙情的な「感嘆法」(Exclamatio) で締めくくる：'Swete is his death...'。これはペトラルカの「愛の殉死」の主題に沿うものであるが，サリーの置かれた宮廷社会で容易に聞かれる感嘆であろう。この詩の主人公を「ぼく」としたが，男の戯曲化された役割から，武勲を求め恋に生きる若き宮廷人にふさわしいと思われるからである。

　モデルから作られた二つのテクストはほぼ忠実な翻訳であるが，ともにモデルから逸脱して個性を見せる。Invention（題材の発見）を他（ペトラルカ）に依存したが，二人の英詩人はその枠内で個性的な invention を作り上げ，この時期の翻訳詩の一側面を表していると言えよう。なお，戯曲化の観点からは，この詩集の読みである「外套」のほうが写本の「目差し」(looke) に勝るであろう。

SS 初版 (1557) には Q. Horatius Flaccus (BC 65–8) の *Carmina* II, 10 の英訳が 2 篇ある（再版にはもう 1 篇）。しかし，冗長な一方の訳を除きサリーのものと，20 数年後のシドニー (Sir Philip Sidney) の訳を取り上げたい。

　以下，原文に続き，英語訳と日本語訳を試みる。

Horatius, *Carmina* II, 10 (Rollins II, 152–153)

Rectius vives, Licini, neque altum
semper urgendo neque, dum procellas
cautus horrescis, nimium premendo
　　litus iniquom.

Auream quisquis mediocritatem　　　　　　　　　　5

diligit, tutus caret obsoleti
sordibus tecti, caret invidenda
    sobrius aula.

Saepius ventis agitatur ingens
pinus et celsae graviore casu   10
decidunt turres feriuntque summos
    fulgura montis.

Sperat infestis, metuit secundis
alteram sortem bene praeparatum
pectus. Informis hiemes reducit   15
Iuppiter; idem

Summovet. Non, si male nunc, et olim
sic erit: quondam cithara tacentem
suscitat Musam neque semper arcum
    tendit Apollo.   20

Rebus angustis animosus atque
fortis appare: sapienter idem
contrahes vento nimium secundo
    turgida vela.

〔英訳〕
Better you shall live, Licinius, neither to deep seas
by always driving nor, while at storms
careful you tremble, by just too much keeping
    close to the sea-shore.

Whoever the golden mean   5
esteems, safe is without shabbiness
of the decayed house, is sober away
    from envious Court.

Most often by winds is tossed the huge
pine and with graver crash the lofty   10
towers fall, and strike the summit of
    the mount the bolts of lightning.

> Hopes in danger, fears in prosperity
> a mind well prepared for either
> fortune. Ugly winters Jupiter 15
>   brings back; the same
>
> Drives off. No, if it be ill now, yet hereafter
> it shall [not] be thus: some day the lute
> shall arouse Muse now silent, nor always his bow
>   Apollo draw. 20
>
> In hard state show you courageous
> and strong: yet wisely
> you should furl, in too favourable wind,
>   the prosperous sails.

リキニウスよ，いつも大海に打って出ることもなく，また嵐の時怯えて岸辺に近寄りすぎもしないで，きみはより良い生き方をして欲しい。

黄金の中庸を心する者は朽ちた家のむさくるしさもなく安全だ。宮廷の嫉妬もなく落ち着いていられる。

巨大な松は真っ先に強風を受け，聳える塔は倒れると無残に崩れ，山の頂は稲妻が打つ。

心を運・不運双方によく備えておけば，危機に際して希望を持ち，栄えたときに恐れを抱く。ユピテルは険悪な冬をもたらすが，それを追っ払いもする。

今悪くとも，これからも同じではあるまい。いつかアポロの竪琴が今は黙するムーサを覚まし，何時までも弓を引きはしないであろう。

困難にあたっては勇気を出し雄々しく振る舞うのだ。しかし順風にあたっては，思慮深く満帆をたたむがよい。

アリストテレスは，徳としての「中庸」について過超と不足の中位を説く（『ニコマコス倫理学』，特に第 2 巻）。ホラティウスはこれを受けていると思われる

が，人生航路においてこの中庸の生き方を，幸福をもたらす正しい生き方として息子Liciniusに勧める。内容は次のように展開する。

第1聯：両極端ではなく中位に位置することはより良い（正しいrectius＜rectus）生き方をすることだ。

第2聯：中庸を旨とする者は，家庭では安全で（tutus）いられるし，宮廷の嫉妬とも無縁で心落ち着いて（sobrius）いられる。

第3聯：高い位置にあると危険や破壊を被る。（中位にあればこともなく安全だ。）

（第4聯以下，中庸の具体的な徳目が示される。すなわち，希望（sperat），恐れ（metuit），勇気（animosus），果敢（fortis），思慮（sapienter））。

第4聯：運・不運双方にあって心すべきことは，希望（不運の時），恐れ（幸運の時）だ。

第5聯：運命は好転する（神意）。

第6聯：勇気，果敢（不運の時），思慮（幸運の時）が必要。

このように中庸は，有為転変の人生にあって幸福を得るための心のあり方を示す。

このモデルにたいしてサリーのテクストは以下の通りである。

No. 28　Praise of meane and
　　　　　　　constant estate.
OF thy lyfe, Thomas, this compasse well mark:
Not aye with full sayles the hye seas to beat:
Ne by coward dred, in shonning stormes dark,
On shalow shores thy keel in perill **freat**.
Who so gladly **halseth** the golden meane, 　　　　　5
Uoyde of dangers aduisdly hath his home
Not with lothsom muck, as a den vncleane:
Nor palacelyke, wherat disdayn may **glome**.
The lofty pyne the great winde often riues:

With violenter swey **falne** turrets stepe: 10
Lightninges assault the hye mountains, and **cliues**,
A hart well stayd, in **ouerthwartes** depe,
Hopeth amendes: in swete, doth feare the sowre.
God, that sendeth, withdraweth winter sharp.
Now ill, not aye thus: once Phebus to lowre 15
With bow vnbent shall cesse, and frame to harp
His voyce. In straite estate appere thou stout:
And so wisely, when lucky gale of winde
All thy puft sailes shall fil, loke well about:
Take in a ryft: hast is wast, profe doth finde. 20

 4 *freat* to fret, i.e., rub, cause...to graze
 5 *halseth* to halse, i.e., embrace
 8 *glome* to gloom, i.e., frown
 10 *falne* fallen　三人称複数現在。
 11 *cliues* cliffs
 12 *ouerthwartes* adversity

「中庸を得た揺るぎない生活のすすめ」
トマスよ，君の生き方についてこの中庸を心得給え。
それは，いつも帆を張りつめて大海原を航海せず，
また，臆病風に吹かれて陰鬱な嵐を避けながら，
浅い岸辺で竜骨を擦り切らす危険を冒さないことだ。
黄金の中庸をすすんで心する者は誰でも， 5
熟慮の上，家庭を危険の無いようにし，
汚いごみいっぱいの不潔な穴ぐらのようでも，
軽蔑して顔をしかめる宮廷のようでもいけない。
聳え立つ松を強風がしばしば引き裂く。
急な小塔はもっと激しく揺れて崩れる。 10
高山と断崖は稲妻が襲う。
落ち着いた心は，深い逆境にあって
改善を目指し，喜びにあって苦しみを恐れる。
厳しい冬を神は送り給うが，やがて退去させ給う。

今は病んでも，やがては癒える。太陽神もいずれ　　　　　　　　15
弓を置いて笑顔を取り戻し，竪琴に合わせて歌おう。
危急の場合に雄々しくあれ。
幸運にも順風満帆の時にこそ，
心して慎重に，よく周囲を見渡すことだ。
縮帆を巻け。急いては仕損じる。これは自明の理だ。　　　　　20

はじめにサリー訳の英語について古語の使用を指摘しておきたい（テクスト中太字で示した）。古語使用はSS詩人達に共通する時代的な特徴であるが，対照的にシドニーには無い。ちなみに散文は学者気取りの学術用語（inkhornisms）を積極的に用いるが，SSではワイアットが 'the bright *transplendant* glasse'（No. 104, 1.49 = brilliantly translucent）を用いるだけである。この秀歌集は時代の衒学趣味とは無縁である。

サリーは最終行の「急いては仕損じる。これは自明の理だ」を付け加え，そして「改善」（amendes）(13)を付け加えた。何故逆境に陥ったか，どうすればこれから抜け出せるか，改善を目指せよ，と言うのである。「よく周囲を見渡す」(19)とは冷静で合理的な（rational）精神の働きを促していると思われる。指摘した最終行の付言 'hast is wast' も同じであろう。これは，'Haste makes waste' という当時のことわざをもとにして，より直截で力強い。

サリーは個人の自立した精神，しかも（モデル同様の）雄々しさ，力強さに支えられた近代的・合理的精神を主張していると思われる。

    Sir Philip Sidney, from *Certain Sonnets* 12
    Translated out of Horace, *which beginnes* **Rectiùs viues** (c1581)

    You better sure shall live, not evermore
        Trying high seas, nor while Sea rage you flee,
        Pressing too much upon ill harbourd shore.

    The golden meane who loves, lives safely free
        From filth of foreworne house, and quiet lives,　　5
        Releast from Court, where envie needes must be.

> The wynde most oft the hugest Pine-tree greeves:
>   The stately towers come downe with greater fall:
>   The highest hills the bolt of thunder cleeves:
>
> Evill happes do fill with hope, good happes appall   10
>   With feare of change, the courage well prepared:
>   Fowle Winters as they come, away they shall.
>
> Though present times and past with evils be snared,
>   They shall not last: with Citherne silent muse
>   Apollo wakes, and bow hath sometime sparde.   15
>
> In hard estate with stowt shew valor use,
>   The same man still in whome wysdome prevailes,
>   In too full winde draw in thy swelling sailes.

いつも大海原に出ようとしたり，嵐の海を逃れて船泊まりの無い岸を目指そうとしなければ，きみは必ず良い生き方ができよう。

黄金の中庸を愛する者は，朽ちた家の汚物とは無縁に安らかに過ごし，嫉妬が渦巻く宮廷から解放されて静謐な人生を送ることができる。

風は一番高い松の木を真っ先に痛めつける。堂々たる塔はそれだけ倒れるとひどい。丘の高い頂は稲妻が裂く。

よく準備のできた精神は，不運の時には希望に満ち，幸運の時には暗転の恐れに慄く。厳しい冬は来もすれば，必ず去りもする。

現在も過去も不運に捕えられていようとも，長く続きはしない。アポロは竪琴を弾いて黙するミューズを起こす，いずれは弓を置くのだ。

危急の場合に凛々しく胆力を見せるのだ。知恵を使い，うろたえてはならない。順風の時は満帆を下ろしてほしい。

シドニーの訳はモデルに忠実である。その中でも彼の特徴が出される。最終聯，'The same man still in whome wysdome prevailes' に見られる 'wysdome'

を生き方のキー・ポイントとしている。危急の場合，うろたえて自分を見失わないように知恵を働かせる，と言う。それは，困難な時にこそ個人の自立した判断が求められるという教えである。シドニーはホラティウスの 'sapienter' (22)，サリーの 'wisely' (18) をこのように重要な概念として自立させている。モデルの 'animosus', 'fortis' をサリーは 'stout', シドニーは 'stowt', 'valor' で受け継いでいる。シドニーはホラティウスにより近いが，サリーと共に困難に際しての英国人の沈着と気骨を伝えていると思われる。

　古典のキリスト教化という視点で最後に付け加えておきたい。この詩は幸福な人生をおくる指針を述べたものである。ホラティウスは精神の思慮深さと剛毅をもって幸福の基盤とする。サリーもシドニーもこれに倣う。栄えたときに恐れを知り，喜びにあって苦しみを恐れ，幸運にあって暗転を恐れる——，これは「忍耐」と言い換えることができよう。キリスト教的な忍耐は，例えばミルトンによると次のように定義される：「幸，不幸いずれの場合にあっても，己を制して等しく耐え，慣れることによって，たとえば喜びを感ずる際にも，畏れと敬虔な悲しみを交えて感ずるようになってもらいたい。そうすれば，お前は最も安らかにその生涯をおくることができる」(『失楽園』11巻361–365)。モデルの枠組みの中にあるとはいえ，サリーとシドニーのテクストに接して，読者は容易にキリスト教的な忍耐を読み取るであろう。

SS 即ち『トテル詩選集』は周知のごとく人文主義の影響を色濃く受けて，その多くが古典，中世，近代初期の外国文芸からこれまで経験したことのない題材を導入して新しい詩歌が作られた。メイスン (Mason) は真の人文主義者について，今もなお生き続ける最高の形で古典作品を「翻訳した」詩人として位置づけている (289)。我々が扱った作品は原作を単に英語で置き換えたものではなく，新しい詩人の息吹きによって新たな自立した生命を持ったように思われる。

テクスト

Durling, R. M. (tr. and ed.) (1976) *Petrarch's Lyric Poems*. Cambridge, Mass. and London: Harvard University Press.

Fowler, Alastair (ed.) (1998) *Paradise Lost*, Second Edition. London and NY: Longman.

Ringler, Jr., W. A. (ed.) (1962) *The Poems of Sir Philip Sidney*. Oxford: The Clarendon Press.

Rollins, H. E. (ed.) (1966) *Tottel's Miscellany (1557–1587)*, Revised Edition, 2 vols. Cambridge, Mass.: Harvard University Press.

上利政彦（訳注）（2010）『トテル詩選集　歌とソネット　1557』九州大学出版会.

高田三郎（訳）（1971, 2006）『ニコマコス倫理学』（上下）岩波書店.

平井正穂（訳）（1981）『失楽園』（上下）岩波書店.

参考文献

Berdan, J. M. (1961) *Early Tudor Poetry 1485–1647*. NY: Macmillan.

Mason, H. A. (1980 [1959]) *Humanism and Poetry in Early Tudor Period*. London: Routledge and Kegan Paul.

文学テクストの重層性
――『失楽園』最終部について――

上 利 政 彦

『失楽園』 *Paradise Lost* はアダムとイーヴの楽園追放の場面で終わる。

> High in front advanced,
> **The brandished sword of God** before them blazed
> Fierce as a comet; which with torrid heat,
> And vapour as the Lybian air adust,   635
> Began to parch that temperate clime; whereat
> In either hand the hastening angel caught
> Our lingering parents, and to the eastern gate
> Led them direct, and down the cliff as fast
> To the subjected plain; then disappeared.   640
> They looking back, all the eastern side beheld
> Of Paradise, so late their happy seat,
> Waved over by ***that flaming brand***, the gate
> With ***dreadful faces*** thronged and ***fiery arms***:
> Some natural tears they dropped, but wiped them soon;   645
> The world was all before them, where to choose
> Their place of rest, and providence their guide:
> They hand in hand with wandering steps and slow,
> Through Eden took their solitary way.
> (Fowler's edition より。太字斜体付加)

この箇所は聖書の記述に基いていることは周知の通りである：

> Therefore the Lord God sent him forth from the garden of Eden, to till the ground from whence he was taken. So he drove out the man; and he placed at the east of the garden of Eden Cherubims, and a flaming sword which turned every way, to keep the way of the tree of life. (AV: Gen.3.23–24)
> そこで主なる神は彼をエデンの園から追い出して，人が造られたその土を耕させられた。神は人を追い出し，エデンの園の東に，ケルビムと，回る炎のつるぎとを置いて，命の木の道を守らせられた。(『聖書』日本聖書協会 1966)

　神は，何者も生命の木に近づかないようにと，ケルビムと回る炎の剣をエデンの東門に配置された理由が述べられている。ミルトンでは神の剣が，これに先立って二人を楽園の出口へと先導する大天使ミカエルによって振り回されている (632–633)。聖書には無いこの記述中の「神の剣」は温暖な楽園の土地を焦がす。この神の剣は次には聖書の記述に沿って現れる (643)。「燃え，回転する剣」は，聖書の記述に見られる通り，「生命の木の守護」のために置かれたと当然ミルトンは理解している。

　更に，これは，堕落した二人を楽園から追放するにあたって，神が天使ミカエルに命じた通りに実践されたものである。

> Take to thee from among the cherubim　　　　　　　　　　100
> Thy choice of flaming warriors, lest the fiend
> Or in behalf of man, or to invade
> Vacant possession some new trouble raise:
> Haste thee, and from the Paradise of God
> Without remorse drive out the sinful pair,　　　　　　　　105
> From hallowed ground the unholy, and denounce
> To them and to their progeny from thence
> Perpetual banishment.
> 　..........
> And on the east side of the garden place,
> Where entrance up from Eden easiest climbs,
> Cherubic watch, and of a sword the flame　　　　　　　　120
> Wide waving, all approach far off to fright,

And guard all passage to the tree of life:
Lest Paradise a receptacle prove
To spirits foul, and all my trees their prey,
With whose stolen fruit man once more to delude. (11.100–108, 118–125)

汝はケラビムの中からえり抜きの炎を放つ戦士を
引き連れて，悪魔が人間を汚すためであれ，
無人の住みかを荒らすためであれ，
新たな騒動を起こさないようにするのだ。
一刻も早く，神の楽園から容赦なく
罪深い二人を，不浄の二人を神聖な土地から
追い出し，彼らとその子孫への永久の追放を
申しつけてほしい。
………
エデンから入って一番登りやすい
庭園の東側に警備のケラブを配備し，
剣の炎の大きくはためくに合わせ，
如何とも近づくことならぬ，とおどして，
生命の木に通ずる道すべてを固めるのだ。
楽園が汚れた霊たちの巣窟となり，
楽園の木がすべてその餌食となって，
盗った実で再び人間を欺いてはならぬからだ。

　ここでは，不浄となった二人の楽園追放と，生命の木を含むあらゆる神の木がサタンら悪霊によって盗まれないように，次にそれが人間をたぶらかすのに使われることがないように，と述べられている。なお，「剣の炎の大きくはためく」(120-121) のは，全天の回転を表すアレゴリーという見解もあるようだ (Fowler 注)。
　では *Paradise Lost* ではこれ以上の意味は読み取れないのであろうか。
　カルヴィンは比喩 (allegory) 的な解釈を全く容れないが，アウグスティヌスはこれを容れている。これまでミルトン研究ではアウグスティヌスとの関

係は勿論論じられてきたが (Lewis[2], Fiore)，剣の回転との関係は指摘されてこなかったようだ。しかしアウグスティヌス研究では当然論じられている。わが国では清水正照氏は次のように指摘されている。「『創世記について　マニ教徒駁論』(2.23, 35) でケルビムは知恵の充溢を，回転している剣は時間的な刑罰を意味しており，剣が火焔であるのは，火焔がすべての苦しみを燃やし尽くして，正義をいっそう純化するためであると考えている。つまり人は苦しみを忍耐し，知恵の充溢を経なければ生命の樹に到達できないというのである」(清水459, n.118)。これはキリスト教徒の信仰の道を示したものである。この聖書解釈をミルトンは知っていたのか。もし知っていたとしてこの作品にあてはまるのか。その意図と作品の思想に対応するのか。まずアウグスティヌスを詳しく見てみよう。

　アウグスティヌスの解釈は以下の通りである：

35. *Posuit autem deus Cherubim et flammeam frameam quae versatur,* quae uno nomine versatilis dici potest, *ad custodiendam viam arboris vitae*. Sicut illi volunt, qui Hebraea verba in scripturis interpretati sunt, Cherubim Latine scientiae plenitudo esse dicitur. Flammea vero framea versatilis temporales poenae intelleguntur, quoniam tempora volubilitate versantur. Propterea et flammea dicitur, quia urit quodammodo omnis triblatio. Sed aliud est uri ad consumptionem, aliud est uri ad purgationem. Nam et apostolus dicit: *quis scandalizatur, et ego non uror?* Sed iste affectus purgabat eum magis, quia de caritate veniebat. Et illae tribulationes quas iusti patiuntur, ad ipsam pertinent flammeam frameam, *quoniam in igne probatur aurum et argentum, et homines acceptabiles in camino humiliationis*; et iterum: *vasa figuli probat fornax, et homines iustos temptatio tribulationis*. Quoniam ergo *quem diligit deus corripit et flagellat omnem filium quem recipit,* sicut dicit et apostolus: *scientes quoniam tribulatio patientiam operatur*, *patientia probationem* et legimus et audimus et credendum est arborem vitae plenitudine scientiae et flammea framea custodiri. Nemo ergo potest pervenire ad arborem vitae nisi per has duas, id est tolerantiam molestiarum et scientiae plenitudinem.
36. Sed tolerantia molestiarum omnibus fere in hac vita subeunda est tendentibus ad arborem vitae, plenitudo autem scientiae videtur paucioribus provenire, ut quasi non omnes, qui perveniunt ad arborem vitae, per

scientiae plenitudinem veniant, quamvis omnes tolerantiam molestiarum, id est flammeam frameam versatilem sentiant. Sed si attendatur quod apostolus dicit: *plenitudo autem legis caritas*, et videamus eandem caritatem praecepto illo gemino contineri: *diliges dominum deum tuum ex toto corde tuo et ex tota anima tua et ex tota mente tua*, et *diliges proximum tuum tamquam teipsum; in quibus duobus praeceptis tota lex pendet et prophetae*, sine dubitatione intellegimus ad arborem vitae non solum per flammeam frameam versatilem, id est per tolerantiam temporalium molestiarum, sed etiam per plenitudinem scientiae, id est per caritatem veniri; quia *si caritatem*, inquit, *non habeam, nihil sum*. (*De Genesi: Contra Manichaeos* II, xxiii, 35–36: Weber 158–160)

35. 神がエデンの東に置かれたケルビムと燃える槍（ここでは 剣ではなく槍が使われている）(Gen.3.24) は知識の充足 (scientiae plenitudo) を意味する。回転する燃える槍 (flammea framea quae versatur) は神により正しい人に科せられる時間的（現世的）懲罰を意味する。時間はその性質上回転するからである。燃えるのは，すべて苦難は燃えるものだからである。しかし，燃えて尽きるものもあれば，浄化するものもある。パウロは言う，「だれかが罪を犯しているのに，わたしの心が燃えないでおれようか。」(2Cor.11.29) この感情はむしろパウロを純化していた。それは愛 (caritas) から発せられたからだ。正しい人が受ける艱難はこの燃える槍に属するものである，「何故なら，金銀は火の中で試され，神に良しとされる人は悲痛のかまどで試されるからである」(Sirach 2.5)。更に，「炉は焼物職人の器を試し，艱難の試練は義人を試す」(Sirach 27.5)。それ故，「主は愛する者を訓練し，受け入れるすべての子を，むち打たれるのである」(Heb.12.6)。だから，聖パウロが言うように，「艱難は忍耐を生み出し，忍耐は練達を生み出すことを知っているから」(Rom.5.3–4)，生命の木が知識の充足と燃える槍とによって守られるものと書いてあり聞くので，信じなければならない。それ故，これら二つ，即ち艱難の忍耐と知識の充足による以外に何人も生命の木に到達することはできない。

36. しかし，艱難の忍耐は，生命の木を求めるすべての人々がこの世で受けるべきものであるが，反して知識の充足はずっと少数の人々にのみ

可能と思われる。従って，万人が艱難の忍耐すなわち回転する燃える槍を経験するけれども，生命の木に至る者すべてが知識の充足に頼るわけにはいかない。しかしパウロの言葉に耳をかたむければ：「だから，愛は律法を完成するものである」(Rom.13.10)，そして次の二つの教えに同じ愛が込められているのを知るならば：「イエスは言われた，『心をつくし，精神をつくし，思いをつくして，主なるあなたの神を愛せよ』」(Matth.22.37) と，「『自分を愛するようにあなたの隣り人を愛せよ』。これら二つのいましめに，律法全体と預言者とが，かかっている」(39-40) との二つである，もしこれらを知るならば，回転する燃える槍すなわち時間的艱難の忍耐によるのみならず，知識の充足すなわち愛によっても，人は生命の木に至る，このことをはっきりと我々は理解するのである。パウロが言うように，「もし愛がなければ，わたしは無に等しい」(1Cor.13.2) からである。

永遠の生命（即ち生命の木）を得る困難な方法（知識の充足），または誰にでもできる方法 (caritas) と忍耐をアウグスティヌスは説く。これがミルトンのテクストの背後にあるとすれば，楽園から追放されようとしているアダムとイーヴは「世界」(12.646) を前にして，悪 (Satan) との戦いに勝って永遠の生命を得る方法を教わっていることになる。ケルビムと燃える剣は，二人が愛と忍耐の教えを心に刻んでいることを表していると思われる。

忍耐は「神の摂理と御力と善意を確信して，約束されることを私たちが心穏やかに受け入れるとき，そしてまた心静かに耐える目の前の災いを，至高の父が私たちの善のために送られたものとして耐えるときに，見られる徳である」とミルトンは『キリスト教教義』(*CPW* 6.662) の中で述べる。神意を心穏やかに受け入れ，艱難を神から送られたものとして耐えること，これが忍耐と言うのである。アダムとイーヴは天使ミカエルが語る人類の未来史から，神の恩寵 (supernal grace) が人の罪深さと戦うのを知って真の忍耐を学ぶ (11.359-362)。即ち，人の忍耐の原型は，人の罪深さと戦うキリストの愛に見られるのである。つまり，キリストにおいて愛は忍耐であるということができる。

忍耐と愛について，大天使は次のように言う：

> only add
> Deeds to thy knowledge answerable, add faith,
> Add virtue, *patience*, temperance, add *love*,
> By name to come called *charity, the soul*
> *Of all the rest*: (12.581–585 斜体付加)

　　　　ひたすらに汝の知識に
応える行為を加えよ，信仰を加えよ，
徳と忍耐と節制を加えよ，愛を加えよ，
いずれ charity と呼ばれ，一切の
魂となる愛を。

　ミカエルは，これによって人は「はるかに幸せな楽園」(12.587) を獲得すると言ってアダムを激励する。命じられた持ち場に急ぐケルビムが丘から平地に降る様子は，流星のごとく (meteorous) (629) 地面を這い，夕霧 (evening mist) (629) が家路を急ぐ農夫のかかとにまとわりつくようだ。エデンは最早や永遠ではない。ときは夕刻，罪を犯した二人は既に時間の世界にいる。二人は安息の地を求めて荒野の長い道のりをさまよわねばならないが，そのための精神的武器はさずかっている。ケルビムは，夕霧が農夫を憩いの場に導くように，二人を安息の場へと導いてくれる。そして燃える剣は，二人が艱難を耐え永遠の生命に到達せよとの神の思し召しだ。「真理のために受難することは最高の勝利に至る勇気であり，信仰厚き者にとり死は生命への入り口である」'suffering for truth's sake / Is fortitude to highest victory, / And to the faithful death the gate of life' (12.569–571) と言うように，アダムは「忍耐の勇気と英雄的殉死」'fortitude / Of patience and heroic martyrdom' (9.31–32) という忍耐の原型をキリストにおいて理解しているのである。

　聖書に基く楽園追放の場面にアウグスティヌスは二つの霊的な意味を読み取った。ミルトンは *Paradise Lost* の最終場面までに忍耐と愛 (charity) の二つのすすめを十分に説明した。アウグスティヌスをこの場面に読み込むこと

はキリスト教徒の原型としてのアダムとイーヴをより明白にしたことになろう。

ここで再び聖書の記録を見よう：'he [Lord God] placed at the east of the garden of Eden Cherubims, and a flaming sword which turned every way, to keep the way of the tree of life.' (AV: Gen.3.24)。*Paradise Lost* では，ケルビムが打ち振る神の剣（12.633）は楽園の東側いっぱいに振られ，門にはケルビムの恐ろしい顔と炎の武器が群がっていた，とある：

Waved over by that flaming brand, the gate
With ***dreadful faces*** thronged and ***fiery arms***:
(12.643–644. brand, i.e., sword (poetic): Fowler)

644行目は聖書もアウグスティヌスも触れない。何故「恐ろしい」のか，何故「剣」のほかに「武器」を加えたのか。

　楽園追放はたしかに神の慈愛と正義（'mercy and justice', *PL* 3.132）を顕かにするものである。加えて，この最終場面にはもう一つのテクストが背後にあるように思われる。それは文芸上の「模倣論」に関わる。その枠組みと展開を1964年C. S. ルイスは次のように語っている。中世におけるモデルとしての世界観はルネサンス期を経て17世紀へ，そしてそれを跨ぐまで，個人の創作の枠組みをつくった（Lewis 13）。創作とはシステムとして蓄積されてきた歴史の中から継承に値するものを選ぶことであり，その結果としてのテクストはモデルの模倣であった（歴史的素描の試みは『英詩評論』21号参照）。17世紀，ミルトンもこの伝統に無縁ではない。*The Reason of Church-Government* 『教会統治の原則』（1642）の中で，キリスト教叙事詩人として「全土にわたり我が同胞が持つ最も秀れ最も賢明な資質を母国語にて代弁する語り部」'an interpreter & relater of the best and sagest things among mine own Citizens throughout this Iland in the mother dialect' （*CPW* 1.811–812）にならんとの決意を述べている。続いて，己れの国のために叙事詩を書いたギリシャのホーマー，ローマのヴァージル，イタリアのタッソー，ヘブライの『ヨブ記』の

作者に言及する (813)。この直前,アリオストーの例をにらみながら彼は,ラテン語で書くならばラテン詩人の中で第2位になることさえ難しいとほのめかしている：'it would be hard to arrive at the second rank among the Latines' (810–811; n.71 を参照)。彼はタッソーやアリオストー（あるいはダンテ）が考えたと同様にヴァージルをモデルと考えていて,「彼に次いで第2位にさえ…」と言っているように思われる。モデルとテクストの関係から言えば,ヴァージルの *Aeneid* をモデルとして Christian epic を「英語で」書くという決意を読み取ることができる。

Paradise Lost に至る前に,この 1642 年の決意はまず prose epic である『英国民の擁護』*A Defense of the People of England* (1651) に結実する。それは 12 章から成り,*Aeneid* の 12 歌を踏襲するかのような構成を持つ。続いて *A Second Defence* (1654) の中でミルトンは「模倣」の方法について述べている：'the epic poet ...undertakes to extol, not the whole life of the hero ..., but usually one event of his life (the exploits of Achilles at Troy, ... or the return of Ulysses, or the arrival of Aeneas in Italy) and passes over the rest' (*CPW* 4.pt.1.685)「叙事詩人は…主人公の全生涯ではなく,通常一つの事件（トロイでのアキレスの武勇,ユリシーズの帰郷,アエネーアースのイタリア上陸など）を称揚することを努めとして,他は無視する。」これは二つのテクストを念頭に置いたものであろう。即ち,アリストテレス（「ホメーロスは,…トロイアー戦争さえも,それが初めと終わりをもっているにもかかわらず,その全体をそのまま詩につくることは試みなかった…。実際にはホメーロスは,（トロイアー戦争の全体から）一部分だけを取りあげ,でき事の多くを場面として用いた」（松本・岡訳『詩学』23））と,以下に述べるホラティウスである。

　ギリシャのモデルを凌駕しようとしたローマ詩人の努力についてホラティウスは言う：「我がローマ詩人たちはギリシャ詩歌のあらゆる文体を試してみたし,彼らの足跡を敢えて離れ我が母国の偉業を歌い上げて不名誉の誇りをうけることはない」（*Ars Poetica* 285–287）。ローマ詩人にとって模倣は継承と創造のための文化運動であった。ホラティウスが,独創性を求める詩人に勧める重要なポイントは,よく知られた題材（fama 119, publica materies 131）を

如何に利用するかであり，新たな題材を工夫するよりも悲劇に (in actus) (129) 仕立てるほうが独創的になると言う (128–130)。更に安易な真似を戒め，叙事詩の事件についてホーマーが見せる技を模倣するように奨める (131–152)。彼はアリストテレス (『詩学』第 23 章) に依拠しながら (岡 272. 注 11)，トロイ戦争をヘレンの誕生から始めることをせず (147)，絶えず結末に向かって急ぎ，「事件の中核から始める」(in medias res) (148) に見られる「配置」，「選択」(relinquit 150)，「虚実混合」(創意となる) (mentitur...veris falsa remiscet 151) を奨める。従って，上でミルトンはホラティウスの「選択」に言及していることになる。なお，ドライデン (John Dryden) はヴァージルが題材を common fame から得ていると言っているのは (Ker II.199)，ホラティウスの fama, publica materies に拠っていると思われる。

Paradise Lost は，ホラティウスに見られる古典模倣論の伝統の中で *Aeneid* をモデルとして書かれた叙事詩ということになろう。結論的に言えば，ミルトンは構造的には *Aeneid* の「航海」，「歴史」，「追放」，「戦い」を選んだ。これらは，ドライデンの表現では，建物の柱にあたるものである (Ascham 125 が念頭にあるのかも知れない)。アエネーアースの追放はサタンと人 (アダムとイーヴ) が担い，ローマを建設することになるトロイ人の再生の歴史は，人の堕落と再生の連続の末，キリストによる人類再生の歴史にとってかわる。敗北・追放ののちアエネーアースの遭難と航海は，サタンが演ずる。イタリア上陸後，イタリア建国のためトゥルヌスに対するアエネーアースの戦いは，サタンの二つの戦い (天上における神と御子に対する戦いと，アダムとイーヴに対する誘惑という心理的戦い) に変えた。

我々が上に選んだテクストは *Paradise Lost* 中，人が楽園から追放される場面である。第一の追放では，御子の武力によってサタンと一味が天上から排除される：

>   Him the almighty power
> Hurled headlong *flaming* from the ethereal sky
> With hideous *ruin and combustion* down
>   To bottomless perdition, ... (1.44–47 斜体付加)

文学テクストの重層性

　　　　　その者を全能の神は力いっぱい
清らかな天空から真っ逆さまに投げおとされた。炎に包まれると，
恐ろしい転落と共に怯えながら，下へ，
底なしの破滅へと落ちていった。

火炎に包まれた墜落は神の怒りの象徴である。この場面は更に以下のように詳述される。

> [the Son] Drove them before him *thunderstruck*, pursued
> With *terrors* and with *furies* to the bounds
> And crystal wall of heav'n, which op'ning wide,　　　　860
> Rolled inward, and a spacious gap disclosed
> Into the wasteful deep; the monstrous sight
> Strook them with *horror* backward, but far worse
> Urged them behind; headlong themselves they threw
> Down from the verge of heav'n, *eternal wrath*　　　　865
> *Burnt* after them to the bottomless pit. (6.858–866 斜体付加)

御子は雷電で打って一味を追いたて，
恐怖と憤怒をもって天の端，水晶の壁まで
追撃すると，それは大きく開いて
内側に回転し，荒涼たる深みに向って
広大な空洞を露わに見せた。みな奇怪な光景に
恐怖に打たれて後ずさりした，が背後から
息詰まる恐怖が背を押した。一味は逆さまに
天の端から墜落した。永遠の憤怒が
彼らを追って底なしの地獄まで燃えた。

御子の立位に対する嫉妬から神の王国に謀反をおこした天使が，サタンとなって一味を率い戦いを挑んだその結果被った敗北である。サタン自身が語る状況は次の通りである：

> the *sulphurous* hail
> Shot after us in storm, o'erblown hath laid
> The *fiery* surge, that from the precipice
> Of heaven received us falling, and the *thunder*,
> Winged with *red lightning* and impetuous *rage*,　　　　175
> Perhaps hath spent his shafts, and ceases now
> To bellow through the vast and boundless deep.（1.171–177 斜体付加）

　　　　　　我々の背後から嵐のように
　射かけられた硫黄のあられ弾が止んで，
　天の絶壁から墜落した我らを受け止めた
　うねる火焔も静まった。赤い稲妻と
　激しい突風の翼もつ雷鳴も
　射矢を尽くしたのであろう，今は
　広大無限の深みに轟きわたることはない。

　これは *Aeneid* 的エピックの伝統に則るものである。第二の追放においても，神に対する謀反ゆえに人は楽園から排除されなければならない。しかも天と違って地上の楽園は修復されるものではなく消滅する定めにある。しかし第二もエピック的であって，第一との共通点を持っている。即ち，恐怖（威嚇）と火炎である。特に 859 行目 'terrors and ... furies' は 'dreadful faces...and fiery arms' (12.644) を想起させる。聖書にもアウグスティヌスの釈義にも見られない恐怖と武力のイメジ (arms) を付加したことは叙事詩の伝統を踏まえた結果と思われる。*Aeneid* では，凶暴極まりない女神ユーノーが剣を帯び，西城門を占拠する (II.612–613)，女神パラスが城塞頂上を占領し，武器は雷雲とともに猛り狂うゴルゴンの如く輝く (II.615–616)。指摘されるように (Bowra 41; Martindale 134; Steadman 56–57)，アエネーアース一族郎党を追い出す，トロイに敵対する偉大な神々の恐ろしい形相が出現する：'apparent *dirae facies* inimicaque Troiae/ numina magna deum.'「そしてトロイに敵対する恐ろしい顔が浮かび出る，それは偉大な神々の神霊なり」(*Aen*. II.622–623 斜体付加)。

　1642 年，ミルトンはキリスト教徒であることを特に意識して，ホーマー，

ヴァージルやカトリックのタッソーと違って,「キリスト教徒であることの優位に応じて」'in my proportion with this over and above of being a Christian' (*CPW* 1.812) 叙事詩人として同胞を教化するとの決意を述べた。そして 1651 年,散文叙事詩と称しうる *A Defence of the People of England* において英国の自由擁護のために尽くし,その大義を国内外に擁護して同胞の栄誉を高め後世への模範としたと,のち *A Second Defense* (1654) において自らを称えた (*CPW* 4.pt.1.684–685)。そして今,*Paradise Lost* において,キリスト教叙事詩であるが故にヴァージルを凌駕する (emulate) という生涯の仕事を成し遂げようとする。

　ヴァージルの神々のあるものはアエネーアースに敵対した。ミルトンもアダムとイーヴを追放する恐ろしい,火炎を振る天使軍を配置した。叙事詩的装置は共通するが,彼らは人の新たな旅の出発を見守っている。一見恐怖に満ちているけれども,すべて神の恩寵が働いている。アウグスティヌスのキリスト教釈義とヴァージル的要素の融合,すなわちキリスト教と叙事詩の伝統の融合は,さらに精神性と物質性・身体性の対比によって見事に締めくくられることになる。堕落以前の楽園では,アダムとイーヴは完全で欠けるところなく,アダムは「自らの完全無欠な美徳という供をつれて」いて (5.351–353 平井正穂訳),イーヴには「魅惑的な優美がそなわり,女王にかしずく風情であった」(8.60–61)。しかし堕落した今は,二人共に「摂理」Providence を導き手として荒野に旅立つことになる。摂理は人の小さな振る舞いにも及ぶとして,ミルトンは『ヨブ記』34.21 から引用している:「神の目が人の道の上にあって,そのすべての歩みを見られるからだ」'for his eyes are turned towards each man's ways, and he counts all his steps" (*CPW* 6.329)。一方アエネーアースは「聖物と一族の守り神」'sacra…patriosque Penatis' (*Aen.* II.717),「神々の聖なる像,トロイの守り神」'effigies sacrae divum Phrygiique Penates' (3.148) と呼ぶ一族の宝物に守られてトロイ城をあとにし,目指す約束の地イタリアに苦難の旅に出る。ミルトンはこの最終場面において,楽園をあとに安息の地に向けて孤独の旅に出る二人に,偶像の守り神とは対照的に,生ける神の摂理を導き手として対置することによって,キリスト教叙事詩の意味を闡明にしたと思われる。

テクスト

Ascham, Roger（1934 [1570]）*The Scholemaster*（ed. D. C. Whimster）. London: Methuen.

Augustine（1998）*De Genesi: Contra Manichaeos*（CSEL 91）（ed. Dorothea Weber）. Vienna: Verlag der Österreichischen Akademie der Wissenschaftten.

Dryden, John（1961）*Essays of John Dryden*, 2 vols.（ed. W. P. Ker）. NY: Russell and Russell.

Horace（1999）*Satires, Epistles and Ars Poetica*（Loeb Classical Library 194）（trans. H. R. Fairclough）. Cambridge, Massachusetts: Harvard University Press.

Milton, John（1998）*Paradise Lost*, Second Edition（ed. Alastair Fowler）. London and NY: Longman.

Milton, John（1953–82）*Complete Prose Works of John Milton*（CPW）（ed. D. M. Wolfe）. New Haven: Yale University Press.

Virgil（1960 [1934]）*Aeneid*, 2 vols.（Loeb Classical Library 64）（trans. H. R. Fairclough）. Cambridge, Massachusetts: Harvard University Press.

清水正照（訳）（1995）『アウグスティヌス　創世記逐語的注解』九州大学出版会.

平井正穂（訳）（1981）『失楽園』（上下）岩波書店.

松本仁助・岡道男（訳）（2003）『アリストテレース詩学　ホラーティウス詩論』岩波書店.

参考文献

Bowra, C. M.（1957）*From Virgil to Milton*. London: Macmillan.

Fiore, P. M.（1981）*Milton and Augustine*. University Park and London: Pennsylvania State University Press.

Lewis, C. S.（1964）*The Discarded Image*. Cambridge: Cambridge University Press.

Lewis[2], C. S.（1942）*A Preface to Paradise Lost*. Oxford: Oxford University Press.

Martindale, Charles（2002）*John Milton and the Transformation of Ancient Epic*. London: Bristol Classical Press.

Steadman, J. M.（1984）*Milton's Biblical and Classical Imagery*. Pittsburgh: Duquesne University Press.

上利政彦（2005）「ルネサンス模倣論とミルトン」『英詩評論』21（中四国ロマン派学会）42–51.

第 4 部

歴史辞書を読む

語学研究における辞書の役割
―― 初期の英語辞書を中心にして ――

和 田　章

はじめに

語義集で様々な配列法が試みられて[1]，検索に便利なアルファベット順配列が定着し，17世紀に英語辞書は十分な学識のない人の教化を目的として始まった。これらの辞書は今日の精緻な辞書より簡単とはいえ，その方式，内容から英語の種々の語の歴史を読み取ることができる。これらの辞書は，当時の難解語が対象であり，時の流れに揉まれ今では多くが平易語である。このような語は過去を背にして現在を生きている歴史の産物である。18世紀になると，英語辞書は難解語に加え平易語も扱う。しかし Johnson (1755) 以前の18世紀前半の辞書では，平易語は，自明の語という理由なのか，記述が簡単か，その多数が取り上げすらされていない。

　本論の大区分は，三つとし，1では，初期時代の英語辞書，特に17–18世紀の英語辞書数点を紹介する。これらの辞書と比較のため又は補足として，*OED* はじめ現代の辞書にも適宜言及する。(1.3–1.11)

　2, 3 は，語学研究における辞書の役割をこれらの英語辞書その他を利用して示す一つの試みである。

　2 では，これら初期の英語辞書が扱う語が今日とは異なる考え，解釈を示す例を二，三述べる。語の現代とは異なる過去の意味を見逃さないためには，英語辞書の王者 *OED* はじめ初期の辞書は強力な助けとなる。(2.1–2.7)

---

[1]　語彙集の配列順の推移は Murray (1900: 10–12) と，林 (1985: 5–7) が詳しい。

3 では，これら英語辞書に加え 15–17 世紀の羅英，伊英，仏英などの 2 言語辞書も利用して，英語の四季語のうち春と秋の呼称が不安定な変遷を経て spring と autumn / fall に定着することを扱う。(3.1)

付記として辞書関連文献の簡単な紹介をする。(3.2)

略号

Early ModE	Early Modern English
EETS, o.s. / e.s.	Early English Text Society, original series / extra series
ME	Middle English
n. s.	noun substantive[2]
OE	Old Englsih
ON	Old Norse
q.	quoted, quotation

文献の略号は，編・著者名と括弧内に出版年を記す。編・著者名のない略号は参照文献の欄に記してある。その他説明を脚注でしている略号もある。

1　初期の英語辞書——難語辞書から一般語辞書へ——

難語辞書 (1604–1676) と一般語辞書 (1702–1721) は，後続の辞書になるほどに内容を充実させ，英語辞書発達の歴史をしるした。難語辞書は，柱の外来語に加えて専門用語，古語，固有名，方言，隠語にも記述を広げ，18 世紀には，これらに加え誰しも知る平易語が英語辞書で扱われた。

1.1　英英辞書不要の考え

16 世紀には，羅英辞書，伊英辞書など，外国語を英語で説明する 2 言語辞書

---

[2]　本論では，Johnson (1755) と Todd's Johnson (1818) の用例に現れる。今日の通常の呼称 adjective 及び noun をかつて noun adjective と noun substantive に分ける呼称があった。

はあり，母語を母語で説明する英英辞書はなかった。生国の空気を吸い，母乳を吸えば覚える生得の英語に解説書は不要という大真面目な言い分を，Murray (1900: 26-27) は，昔物語として語っている。

1.2　Edmund Coote (1596) *The English Schoole-maister*
　　――英英辞書の先駆け――

母語の英語にも，印刷本の流布による読者層の拡大，外来語の流入，なかんずく 16 世紀のラテン語の洪水で，これら難解語を理解しない人々に解説書が必要となった。それに応えた書に Edmund Coote (1596) がある。本書巻末の語彙表 (*A Table*) は，約 1,500 語を収録し (林 1985: 139)，難解語がアルファベット順に配列され，語釈は「平易な英語で」を旨とした。語釈なしで見出しだけの語は正しい綴字を示すためとある (e.g. anchor)。ラテン語由来の見出し語はローマン体で (e.g. agent **doer**)，フランス語由来の見出し語はイタリック体 (e.g. *accord* **agreement**) で示され，ギリシア語由来の語は，g./gr. が語釈の前に付される (e.g. agonie g. **heauie passion**)。語の由来の区別は，語の難易度などの手掛りとなり得たろうし，又後世の英語辞書の語源項目の萌芽でもあろう。本書翻刻版（南雲堂，1971 年）の解説者豊田昌倫氏は，「難解な語に英語による説明を並置する Coote の語彙表は，英語辞典の雛形ともいうべきものであり… Robert Cawdrey の *A Table Alphabeticall* ... (1604) に大きな影響を及ぼすことになる。」(p. 375) と述べている。実際 Coote (1596) の記述形式，内容の大部分が Cawdrey (1604) へ移動している。

1.3　難語の解説から始まった英語辞書 Robert Cawdrey, ed. (1604) *A Table Alphabeticall*

Coote (1596) の方式を踏襲し，見出し語[3] を増やし，解説内容を追加した，

---

3) Cawdrey (1604) の語数は，Schäfer (1970: 35) によると約 2,500 で，林 (1985: 144, 263) によると約 3,000 である。私が数えた見出し語数は，2 桁数字を無視するなら，2,500 以上 2,600 以下である。

Robert Cawdrey, ed. (1604) が，英語辞書の嚆矢であった。本書をどんぐりの種として，オークの大木に育ったのが *OED* だと譬えられることもある[4]。

A Table Alphabeticall は更に，「難解ではあるが…通常用いられる英語を書き理解することを教え，貴顕の女性，その他読み書きを不得手とする人々のために難語を平易な言葉で説明し」と続く。

難語は French, Latin, Greek 由来の語が主である。見出し語に続く (g.), (gr.) は，ギリシア語系を表す。見出し語の前の § は，フランス語系を表す。記号なしの語はラテン語由来と断ってあるものの，その他の外来語 (e.g. **abba**, father. [Aramic]; **ay**,[5] euer, at any time, for euer [ON]) 又本来語 (e.g. **throtle**, strangle, hang or torment / **thwite**, shave) にも記号はない。語釈の前の (k) は，a kind of の略号である。

(1) 　§**ABandon**, cast away, or yéelde vp, to leaue, or forsake. / **absurd**, foolish, irksome. / §**action**, the forme of a suite / **admire**, maruell at, or be in loue with / **admission**, receiuing, or leaue to enter into a place, accept. / **adorne**, beautifie, apparell, prepare. / **agonie**, (gr) heauie passion, anguish, griefe / **apt**, fit. / **azure**, (k) of colour. / § **cancell**, to vndoe, deface, crosse out, or teare / **centre**,[6] (g) middest of any round thing or circle.

400 年以上経過した今では，上の見出し語は難解の段階は脱している。

1.4　Cawdrey (1604) 後の難語辞書

続く難語辞書は，17 世紀の間収録語数を増やしつつ出版された。以下次の書を取り上げた。収録語数付きの辞書は林 (1985: 263) による。

---

4)　*OED* (1933) Historical Introduction, vii.

5)　Ay の難語扱いは，archaic or obsolete という意味合いであろう。Bullokar (1616) と Cockeram (1626[2]) は，古の作家が用いただけの古い語に星印 (*) を付すと述べ (to the Reader), **Aye*, For euer. としている。

6)　16–18 世紀では *center* の方が広く普及しており，Johnson (1755) *centre* がイギリス綴りを決定づけた (*OED* centre, center)。本論で扱う文献の例は次の通り。Coote (1596) centre / Cawdrey (1604) centre / Bullokar (1616) *Center* / Cockeram (1626[2]) *Center* / Blount (1656) centre / Phillips (1658) *Center* / Coles (1676) *Center, -tre,* / Kersey (1702) Center / Bailey (1721) CENTER / Dyche-Pardon (1754[8]) CE′NTER or CE′NTRE.

John Bullokar, ed. (1616)（収録語数 6,000）

Henry Cockeram, ed. (1626²) 第 1 版は 1623 年。

Thomas Blount, ed. (1656)

Edward Phillips, ed. (1658)（収録語数 11,000）

Elisha Coles, ed. (1676)（収録語数 30,000）

これら難語辞書は，現在の我々には，一般語，古語，廃語などへの過程を知る上で好都合な手掛りとなる。

1.5　John Bullokar, ed. (1616) *An English Expositor*

この難語辞書で，Cawdrey (1604) よりも法律などの専門用語が格段に増えた。また Bullokar は，Cawdrey (1604) が記さなかった古語の印として * を付した[7]。* 付きの語数は，Schäfer (1970: 36) によると 140 を超える。

(2)　　***Alnath**. A starre in the hornes of the signe *Aries*.[8] / ***Bargaret**. A kind of dance.

(3)　　**Abate**. To make lesse: In our common Law it signifieth, to enter into any inheritance, before the right heire take possession, with intent to keepe the said heire out of it. / **Abatement**. The action or enterprise of him which abateth in the common Lawe.[9]

1.6　Henry Cockeram, ed. (1626²) *The English Dictionarie: or, An Interpreter of Hard English Words*

この辞書は 3 部構成で，第 1 部は，現用の選り抜かれた語集（"the choicest words ... now in vse"）が中心で，同時に廃用の語も * 印付きで扱っている。

---

7) "euery word marked with this marke * is an olde word, onely vsed of some ancient writers, and now growne out of vse"（An Instruction to the Reader）

8) Alnath は Cawdrey (1604), Cockeram (1626²) になく，Blount (1656), Phillips (1658), Coles (1676) に受け継がれる。

9) Cf. Schäfer (1970: 35): Particularly conspicuous among Bullokar's new lemmas are the legal terms often introduced with a reference to "our common law."

(4) ***Abandon***. To forsake, or cast off. / ***Abate***. To make lesse, diminish, or to take from. / *Abbreuiate*. To make short, to abridge. / *Abhorre*, To shunne or disdaine. / ***Bardes***, Ancient Poets. / *Barrester*, One allowed to plead at a barre. / *Calculate*, To reckon, to cast account. / *Compose*, To frame, to set together. / *Experiment*, To find by tryall. / **Probabilitie**, Great appearance of truth.

第 2 部は，日常語（"vulgar [= Common, much vsed] words"）が見出し語でそれに対応する洗練された表現が説明される。いわば第 1 部の見出し語と語釈を逆転させた扱いで，これさえ利用すれば，平凡な表現も洗練された優雅な文体に変換できると，Cockeram は言い，凡人も Oxford 大学学生クラブ弁論会に一矢報いる書き方が可能と，Murray (1900: 29)[10] は持ち上げた。

(5) **To Abate or take away**, *Deduct, Deduce*.[11] / **to Agree**, *Concurre, Cohere, Condog, Condiscend*. / **a casting of Accompt**, *Calculation*. / **the Art of well-speaking**, *Rhetoricke*. / **a Doing againe**, *Iteration*. / **ill Doing**, *Maleficence*.

第 3 部は，Gods and Goddesses, Men and Women, etc. の豆百科事典である。

(6) ***Apollo***, and *Æsculipius*, gods of Phisicke and Surgerie. / ***Pytho***, the goddesse of eloquence.

1.7　Thomas Blount, ed. (1656) *Glossographia: or A Dictionary, Interpreting all such Hard Words ... as are now used in our refined English Tongue*

1.7.1　語源付きの辞書

本書は，見出し語に続き（　）内に語源を示す。（　）内に語形のみの例は大

---

10) "The plain man or gentlewoman may write a letter in his or her natural language, and then by turning up the simple words in the dictionary alter them into their learned equivalents. Thus ... 'he and I are of one age' [may be altered] into *we are coetaneous*, ... — a useful expression to hurl at an opponent in the Oxford Union."

11) 第 1 部の難語である見出し語 *Abate を第 2 部で，平易な語の見出し語とするのは，矛盾である。この項は，見出し To Take away で扱うべきだったろう。

方ラテン語由来，ときにギリシア語由来である。

(7) **Accurate** (*accuratus*) curious, diligent. / To **Cheve** (*Sax.*) to thrive. *Chaucer*. / **Largesse** (Fr.) bounty, liberality; handfuls of money cast among people, or a Donative bestowed on Souldiers. / **Monks** (from the Gr. *monos*, because they live alone or solitary) a sort of religious people, whereof there are divers sorts, as those of St. *Benedict*, St. *Bazil*, St. *Hierome*, &c.

1.7.2 事典風な詳細な説明

学術，宗教，制度，法などの語（多くは名詞）の説明は一般に長く詳細である。引用は短い説明の例である。

(8) **Accent** (*accentus*) tune, tenor, the rising and falling of the voice, the due sound over any word or letter, or the mark of any letter which directs the pronunciation. There are also *Accents* of sentences; As in the close of a Period we let fall the voice, in a demand raise it.

1.8 Edward Phillips, ed. (1658) *The New World of English Words: or, a General Dictionary*

本書には書名に "*a General Dictionary*" とあるものの，一般語辞書ではなく難語辞書である。Phillips の dictionary の解釈は，

(9) ***Dictionary***, (lat.) called in Greek a Lexicon, a Book wherein hard words and names are mentioned and unfolded.

で，外来系難語と芸術，専門語，詩語，等々を扱う。特に固有名が多く，人名 (given names) には本来の意味の説明が付く。

1.8.1 外来語（専門語を含む）

(10) To ***Adjourn*** (French) to warn one to appear at the day appointed, also to put off a day. A word used in Common Law. / ***Adjunct***, (Latin) a quality adhering to any thing, as heat to fire, greenness to grass, &c. a term used in logick. / ***Bucoliks***, (Greek) pastoral songs.

1.8.2　Old Words[12]

(11)　***Agast***, (old word) dismaid with fear.[13] / ***Ay***, (old word) an Egg. / ***Aye***, (old word) for ever. / ***Bargaret***, (old word) a Sonnet, or Ballet.

1.8.3　地名・人名 (surnames & given names)

(12)　***Budaris***, a Citie of Germany, belonging to the Pals-grave, now called *Heidelbergh*. / ***Sidneys***, the sirname of a very honourable Family, whose chief seat is *Pensherst* in *Kent*; they derive themselves from *William de Sidney* Chamberlain to King *Henry* the second; but the flower and chief glory of this Family, was that most accomplisht Gentleman Sir *Philip Sidney* [.] / ***Charles***, a proper name contracted from the Dutch words *Gar*, and *Ethel*, signifying all Noble.[14] / ***Daniel***, (Hebr.) judgement of God. / ***Eadgar***, (Sax.) happy power.

1.8.4　†印付きの見出し語

Phillips は The Preface (c2–c2b) で，†付きの語は，自然で気取らない表現には勧められない不自然な語であると述べている。

(13)　†***Abaction***, (Latin) *a driving, or forcing away.* / †***Bulimy***, (Greek) insatiable hunger.

1.9　Elisha Coles, ed. (1676) *An English Dictionary*

語数は，今までのどの辞書よりも多く，Coles は "almost thirty thousand" (*To*

---

12) Phillips (1658) は，古語，廃語には，見出しの後に (old word) と記し，次節の Coles (1676) も，old word の省略記号 *o.* を付す。先に述べた Bullokar (1616)，Cockeram (1626²) は本来語の古語，廃語に * を付す。
　Phillips (1658) の (old word) と (Saxon) [e.g. **Scyld**, (Saxon) debt, or default.] の区別は判然としない。*MED*, shild が OE の例のみ引用していることからして，まして 17 世紀では scyld は (old word) であったろう。

13) Cf. Bullokar (1616), Cockeram (1626²) の agast には古語の印 * は付されていない: ***Agast***, Amazed with feare, dismaide.

14) 今日では別の解釈がなされている。Cf. Withycombe. (1950²): **Charles** (m.) : ...Old German *carl* (Old English *ceorl*) 'a man'. *Karl* or *Carl* was latinized as Carolus, whence the French Charles....

the Reader) と記す。ラテン語，ギリシア語，フランス語，ヘブライ語等の外来語と，Blount などが多くは扱わなかった "Old Words" も現用の語にも光を当てるとして，採用された。高尚な表現のためには "Latin, Greek or French" の印 (*l., g., f.*) 付きの語を参照するようにと Coles は言っている。

1.9.1 Old Words（略号 *o.*）

(14) ***Agast***, *o. Amazed.* / ***Algate***, *o.* Altogether, if so be, notwithstanding. / ***Chepe***, *o.* buy. / ***Chese***, *o.* chose.

Old Words には，OE 系の語の他に外来借用語も含まれる。

(15) ***Desidery***, *o.* desire, lust. ◊ *OED*, desidery, [a. OF. ...] *Obs. rare* c1450–1513.

1.9.2 French

(16) ***Affront***, *f.* wrong. / ***Chivalrie***, *f.* horsemanship, also a tenure by Knights service. / ***Embellish***, *f.* beautify.

1.9.3 Latin

(17) ***Agent***, *l.* Doer, also a dealer for another. / ***Diary***, *l.* a day-book. / ***Pejorate***, *l.* to make or grow worse.

1.9.4 Greek

(18) ***Agony***, *g.* Extream anguish of mind or death. / ***Atheism***, *g.* the Doctrine of an | ***Atheist***, who believes there is no God.

1.9.5 Canting

Coles は，洗練表現に加え，巷の方言，隠語（"Canting"）に注目した。"Canting Terms" の理解で，財布をすられたり，喉を搔っ切られたりされないで済むと Coles は言う (*To the Reader*): "It [*i.e.* to understand the Canting Terms] may chance to save your throat from being cut, or (at least) your Pocket from being pickt."

略号：C. (*Canting*)

(19) **_Darkmans_**, *c.* night, evening. ◊*Thieves' cant.* (*OED*) / **_Dimber_**, *c.* pretty. ◊ q. in Partridge *DU*³. / **_Dup_**, *c.* enter [the house] ◊ q. in Partridge *DU*³. / **_Ken_**, *c. a* house. / **_Milken_**, *c.* a house-breaker. ◊ Cf. *OED*, mill-ken. / **_Mill_**, *c.* to steal.

1.9.6　Dialects

方言区分は 10 以上で，小規模辞書にしては細かい。

(20) **_Daft_**, *No[ttinghamshire]*. stupid, blockish. / **_Dazed_** [bread,] Dough-baked, *Li[ncolnshire]*. / I's *Dazed*, I'm very cold, no. / **_Doundrins_**, *Der[bishire]*. afternoons drinkins. ◊ Cf. *EDD*, DOWNDRINS, *sb. pl.* downdring Der. Afternoon 'drinkings.'; *EDD*, DRINKING, *sb.* 1. Food taken between regular meals[.] / **_Eem_**, *Che[shire]*. to have leisure, to spare time.

1.10　John Kersey, ed. (1702) *A New English Dictionary*

18 世紀初頭，難語・術語（"*Difficult Words and Terms of Art*"）と一般語も含めた辞書が出版された。これは当初の一般語の記述方法を知る上で貴重な文献と言えよう。

1.10.1　前置詞などの不変化詞

機能語には語釈なしで用例一つの記述が目立つ。

(21) **About**, as *about Noon*. / **At**, *as*, *at first sight*. / **Before**, *long before*. / **In**, *as in times pass'd*. / **On**, *or* upon [.] / **Upon**, *or on*; as *upon that day*. / **With**, as *I was with him*.

(22) **As**, even as, like as, *&c.* / **Back**, *as to give back*, or *recoil*. / **The**, *as* the *one of them is living* the *other dead*.

1.10.2　動詞

語釈のある例，用例のみの例が混在する。語釈も同義語による例が多く，多義語 come, cut, etc. の語釈は，誰しも知る語で語釈は不必要ということなのか，"(*in all senses*)" と記している。動詞の見出しには to が付される。助動

詞 may すら To may が見出しである。

1.10.2.1 見出しのみ

(23) *A* **Cry**, *and to* **cry**. / **Drink**, *and to* **drink**.

1.10.2.2 説明が (*in all senses.*), (*in all its senses*) の動詞

(24) *To* **come** / *A* **Cut**, *and to* **cut** / *To* **draw** / *A* **Fall**, *and to* **fall** / *To* **give** / *To* **go** / *To* **Keep** / *A* **Look**, *and to* **look** / *To* **make** / *A* **Play**, *and to* **play** / *To* **put** / *A* **Set**, *and to* **set** / *A* **Stand**, *and to* **stand** / *Use*, *and to use* / **Will**, *and to* **will** [.] ◊多義語 be, do は *To* **be**, or exist. / *To* **do**, or *act*, &c. とあるのみ。

1.10.2.3 動詞の見出し語に連語を添えて語釈に代える

連語のみの例と，これに語釈が併記される例がある。

(25) *To* **dream** *a dream in ones sleep*. / *To* **drive**, *a cart*, *coach*, *cattel*, &c. *or to force*. / *To* **fly**, *as a bird does*; *to run away*, *or escape by flight*.

1.10.2.4 助動詞と本動詞の区別

(26) **Have**; as, *I have loved*. / *To* **have**, *possess*, *obtain*, &c.

1.10.2.5 助動詞

(27) *I* **can**, or *am able*. / *I* **Cannot**, or *am not able*. / **Can't**, *for cannot*. / *To* **may** or *can*; as *if you will you may*. / **Must**, as *it must be done*. / **Ought**, or *should*, as *it ought to be so*. / **Shall**, *the sign of the future Tense*; as *I shall live*.

1.10.2.6 過去形などの不規則な活用形

(28) *I* **came**, or *did come*. / **Done**, or *acted* (*from to do*.) ◊ did の見出しなし。/ **Gone** (*from to* go.) *I* **Went**, or *did goe*. / **Knew**, (*from to* know) ◊ 見出しのみ: **Known**. / **Might**, as *I might* (*from to* may.) / *I* **saw**, or *did s[e]e*. **Seen** (*from to* see.) / *It* **should**, or ought. / **Was**; as *I was with him*. **Were** (*from to* be;) as *I wish he were gone*. / *I* **VVould** (*from to* will.).

1.10.2.7　動詞と同形名詞，動詞の派生形を利用

(29)　　To **care**, or *take care*. / To **lie**, or *tell a lie*. To **ly**, or *tell a lie*. / To **want**, *to be wanting*, or *to stand in need of*.

1.10.2.8　同義語による語釈

同義語での説明は簡単で済む。これは，今日の辞書も使う便宜手段である。

(30)　　To **begin**, or *commence*. / To **commence**, *to begin*; or *to take a degree*.

1.10.3　形容詞

(31)　　**Best**, beyond compare. / **Better**, or *of more worth*. / **Good**, *honest, just, profitable, convenient, fair, kind, pleasant*, &c.

1.10.4　名詞

語釈付きの例は多くなるが，卑近な事物を表す語では，語釈は概して簡単で，見出しのみの語又は見出しすらない語もある。加算名詞の見出しに不定冠詞が付されている。この種の語の基本形という理解があるのだろう。以下の引用に不定冠詞の字体がイタリック，ときにローマンという不統一がある。これは原著の字体のまま引用した結果である。また，上記引用で既出している語釈の前のローマン体 or に加え，以下の引用には，見出し語の異綴りの前でイタリック体 *or* が用いられている。

1.10.4.1　動物・植物

(32)　　An **Animal**, or *living creature*. / A **Beast**, or *brute-beast*. / A **Deer**, *a wild beast*. / A **Horse**, *a labouring Beast*. / A **Hound**, or *hunting-dog*. / A **Lion**, *a wild beast*. / A **Monkey**, or *Ape*.

(33)　　"*a beast*" のみの語釈：An **Ape**, A **Bull**, A **Cow**, A **Dog**, An **Elephant**, A **Fox**, A **Goat**, A **Hog**.

(34)　　A **Bird**, or *fowl*. / A **Capon**, or *gelt Cock*. / An **Eagle**, *a bird of prey*. / A **Foul**, or *great bird*. / An **Ostrich**, *or* estrridge, *a great African fowl*.

(35)　　'*a bird*' のみの語釈：A **Crow**, A **Cuckoo**, A **Duck**, A **Lark**, A **Pigeon**, A **Raven**, A **Sparrow**, A **Swallow**.

(36)　　見出しのみ：*A* **Fish**.

(37) "*a fish*" のみの語釈: *A* **Bream**, *A* **Carp**, *An* **Eel**, *A* **Herring**, *A* **Salmon**.
(38) *A* **Mackerel**, *a sea-fish.* / *A* **Tench**, *a fresh-water fish.*
(39) 樹木: *A* **Birch-tree**. / **Fir**, or *a Fir-tree.* / *An* **Oak** or *oak tree.*
(40) **Go-to-bed-at-noon**, *an herb.* ◊ a dialectal name for GOAT'S-BEARD 2. (*OED*, go, *v.* VIII. go-to-bed-at-noon.)

1.10.4.2 食品

(41) *A* **Pie**, or *pasty.* / *A* **Pudding**, (*a dish well known in* England.)
(42) 見出しのみ: *A* **Bisket**. / **Bread**. / **Butter**.
(43) **Ale**, *a well known drink.* / **Tea**, *a plant, and the liquor made of its leaves.*
(44) "*a fruit*" のみの語釈: *A* **Chesnut**, *A* **Cucumber**, *A* **Fig**, *A* **Lemmon**.
(45) *An* **Apple**, *a known fruit.* / *A* **Radish**, *a root.* / **Spinage**, *a pot herb.*
(46) **Beef**, *the flesh of an Ox or Cow.* / **Mutton**, or *sheep-flesh.*

1.10.4.3 身体とその部分

(47) *A* **Body** (*in all senses*) / *A* **Foot** (*in several senses*) / *The* **Leg**, *from the knee to the ankle.* / **Stomack**, *that part which digests the food*[.]

1.10.4.4 数

(48) **One** *in number.* / **Ten**, *in Number*; as *the ten Commandments.* / *A* **hundred** (*in number*) or *the division of a County in* England. / *A* **Thousand** *in number*; as *a thousand pounds.* / *A* **Million**, or *Ten hundred thousand.*

1.10.4.5 複合語・派生語の記述

(49) A **Head**, *and to* **head** (*in all senses.*) | A **Block-head**. | *The* **Head-ach**, *or* head-ake. | A **Head-band** *for a book.* | ....
(50) *The* **heart**. | *The* **Heart-strings**. | A **Sweet-heart**. | **Heart-burning**, *a disease*, or *a grudge*. | **Hearted**; as, | **Faint-hearted**, or *cowardly*. | .... *To* **hearten up**, *animate* or *encourage*. | ...**Heartiness**, or *sincerity*. | **Heartlesness**, *being out of heart*. | **Hearts-ease**, or *content; also an herb*. | **Heartless**, *cowardly*, or *formal*. | **Hearty**, *cordial and sincere*, or *lusty*.
(51) **Pleasant**, *delightful, merry*, or *witty*. | **Pleasantness**. | *To* **please**, *to*

give content, *to delight*, or *humour one*, &c. | **Pleasurable**, *pleasant*, or *agreeable*. | **Pleasure**, *delight*, *content*, *satisfaction*, *a good turn*, &c.| *To* **pleasure**, *do one a pleasure*, or *gratify him*.

1.10.4.6　詳しい説明付きの語

(52)　A **Parliament**, or *general Assembly of the Estates of a Kingdom; in* England *of the three Estates*, viz. *King, Lords Spiritual and Temporal, and Commons*.

1.11　Nathan Bailey, ed. (1721) *An Universal Etymological English Dictionary*

Kersey (1702) のAの1番目の見出し語は **AN ABaisance** で *To* **abandon** へと続くのに対して，Bailey (1721) の見出し語 **To ABANDON** の前に13の見出しがあり，Bailey (1721) は辞書の規模として一歩進んでいる。

　Bailey (1721) は dictionary を次のように定義する。

(53)　**DICTIONARY**, [*Dctionnaire, F. of Dictionarium, L.*] a Collection of all the Words of a Language, explain'd in Alphabetical Order.

しかし本書は "a Collection of all the Words" からはほど遠く[15]，上の定義に用いられている a, all, in は見出しとして現れない。このような不十分な点はあっても，一般語の大幅な採用は英語辞書の前進と言える。

　見出し語に続く［…］は語源欄で，今日では否定されている語源説もあるが，由来する言語名に加えその語形も記したのは評価できよう。以下語源欄は，必要の場合のみ記す。

1.11.1　小辞（前置詞・副詞・冠詞など）

基本語彙中の基本の語釈が，簡単である。見出しすらない語もある。

(54)　**ABOVE**, aloft, higher. / **ABOUT**, as round about, near in Time and Place. / **ABOUT**, *i.e.* doing or about to do, as I am about. / **AGAINST**,

---

15)　Starnes & Noyes (1991: 100): A conservative estimate places Bailey's vocabulary at about 40,000 words[.]

opposite to. / **BY**, beside, or nigh. / **FOR**, a causal Particle. / **ON**, upon. / **THE**, an Article used before Nouns, &c. / **UNDER**, beneath. / **UP**, aloft, high, above. / **UPON**, on some Thing. / **WITH**, a Particle denoting Company or Union, &c.

（55）　**AND**, a Conjunction. / **BUT**, besides, except. / **SINCE**, from that time.

（56）　見出し語と語源のみ：**AFTER**, [from Æfter, *Sax.*] / **AT**, [Æt, *Sax.*] / **BETWEEN**, [Betwýnan *Sax.*] / **BETWIXT**, [Betwix *Sax.*]

見出しなし：**IN, THROUGH.** / **BECAUSE** / 名詞の記載のみ：**AS** / 名詞, 動詞の記載のみ：**BACK**

1.11.2　接頭辞・接尾辞

OE 系の接辞と接辞付きの派生語は手薄である。

1.11.2.1　For-

接頭辞 for- の説明と語釈付き見出しは古語を含め次のような例：

（57）　**FOR**, in Composition denyeth and depriveth, as forbid, forbear, &c. [:]
To **FORDO**, to undo. *Spencer*. / To **FORDOE**, to kill. *O[ld Word]* / To **FORGET**, to let slip out of Memory. / To **FORGIVE**, to pass by a Fault, quit a Debt, &c. / To **FORGOE**, to forsake, give up, quit, &c. a Pretence, &c. / To **FORSAKE**, to leave or quit. / To **FORTHINK**, to be grieved in mind. *O[ld Word]*

1.11.2.2　Un-¹: 否定を表す

（58）　**UN**, a Negative Particle which is joined to abundance of *English* Words, and deprives them of their native Sense[:]
A **LIE**, an untruth. / **UNCOUTH**, foreign, barbarous, harsh, not to be understood[;] also strange, unusual. / **UNKEN'D**, unknown. *Spencer*. / **UNNATURAL**, against Nature; monstrous[.] / **UNTHEWED** Unmannerly. *O[ld Word]*

語釈に見る untruth, unusual, unknown, unmannerly は見出しなし。見出し語選択の重点は，古風な語にある。

1.11.2.3　Un-²: 単純動詞の行為の反対・取り消し・除去を表す接頭辞

この接頭辞の見出しはなく，次のような例：

(59)　To **UNBEND**, to loosen ..., to ease ... ones mind. / To **UNDOE**, to take to pieces what was put together; also to ruin. / To **UNYOKE**, to take off the Yoke from a Beast; to free out of Bondage or Slavery.

他10例余は，航海（e.g. To **UNCLOY** a Piece; To **UNRIG** a Ship），狩猟（e.g. To **UNSTRIKE THE HOOD**），錬金（e.g. To **UNLUTE**）などの術語，古語（e.g. To **UNPLITE**）など。

1.11.2.4　形容詞形成接尾辞 (1) -ISH

接尾辞 -ish も，これを含む形容詞も，ENGLISH, BRITISH などの民族を表す語を除き，他に例を見ない。-ish を伴う語は語釈に用いられ，見出し語にならない規則的な屈折語尾を伴う変化形と同じ扱いに見える[16]。

(60)　**FUTILE**, foolish, silly. F. / **SILLY**, [some derive it of Sillus, L. ... but Skinner rather of **selig**, Teut. Pious, because such are commonly plain-hearted] simple, foolish.

1.11.2.5　形容詞形成接尾辞 (2) -FUL

(61)　**BEAUTEOUS, BEAUTIFUL**, comly, handsome, fair, fine. / **FAITHFUL**, Honest, Sincere, Trusty. / **GRATEFUL**, willing to reward, or make amends for, that acknowledges a favour done, thankful; also agreeable, pleasant. / **THANKFUL**, full of Thanks, Grateful.

語釈の中で見られ見出しにならない語の例：

(62)　**CRUEL**, painful. / **LUCRATIVE**, gainful[.] / **MERRY**, chearful[.] / **TERRIBLE**, dreadful, fearful.

1.11.2.6　副詞形成接尾辞 -LY

(63)　**EREWHILE**, lately[.] / **OFTEN**, frequently. / **RECENT** ... lately done[.]

---

16)　ただし Bailey (1721) で比較級・最上級語尾を伴った young は，見出し語で，語釈まで付されている。これは，例外的な扱いだろう。**YOUNGER**, more young. / **YOUNG-EST**, the most Young of all.

1.11.2.7　名詞形成接尾辞 -NESS

接尾辞 -ness の見出しはなく，またこれを伴う見出し語よりも，外来系抽象名詞の語釈の定番接尾辞として頻用される。

(64)　**BRIGHTNESS**, Lucidity, Shiningness. / **FAIRNESS**, Beautifulness, Clearness[.] / **NOBLENESS**, Nobility or the State of a Nobleman. / **UNSELINESS**, Unhappiness. *O[ld Word]*.

(65)　**CAUTION**, Heedfulness, Wariness[.] / **CURIOSITY**, Inquisitiveness[.] / **DEFORMITY**, Ugliness, Ill-favouredness. / **DENSITY**, Thickness. / **GENEROSITY**, nobleness of Mind. / **INSIGNIFICANCY**, Unprofitableness[.] / **JUSTICE**, Justness ... Rreasonableness[.] / **NOVELTY** ... Newness[.]

1.11.2.8　接尾辞 -ER, -ABLE , etc.

その他，-er, -able などを伴う派生語も，例えば，teacher, teachable がそれぞれ doctor, docile の語釈で用いられている。

1.11.3　代名詞

代名詞の語形変化系列の記述に整合性が見られない。

1.11.3.1　人称代名詞

(66)　**I**, the Pronoun of the first Person singular. / **MINE**, belonging to me. / **THOU**, thee. / **THINE**, of or belonging to thee. / **THEE**, Thou. / **YOU**, thou or ye. / **YOUR**, of or belonging to you. / **HE**, a Pronoun of the 3d Person singular Masculine. / **HIS**, of or belonging to him. / **HIM**, an Oblique Case of the Pronoun *He*. / **IT**, [Hit, *Sax*. Het, *Du*. Id, *L*.] ◊ 語釈なし. / **WE**, Us. / **OUR**, of or belonging to us. / **US**, we. / **THEY**, those persons. / **THEIRS**, of them. / **THEM**, the Pronoun They in an Oblique Case.

見出しなし：**MY, ME / THY / YE / YOURS / SHE, HER, HERS / ITS / OURS / THEIR**.

1.11.3.2　疑問代名詞・副詞

(67)　**VVHAT**, what thing, an Interrogative Pronoun. / **VVHICH**, whether of the two? &c. Or who? / **WHO**, which. / **VVHEN**, at what Time? /

VVHERE, In what Place? / **WHY**, For what Cause or Reason? 見出しなし：/ **WHOSE, WHOM**.

1.11.4　動詞
To be は簡単すぎる扱いで，go, keep, make も簡単な語釈に，ごく少数の成句，専門用語，古語が加わる。総じて，動詞の記述は簡単である。

(68)　To **BE**, to exist. / To **GO**, to walk, move, &c. / To **GO TO GOD**, To **GO WITHOUT DAY**, [*Law Phrase*] to be dismissed the Court. / To **HAVE**, to possess, to hold, to enjoy. / To **KEEP**, to retain, preserve, nourish, observe, look to, &c. / **KEEP YOUR LOOF, KEE[P] HER TO**. [*Sea-Term*] when the Steersman is directed to keep the Ship near the Wind. / To **MAKE**, to cause, to form or frame. / To **MAKE** [in *Law*] to execute or perform. / To **MAKE ONES BEARD**, To deceive or beguile, O[*ld*]. *Phrase*. / To **MAKE**, to hinder, O[*ld Word*]. / To **MAKE FAST**, [*Sea-Term*] to bind or tie. / To **PUT**, to lay, place, dispose, &c.

(69)　見出しのみ： To **MAY OR CAN**, [Magan, Sax.]

(70)　見出しなし： **DO**.

1.11.5　語釈の粗と密
見出しなしの語，見出しのみで語釈なしの語は，機能語（小辞，代名詞類）と接頭辞・接尾辞を伴う語であり，内容語でも熟知されている語に同じ扱いが見られる。例えば動詞 do は語釈では活躍する。

(71)　**To PLEASURE**, to do one a Pleasure. / **To WRONG**, to do injury or injustice. / **WROUGHT**, worked, did work.

(72)　**ELSE**, otherwise.

とあるが，otherwise は見出し項目にはない。Bailey の方針は，familiar な語はできる限り簡単に，他の事項は詳しくということである。

1.11.6　語釈 "... WELL KNOWN"
熟知された語の語釈を "...well known" で簡略化する。

　以下の加算名詞の見出しの不定冠詞の有無の基準は不明瞭である[17]。

---

17)　加算と非加算の意味の区別をＡの有無の別見出しで示している例もある。**BEAUTY**,

(73)　**BULL**, a Beast well known. / **CAT**, a Creature well known. / **CUCKOO**, **CUCKOW**, a Bird well known.[18] / **GOOSE**, a Fowl well known.[19]

(74)　**BUTTER**, a Food well known. / **CHEESE**, an eatable well known. / **ALE**, a Drink well known. / **BEAN**, a well known Pulse.

(75)　To **DREAM**,[20] an Action well known. / To **SNOW**, is what is too well known in *England*, to need Explanation. / **THUNDER**, a Noise well known by all Persons who are not Deaf.

1.11.7　種類の特定区分の言及で僅かに限定的な語釈

(76)　An **HARE**, an Animal well known, and peculiarly so called in the second Year of her Age. / **HOG**, a Swine, a wild Boar in the Second Year.

1.11.8　イギリス諸島外起源の生き物・産物には特性への言及

(77)　**CROCODILE**, a very large Beast in the Shape of a Lizard, living both on the Land and in the Water. *F.* / **ELEPHANT**, the biggest, strongest, and most intelligent of all four footed Beasts. *F.* / **CHA**, the Leaf of a Tree in *China*, which being steep'd in Water, makes the common Drink of the Inhabitants.

1.11.9　詳しい語釈

例えば，想像上の鳥 phoenix の説明は，長さにおいて *OED* のこの語の説明にひけをとらない。

(78)　**PHOENIX**, a Bird in *Arabia*, about the bigness of an Eagle, which is reported to live 600 Years, and that there is but one of them in the World at a Time, and that she having lived that Time, builds her a Nest of combustible Spices, which being set on Fire by the Sun, she fans it with her Wings, and burns her self in it, and that a Worm rises out of her Ashes,

---

　　Comliness, Handsomeness. / A **BEAUTY**, a beautiful, very fair, handsome, or charming Person.

18)　Cf. Johnson (1755): **BIRD**. ... In common talk, *fowl* is used for the larger, and *bird* for the smaller kind of feathered animals.

19)　Cf. Johnson (1755): **FOWL**. ... It is colloquially used of edible birds, but in books of all the feathered tribes.

20)　Cf. 対応する名詞の定義： **DREAM**, an acting of the Imagination in Sleep.

which comes to be a New *Phoenix*.

1.11.10　PROVERBS

Bailey（1721）では諺の引用が多く，又その解説に惜しみなく字数を費やし，詳細な解説に加えてフランス語，ラテン語，ギリシア語，ヘブライ語の対応する諺まで付く。この辞書の諺をすべて集めれば豆諺辞書になるだろう。

> (79)　**HORSE, ... It is a good Horse that never stumbles**. This Proverb intimates to us, that there is no Creature that ever went upon four *Legs*, but has made some false Step or another, and that every Mother's Son of us who goes upon two, hath his *Slips* and his *Imperfections*; that there is no Person in the World without his *weak Side*, and therefore pleads a Pardon for Mistakes, either in *Conversation* or *Action*, and puts a Check upon intemperate *Mockery*, or uncharitable *Censure*. And as we, so the *French* say, *Il n'y a bon cheval qui ne bro*[*n*]*che*, and *Quandoque bonus dormitat Homerus* says *Horace*.

この諺は 'vulgar and rustical' と評されている次の陳述からして，18 世紀でも人口に膾炙されていたと言えよう。

> (80)　　*OED* **vulgar**, *a*. 6. Commonly current or prevalent, generally or widely disseminated, as a matter of knowledge, assertion, or opinion: **a**. Of sayings, statements, facts, etc.
> 　　**1653** W. RAMESEY *Astrol. Restored* To Rdr. 6 But I shall answer in that vulgar and rustical Proverb, it is a good Horse that never stumbles.

フランス語の諺は，引用の諺と殆ど文字通り対応する。Horace の諺は，意味は対応するが，文字通りの対応はない。このラテン語の英語版は，今日 Homer sometimes nods で知られている。しかし Bailey（1721）: HOMER, To NOD のいずれの項にもこれはない。Whiting（1968）H427: Homer sleeps sometimes の引用は a1387 から始まり，Tilley H536: HOMER nods sometimes の引用は 1530 から 1677 DRYDEN *Apol*., p. 112: Horace acknowledges, that honest Homer nods sometimes: he is not equally awake in every line. まである。Homer sleeps / nods sometimes に固まった表現にほぼ近い 1677 の例を除くと，どの引用も，原意を敷衍した様々な表現である。Bailey（1721）が，この時点では，Homer nods sometimes に無言であるのは，これが，知識人の間

ではともかく，一般人の諺でなかったことを暗示しているのだろうか。

1.11.11 Bailey と Johnson

Bailey (1721) は，一般語辞書の充実の余地を残した。その後，改定版 Bailey (1730)，Dyche-Pardon (1735¹)，(1754⁸) と英語辞書は，充実を重ね，これらの下地があって，真に辞典と言える Johnson (1755) が出版される。次の Bailey (1721) の語源欄は，Johnson (1755) の oats の定義と一部重なる。

(81)　Bailey (1721): **OATS**, [Aten, *Sax*, of Etan, *Sax*. to eat, because it is Forage for Horses, generally, and sometimes Provision for Men] a sort of Grain.

(82)　Johnson (1755): **OATS**. *n. s.* [aten, Saxon.] A grain, which in England is generally given to horses, but in Scotland supports the people.

Bailey (本論 1.11.4) の To be, go, keep, make の簡単な記述に対し Johnson (1755) は緻密で，動詞には，語形変化が記され，続く語義区分は，to be が 4; to cut, *v. a.*²¹⁾ は 27 区分の 7 まで cut の語義，区分 8 以降は結合形 (cut *down*, &c.) の語義，to cut *v. n.* は 3 語義区分; to give *v. a.* は 35 区分の 22 まで give の語義，23 以降は結合形 (give *away*, &c.) の語義，to give, *v. n.* は 10 区分の 3 まで give の語義，4 以降は結合形 (give *in*, &c.) の語義である。

Johnson (1755) は辞書編纂者 lexicographer を次のように定義する。

"A writer of dictionaries; a harmless drudge, that busies himself in tracing the original, and dealing the signification of words."（辞書の作者；語の起源を辿り，意味を扱うことにせわしい無害な苦役者。）

無害な苦役者 (a harmless drudge) よりも，序文では，辞書編纂者は一層自虐的に身分の低い苦役の輩 (the humble drudge) とされている。序文のその辺りの大意を和訳で記してみる。

「卑しい生業(なりわい)の者は，汗水流せど，良き展望は望めず，追い掛け来る禍の恐怖を背に感じ，賞賛は望めず非難に曝され，失敗は辱められ，怠慢は罰せられ，成功に拍手喝采なく，勤勉これつとめて報いなしと運命づけられている。

---

21)　Johnson (1755) の動詞見出しに付く *v. a., v. n.* は verb active, verb neuter の略。それぞれ verb transitive と verb intransitive の別名。

この不幸な人間の数の中に辞書編纂者がいる。人類は，辞書編纂者は知の学徒ではなくその奴隷であり，通路の塵を取り払い障害物を取り除くべく運命づけられた，学問のための工兵にすぎずと考えてきた。この通路を学識者と才人は闊歩し，前進を容易ならしめる身分低き苦役の輩（drudge）に笑みの一つだに与えず征服と栄光へと突進する。著者たる者は，辞書編纂者を除き，誰しも賞賛を望み得る。他方辞書編纂者の望みは非難を免れることが関の山で，この消極的な償いすら認められた者は未だ指折り数えるほどもいない。」
(Samuel Johnson, ed. 1755. *A Dictionary of the English Language*, Preface)

Johnson の刺戟的な陳述「[辞書編纂者が整えた] 通路を学識者と才人は闊歩し，前進を容易ならしめる身分低き苦役の輩に笑みの一つだに与えず征服と栄光へと突進する」を平たく言えば，辞書は語学研究の縁の下の力持ちとしての役割を担う，となろう。統語論であれ，意味論であれ，英語の史的研究であれ，そこに，見えても見えなくても，辞書の土台がある。

「辞書編纂者の望みは非難を免れることが関の山」とは，全く逆に Johnson (1755) は，絶賛で迎えられ，フランスアカデミーが総力で編纂したフランス語辞書に匹敵する英語辞書は Johnson の独力で成し遂げられたという評価を得た。以後英単語の綴字，その意味，用法の基準は，Johnson (1755) に仰ぐという権威と栄誉を獲得した。

ここまでを個々の辞書の紹介としておきたい。

2　初期の辞書から読み取るその時代の考え・解釈

辞書は，時代により異なる物事の捉え方を映している。

2.1　生き物の分類変化

2.1.1　WHALE
whale, *noun* の解釈は，魚類から哺乳類へと変化する。

(83)　Kersey (1702): A **Whale**, *a huge sea-fish*. / Bailey (1721): A **VVHALE**, the Greatest of Fishes. / Dyche-Pardon (1754[8]): **WHALE** (S.) the greatest of all fishes.... she [＝the female] has no udder, but nipples and teats, which contain so great an abundance of milk.... / Johnson (1755) & Todd's Johnson (1818): **WHALE**. *n. s.* [...] The largest of fish; the largest of the animals that inhabit this globe. | God created the great *whales*. *Genesis*. / Webster (1828): **WHALE**, *n*. [... This fish is named from roundness, or from rolling; for in Dan. *hvalt* is arched or vaulted; ....] The general name of an order of animals inhabiting the ocean, arranged in zoology under the name *Cete* or *Cetacea*, and belonging to the class *Mammalia* in the Linnean system....

Kersey (1702) から Todd's Johnson (1818) までのいずれも，whale を fish と規定している。Webster (1828) は，語源欄では鯨を "This fish" と呼びながら，語釈では，リンネ式分類で哺乳類 (*Mammalia*) としている。

　歴史辞書 *OED* は，whale の fish から mammal への解釈変化に触れているだろうか。見れば，

(84)　*OED* (1933): **Whale**, *sb*. 1. Any of the larger fish-like marine mammals of the order *Cetacea*［クジラ目］.... | *c* 893 ÆLFRED *Oros*. I. i. §16 Se hwæl bið....

と，whale は哺乳類と規定され，OE から 19 世紀までの例が引用されている。しかし whale, *sb*. に，魚類の一種と解釈されていた時代があったとの言及はない。*OED* 利用者が OE の用例の "Se hwæl" を哺乳類と解釈して，読むことが正しいだろうか。少なくとも OE 時代の解釈ではない。

2.2　病気の解釈の変化

過去の辞書の病名説明に，今日と異なる解釈が，比較的容易に見つかる。

2.2.1　CANCER

POD[1] (1924): **can′cer**, n. ... malignant tumour spreading indefinitely & recurring when removed (often fig. of corruption, militarism, &c.) が現代の辞書に見える。Bailey (1721) と Dyche-Pardon (1754[8]) は，乳癌を主な cancer と

考え，Johnson (1755) は，癌を不治の病としている。

(85) Kersey (1702): A **Cancer**, or *ulcer in a Woman's breast*.
(86) Bailey (1721): **CANCER**, [in *Surgery*] a dangerous Sore, or Ulcer; as in a Womans Breast, &c. / **ULCER**, a running Sore in the soft Parts of the Body, accompanied with Putrefaction. | **CANCEROUS ULCER**, [among *Surgeons*] a large Ulcer, the Lips of which are swollen, hard and knotty, with thick Veins round about full of dark blackish Blood.
(87) Dyche-Pardon (1754[8]): **CA'NCER** (S.) .... In *Physick*, it is a hard and immoveable tumour, of a livid or lead colour, encompassed round with branched turgid veins full of black, muddy blood; it begins without pain, and grows apace, and chiefly afflicts the lax, glandulous parts, especially the breast; it is observable to grow more in barren or single women, than others.
(88) Johnson (1755) & Todd's Johnson (1818): **CA'NCER**. *n. s.* 3. A virulent swelling, or sore, not to be cured.
(89) Webster (1828): **CAN'CER**, *n.* 3. In *medicine*, a roundish, hard, unequal, scirrous tumor of the glands, which usually ulcerates, is very painful, and generally fatal.

2.2.2 体液の異常と思われていた CATARACT

白内障を *POD*[1] (1924) は **căt'arăct**, n. ... opacity of crystalline lens of eye producing partial blindness. と説明する。これとは異なり 'humours' の異常とするのは，Bullokar (1616), Phillips (1658), Dyche-Pardon (1754[8]) である。Johnson (1755) は，視覚の妨げが瞳孔に被さる薄い皮膚のためとする。

(90) Bullokar (1616): *Cataract*. A destillation[22] of humours out of the eyes. / Phillips (1658): *Catarract*, (Greek) ... a disease in the eyes caused by a coagulation of flegme, between the Uveous Tunicle and the Christalline humour, hindring the egresse and ingresse of the visual spirits. / Dyche-Pardon (1754[8]): **CA'TARACT** (S.) ... a distemper in the eyes caused by the congelation of phlegm between uveous coat and crystalline humour.
(91) Johnson (1755): **CA'TARACT**. [In medicine] A suffusion of the eye, when little clouds, motes, and flies, seem to float about in the air;

---

22) destillation. 詳しくは *OED*, distillation †2. *Path*. を参照のこと。

when confirmed, the pupil of the eye is either wholly, or in part, covered, and shut up with a little thin skin, so that the light has no admittance. *Quincy*.

2.3　世界観を映す Center, -tre = the earth

(92)　Bullokar (1616): ***Center***. The point in the midst of a round circle, or the inward middle part of a globe. VVherefore the earth is called the Center of the world, because it is in the midst thereof.

Cockeram (1626²): ***Center***, Blount (1656): **Centre** の定義も上の定義と実質同じで，どれも地球が世界の中心地点にあるという考えに立つ。

他方次は，"supposed" と条件を付けて，この考えから距離を置いている。

(93)　Schmidt, *Shakespeare-Lexicon*, **Centre** = the earth, as the supposed centre of the world[.]

(94)　*OED*, **centre**, *sb*. 2.b. The earth itself, as the supposed centre of the universe.
　　1606 Shakes. *Tr. & Cr.* I. iii. 85 The Heauens themselues, the Planets, and this Center, Obserue degree, priority, and place. (天體其者すら，いや，惑星でも，此地球でも，階級を，先後を，位置を…遵守してゐます (坪内訳) / 天の星々も，惑星も，宇宙の中心であるこの地球も… (小田島訳))

(95)　**1667** Milton *P.L.* I. 74 As far remov'd from God and light of Heav'n As from the Center thrice to th' utmost Pole. (…神の在し給う光の世界から遠ざかること実に甚しく，その距離は，地球からそれを取りまく宇宙の最外郭にいたる距離の三倍はあった。) (平井訳)

地球は宇宙の中心地という考えは，*OED* の定義でその引用を読むより，Bullokar (1616) の定義で読めば，時代の考え，話者の考えに直結する。更に坪内訳の「地球」では，宇宙の中心たる地球を読み取ることはできない。

　歴史原理の *OED* が，過去の見方での表現を過去の見方から記述していないとき，過去の見方に直結する初期の辞書は有用である。

2.4 難語対平易語の CORDWAINER と SHOEMAKER

(96)　Cockeram (1626²) *Second Part*: **a Shoomaker**, Cordwayner.

平易語 shoemaker に対応する難語 cordwainer である。本来スペインのコルドバ革 (cordovan leather) の鞣し職人，又はその商い人を指していた語が，靴職人の意味に転用した語である。

Dekker, *The Shoemakers' Holiday* の種本になった Deloney, *The Gentle Craft, Parts 1 & 2* に Shooemaker(s)（5例），shoomaker(s)（103例）と100例以上現れるところ，cordwainer は1例だけ複数形で，ロンドンの靴職人組合重鎮への作品献呈の辞に見られる。

> (97)　Deloney (the last decade of the 16ᵗʰ c.) *Gentle Craft, second Part* 139. 1–4. To the Master and Wardens of the | worshipfull company of the Cordwaynors | in London, all continuance of health and per-| fect brotherly affection.（尊敬すべきロンドン製靴組合員諸氏の組長並びに役員諸賢へ，末永き御健勝と友愛の誠を献じます。）

OED Cordwainer 1600年の引用は，二つの語の使用域の対比を示している好例であろう。それは，Dekker からの引用で，ロンドン市長が使う一般語の shoemaker に対して，靴職人の親方エアはきばって cordwainer で応じている。

> (98)　1600 Dekker *Gentle Craft* Wks. 1873 I. 44 *L. Ma.* Maister Eyre, are all these Shoomakers? *Eyre.* All Cordwainers, my good Lord Mayor.（[ロンドン市長]：エア殿，この皆々さんは靴作りの方ですか。[エア]：全員製靴業者にございます，市長閣下。）

2.5 HERB は「薬草・香草」よりも広い意味の語

> (99)　Bailey (1721): **BEET**, a Garden Herb. / **CELERY**, a Winter Sallet-Herb. / **LETTICE**, a Garden Herb. / **SORREL**, a cooling Herb of a pleasant sharp Taste, much used in Sallet. / **SPINAGE**,²³⁾ an Herb well

---

23) Cf. the spellings: **SPINACHE**, herb, *blitum, i.* (Levins 1570); Spinacchia, *the hearbe called* **Spinage**. (Florio 1598); Espinars. des espinars: m. **Spinage**, *or* **Spinach**. (Cotgrave

known.

上の語のうち，POD⁵ で herb と定義されているのは lettuce, sorrel である。

(100)　POD⁵ (1969): **lettuce**, n. Herb grown for salad. / **sorrel**, n. Kinds of sour-leaved herb.

(101)　POD⁵ (1969): **beet**, n. Kinds of plant with succulent root used for salad &c. (*red* ～) & sugar-making (*white* ～). / **celery**, n. (Blanched stems of) plant used as salad & vegetable. / **spinach**, n. Plant with succulent leaves eaten boiled.

野菜（**vegetable**, A plant cultivated for food; *esp.* an edible herb or root）の OED の初例は 1767 年。この意味と草本を意味する plant の用法が拡大し，herb は現代では「草本」より「薬草・香草」の比重が大きいのではなかろうか。

(102)　OED (1933): **plant**, *sb.*¹ 2. ... Often popularly restricted to the smaller, esp. herbacious plants, to the exclusion of trees and shrubs. ◊ Cf. POD¹⁰ (2005): **mint**¹ n. 1. a plant used as a herb in cookery.

(103)　Dyche-Pardon (1754⁸): **HERB** (S.) a common name to all plants, whose stalks or stems do not grow large, or united enough to become wood, and so die away every year after their seed is become ripe; of these, in some the root perishes with the stem, as wheat, rye, barley, &c. and so are necessarily raised from the fresh seed every year; and in others the roots last many years, as mint, fennel, &c. some keep their leaves all the year round, and are called ever-greens, as the asarabaca,[24] yellow violet, &c. others shed their leaves, and remain bare part of the year, as fern, coltsfoot, &c. they are further distinguished into kitchen or salled [= salad] *herbs*, and medicinal or physical *herbs*.

上の引用で herb が薬草に限定されない語と分かる。更に

(104)　Dyche-Pardon (1754⁸): **WEED** (S.) a wild herb that grows in gardens without culture[.] / **WEED** (V.) to root or pull up the useless or noxious herbs in a garden from among the flowers, &c.

で，"wild," "useless," "noxious" で形容される草も herb である。ME, Early

1616); **SPI'NACH. SPI'NAGE** *n. s.* [*spinachia*, Latin] (Johnson 1755 & Todd's Johnson 1818); **SPIN'ACH, SPIN'AGE**, *n.* (Webster 1828); **spin'ach, -age**, n. (COD¹⁻⁵ 1911–1964); **spi'nach** n. (COD⁶⁻¹¹ 1976–2004).

[24]　OED (1933), ‖ **Asarabacca** の異綴りの中に asarabaca は記載されていない。

ModE の herb は必ずしも「薬草・香草」ではない。

2.6　ARTERY と VITAL SPIRITS

2.6.1　ARTERY は vital spirits の通る管

Artery（動脈）が，血液以外のものも運ぶ管だとは今日の理解ではないだろうが，17–18 世紀の英語辞書には artery は，the vital spirits, the spirits of life（生気）と血液が流れる管だとある。

（105）　Cockeram（1626²）: ***Arteries***, Hollow sinewes or veines, wherein the spirits of life do walke.

（106）　Blount（1656）: **Artery**（*arteria*）a sinew like to a vein, a hollow vessel, in which the spirits of life mixed with blood do pass through the body. All these kind of veins proceed from the heart, where the vital spirits are made, and are those which pant or beat, called commonly the pulses ....

（107）　Coles（1676）: ***Arteries***, *l*. pulses, hollow vessels like to veins, wherein the thinnest and the hottest bloud（with *the* vital spirits）passeth.

（108）　Phillips（1658）: ***Arteries***,（Lat.）those hollow membranous Vessels like to veins, in which the most thin, and hottest part of the bloud together with the vital spirits pass through the body.

（109）　Bailey（1721）: **ARTERY**, [*Artere, F. Arteria, L.* of ἀρτηρία, *Gr.*] is a sanguiferous Vessel, and generally holds the same Course with a Vein, it conveys Blood and vital Spirits from the Heart, into all the Parts of the Body for their Nourishment, and the Conservation of their vital Heat.

OED, artery, *n*. 2 のノートによると，「古代人は artery を空気を通す管と考えていた。又中世の書物に，この管には揮発性の流体 'vital spirits'（生気）が存在すると記されている。Artery の原義は，空気を運ぶ管であり，この管を揮発性の血液である vital spirits が通過すると考えられていた。William Harvey（1578–1657）の血液循環の原理発見後も，この誤った考えが消滅するには長い時を要した。」18 世紀の Bailey（1721）でも古い考えのままである。

2.6.2 Artery の原義

Vital spirits を運ぶ artery は，ギリシア語 artēría に由来する。

(110)　Liddell-Scott-Jones (1996) *GEL*: ἀρτηρία, ἡ, *wind-pipe*[.] II. *artery*, as distinct from a vein[.]

artēría の第一義は wind-pipe（気管，風管）である。医学者ガレノスの著作の翻訳者内山勝利氏は，ギリシア語の ἀρτηρία (artēría) の訳語として「気息管」を提案する[25]。次のギリシア語由来のラテン語 artēria も「気息管」の意味を受け継いでいる。

(111)　Glare (2012²) *OLD*: **artēria** ~ae Also *f*. ARTĒRIVM. [Gk ἀρτηρία] **1** (sg.) ... windpipe.... **2** (pl.) ... the breathing tubes or passages. **3** An artery. **b** (regarded as conveyers of air).

Artery は，原義に沿えば，血液を通す管ではなく，気息を通す管である。次に vital spirits が気息と整合するか，spirit の意味を見る。

2.6.3 PNEUMA—SPĪRITUS—SPIRIT への流れ

「英語の spirit の初期の用法は，主としてウルガタ聖書 (Vulgate) に由来する。同聖書では spīritus がギリシア語 πνεῦμα (pneûma) そしてヘブライ語 rūaḥ[26] の翻訳語であった。これらの語は Wyclif 以来すべての聖書翻訳で一般的に spirit（又はその異形）に翻訳された。」(*OED*, spirit, 語源欄ノート)

ギリシア語 **πνεῦμα**, 1. *wind*, *air*. 2. *breath*, πνεῦμα βίου *the breath* of life[.] (*Abridged GEL*) の二つの意味は，ラテン語 spīritus にも見られる。

(112)　Glare (2012²) *OLD*: **spīritus** ~ūs *m*. [**SPĪRŌ** to breathe; be alive + **TVS**³] **1** The action of breathing, respiration; (also) a single breath[.] **2** The air breathed into and expelled from the lungs, breath[.] **3** Breath as

---

25)　内山 (2014: 1): 古代ギリシアの医学者ガレノスの著作の一つを訳したとき，「動脈」に当たる「アルテーリアー」という語を，あえて「気息管」としてみた。言葉としても，もともと鼻腔から肺に至る「気管」の語が流用されたものであり，それはプネウマ（気息）を全身に巡らせるための脈管と考えられていた。当時のこうした生理学的知見を明示するためには，言語に即した「気息管」という造語をすることも許されるのではないか。

26)　Souter (1966): πνεῦμα ... Hebrew employed three words for the breath-soul, *nephesh*, *ruach*, *neshāmāh*[.]

the concomitant of life or consciousness[.] **4.** The non-corporeal part of a person... spirit, soul; one's being[.] **8** Air in motion, wind, breeze, air current[.]

ギリシア語 pneûma と Vulgate の spīritus が次例では英訳聖書の spirit ('wind' or 'breath') と対応する[27]。

'Wind' の意味の John 3: 8.

 (113) Greek: τὸ Πνεῦμα ὅπου θέλει πνεῖ,
    Vulgate: Spiritus ubi vult spirat,
    Wyclif (1380): the spirit brethith where he wole,
    Cf. Authorized (1611): The winde bloweth where it listeth,
    新共同訳: 風は思いのままに吹く。

'Breath' の意味の Luke 8: 55.

 (114) Greek: ['Iησοῦς] ἐφώνησε, λέγων, ''Η παῖς, ἐγείρου.' | Καὶ ἐπέστρεψε τὸ πνεύμα αὐτῆς,
    Vulgate: [Iesus] clamavit, dicens: Puella, surge. Et reversus est spiritus eius,
    Wiclif (1380): [ihesus] cried & seide, damysel rise vp, and hir Spirit turned aȝen:
    Cf. 新共同訳: イエスは…「娘よ，起きなさい」と呼びかけられた。すると娘は，その霊が戻って…[28]

英語の spirit は，ギリシア語，ヘブライ語からの翻訳語としてのラテン語 spīritus, 'wind, breath' を介して取り入れたのが始まりということである。

次に息と命との繋がりは，息を与えられることで人は生きる存在になったという考えに見られる。その端的な例は，Genesis 2:7.

 (115) Vulgate: Dominus Deus ... inspiravit in faciem eius spiraculum vitae, et factus est homo in animam viventem.
    AV (1611): And the LORD God ... breathed into his nostrils the breath of life; and man became a liuing soule.
    新共同訳: 主なる神は…［人（アダム）］の鼻に命の息を吹き入れられた。

---

27) 引用の 'wind', 'breath' の解釈は，Souter (1966) πνεῦμα による。

28) 新共同訳は「息を吹き返した」と解釈しない。日本語「霊」が「息」を含意するとは言えまいが，Vulgate の spiritus は Glare (2012²) spīritus 2, 3, 4, 8 の意味を含む語である。

人はこうして生きる者となった。
Lewis & Short (1879) は上の Vulgate を例に次のように語釈している。

 (116) **spīrāculum**, ... *air-hole*... (poet. and in post-Aug[ustan] prose) ...— Also *breath*: vitae, Vulg[ate]. Gen[esis] 2, 7[.]

spīrāculum は spīritus と同じく, spīro の派生語。

2.6.4 ARTERY を流れる命を支える流体の名

一方, 英訳聖書を通して spirit, 'breath' が英語化され, 息は命と繋がる考えがあり, 他方, 古の医学の考えとして, artery を流れて命を支える揮発性の流体 vital spirit(s) がある。二つの筋からの生命活動に関わる思想が, 共に spirit で表されている。Artery を流れ体内をめぐる spirits は 3 種類, 別の説で 2 種類と Bailey (1721) は記している。

 (117) Bailey (1721): **SPIRITS**, [in an *Animal Body*] were reckoned of 3 Sorts; the *Animal Spirits* in the *Brain*, the *Vital* in the *Heart*, the *Natural* in the *Liver*; but late Authors distinguish them only in 2 Kinds, the *Vital* and *Natural*, (which are the same) in the Mass of Blood.[29]

 (118) Bailey (1721): **THE ANIMAL SPIRITS**, [among *Naturalists*] are a very thin Liquor, which distilleth from the Blood in the external or cortical Substance of the Brain, and are by the proper Ferment of the Brain exalted into Spirit, and thence through the Medullar Substance of the Brain, the *Corpus Callosum* and *Medulla Oblongata* are deri'vd into the Nerves, and in them perform all the Actions of Sense and Motion.

 (119) Bailey (1721): **THE VITAL SPIRITS, THE NATURAL SPIRITS**, [among *Naturalists*] are the most Subtil Parts of the Blood, which cause it to act and ferment, so as to make it fit for Nourishment.

2.6.5 VITAL SPIRITS

 (120) *OED* (1933): **vital**, *adj*. **2**. Maintaining, supporting, or sustaining life. †**a**. *Vital spirit, spirits*... *Obs*. Freq. in the 16th c., chiefly in pl.

---

[29] Cf. *OED* (1933): **spirit**, *sb*. **16**. One or other of certain subtle highly-refined substances or fluids (distinguished as *natural, animal,* and *vital*) formerly supposed to permeate the blood and chief organs of the body. In later use only *pl*. その他 natural spirits, animal spirits の詳細は *OED*², natural, *a*. 12.a.; *OED* (1933), animal, *adj*. †1. を参照。

(a). **1715** POPE *Iliad* III. 366 The vital spirit issued at the wound. (6th q.)
(b) **1667** MILTON *P.L.* v. 484. (5th q.)

上の引用 (a) は，生贄の仔羊が喉を切り裂かれた描写の続きで，Pope は，生気を奪われ息絶える様を artery に流れる「生気が傷口から流失した」と表現した。生き物は息で生きるという考えであろう。原文は

(121) Homer *The Iliad* (Loeb Classical Library, 1999), 3.294: Θυμοῦ δευομένους (q. Liddell-Scott-Jones (1996) *GEL*, **δεύω** (B) '*reft of* life'); Cf. (生気を奪われて)(松平訳); *Abridged GEL*, **θῡμός**, ὁ, (θύω) 1. *the life, breath*[.] 2. the soul[.] 3. the mind[.] θυμοῦ は単数属格。

Latin *spīritus*, Greek θῡμόσ (thūmós) の意味は共に「息，命，精神」[30]。
Milton (120) (b) の詩行は，

(122) Fowler, ed. (1998) *P. L.* V. 482-485: flowers and their fruit | Man's nourishment, by gradual scale sublimed | To vital spirits aspire, to animal, | To intellectual…. (花が咲き果実が生ずると，これが人間の滋養物となり，| 次第に階梯を経て上昇してゆき，生気へ，精気へ[31]，知力へ，と向かい)(平井訳)

2.7 PHILOSOPHY, SCIENCE 及び ART
―― 共有する意味の弱化と分化した意味の優位 ――

Philosophy はギリシア語 philosophía (= love of knowledge and wisdom) に遡り，science と art はラテン語 scientia (= knowledge) と ars (= practical skill) に遡る。英語は，この三つの語を中英語期にフランス語から借用した。3 語とも知に関わる意味が共通する。philosophy は「(知・叡智への) 愛」(1340–

---

30) Cf. 大野・佐竹・前田 (1974): いき【息】《生キと同根》… ▷ 息と生キとを同根とする言語は，世界に例が少なくない。例えばラテン語 spiritus は息・生命・活力・魂，ギリシア語 anemos は空気・息・生命，ヘブライ語 ruah は風・息・生命の根源の意。日本の神話でも「息吹(いぶき)のさ霧」によって生まれ出る神神があるのは，息が生命を意味したからである。

31) 「ミルトン当時の人々は，自 然 の 気 [natural spirits] は肝臓で造られ，生　気 [vital spirits] は心臓で造られ，この生気から精気 ("animal spirits" …) が生じ，これが血液の中を流れて頭脳その他にいたり，各種の思考や運動を可能ならしめている，と考えていた。」(平井訳『失楽園』(上) 四巻，八〇六行「精気」の訳注)

1775)³²⁾，science は「知識」(a1340–1882)，art は「(知識・実践から得た) 腕前」(c1225–1849) がそれぞれの第一義である。三つの語は，大差というより，知を共有する仲間の語として歩み始め，今日では，philosophy は (人文科学分野の) 哲学が，science は自然科学が，art は芸術が，仲間というより別の知の分野を強調する意味を際立たせる。

2.7.1 PHILOSOPHY

17世紀の難語辞書では，philosophy は，学問・学術一般を意味する。

(123) Cawdrey (1604): **philosophie**, (g) study of wisdome[.]

(124) Bullokar (1616): **Philosophie**. The study of wisedome: a deepe knowledge in the nature of things. There are three different kindes hereof. **1.** *Rationall* Philosophy, including Grammer, Logick, and Rhetorick. **2.** *Naturall* Philosophy teaching the nature of all things, and conteining besides Arithmetick, Musick, Geometry and Astronomy. **3.** *Morall* Philosophy, which consisteth in the knowledge and practise of ciuilitie & good behauiour.

(125) Cockeram (1626²): ***Phylosophie***, The study of wisedome. |**Phylosopher**, A louer of wisedome.

(126) Blount (1656): **Philosophy** (*philosophia*) the love or study of wisdom; a deep knowledge in the nature of things; There are three different kinds thereof. 1. *Rational Philosophie*, including Grammer, Logick, and Rhetorick; and this dives (sic) into the subtilty of disputations and discourse. 2. *Natural Philosophie*, searching into the obscurity of natures secrets, containing besides, Arithmetick, Musick, Geometry, and Astronomy. 3. *Moral Phylosophy*, which consists in the knowledge and practise of civility and good behavior.

(127) Phillips (1658): **Philosophical**, (Greek) belonging to a Philosopher or **Philosophy**, *i*.³³⁾ the love and study of wisdom, knowledge of natural causes.

(128) Coles (1676): **Philosophy**, g. the study of wisdom, or knowledge in things Rational, Natural and Moral.

---

32) ( ) 内の数字は *OED* の第一義の初例と最終例の年号。

33) *i*.: †*i*. the earlier equivalent of *i.e.* = *id est* (L.) that is (to say). (*OED*, **I**, III. Abbreviations.)

纏めれば，17世紀の難語辞書の philosophy は，the study of wisdom（英知の探求）が意味の根幹であり，これを3区分して，(1) rational philosophy（明理・弁理の学）[34] は文法，論理学，修辞学も含み，(2) natural philosophy（自然哲学）は，自然界の秘密の解明であり，算術，音楽，幾何，天文学も含み，(3) moral philosophy（道義学）は礼節と正しい行いの知識と実践よりなる。

3種の philosophy（哲学[35]）は，知への愛で統合されて，自然科学と精神科学（社会科学・人文科学）に分化していない学術一般を表し，17世紀の難語辞書の philosophy の意味でもある。錬金術師（alchemist）が求めていた金銀に変換できる物質の名が philosophers' stone（哲学者の石）で，Ph.d.（＝ Doctor of Philosophy 哲学博士）が法学，医学，神学以外の学問分野の博士号であることから，philosophy が広い意味の呼称であったことが窺える。

これに対して18世紀の間に学問が，自然科学（science）と精神科学（社会科学，人文科学）の分化と独立により，人文科学の一部門としての philosophy の意味が優勢となった。

2.7.2　SCIENCE

17世紀の難語辞書では science も philosophy と同じく学問・学術を意味し

---

34) rational philosophy: これは廃用表現であり，この区分は，すでに18世紀の Bailey (1721), Dyche-Pardon (1754[8]) の philosophy では見られない。*OED*（rational **A.** *adj*. 2.）の説明は "Of, pertaining or relating to, reason, Chiefly in *rational faculty*, *nature*, *power*, etc. Also † *rational philosophy*, mental philosophy." である。井上・有賀（1884）『哲學字彙』の訳語「mental philosophy 心理学」は，psychology の定訳となっている今日では，心理学が文法，論理学，修辞学を含むとも言えないし，この訳語は rational philosophy には不適である。暫定的に"明理・弁理の学"としておこう。

35) 仏語 Philosophie *sf*.，英語 philosophy の「哲学」以前の訳語として「聖学」（*Nouveau dictionnaire français-japonais*, 1871），「理学」（前田・高橋（編）『大正増補和譯英辭林』1886）があった。西欧語のフィロソフィーをはじめて「哲学」と訳出したのは，荒川他（編）(1977: 973) によると，西周『百一新論』(1874) であった。訳語「哲学」の普及に，井上・有賀（編）『哲學字彙』再版（1884）の力があったろうが，philosophy「理学，哲学」，「哲学，理学」の訳語並列は明治期の英和辞典でしばらく続いた。島田（編）『雙解英和大辭典』（第9刷，1899）では，まだ「格物窮理，理學，哲學」で，しかも「理学」は science の訳語の一つでもある。しかし和田垣（編）『新英和辭典』初版 [1901] 7版 (1902) になると，philosophy は「哲學，原理の學，理論」であり，「理學」は philosophy ではなく science の訳語の一つである。

た。Blount (1656) Science と Phylosophie を比べると，seven liberal Sciences は philosophy 第 1 類 Rational Philosophy と第 2 類 Natural Philosophy の内容と合致する共通性と，第 3 類 Moral Philosophy が Science にはない違いがある。このように大筋では，両語は同義の重なりを共有して歩み始めている。

(129)　Cawdrey (1604): **science**, knowledge or skill[.]
(130)　Bullokar (1616): **Science**. Knowledge.
(131)　Cockeram (1626²): *Science*, Knowledge.
(132)　Blount (1656): **Science** (*scientia*) cunning, skill, learning, knowledge. The seven liberal Sciences are these, *Grammer, Logick, [R]hetorick, Astrology, Geometry, Arithmetick* and *Musick*.
(133)　Phillips (1658): ***Science***, (lat.) knowledge, skill, or learning.
(134)　Coles (1676): ***Science***, *l*. skill, knowledge. *Liberal Sciences*, Grammar, Logick, Rhetorick, Musick, Arithmetick, Geometry, Astronomy.

2.7.3　SCIENCE と ART

Seven liberal sciences は seven liberal arts とも呼ばれる[36]。学も術も排他的に区別しなかった時代の呼称で，大学が授ける称号 'Bachelor of Arts','Master of Arts' もそれを証する。

(135)　Bailey (1721): **LIBERAL ARTS AND SCIENCES**, are such as are fit for Gentlemen and Scholars, as Mechanick Trades and Handicrafts are for meaner People.

しかし Dyche-Pardon (1754⁸) は，art は実践による知で，science は熟察による理論であるのに，二つを同一視する混同が頻繁であると警告している。

(136)　Dyche-Pardon (1754⁸): **ART** (S.) the skill or knowledge of doing, acting, or performing any thing regularly by proper instruments, fit methods, and due ways; and differs from a science, which properly is the contemplation of the theory, or abstracted relation that one thing bears to another; though these terms are frequently confounded.

二つの語の用法を，何故混同としたのか。18 世紀には，理論が術との間に不均衡を生じる程発達したのに，science と arts[37] が峻別されていない不満が

---

36)　7 科目に 'liberal' が付くのは，ローマで自由民のみが学ぶことが許されたから。
37)　Science の知を art の術で実践する相補関係の表現は *OED*, art, *sb*. 8. の 1489–1870 の引用が参考になる。

混同とする背景ではなかろうか。上の引用に science の優勢な意味が自然科学となる先駆けを垣間見るようだ。

2.7.4　崩れた等位関係
知的追究を旨とする science の突出した発達は，自然科学という意味を際立たせ，science は，知の愛を旨とする philosophy とも知の実践で相補っていた art とも等位関係を崩し，結果学術体系が変革したということだろう。

2.7.5　PHILOSOPHY の和訳「哲学」の問題点
古典期ギリシア語（紀元前5–4世紀）の philosophía を発端とする西欧語の語形（英語の philosophy など）は，広範囲な学問，学術の意味から限定的な分野の学問の意味が優勢となるまでの歴史を経ており，他方和訳「哲学」[38]は，特化された人文科学分野の philosophy の意味がすでに優勢であった明治期の登場で，この優勢な意味以前の歴史を歩んでいない。そこで和訳「哲学」が，philosophy の優勢な意味以前の philosophy の翻訳に適用されると，原文の意味通りには解釈され難い例が出る。16–17 世紀の philosophy の意味は，学問，学術で，その3分野の一つに自然哲学がある。例えば，Shakespear, *Hamlet*, I. v. 166–67; II. ii. 384–85[39] の philosophy である。

(137)　Shakespeare, *Hamlet* I. v. 166–67. There are more things in heaven and earth, Horatio, Than are dreamt of in your philosophy.

(138)　*Hamlet* II. ii. 384–85. ['Sblood,] there is something in this more

---

38)　*OED* が philosophy (*n.* 5.) で現在最も普通の意味 (Now the most usual sense.) とする初例は 1794 年からで，第3例は，井上哲次郎・有賀長雄（編）再版 (1884)『哲學字彙』が依拠した Fleming の書からで，philosophy は「諸原因と諸原理の科学で，哲学はすべての知とすべての存在が究極的に依存する根本原理の究明である」と定義される："1857 William Fleming, *The Vocabulary of Philosophy* 381 Underlying all our inquiries into any of these departments [God, nature, or man], there is a <u>first philosophy, which seeks to ascertain the grounds or principles of knowledge, and the causes of all things. Hence philosophy has been defined to be the science of causes and principles. It is the investigation of those principles on which all knowledge and all being ultimately rest</u>."（下線筆者）

39)　テクストの行数は編者により異なる。ここはグローブ版の行数で記した。

than natural, if philosophy could find it out.

この2箇所の philosophy は,次の Shakespeare の語彙集,注釈書では「自然哲学」と解釈されている。

- (139) Alexander Schmidt, ed. *Shakespeare-Lexicon*, 3rd ed. (1902); 4th ed. (1923) rev. & enlarged by Gregor Sarrazin, Supplement: **Philosophy**: *in your p*. Hml. I, 5, 167 = "natural philosophy", ("Naturphilosophie, Naturwissenschaft").
- (140) John Dover Wilson, ed. (2nd ed. 1936; rpt. 1957) *Hamlet*, GLOSSARY, **PHILOSOPHY**, natural philosophy, science as then understood (including demonology); I. 5. 167; 2. 2. 371.
- (141) G. Blakemore Evans, ed. (1974) *The Riverside Shakespeare*, note to *Hamlet* I. v. 167: **philosophy**: i.e. natural philosophy, science.
- (142) David Crystal, and Ben Crystal, eds. (2002) *Shakespeare's Words*, **philosophy** (*n.*) natural philosophy, i.e. science **Ham** II. ii. 366 [Hamlet to Rosencranz, of the current situation] *there is something in this more than natural, if philosophy could find it out*[.]

Shakespeare は明示的に natural philosophy(自然哲学)と表現していないが,philosophy 一語に自然哲学が含まれることは,上の諸家の解説からも,*OED* philosophy, sb. 3. (=*natural philosophy*.) の引用例からも分かる。

　場と文脈から自然哲学の解釈に沿い,特に I. v. 166–67 では,ハムレットが父王の亡霊出没の場で人の想像を絶する超自然的現象は起こるものだと語っていると取るのは無理のない解釈であろう。

　いくつかの『ハムレット』の二つの箇所の和訳は「哲学」[40] である。この和訳は自然哲学説の否定によるのか,否定しないまでも philosophy は如何なる学も「哲学」ということなのか。あるいは,I. v. 167 の「哲学」は,この箇所を引用する *OED*, philosophy, sb. 8.[41] が典拠かもしれない。自然哲学説を否定せず「哲学」とするには,日本語「哲学」に自然哲学,今日の言葉でいう自然科学の意味が一般的であることが前提だろう。

　無難な訳は,野島秀勝訳(2002)の上に挙げた *Hamlet* の2箇所の訳と坪内

---

40) 市河・松浦 (1949),三神 (1961),小津 (1972),永川 (1979),小田島 (1986)。

41) A particular system of ideas relating to the general scheme of the universe; a philosophical system or theory. (With *a* and *pl.*) 1390 GOWER....

逍遥 (1933) と澤村寅二郎 [1935] (1942) の *Hamlet*, II. ii. 385 の訳である。

　野島訳　I. v. 166–67: ホレイショー，この天地のあいだには，人間の学問などの夢にも思いおよばぬことが，いくらでもあるのだ。/ II. ii. 384–85: たしかに，これには何か自然の道理を越えたものがある，かりに自然哲学がその理由を見出すとしても。

　坪内訳　II. ii. 384–85: あッぱれ，是にこそ尋常(よのつね)ならぬ理合(りあい)があらうて，學問で探られるものなら。

　澤村訳　II. ii. 384–85: いや全く少し妙だよ，ちょっと理窟では割り出せないが。

しかし坪内 (1933) と澤村 [1935] (1942) も I. v. 167 の訳は「哲学」である。いずれにせよ，16–17 世紀の philosophy の訳語としては，広義の「学問」，「学術」又は「自然哲学」の方が的確なことがある。

3　言語変化を出版年順の辞書で読み取る

同じ語を出版年順に辞書で当たると，記述に変化が見られることがある。その変化が，言語変化と関わるとき，英語史の問題提起の糸口となる。

3.1　英語の四季の名称

英語の四季の名称の歴史では，*summer*, *winter* は一定で安定しているのに対し，春と秋の呼称は多様で揺れながらの歩みであった。OE, ME, Early ModE のいくつかの例を挙げれば，春は *lent*(*en*), *veer*, *prime-temps*, *prime-time*, *spring*, etc. であり，秋は *harvest*, *autumn*, *fall of the leaf*, etc.[42] である。これらの語の *OED* による季語用法の初出年代と，廃用には最終例の年代も記す。

---

[42]　春，秋のその他網羅的な 1100–1900 年にかけての呼称は，Fischer 1994: Figures 2–7, pp. 82–85, 87 にある。

春	秋
len(c)ten ....(c1000–a1310)	harvest ....(902–1774)
lent ....(c1275–1387)	
vere ....(c1325–1583)	autumn ....(c1374–)
prime-temps ....(c1400–1484)	
prime-time ....(1503–1609)	
the spring of the year ..(1530–? *Obs*.)	fall of the leaf ....(1545–1846)
spring of the leaf ......(1538–1670)	fall ....(1599–)
spring ....(a1547–)	the fall of that/ the year ..(1851–)

len(c)ten, *lent* は季節的意味を ME で失い，語形 *lent* が宗教的意味の四旬節で残り，対して *harvest* は18世紀後半で季節の意味を失い，収穫（期）の意味で残った。以下 spring と autumn / fall に至る変動のあらましである[43]。

3.1.1　ME, Early ModE の2言語／3言語辞書に見る英語の1番目と3番目の季節の呼称

英英辞書の嚆矢 Cawdrey (1604) 以前は，ラテン語を英語で語釈する羅英辞書，逆方向からの英羅辞書がいくつか出ていた。16世紀末 (1598) には伊英辞書，17世紀 (1611) には仏英辞書がある。これら外国語辞書は，作成当時の英語資料として，*OED* の引用例などで，活用されている。

　ここでは，ラテン語の春 (ver)，秋 (autumnus)，イタリア語の春 (primavera)，秋 (autunno)，フランス語の春 (printemps)，秋 (automne) に対応する英語の推移を，c1440年から1611年までの辞書9点で時代順に示す。ラテン語／イタリア語／フランス語の夏 (Lat. aestas, estas / It. està, estade, estate / Fr. esté)，冬 (Lat. hiem(p)s, hyem(p)s / It. inuerno / Fr. hyver) に対応する英語は，以下の諸外国語辞書で，summer と winter であるから，引用は省く。

　c1440–1500年までの4点の辞書で，ラテン語 autumpnus の英語対応語として harvest が見られる。対してラテン語 ver の見出しは，c1440 *Medulla Grammaticae* のみにある。しかし羅英辞書でありながら，ver の英語対応語を挙げずラテン語で「草本が青々となる月」と語釈している。

---

[43]　英語の四季の名称の記述のうち 3.1–3.1.1 は，Wada (2013: 27–52) と Wada (2014: 100) を要約した。季語 autumn の定着を扱う 3.1.2–3.1.5.3 は新しく本論で追加した。

1538年以降の5点の辞書のうち，羅英辞書3点は ver, autumpnus の英語対応語を挙げ，続く伊英辞書，仏英辞書も春と秋の英語対応語を挙げている。これら1538年以降の辞書では，春は，spring を中核とした句形式表現が大勢で，Cooper (1578) と Cotgrave (1611) にのみ (the) spring が見られる。

　秋は，harvest が c1440–1611 の9点の辞書のうち，Florio (1598) を除く，8点に見られる。対する autumn は，1552年以降の4点の辞書でようやく現れる。そのうち3点は，Florio (1598) を除き，harvest と並置されている。

(143)　c1440[44)] *Medulla Grammaticae* (Medieval Latin-English): **Autumnus, -i, Autumpnus, -i,** *harvest.* / **Ver, -eris,** mensis in quo herbe virescunt.

(144)　c1460 *Promptorium Parvulorum* (English-Medieval Latin): **Hervest**: *Autumpnus, -i* ....

(145)　1483 *Catholicon Anglicum, an English-Latin Wordbook*: **Harvest**; *Autu*mpn*us, messis.*

(146)　1500 *[H]ortus Vocabulorum* (Medieval Latin-Latin + English equivalent): **Autumpu*u*s** [sic] ... heruest.

(147)　Elyot (1538) (Latin-English): **Autumnus**, haruest. / **Ver, ueris**, the spryng of the yere.

(148)　Estienne (1552) (Latin-English-Gallic): **Autúmnus, ni**, m.g. Autu*m*ne, or haruest the fourth part of the year ensuing summer[.] / **Ver** ... the springe tyme of the yeare.

(149)　Cooper (1578) (Latin-English): **Autumnus**. Virg. *Autumne or haruest time, from the vj. of August, to the vj. of Nouember.* / **Ver, veris**, n.g. *The spring time....* Adolescit ver. Tac. *Spring time groweth toward an ende....* Ineunte vere. Cic. *At the beginning of spring....* Rubens ver. Virgli. *The spring bringeth foorth faire redde flowres.* / **Vernus**, Adiect. *Of the spring time....* Tempus vernum. Hor. *The spring.*

(150)　Florio (1598) (Italian-English): **Autunno**, *the autumne or fall of the leafe.* / **Primauera**, *the spring time of the yeere.*

(151)　Cotgrave (1611) (French-English): **Automne**: m. *Autumne, or haruest time.* / **Printemps**: m. *The Spring, or Spring time.*

---

44)　*Medulla Grammaticae* の編纂年は，Trembley, ed. (2005: 3): "The HARL. Ms. 1738, which was written around the year 1440, and ... was used as the basic text of the present publication." による。

以上簡略化して纏めれば次の通り：

春	秋
c1440 *MG* (　)	harvest
c1460 *PP* (　)	harvest
1483 (　)	harvest
1500 (　)	harvest
1538 the spring of the year	harvest
1552 the spring time of the year	autumn, harvest
1578 (the) spring time, (the) spring	autumn, harvest time
1598 the spring time of the year	the autumn, fall of the leaf
1611 The spring, spring time	Autumn, harvest time

3.1.2　難語英語の辞書で扱われている autumn

前節 3.1.1 を見る限り，16 世紀には，autumn は広まったかに見える。しかし，17 世紀の難語辞書 6 点のうち 5 点では，四季名は autumn のみ見出し語で，その他の季節を表す名詞は見当たらない。残る 1 点では形容詞 autumnal を除き，名詞形の四季語はすべて欠けている。

(152)　Cawdrey (1604): **autumne**, the haruest[.]

(153)　Bulloker (1616): ***Autumne***. Haruest time: one of the foure quarters of the yeare; the other three are winter, spring-tide, and sommer. ***Autumnal***. Of, or belonging to Autumne.

(154)　Cockeram (1626²): ***Autumne***, Haruest time. ***Autumnall***, Belonging to Autumne.

Cockeram は，第 2 部でもありふれた語 harvest time に対応する洗練表現は autumn であるとして次のように記している。

(155)　Cockeram (1626²): **Haruest time**, *Autumne*. **to Haruest belonging**, *Autumnall*.

(156)　Blount (1656): **Autumnal** (*autumnalis*) belonging to harvest of Autumn, which is from the sixth[45] of *August* to the sixth of *November*;

---

45)　イギリスでは，1656 年はまだユリウス暦の時代で，1752 年に the Gregorian Calendar (Sept. 2 followed by Sept. 14) (Görlach 2001: 11) が採用された。Dyche-Pardon (1754⁸) **GREGO'RIAN CALENDAR** (S.) は "the old stile [*i.e.* the Julian Calendar] being now 11 days behind the new[.]" と記している。

and is one of the four Quarters of the year; Others reckon Autume to begin at the Æquinoctium, *i.*[46] about the twelfth of *September*, and to end at the Solstice or shortest day, about the eleventh of *December*.

(157)　Phillips (1658): ***Autumnal***, (Lat.) belonging to Autumne, one of the four quarters of the year.

(158)　Coles (1676): ***Autumnal***, belonging to | ***Autumn***, *l*[*atin*] the Harvest-quarter.

これに対し，17世紀のこれら難語辞書では，季節語 spring は，難語 vernal, adj. を平易な表現で説明する文中の語として用いられている。

(159)　Cawdrey (1604): ◊ 見出し vernal なし。

(160)　Bulloker (1616): ***Vernall***. Of or belonging to the spring.

(161)　Cockeram (1626²): ***Vernall***, Belonging to the spring.

(162)　Blount (1656): **Vernal** (*vernalis*) of or belonging to the Spring of the year.

(163)　Phillips (1658): ***Vernal***, or ***Vernant***, (lat.) flourishing or belonging to the Spring.

(164)　Coles (1676): ***Vernal***, *l*[*atin*] of the spring.

3.1.3　Skinner (1671) に見出し語 Autumn がないこと

英語語源辞書 Skinner (1671) の季語は Spring, Summer, Harvest, & Winter であり，Autumn は見られない。春，秋，冬はラテン語の対応語 ver, autumnus, hiems が付され，夏は太陽が支配する時季との説明がある。

(165)　**Spring**, Ver[.] / **Summer**, ... Tempus Solis, sc. in quo Sol, dominatur[.] / **Harvest**, ... Messis, *Ælfrico* Autumnus[.] / **Winter**, ... Hyems[.]

17世紀の難語辞書が一様に季語は autumn のみを取り上げ，同じ世紀の英語語源辞書では，四季語のうち秋は harvest に譲り autumn が出てこない。

OED の autumn と spring の初例は，それぞれ c1374年と a1547年で，autumn が 150年以上前に現れていても，spring が先に一般化したことを17世紀の辞書が語る。刈り入れと秋という時を表す harvest の座に，autumn が納まるのに手間取ったのは農耕社会の生活感覚があったのだろうか[47]。

---

46)　*i.*: *i.e.* を意味する廃用の表記法。脚注33) を参照。

47)　18世紀後半から工業化するイギリス社会で，秋と農事の収穫への関心が薄れること

3.1.4 18世紀の辞書の harvest

18世紀の辞書では，Kersey (1702) で四季名は出揃う。但し，*The* Spring-time は見出しのみで，語釈が不必要な語の扱いである。Bailey (1721) で四季語は語釈を伴う見出しとして揃う。これら辞書が，同意語 harvest で autumn の語釈としていない点は，17世紀の難語辞書の autumn の語釈との違いである。18世紀の辞書の harvest の語釈の比重は，むしろ収穫（期）にある。

(166)　Kersey (1702): *A* **Season**, or *proper time*. ◊ 季節の語釈はない。
The **Spring-time**. / **Summer**, *the hot season of the year*. / **Autumn**, *the season for Harvest and Vintage*. / *The* **Winter**, or *winter-season*. / *A* **Harvest**, or *crop of corn*.

(167)　Bailey (1721): **SEASON** (S.) one of the 4 Quarters of the Year, which are *Spring*, *Summer*, *Autumn*, and *Winter*[.]
A **SPRING**, ... also one of the 4 Seasons of the Year[.] / **SUMMER**, one of the 4 Seasons of the Year. / **AUTUMN**, the Season of the Year which begins quickly after Harvest, when Grapes and other Fruits are gathered. ◊ この "Harvest" の意味は「刈取り」。/ **WINTER**, one of the Seasons of the Year.
HARVEST, the Time of reaping corn.

(168)　Dyche-Pardon (1754[8]): **SEA′SON** (S.) one of the four quarters of the year[.]
SPRING (S.) ... the season of the year that immediately follows winter, and in which nature seems as if it was new raised or born, by the sprouts of the trees, plants, flowers, &c.... / **SU′MMER** (S.) that part of time or season of the year that the days are longest and hottest, and consequently the fruits, plants, &c. brought to ripeness fit for laying up in stores[.] / **AU′TUMN** (S.) the third season of the year, or that wherein the harvest or summer fruits are gathered; it begins that day when the sun's meridian distance from the Zenith, being on the decrease, is a mean between the greatest and least, which is about the sun's entering[.] In *Alchymy*, it is the time or season that the operation of the philosopher's stone is brought to perfection. Some nations computed their years by *autumns*, and the *English Saxons* by winters. / **WI′NTER** (S.) that season of the year when

---

　　はなかっただろうか。ただ harvest (= autumn) の用例が18世紀末までは続かなかったという辞書の記述材料だけでは，確言は無理である。

the days are shortest and the weather coldest and wettest, &c.
HA′RVEST (S.) the time or season that the corn, &c. is ripe and fit to get into the barns, &c.

この説明は,「収穫期」と解釈できるものの,収穫が秋という時を含意するので,秋の内包的意味は読み取れよう。

(169)　Johnson（1755）: **HA′RVEST**. *n. s.* 1. The season of reaping and gathering the corn.
　　As it ebbs, the seedsman | Upon the slime and ooze scatters his grain, | And shortly comes to *harvest*. Shakes[*peare*]. *Ant. and Cleopatra.* [II. vii. 24–26]（水が退くと,農夫がぬらぬらしてゐる泥の中へ穀物を蒔く,すると,程なく収穫時となるのです。）(坪内訳)

3.1.5　英訳聖書の秋
3.1.5.1　*OED* の autumn の初例と第 2 例 1526 TINDALE
OED の autumn の初例は Chaucer *Boeth.* の Autumpne である。

(170)　c1374 CHAUCER *Boeth.* ɪv. vii. 144 Autumpne comeþ aȝeyne heuy of apples.

これは次のラテン語原典 autumnus の殆ど音写と言えよう。

(171)　Boethius, *De consolatione philosohiae*, ɪv. vi. 28. Remeat pomis grauis *autumnus*[.]

"Remeat pomis grauis" は本来語 "comes again heavy of apples" で訳され,"Autumpne" だけは新奇な外来語である。第 2 例も聖書からの翻訳である。

(172)　1526 TINDALE Jude 8 *Trees* rotten *in authum*.

OED 引用の Jude 8[48) の続きも記せば,次のようになる。

(173)　Tyndale（1526）Judas: Trees rotten *in authum*, vnfrutfull, twyse deed, and plucked vppe by the rotes.

ギリシア語原典は次のようになっている。

(174)　*Hexapla*（1841）, ΕΠΣΤΟΛΗ ΙΟΥΔΑ (The Epistle of Jude) 12: δένδρα φθινοπωρινά, ἄκαρπα, (literally: trees *autumnal*, fruitless,)

φθινοπωρινά (phthinopōrinà), 'autumnal' が *in authum* と表されたことは,

---

48)　1526 Jude 8 は 1534 訳 *Hexapla*（1841）では Jude 12 に対応する。他の引用のテクストも Jude 12 である。

すでに英語化された autumn の存在と，ギリシア語からの英語訳とはいえ，Vulgate の arbores *autumnales*（trees *autumnal*）も考慮すべきかもしれない。

(175)　Epistola Catholica B. Iudae Apostoli Summarium. 12: arbores *autumnales*, infructuosae....

3.1.5.2　Tyndale, tr. 1534 Jude 12 での変化

Tyndale の 1534 年訳では，autumn が未だ難語であるのか，at gadringe tyme へと変わる。*Hexapla*（1841），Jude 12 の時代順に Wiclif（1380）以下の諸訳では秋の表現に揺れがある。Geneva（1557）と Authorized（1611）は秋を明示的に表していない。以下 6 例は *Hexapla*（1841），Jude 12 の引用。

(176)　Wiclif（1380）: *heruest* trees with out fruyt[.]
(177)　Tyndale（1534）: trees with out frute *at gadringe tyme*, twyse deed and plucked vp by the rotes.
(178)　Cranmer（1539）: trees with out frute *at geatherynge tyme*[.]
(179)　Geneva（1557）: corrupt trees, and without frute[.]
(180)　Rheims（1582）: trees of *autumne*, vnfruiteful[.]
(181)　Authorized（1611）: trees whose fruit withereth, without fruit[.]

19 世紀以降の英訳と邦訳。

(182)　Revised Version（1881）: The General Epistle of Jude. p. 509. *autumn* trees without fruit, twice dead, plucked up by the roots[.]
(183)　*NEB*（1970）: A Letter of Jude 12. trees that *in season* bear no fruit[.]
(184)　文語訳：ユダの書 12. 枯れて又かれ，根より抜かれたる果(み)なき秋の木
(185)　新共同訳：ユダの手紙 12. 実らず根こぎにされて枯れ果ててしまった晩秋の木

3.1.5.3　Spring よりも時を要した autumn の一般語化

OED では，autumn の初例が ME 後期で，16 世紀初出の spring を引き離している。しかし難語辞書の二つの語の扱いから見ると，spring が先に一般語化したらしい。Spring は，外来語の難語の形容詞 vernal の語釈に用いられても，難語としての見出し語ではない。対して autumn は難語辞書の見出し語である。英訳聖書の諸訳の間で秋の表現が一定でないのも，autumn の一

般語化がすんなりと行かなかったことを示唆しているようである。

3.2 辞書に関する文献

辞書及び辞書に関する文献を挙げるとすれば，以下の書で他の辞書関係の多数の文献を知ることができる。

1. Alston, R. C., ed. (1966) *A Bibliography of the English Language from the Invention of Printing to the Year 1800*. Vol. 5: *The English Dictionary*. Leeds: E. J. Arnold & Son.

    1800 年までの英語辞書の書名の第 1 版から，増刷された刷のすべてと，所蔵する世界の主要図書館・研究機関を網羅した書誌。

2. Berg, Donna Lee. (1993) *A Guide to the Oxford English Dictionary*. Oxford, and New York: Oxford University Press.

    Part I: A User's Guide to the *OED*. Part II: A Companion to the *OED* の 2 部構成で，"*A Guide to the OED* is designed, like a map, to provide users with directions and information, when needed, with a minimal amount of effort." (Foreword) とある。*OED* 編者達の略歴，*OED* 成立の関連事項として Johnson (1755) から始まる年代記もある。

3. 早川勇（著）(2006)『日本の英語辞書と編纂者』（愛知大学文學會叢書 XI）横浜：春風社.

    1755–1946 年に編集された英和，和英の辞書とそれらの編集に関連する英語辞書の目録とその編纂者の簡便な経歴を含む。

4. 林哲郎（著）(1985)『英語辞書発達史』東京：開文社.

    OE 期のラテン語に意味上対応する英語をほどこす類語集 (vocabulary)，註解 (gloss)，註解集 (glossary) などを濫觴として 19 世紀までの英語辞書の発達を跡付けた緻密な研究書。

5. Hayashi, Tetsuro, (1978) *The Theory of English Lexicography 1530–1791*. Amsterdam: John Benjamins.

    上の和文の著書が "dictionary-users" の立場からの記述に対し，英文の著書は，"dictionary-makers" の立場から辞書編纂方針に主眼がある。

6. 今里智晃・土屋典生（著）(1984)『英語の辞書と語源』（スタンダード

英語講座，4) 東京: 大修館.
　付録の辞書関連文献紹介は英語研究に必要な文献である。一般英語辞書の項目は〈イギリス出版〉〈アメリカ出版〉〈英和辞書〉〈和英辞書〉，特殊辞書は〈發音〉〈語源〉〈類義語・同意語・反意語〉〈語法・イデイオム〉〈俗語・方言・地域語〉〈OE・ME〉〈英語学・言語学〉〈諺・引用句〉〈雑学〉に簡明適切な解説がある。参考図書の解説も有益。

7. Murray, James A. H.（1900）*The Evolution of English Lexicography*. Oxford: Clarendon.
　イギリス史と歩調を合わせて発達し *The Oxford English Dictionary* に至る英語辞書編纂の歩みを簡潔骨太にまとめた講演の記録。

8. 永嶋大典（著）(1970)『蘭和・英和辞書発達史』東京: 講談社.
　英和辞書が蘭和辞書から展開される日本文化史の一面を言語文化研究（philology）の立場から広範な資料を過不足なく駆使して解明した。

9. 大泉昭夫（編集）(1997)『英語史・歴史英語学―文献解題書誌と文献目録書誌』第 I 部　文献解題書誌，VIII. 辞書学・辞書編纂論（pp. 90–99）; 第 II 部　文献目録書誌，XI. LEXICOLOGY, SEMANTICS & ETYMOLOGY（pp. 249–269）; XII. LEXICOGRAPHY（pp. 271–293）.（英語学文献解題，第 3 巻）東京: 研究社.
　辞書全般の文献目録が参考になる。

10. 惣郷正明（著）(1973)『辞書風物誌』東京: 朝日新聞社.
　2,500 冊を超える辞書を集めた著者の英語も含め辞書一般について，辞書にまつわるエピソードもまじえ，話題豊富な新聞人の辞書案内。

参照文献

辞書・辞書関連書
Abridged GEL　　　See Anonymous ed., rev. [1871]（1966）
Catholicon Anglicum.　　See Anonymous ed.（1483）
COD[1-11]　　See Fowler, H. W., and F. G. Fowler, eds.
EDD　　See Wright, Joseph, ed.
[H]ortus Vocabulorum.　　See Anonymous ed.（1500）
MED　　See Kurath, Hans, Sherman M. Kuhn, and Robert E. Lewis, eds.

MG / *Medulla Grammaticae*　　See Tremblay, Florent, ed.
OED　　See Murray, James A. H. et al., eds.
POD[1–11]　　See Fowler, F. G., and H. W. Fowler, eds.
PP / *Promptorium Parvulorum, The*　　See Galfridus Grammaticus, ed. (c. 1460)
Todd's Johnson (1818)　　See Johnson, Samuel, ed., and H. J. Todd, rev.
　　　　　　　　　　（以上は編・著者名で始まらない略号，書名である。）

Alston, R. C., ed. (1966) *A Bibliography of the English Language from the Invention of Printing to the Year 1800*. Vol. 5: *The English Dictionary*. Leeds, UK: E. J. Arnold & Son.

Anonymous ed. (1483) *Catholicon Anglicum, an English-Latin Wordbook*. Sidney J. H. Herrtage, ed. 1881. EETS, o. s. 75. Rpt. 1973. Millwood, NY: Kraus Reprint.

Anonymous ed. (1500) *[H]ortus Vocabulorum*. Rpt. 1968. R. C. Alston, ed., English Linguistics 1500–1800, no. 123. Menston, Yorkshire, UK: Scolar Press.

Anonymous ed., rev. [1871] (1966) *A Lexicon Abridged from Liddell and Scott's Greek-English Lexicon*. Oxford: Clarendon. [Abbrev. *Abridged GEL*]

Bailey, Nathan, ed. (1721) *An Universal Etymological English Dictionary*: | COMPREHENDING | The Derivations of the Generality of Words in the | *English* Tongue, either Antient or Modern, from the Antient *British, Saxon, Danish, Norman* and Modern *French, Teutonic, Dutch, Spanish, Italian, Latin, Greek,* and *Hebrew* Languages, each in their Proper Characters. | AND ALSO | A Brief and clear Explication of all difficult Words derived from any of the aforesaid Languages; and Terms of Art relating to Anatomy .... | Together with | A Large Collection and Explication of Words and Phrases us'd in our Antient Statutes ... and Processes at Law; and the Etymology and Interpretation of the Proper Names of Men, Women, and Remarkable Places in *Great Britain*: Also the Dialects of our different Counties. | Containing many Thousand Words more than ... any *English* Dictionary before Extant. | *To which is Added* a Collection of our most Common Proverbs, with their Explication and Illustration. | The whole WORK compil'd and Methodically digested, as well for the Entertainment of the Curious, as the Information of the Ignorant, and for the Benefit of young Students, Artificers, Tradesmen and Foreigners, who are desirous thorowly to underdatnd what they Speak, Read, or Write. Rpt. 1969. Anglistica & Americana, 52. Hildesheim, Ger., and New York, NY: Georg Olms.

Bailey, Nathan, ed. (1730) *DICTIONARIUM BRITANNICUM*: | Or a more COMPLEAT | UNIVERSAL ETYMOLOGICAL ENGLISH DICTIONARY | Than any EXTANT[.] Rpt. 1969. Anglistica & Americana, 50. Hildesheim, Ger., and New York, NY: Georg Olms.

Berg, Donna Lee (1993) *A Guide to the Oxford English Dictionary*. Oxford, UK, and New York, US: Oxford University Press.

Blount, Thomas, ed. (1656) *GLOSSOGRAPHIA*: OR A DICTIONARY, Interpreting all such | Hard Words, | Whether *Hebrew, Greek, Latin, Italian, Spanish, French, Teutonick, Belgick, British* or *Saxon*, as are now used in our refined *English Tongue*. | Also the Terms of *Divinity, Law, Physick, Mathematicks, Heraldry, Anatomy, War, Musick, Architecture*; and of several other *Arts* and *Sciences* Explicated. | With *Etymologies, Definitions*, and *Historical Observations* on the same. | Very useful for all such as desire to understand what they read. Rpt. 1972. Anglistica & Americana, 32. Hildesheim, Ger., and New York, NY: Georg Olms.

Bulloker, John, ed. (1616) *AN ENGLISH EXPOSITOR*: | TEACHING THE INTER- | pretation of the hardest words vsed | in our Language. | WITH SVNDRY EX- PLICATI- | ons, Descriptions, and Discourses. Rpt. 1971. Anglistica & Americana, 71. Hildesheim, Ger., and New York, NY: Georg Olms.

Cawdrey, Robert, ed. (1604) *A | Table Alphabeticall*, con- | teyning and teaching the true | vvriting, and vnderstanding of hard | vsuall English wordes, borrowed from | the Hebrew, Greeke, Latine, | or French. &c. | With the interpretation thereof by | *plaine English words, gathered for the benefit & | helpe of Ladies, Gentlewomen, or any other | vnskilfull persons*. | Whereby they may the more easilie | and better vnderstand many hard English wordes, vvhich they shall heare or read in | Scriptures, Sermons, or elswhere, and also | be made able to vse the same aptly | themselues[.] Rpt. 1970. The English Experience, 226. Amsterdam, Neth.: Theatrum Orbis Terrarum, and New York, NY: Da Capo Press. [abbrev. Cawdrey (1604)]

Cockeram, Henry, ed. [1623] (1626²) *THE | ENGLISH | DICTIONARIE: | OR,| AN INTERPRE- | TER OF HARD ENG- | lish Words*: | Enabling as well Ladies and Gen- | tlewomen, young Schollers, Clarkes, Mer- | chants; as also Strangers of any Nation, to the vnderstanding of the more difficult Authors | already printed in our Language, and the more speedy attaining of an elegant perfection of the English tongue, both in rea- | ding, speaking, and writing. | *The second Edition, reuised and | enlarged*. [1st ed. 1623]. Rpt. 1970. Anglistica & Americana, 54. Hildesheim, Ger., and New York, NY: Georg Olms.

Coles, Elisha, ed. (1676) *An | English Dictionary*: | EXPLAINING | The difficult Terms that are used in | Divinity, Husbandry, Physick, Phylosophy, | Law, Navigation, Mathematicks, and other | Arts and Sciences. | CONTAINING | Many Thousands of Hard Words | (and proper names of Places) more than are in | any other English Dictionary or Expositor. | TOGETHER WITH | the Etymological Derivation of them from their | proper Fountains, whether Hebrew, Greek, | Latin, French, or any other Language. | In a Method more comprehensive, than any that is extant. Rpt. 1973. Anglistica & Americana, 76. Hildesheim, Ger., and New York, NY: Georg Olms.

Cooper, Thomas, ed. (1578) *Thesaurus Linguae Romanae et Britannicae*. Rpt. 1975. Anglistica & Americana, 111. Hildesheim, Ger., and New York, NY: Georg Olms.

Coote, Edmund (1596) *The English Schoole-maister*. 大塚高信（編）(1971) 英語文献翻刻シリーズ，第1巻：pp. 207–332, 豊田昌倫（解説）pp. 365–380. 東京：南雲堂.

Cotgrave, Randle, ed. (1611) *A Dictionarie of the French and English Tongues*. Rpt. 1950. Columbia, SC: University of South Carolina Press, 2nd printing 1968.

Crystal, David, and Ben Crystal, eds. (2002) *Shakespeare's Words: A Glossary and Language Companion*. London, UK: Penguin Books.

Dyche, Thomas, and William Pardon, eds. [1735] (1754⁸) A | NEW GENERAL | ENGLISH DICTIONARY; | Peculiarly calculated for the | USE and IMPROVEMENT | Of such as are unacquainted with the | LEARNED LANGUAGES. | Wherein the Difficult WORDS, and Technical TERMS made use of in | ANATOMY, [etc.] | Are not only fully explain'd, but accented on their proper Syllables, to prevent a vicious | Pronunciation; and mark'd with Initial LETTERS, to denote the Part of Speech .... | To which is prefixed, | A Compendious ENGLISH GRAMMAR ... by the due Application whereof, such as understand | *English* only, may be able to write as correctly and elegantly, as those who have been some | Years conversant in the *Latin, Greek*, &c. Languages. | TOGETHER WITH | A SUPPLEMENT, | Of the Proper NAMES of the most noted | KINGDOMS, PROVINCES, CITIES, TOWNS, RIVERS, &c. | .... | AS ALSO | Of the most cerebrated Emperors, Kings, Queens, Priests, Poets, Philosophers, Generals, &c. ... | THe WHOLE Alphabetically digested, and accented ... as the preceding Part; ... for the Use of such, as have but an | imperfect Idea of the *English* Orthography. 8th ed. London: Richard Ware. [Abbrev. Dyche-Pardon (1754⁸)]

Elyot, Thomas, ed. (1538) *Dictionary* [Latin-English]. Rpt. 1970. Menston, Yorkshire, UK: Scolar Press.

Estienne, Robert, ed. (1552) *Dictionariolum Puerorum Tribus Linguis Latina Anglica & Gallica*. Rpt. 1971. The English Experience: Its Record in Early Printed Books Published in Facsimile, no. 351. Amsterdam, Neth.: Theatrum Orbis Terrarum, and New York, NY: Da Capo Press.

Florio, John, ed. (1598) *A Worlde of Wordes*, Or Most copious, and exact *Dictionarie* in Italian and *English, collected by* IOHN FLORIO. Rpt. 1972. Anglistica & Americana, 114. Hildesheim, Ger., and New York, NY: Georg Olms.

Fowler, H. W., and F. G. Fowler, eds. (1911) *The Concise Oxford Dictionary of Current English*. Oxford: Clarendon; 2nd ed. 1929, H. W. Fowler, rev.; 3rd ed. 1934, H. W. Fowler and H. G. Le Mesurier, revs.; 4th ed. 1951, E. McIntosh, rev.; 5th ed. 1964, E. McIntosh, rev.; 6th ed. 1976, J. B. Sykes, ed.; 7th ed. 1982, J. B. Sykes, ed.; 8th ed. 1990, R. E. Allen, ed.; 9th ed. 1995, Della Thompson, ed.; 10th ed. 1999, Judy Pearsall, ed.; 11th ed. 2004, rev. 2006, Catherine Soanes, and Angus Stevenson, eds. *Concise Oxford English Dictionary*. [Abbrev. *COD*¹⁻¹¹]

Fowler, F. G., and H. W. Fowler, eds. (1924) *The Pocket Oxford Dictionary of Current English*. Oxford: Clarendon; 2nd ed. 1934, H. W. Fowler and H. G. Le Mesurier, revs.; 3rd ed. 1939, H. G. Le Mesurier, rev.; 4th ed. 1942, H. G. Le Mesurier and E. McIntosh, revs.; 5th ed. 1969, E. McIntosh, rev.; 6th ed. 1978, J. B. Sykes, ed.; 7th ed. 1984, R. E. Allen, ed.; 8th ed. 1992, Della Thompson, ed.; 9th ed. 2001, Catherine Soanes, ed. *The New Pocket Oxford Dictionary*; 10th ed. 2005, Catherine Soanes, Sara Hawker, and Julia Elliott, eds. *Pocket Oxford English Dictionary*; 11th ed. 2013, Maurice Waite, ed. [Abbrev. *POD*[1-11]]

Galfridus Grammaticus, ed. (c. 1460) *The Promptorium Parvulorum: The first English-Latin Dictionary*. A. L. Mayhew, ed. 1908. EETS, e.s. 102. London: Kegan Paul, and Oxford: Henry Frowde, Oxford University Press. [Abbrev. *PP*]

Glare, P. G. W., ed. (2012²) *Oxford Latin Dictionary*. 2nd ed. 2 vols. Oxford: Oxford University Press. [Abbrev. Glare (2012²) *OLD*]

早川勇著（2006）『日本の英語辞書と編纂者』（愛知大学文學會叢書 XI）横浜：春風社．

林哲郎［1968］再版（1985）『英語辞書発達史』東京：開文社．

Hayashi, Tetsuro (1978) *The Theory of English Lexicography 1530–1791*. Amsterdam, Neth.: John Benjamins.

今里智晃・土屋典生（1984）『英語の辞書と語源』（渡辺昇一（編）スタンダード英語講座，4）東京：大修館．

Johnson, Samuel, ed., (1755) *A | DICTIONARY | OF THE | ENGLISH LANGUAGE*: | IN WHICH | The WORDS are deduced from their ORIGINALS, | AND | ILLUSTRATED in their DIFFERENT SIGNIFICATIONS | BY | EXAMPLES from the best WRITERS. | TO WHICH ARE PREFIXED, | A HISTORY of the LANGUAGE, | AND | AN ENGLISH GRAMMAR. Rpt. 1983. Tokyo, Jpn: Yushodo.

Johnson, Samuel, ed., and H. J. Todd, rev. (1818) *A | DICTIONARY | OF THE | ENGLISH LANGUAGE*; | IN WHICH THE WORDS ARE DEDUCED FROM THEIR ORIGINALS; | AND ILLUSTRATED IN THEIR DIFFERENT SIGNIFICATIONS, BY EXAMPLES | FROM THE BEST WRITERS: | TOGETHER WITH | A History of the Language, and an English Grammar. | *WITH NUMEROUS CORRECTIONS, | AND WITH THE ADDITION OF SEVERAL THOUSAND WORDS, | AS ALSO WITH ADDITIONS TO THE HISTORY OF THE LANGUAGE, AND TO THE GRAMMAR*. 4 vols. London: Longman, Hurst, Rees, Orme, and Brown. [Abbrev. Todd's Johnson (1818)]

Kersey, John, ed. (1702) *A New English Dictionary:* | Or, a Compleat | COLLECTION | Of the Most | Proper and Significant Words, | Commonly used in the | LANGUAGE; | With a Short and Clear Exposition of | *Difficult Words and Terms of Art*. | The whole digested into Alphabetical Order; and chiefly designed for the benefit of Young *Scholars, Tradesmen, Artificers*, and the *Female Sex*, who would learn to spell truely; being so fitted to every Capacity, that it may be a continual help to all that want an Instructer. Rpt. from a copy of University Library, Edinburgh. 1969. R. C. Alston, ed., *English Linguistics 1500–1800*, no. 140. Menston, Yorkshire, UK: Scolar Press. [Abbrev. Kersey (1702)]

Kurath, Hans, Sherman M. Kuhn, and Robert E. Lewis, eds. (1952–2001) *Middle English Dictionary*. Ann Arbor, MI: University of Michigan Press. [Abbrev. *MED*]

Levins, Peter, ed. (1570) *Manipulus Vocabulorum: A Rhyming Dictionary of the English Language*. Henry B. Wheatley, ed. (1867) with an Alphabetical Index. EETS, o.s. 27. Rpt. 1969. New York: Greenwood Press.

Lewis, Charlton T., and Charles Short, eds. (1879) *A Latin Dictionary*. Impression of 1998. Oxford: Clarendon. [Abbrev. Lewis & Short (1879)]

Liddell, Henry George, and Robert Scott, eds., rev. by Henry Stuart Jones (1996) *A Greek-English. Lexicon*. Oxford: Clarendon. [Abbrev. Liddel-Scott-Jones (1996) *GEL*]

Murray, James A. H. (1900) *The Evolution of English Lexicography*. The Romanes Lecture. Oxford: Clarendon.

Murray, James A. H. et al., eds. (1933) *The Oxford English Dictionary*. 13 vols. Oxford: Clarendon; 2nd ed. on CD-ROM version 4.0. 2009. Oxford: Oxford University Press. [Abbrev. *OED*; *OED* (1933); *OED*[2]]

永嶋大典（1970）『蘭和・英和辞書発達史』東京：講談社.

大泉昭夫（編）（1997）『英語史・歴史英語学―文献解題書誌と文献目録書誌』（寺澤芳雄（監）英語学文献解題，第3巻）東京：研究社.

Partridge, Eric, ed. (1968[3]) *A Dictionary of the Underworld British & American*. 3rd ed. London: Routledge & Kegan Paul. [Abbrev. Partridge *DU*[3]]

Phillips, Edward, ed. (1658) *THE | NEW WORLD | OF | ENGLISH WORDS*: | Or, a General | DICTIONARY: | Containing the Interpretations of such hard words as are | derived from other Languages; whether *Hebrew*, *Arabick*, ... &c. their | Etymologies and perfect Definitions: | Together with | All those Terms that relate to the Arts and Sciences; whether *Theologie, Philosophy* ... &c. | To which are added | The significations of Proper Names, Mythology, and Poetical Fictions, Histo- | rical Relations, Geographical Descriptions.... as also all other Subjects that are useful, and | appertain to our English Language. | *A Work very necessary ... for all Per- | sons that would rightly understand what they discourse, write, or read*. Rpt.1969. Anglistica & Americana, 48. Hildesheim, Ger., and New York, NY: Georg Olms.

Schäfer, Jürgen (1970) "The Hard Word Dictionaries: A Re-Assessment," *Leeds Studies in English*, n. s. IV, 31–48.

Schmidt, Alexander, ed. (1923) *Shakespeare-Lexicon*. 4th ed. Gregor Sarrazin, rev. 2 vols. Berlin, and Leipzig: Walter de Gruyter.

Skinner, Stephen, ed. (1671) *Etymologicon Linguae Anglicanae*. Rpt. 1970. Anglis-

tica & Americana, 58. Hildesheim, Ger., and New York, NY: Georg Olms.
惣郷正明（1973）『辞書風物誌』東京：朝日新聞社.
Souter, Alexander, ed. [1916] (1966) *A Pocket Lexicon to the Greek New Testament*. Oxford: Clarendon.
Starnes, De Witt T., and Gertrude E. Noyes (1991) *The English Dictionary from Cawdrey to Johnson 1604–1755*. New edition with an introduction and a select bibliography by Gabriele Stein. Amsterdam, Neth. / Philadelphia, PA, US: John Benjamins.
Tilley, Morris Palmer, ed. [1950] (1966) *A Dictionary of the Proverbs in England in the Sixteenth and Seventeenth Centuries. A Collection of the Proverbs Found in English Literature and the Dictionaries of the Period*. Ann Arbor, MI: University of Michigan Press.
Tremblay, Florent, ed. (2005) *A Medieval Latin-English Dictionary Based on a Set of Unpublished 15th Century Manuscripts*, Medulla Grammaticae / Marrow of Grammar, *Kept in the British Museum Library*. Lewiston, NY, Queenston, Ontario, Can., and Lampeter, Ceredigion, Wales, UK: Edwin Mellen. [Abbrev. *MG*]
Webster, Noah, ed. (1828) *An American Dictionary of the English Language*: Intended to Exhibit, **I.** The Origin, Affinities and Primary Signification of English Words, as Far as They Have Been Ascertained. **II.** The Genuine Orthography and Pronunciation of Words, According to General Usage, or to Just Principles of Analogy. **III.** Accurate and Discriminating Definitions, with Numerous Authorities and Illustrations. To Which are Prefixed, an Introductory Dissertation on the Origin, History and Connection of the Languages of Western Asia and of Europe, and a Concise Grammar of the English Language. 2 vols. Rpt. in facsimile [1967] 5th ed. (1987). Prefaced by an Article by Rosalie J. Slater. San Francisco, CA: Foundation for American Christian Education.
Whiting, Bartlett Jere, ed. (1968) *Proverbs, Sentences, and Proverbial Phrases from English Writings Mainly before 1500*. With the Collaboration of Helen Wescott Whiting. Cambridge, MA: Belknap-Harvard University Press.
Withycombe, E. G., ed. [1945] 2nd ed. (1950^2) *The Oxford Dictionary of English Christian Names*. Oxford: Clarendon.
Wright, Joseph, ed. (1898–1905) *The English Dialect Dictionary*. Oxford, UK: Oxford University Press. Rpt. 1981. 6 vols. Tokyo, Jpn: Oxford University Press. [Abbrev. *EDD*]

日本語による辞書・事典
荒川幾男他（編）[1971] 第8刷 (1977)『哲学事典』東京：平凡社.
井上哲次郎・有賀長雄（編）[1881] 再版 (1884)『哲學字彙』東京：東洋館.
大野晋・佐竹昭広・前田金五郎（編）(1974)『岩波古語辞典』東京：岩波書店．[略 大野・佐竹・前田（1974）]

［好樹堂（訳）］（1871）*Nouveau dictionnaire français-japonais*. Changhai: La Mission presbytérienne américaine.
島田豊（編訳）（1892）第9刷（1899）『雙解英和大辭典』東京：共益商社.
前田正毅・高橋良昭（編）［第1版不詳］第4版（1886）『大正増補和譯英辭林』東京：中外堂.
和田垣謙三（編）［1901］（1902）『新英和辭典』東京：大倉書店.

引用作品および研究書
AV（1611）　　See *The Holy Bible*（1611）
Hexapla　　See Anonymous ed.（1841）
NEB　　See *The New English Bible with the Apocrypha*
Revised Version　　See *The New Testament in the Revised Version*（1881）
Vulgate　　See Colunga, Alberto et Laurentio Turrado, eds.
　　　　　　　　　　（以上は編・著者名で始まらない略号．書名である。）
Anonymous ed.（1841）*The English Hexapla Exhibiting the Six Important English Translations of the New Testament Scriptures*. Rpt. 1975. New York, NY: AMS. [Abbrev. *Hexapla*（1841）]
Boethius, Anicius Manlius Severinus. [*De Consolatione Philosophiae*] *The Consolation of Philosophy*, with the English translation of "I. T."（1609）, revised by H. F. Stewart [1918]（1968）. The Loeb Classical Library. London, UK: Heinemann, and Cambridge, MA, US: Harvard University Press.
Colunga, Alberto et Laurentio Turrado, eds.（1965）*Biblia Sacra iuxta Vulgatam Clementinam*. Quarta editio. Madrid: Biblioteca de Autores Cristianos. [Abbrev. Vulgate]
Deloney, Thomas. Francis Oscar Mann, ed.（1912）*The Works of Thomas Deloney*. Oxford: Clarendon.
Fischer, Andreas.（1994）"'Sumer is icumen in': the Seasons of the Year in Middle English and Early Modern English." Dieter Kastovsky, ed. *Studies in Early Modern English*. Berlin, Ger. and New York, NY, US: Mouton de Gruyter, 79–95.
Görlach, Manfred（2001）*Eighteenth-Century English*. Heidelberg, Ger.: Universitätsverlag C. Winter.
The Holy Bible（1611）An Exact Reprint in Roman Type, Page for Page of the Authorized Version Published in the Year 1611. With an Introduction by Alfred W. Pollard. Rpt. 1985. Oxford, UK: Oxford University Press, and Tokyo: Jpn: Kenkyusha. 付：寺澤芳雄（著）（1985）『翻刻版「欽定英訳聖書」—文献学的・書誌学的解説—』東京：研究社. [Abbrev. AV（1611）]
Homer. [$IAIA\Delta O\Sigma$] *The Iliad*. With an English translation by A. T. Murray, Vol. 1 [1924], Vol. 2 [1925], 2nd ed. rev. by William F. Wyatt, Vols. 1 & 2（1999）. The Loeb Classical Library. Cambridge, MA, US, and London, UK: Harvard University Press.

Milton, John (1667) *Paradise Lost*. Alastair Fowler, ed., 2nd ed. (1998) London, UK, and New York, NY, US: Longman.
The New English Bible with the Apocrypha [1961] 2nd ed. (1970) n. p.: Oxford University Press, and n. p.: Cambridge University Press. [Abbrev. *NEB* (1970)]
The New Testament in the Revised Version (1881). World's Classics 346 [1929] (1951). London: Oxford University Press. [Abbrev. Revised Version (1881)]
Pope, Alexander, tr. (1715–20) *The Iliad*. Henry W. Boynton, ed. (1903) *The Complete Poetical Works of Pope*. Boston, MA: Houghton Mifflin.
Shakespeare, William
    Evans, G. Blakemore, textual ed. (1974) *The Riverside Shakespeare*. Boston, MA: Houghton Mifflin.
    Neilson, William Allan, and Charles Jarvis Hill, eds. (1942) *The Complete Plays and Poems of William Shakespeare*. Boston, MA: Houghton Mifflin. The line-numbering of the *Globe* edition has been adhered to.
    Wilson, John Dover, ed. [1934] 2nd ed. [1936] (1957) *The Tragedy of Hamlet, Prince of Denmark*. Cambridge, UK: Cambridge University Press.
Tyndale, William, tr. (1526) *The New Testament of Our Lord and Saviour Jesus Christ:...* Being the First Translation from the Greek into English[.] With a Memoir of His Life and Writings, by George Offor (1836). London: Samuel Bagster. [Abbrev. Tyndale (1526)]
Wada, Akira (2013) "The Meaning of 'somer' in *It is not one swalowe that bryngeth in somer* Translated from *Una hirundo non facit ver*." *ERA* 30, 1 & 2: 27–52.
Wada, Akira (2014) "Corrigenda and Addendum." *ERA* 31, 1 & 2: 100.

引用作品（日本語訳）
『舊新約聖書』文語訳［第 1 版不詳］(1969) 東京：日本聖書協会.
シェイクスピア（作）・坪内逍遥（訳）(1935)『アントニーとクレオパトラ』東京：中央公論社.
シェイクスピア（作）・坪内逍遥（訳）(1934)『トロイラスとクレシダ』東京：中央公論社.
シェイクスピア（作）・小田島雄志（訳）(1986)『トロイラスとクレシダ』（シェイクスピア全集 IV）東京：白水社.
シェイクスピア（作）・市河三喜・松浦嘉一（訳）(1949)『ハムレット』（岩波文庫）東京：岩波書店.
シェイクスピア（作）・小津次郎（訳）［1972］第 8 刷 (1999)『ハムレット』（筑摩世界文學大系 16）東京：筑摩書房.
シェイクスピア（作）・小田島雄志（訳）(1986)『ハムレット』（シェイクスピア全集 III）東京：白水社.
シェイクスピア（作）・澤村寅二郎（対訳）［1935］第 3 版 (1942) *Shakespeare's Hamlet*. 東京：研究社.

シェイクスピア（作）・坪内逍遥（訳）（1933）『ハムレット』東京：中央公論社.
シェイクスピア（作）・永川玲二（訳）（1979）『ハムレット』（世界文学全集 4）東京：集英社.
シェイクスピア（作）・野島秀勝（訳）（2002）『ハムレット』（岩波文庫）東京：岩波書店.
シェイクスピア（作）・三神勲（訳）（1961）『ハムレット』（世界文学全集 3）東京：河出書房新社.
『聖書』新共同訳［1987, 1988］（2005）東京：日本聖書協会.
ホメロス（作）松平千秋（訳）（1992）『イリアス』（上下）（岩波文庫）東京：岩波書店.
ミルトン（作）平井正穂（訳）（1981）『失楽園』（上下）（岩波文庫）東京：岩波書店.

月刊誌
内山勝利（2014）「原義に遡行する」『図書』第 779 号：1.

索 引

ア行

アウグスティヌス（Aurelius Augustinus） 269–274, 278, 279
　『創世記について　マニ教徒駁論』270–272
上利　学　61
秋元実治　158
アクティヴ・ゾーン（active zone）　176
アスカム（Roger Ascham）　276
アリオストー（Ludovico Ariosto）　275
アリストテレス（Aristotle）
　『詩学』　275
　『ニコマコス倫理学』　259
アレゴリー　269
異化（estrangement（ostranenie), de-familization）　33, 60, 61
生き物の分類変化（2.1）　304
池上嘉彦　38, 171–173
石川慎一郎　58
意識の流れ（stream of consciousness）　31, 180, 210, 211, 217, 218, 224, 227
一貫性（coherence）　37–40, 200
一般語（共通語）　v, 236, 237, 244, 245, 247
意図性（intentionality）　40
意味
　〜の曖昧性　240
　〜の下降　239
　〜の構造的弛緩　240
　〜役割（semantic roles）　41
イメージスキーマ変換　174
ヴァージニア・ウルフ　（→ Woolf, Virginia）
ヴァージル（Virgil）　250, 276, 278, 279
　Aeneid　250, 275, 276, 278
ウィルソン（Thomas Wilson）　246
　The Art of Rhetorique（1553）　246
　The Rule of Reason（1551）　246
英英辞書不要の考え（1.1）　284
『英語英文學研究』　68
『英語年鑑』
　〜の「文体論研究」　68
英語の四季の名称（3.1）　320
英訳聖書の秋（3.1.5）　326
エリオット（Sir Thomas Elyot）　246
　The Book Named The Governour（1531）　246
大堀壽夫　39, 45
音声文体論（Phonostylistics）　56, 182, 188
音脱落（elision）　156
恩寵（supernal grace）　272, 279　（→摂理）

カ行

解決（Resolution）　43, 44
回復
　不幸からの〜（liquidation of misfortune）　42
会話分析（Conversation Analysis）　50
核強勢（nuclear stress）　191, 194
片見彰夫　40
語られた世界，語られるもの，ナラティブの内容（the narrated）　39, 45, 47
　〜 vs 語り（narration）　45
カタルシス論（catharsis）　43
価値の両面性　235
カルヴィン（Jean Calvin）　269
河井迪男　31
川口喬一　227n
川端康成
　『雪国』　58, 172, 176
含意（implicature）　40, 51, 167, 200, 218
含意された作者（Implied Author）　46, 46n, 47

観念主義／論（idealism）
  Vossler の〜　17, 18, 20
関連性理論（Relevance Theory）　26, 63, 64
キーワード　61, 140, 141, 143, 146, 155, 157
記述言語学（Descriptive Linguistics）　vi, 25
機能（functions）
  物語中の〜　41
キャクストン（William Caxton）　240, 245–247
  Eneydos　243, 246, 247
  Le Morte Darthur（1485）　231, 242, 247
  〜とマロリー　242, 243, 245
  〜による活版印刷　246, 247
ギャップ（gaps）
  文学テクストの中の〜　56
協調性の原則（Cooperative Principle）　38
キリスト教
  〜叙事詩　274, 275, 279
  〜信仰　252, 270
  〜的人文主義　252
  〜的な忍耐　264
  古典・〜両世界観　252
近代性（modernity）　249
  英語史における〜　247
  マロリーの〜　245
崩れた等位関係（2.7.4）　318
グリモールド（Nicolas Grimald）　231, 233, 245, 246, 249–252
厨川文夫　235, 241–243
グレンデル（Grendel）　22, 234, 235
形式主義（Formalism）　24, 33, 34
形式的連結（formal links）　39
結束性（cohesion）　38–40
言語使用域（register）　15, 25, 27, 31
言語選択の同質性
  キャクストンとマロリーの〜　243
言語変化を出版年順の辞書で読み取る（3）　320
行為者（actants）　44
  〜モデル（Actantial Model）　44

構成原理（constitutive principles）　40
構造主義文学理論　55
効率性（efficiency）　40
声（voice）
  語る〜（narrating voice）　46
  虚構テクスト外の〜（extrafictional voice）　46, 47
コード（code）
  意味素，すなわち，コノテーションの記号内容の〜（Les Sèmes ou signifies de connotation）　54
  解釈学的〜（Code herméneutique）　54
  行動の〜（Code des Actions）　54
  象徴の場の〜（Le Champ symbolique）　54
  文化的あるいは参照の〜（Codes culturels ou de références）　54
小迫　勝　65
古フランス語（OF）　147
語法研究（usage studies）　4, 27, 29, 32
コロケーション（collocation）　58, 85, 158, 165–167

サ行

斎藤兆史　65　（→ Saito, Yoshifumi）
  〜の創造的文体論（Creative Stylistics）　65
作者の意図（author's intent）　62, 204, 210, 211
サリー伯爵（Henry Howard, Earl of Surrey）　250, 253, 255–257, 260–262, 264
  〜の Aeneid 訳　250
  〜訳における古語の使用　262
参加者（participants）　51, 190
散文語
  詩語と〜　237, 240, 245–247
シークエンス（sequence）　42
シェイクスピア　（→ Shakespeare, William）
思考（Thought）
  〜行為の物語的報告（Narrative Report of

a Thought Act（NRTA）　*168, 170*
　　間接〜（Indirect Thought（IT））　*102, 168*
　　自由間接〜（Free Indirect Thought（FIT））
　　　93, 94, 102, 103, 114, 168–170
　　自由直接〜（Free Direct Thought（FDT））
　　　168, 170
　　直接〜（Direct Thought（DT））　*168–170*
辞書に関する文献（3.2）　*328*
自然ナラティブ　*43, 44, 44n*
　　〜と虚構ナラティブ　*44n, 212*
事態把握（construal）
　　主観的〜 vs 客観的〜　*172, 173*
実在論（positivism）
　　Bally の〜　*18*
詩的機能（poetic function）　*34, 56*
詩的効果（poetic effects）　*63, 64*
視点構成
　　自己中心的〜（ego-centric viewing arrangement）　*176*
　　主観性の〜　*176*
　　標準〜（canonical viewing arrangement）　*176*
シドニー（Sir Philip Sidney）　*257, 262–264*
篠田義博　*62*
清水正照　*270*
社会言語学（Sociolinguistics）　*4, 26–29, 31–33, 43, 59, 155, 157, 162, 188, 196*
18 世紀の辞書の harvest（3.1.4）　*325*
受益者（Receiver）　*44*
主客
　　〜分離の視点的な構図　*176*
　　〜融合の視点的な構図　*176*
主体（Subject）　*44, 58, 171, 172, 174, 176*
主題―題術（theme–rheme）構造　*203*
主題／トピック（theme/topic）　*51, 140, 211, 213, 218, 219, 223, 228*
　　〜的解釈　*217*
主題化（thematization）　*209, 211*
　　談話的〜　*iv, 209, 209n, 211*
受容理論（Reception Theory）　*26*

情動的文体論（Affective Stylistics）　*26, 55, 56*
情報性（informativity）　*40*
初期中英語期　*148*
初期の英語辞書（1）　*284*
初期の辞書から読み取るその時代の考え・解釈（2）　*304*
助力者（Helper）　*44*
心的態度　*12, 14, 20*
心的表象（mental representation）　*64, 65*
新批評（New Criticism）　*46n, 55*
人文主義　*264*
　　〜運動　*231, 249, 250, 252*
　　〜詩人　*249, 252*
　　キリスト教的〜　*252*
推意
　　弱い〜（weak implicatures）　*63, 64*
遂行部分（performative part）　*211*
スウィート（Henry Sweet）　*232*
スキーマ
　　PLANT 〜の構造　*62*
スタイル　*i, iii, 3n, 4, 48, 56, 58, 173, 174, 176, 177, 188, 189, 195, 196*（→ 文体）
　　個別的な〜　*174*
　　認知言語学による〜の概念　*177*
　　発音の〜　*56*
スタンザ形式　*140*
図（figure）と地（ground）　*61*
　　〜の文化と反転　*174*
スペンサー（Edmund Spenser）　*233*
成員カテゴリー化装置（membership categorization devices）（MCD）　*50*
精神分析　*44n*
生成文法（Generative Grammar）　*26, 36, 38, 39, 84*
世界観を映す Center, -tre = the earth（2.3）　*307*
摂理（Providence）（vs 偶像）　*279*
瀬戸賢一　*63*
ゼロ冠詞　*31*

前景化（foregrounding）　*33, 61*
　　～と背景化（backgrounding）　*174, 187*
選択　*10, 12, 29, 36, 59, 64, 85, 86, 185*
全知全能（omniscience）　*47*
創造性（creativity）
　　通常の話（common talk）の～　*48*

タ行

体系文法（Systemic Grammar）
　　～のシステム（systems）　*43*
題述／コメント（rheme/comment）　*211, 213, 218, 229*
対象（Object）　*44*
対立者（Opponent）　*44*
タッソー（Torquato Tasso）　*274, 275, 279*
田畑智司　*58*
田淵博文　*65*
ダンバー（William Dunbar）　*233*
談話（discourse）　*36–38, 177, 191, 200*
　　～は文脈（context）内に置かれた一貫性（coherence）を持ったテクスト　*38*
　　～標識（的機能）　*48, 159–162, 193*
　　～分析（Discourse Analysis）　*26, 33, 39, 45, 48, 50, 59*
　　越境する～　*218*
　　フィクションの～　*209*
チーク（Sir John Cheke）　*233, 249*
チョーサー（Geoffrey Chaucer）　*231, 233, 240, 245, 246*　（→ Chaucer, Geoffrey）
通常の非流暢的特徴（normal non-fluency features）　*49, 66*
　　relaxation の標識としての～　*193*
適切性（appropriateness）　*40*
テクスト（text）　*i, 37* et passim
　　～から談話へ　*36*
　　～間相互関連性（intertextuality）　*40*
　　～言語学（Text Linguistics）　*38–40*
　　～性（textuality）　*40*
　　～世界（Text World）　*64*
　　～世界理論（Text World Theory）　*64*
　　～とは結束性（cohesion）を持った言語の連鎖　*38*
　　～に込められたイデオロギー　*52*
　　～の生成　*38, 39*
　　～の定義　*37*
　　～部門（textual component）　*iv, 213, 214*
　　～文法（Text Grammar）　*36*
　　虚構～　*46, 48*
　　虚構～外の声（extrafictional voice）　*46, 47*
　　ポスト構造主義的文学～分析　*53*
寺澤　盾　*240*
頭韻（詩／法）　*186, 194, 233, 235, 240–242, 245, 247*
同義語による語釈（1.10.2.8）　*294*
動作主（Agent）　*51, 190, 191*
登場人物（dramatis personae）　*41, 44*
統制原理（regulative principles）　*40*
トテル（Richard Tottel）
　　Songes and Sonettes（1557）（『歌とソネット』）　*iv, 231–233, 246, 249, 257, 262*
　　Tottel's Miscellany（『～詩選集』）　*iv, 249, 250, 264*
豊田昌倫　*3n, 11, 56, 65, 68, 182–197, 285*
ドライデン（John Dryden）　*276*

ナ行

内的独白（interior monologues）　*31, 226*
内部言語形式と外部言語形式　*23*
ナラティブ（narrative）　*39, 41–44, 177, 211, 212, 215, 216, 218*
　　自然～と虚構～　*44, 44n, 212*
　　反射体モードの～（reflector-mode narrative）　*47*
ナラトロジー（Narratology）　*41, 47*
ナレーター（narrator）　*43* et passim
　　～とナレーティー（narratee）　*45, 178, 211*
　　1人称～（first-person narrator）　*45, 52, 62, 178*
　　作者的～（an authorial narrator）　*47*

索引　343

　作者と〜　*43*
　3人称〜（third-person narrator）　*46*, *178*
　信頼できない〜（unreliable narrator）　*181*
　全知の〜（omniscient narrator）　*179*, *181*
　全能者としての〜（Narrator as God）　*179*
　脱特権化された〜（De-authorized Narrator）　*180*
　プロローグを提供するものとしての〜（Narrator as Prologist）　*178*
　物語に参加しない，物語世界外的〜（a heterodiegetic and extradiegetic narrator figure）　*47*
難語
　〜英語の辞書で扱われている autumn（3.1.2）　*323*
　〜対平易語の CORDWAINER と SHOEMAKER（2.4）　*308*
　〜の解説から始まった英語辞書 Robert Cawdrey, ed.（1604）（1.3）　*285*
　Cawdrey（1604）後の〜辞書（1.4）　*286*
西岡啓治　*58*
西田幾多郎
　〜の「も」の用法　*14n*
西原貴之　*65*
日本英文学会中国四国支部　*68*
日本中世英語英文学会　*68*
日本文体論学会　*68*
忍耐（patience）　*270–273*
　〜と愛（charity）　*272*, *273*
　〜と知識　*271*
　キリスト教的な〜　*264*
認知言語学（Cognitive Linguistics）　*26*, *59–62*, *64*, *171–177*

ハ行

媒介（mediation）　*43*, *203*, *204*, *213*, *218*
　〜者　*203*
媒体（medium）　*27*, *33*
　発話〜　*192*
派遣者（Sender）　*44*

橋本　功　*63*
芭蕉
　『奥の細道』　*172*
発信者（encoder）（＝作者）　*iv*, *12*, *14*, *30*, *44–47*, *53*
　〜の心的態度　*20*
発話（Speech）（→ 話法）
　〜意図　*iii*, *iv*
　間接〜（Indirect Speech）　*93*
　自由間接〜／思考（Free Indirect Speech / Thought）　*93*, *94*, *114*, *168–170*
　直接〜（Direct Speech）　*93*, *102*
　物語世界を文脈とする〜　*204*
花輪　光　*36*
場面性（situationality）　*40*
美学的反応理論（Theory of Aesthetic Response）　*56*
東森　勲・吉村あき子　*63*
批評的言語学（Critical Linguistics）　*39*, *51*, *52*, *132*
批評的談話分析（Critical Discourse Analysis）（CDA）　*38*, *39*, *50*, *52*, *85*, *132*
評価（Evaluation）　*4*, *43*, *44*
病気の解釈の変化（2.2）　*305*
表出（Presentation）
　Speech and Thought 〜　*102*
標準英語　*190*, *246*, *247*
平井正穂　*279*, *307*, *314*
平山直樹　*48*
浮網茂信　*162–165*
福元広二　*48*, *158–162*
文学　*i*, *3* et passim
　〜意味論（Literary Semantics）　*68*
　〜規則（literary rules）　*38*
　〜教育　*65*
　〜言語　*4* et passim
　〜語用論（Literary Pragmatics）　*57*
　〜性（literariness）　*38*
　〜性の連続　*83*
　〜的効果　*27*

～テクスト　*i*, *4* et passim
～テクスト文法（Literary Text Grammar）　38
～批評　*4*, *4n*, *5*, *33*
紛糾（Complication）　*39*, *43*, *44*
分詞
　～形容詞　*28*, *29*
　～の叙述的用法（predicative use of past participle）　*29*
　古典ラテン語や古典ギリシャ語の～　*29*
文体（style）　*3* et passim
　～の定義　*3–9*
　越境の～　*224*
　音声面での～　*56*
　機能主義的～（functional styles）　*57*
　古典主義詩人達の～　*7*
　精神的～（mind style）　*59*, *61*
　Shakespeare の～　*7*
文体論（Stylistics）　*i–iii*, *3* et passim　（→ Stylistics）
　～の教育的効果　*65*
　～の通時的概観　*9–26*
　音声～（Phonostylistics）　*56*, *182*, *188*
　機能主義的～（Functional Stylistics）　*56*
　教育的～（Pedagogical Stylistics）　*65*
　狭義の～　*4*, *5*, *33*
　形式～（Formal Stylistics）　*33*, *34*
　言語学的～（Linguistic Stylistics）　*5*
　広義の～　*ii*, *3n*, *4*, *33*, *63*
　コーパス～（Corpus Stylistics）　*58*, *83*
　社会言語学的な～　*4*, *28*, *29*, *31–33*, *188*
　情動的～（Affective Stylistics）　*26*, *55–56*
　心理学志向の～　*26*
　創造的～（Creative Stylistics）　*65*
　認知～（Cognitive Stylistics）　*59*, *60*, *62*, *173*, *176*
　表現的～（Expressive Stylistics）　*15*
　フェミニスト～（Feminist Stylistics）　*52*
　文学的～（Literary Stylistics）　*15*
　変種（variation）としての～　*27*

文法化　*158*, *161*
文脈（context）　*iii*, *11*, *12*, *27*, *31*, *37*, *38*, *40*, *48*, *55*, *57–58*, *140*, *141*, *185*, *204*, *319*
　～的連結（contextual links）　*40*
　社会的～　*8*
平行性（parallelism）　*33*, *39*
ベイコン（Sir Francis Bacon）
　『エッセー』（Essays）　*58*
ベーオウルフ（Bēowulf 登場人物名）　*234*, *235*　（→ *Beowulf*）
ペトラルカ（Francesco Petrarca）　*253*, *254*, *256*, *257*
変奏（variation）　*191*, *192*, *195*, *234*
ホーマー（Homer）　*252*, *274*, *276*, *278*
　～の並列的な文　*21*
ホラティウス（Horatius）　*259*, *264*, *275*, *276*
　Carmina II, 10　*257*

マ行

マクロ構造（macrostructures）　*38*
松井信義　*48*
マッピング（mapping）　*62*
マロリー（Sir Thomas Malory）　*iv*, *231–248*
　Le Morte d'Arthur（『アーサー王の死』）　*61*
　～の近代性　*245*
　～の Winchester 写本　*242*
水野和穂　*58*
ミルトン（John Milton）　（→ Milton, John）
民族心理学　*21*
民族精神
　言語における collective な～　*21*, *24*
無韻詩　*250*
矛盾指示（double reference）　*236*
村上彩実　*65*
メイスン（H. A. Mason）　*264*
名声（観）　*252*
命題（proposition）　*42*, *85*, *211*, *213*
メタファー（metaphor）　*62*, *63*
メタ物語世界的（metadiegetic）　*45*

索引

メトニミー（metonymy）
　〜の認知プロセス　*174, 175*
　焦点化と身体部位の〜　*174, 175*
モア（Sir Thomas More）
　The History of King Richard III（1513）
　246
モデルとテクスト　*iv, 249, 275*
物語性（narrativity）
　文間の〜　*38*
物語世界外的（extradiegetic）　*45*
物語世界的（diegetic），もしくは物語世界内的（intradiegetic）　*45*
模倣論　*274–276*

ヤ行

八木克正　*58*
山口美知代　*168–170*
山崎のぞみ　*48*
山梨正明　*60, 173–177*
山本忠雄　*9n, 14n, 59*
結城英雄　*227n*
有効性（effectiveness）　*40*
容認可能性（acceptability）　*40*
容認発音（RP）　*184*
『ヨブ記』　*274, 279*

ラ行

ルーキウス（Emperor Lucius）　*242*
レシ（the récit）　*41, 42*
レトリック　*12, 13*
　イギリス労働党が用いる〜　*51*
　大衆紙の〜　*191*
　リベラル・アーツの3分野（the trivium of grammar, logic and rhetoric）としての〜　*13*
レベル
　作者―読者（author-reader）の〜　*46, 204*
　登場人物―登場人物（character-character）の〜　*46*
　発信者（encoder）（＝作者）―受信者（decoder）（＝読者）の〜　*46*
レン（Charles L. Wrenn）　*234*
ロシアフォルマリズム（Russian Formalism）　*33*
ロンドン地域言　*245*

ワ行

ワイアット（Sir Thomas Wyatt）　*231–233, 245, 253–256, 262*
脇本恭子　*48*
話者
　〜／作者の表現レベルの変異性　*174*
話法（→ 発話）
　間接〜（Indirect Speech）　*168–170*
　自由間接〜（Free Indirect Speech）　*168–170, 227*
　直接〜（Direct Speech）　*168–170*
　発話（Speech）と思考（Thought）を合わせたものとしての〜　*168*
割り込み（interruption）　*49, 50*

A

Abbott, H. Porter　*47*
Adamson, Sylvia　*19, 19n, 25*
Agari, Masahiko（上利政彦）　*231, 233*
allegory（アレゴリー）　*269*
Amis, Kingsley　*189, 194*
　Girl, 20　*189*
　I Like It Here　*194*
　King's English　*188*
Ancrene Wisse　*149*
Aristotle　*12, 13, 43, 221, 222*
　Art of Rhetoric　*13*
Aronstein, Philipp　*21–25*
ARTERY
　〜と VITAL SPIRITS（2.6）　*310*
　〜の原義（2.6.2）　*311*
　〜を流れる命を支える流体の名（2.6.4）　*313*
Ascham, Roger　*276*

Auden, Wystan H.
　'Musée des beaux arts'　*83, 92*
Austen, Jane　*61, 168–170*
　Emma　*169*
Austin, John L.　*211, 213*
autonomy of the text（テクストの自律性）　*83, 91, 92*

B

Bailey, Nathan, ed.（1721）(1.11)　*296*
　〜と Johnson（1.11.11）　*303*
　PROVERBS（1.11.10）　*302*
　イギリス諸島外起源の生き物・産物には特性への言及（1.11.8）　*301*
　詳しい語釈（1.11.9）　*301*
　語釈 "... WELL KNOWN"（1.11.6）　*300*
　語釈の粗と密（1.11.5）　*300*
　種類の特定区分の言及で僅かに限定的な語釈（1.11.7）　*301*
　小辞（1.11.1）　*296*
　接頭辞・接尾辞（1.11.2）　*297*
　代名詞（1.11.3）　*299*
　動詞（1.11.4）　*300*
Bakhtin, Mikhail　*53, 107*
　dialogic（対話的）　*53*
Bally, Charles　*12–18, 24, 25*
Barthes, Roland　*53–55*
　«La mort de l'auteur»（「作者の死」）　*53*
　S/Z　*54*
Bateson, Frederick W.　*83, 91*
Baudelaire, Charles
　'Les Chats'　*35, 36*
Beardsley, Monroe C.　*91*
Beckett, Samuel　*114*
Benveniste, Émile　*53*
Beowulf　*ii, iv, 22, 233, 235, 238–240*
Berdan, John M.　*249*
Bex, Tony　*33*
Bex, Tony, Michael Burke and Peter Stockwell　*132*

Biber, Douglas　*192*
Biguenet, John and Rainer Schulte　*124*
the Birmingham School of Discourse Analysis　*50*
Blake, Norman F.　*243, 246*
blending conceptual 〜　*133, 134*
Blount, Thomas, ed.（1656）(1.7)　*288*
Boase-Beier, Jean　*iii, 25, 60, 64, 82, 86, 87, 123–138*
Boase-Beier, Jean, Antoinette Fawcett and Philip Wilson　*86*
Boccaccio, Giovanni
　Décaméron（『デカメロン』）　*41–43*
Booth, Wayne C.　*46, 46n*
Bowra, Cecil M.　*278*
Bray, Joe　*19, 68*
Brazil, David　*105*
Bremond, Claude　*43*
the British National Corpus　*92*
Brook, George L.　*160*
the Brown Corpus　*144, 144n*
Brueghel, Pieter　*92*
Bullokar, John, ed.（1616）(1.5)　*287*
Burke, Michael　*67*
Burney, Fanny
　Evelina　*31*
Burton, Deirdre　*84, 103–105, 108*

C

Carston, Robyn and Seiji Uchida　*63*
Carter, Ronald　*26, 48, 49, 59, 65, 68, 84, 92, 101–103*
Carter, Ronald and Michael N. Long　*186*
Carter, Ronald and Walter Nash　*83, 92*
Carter, Ronald and Peter Stockwell　*117*
Catford, John C.　*128*
Catullus, G. Valerius　*129*
Cawdrey, Robert, ed.（1604）(1.3)　*285*
Celan, Paul　*86, 133, 134*
　'Espenbaum'　*134*

Chancery Standard（法務行政府基準） *246*
Chandler, Raymond
 The Lady in the Lake *36*, *100*
characterization（特徴づけ） *48*, *160*
Chatman, Seymour *43*
Chaucer, Geoffrey *ii*, *58*, *61*, *139–143*, *148*, *149*, *151*, *152*, *162*, *231*, *289*
 Boethius *326*
 Knight's Tale *140*, *150*
 Melibee *58*
 The Prioress's Prologue and Tale *139–143*
 Troilus and Criseide (/Criseyde) *61*, *149*, *152*
Chloupek, Jan *57*
choice（選択） *11*, *59*, *64*, *86*, *107*, *108*
 the notion of stylistics as the result of ~s *132*
 stylistic ~（文体的選択） *86*, *126*
Chomsky, Noam *36*, *38*, *100*, *126*
Christie, Agatha *195*, *196*, *206*, *207*
 The Body in the Library *196*
 The Curtain *198*, *199*
 Nemesis *196*
 Ordeal by Innocence *196*
 Third Girl *196*
Clark, Billy *63*
Clark, Kate *85*, *103*, *109*, *110*
Coates, Jennifer *152*, *153*
Cockeram, Henry, ed. (1626²)(1.6) *287*
cognitive subordinatings *104*
Coles, Elisha, ed. (1676)(1.9) *290*
collocation（コロケーション） *105*
 anomalous ~ *167*
context（文脈） *8*, *12*, *35*, *37*, *38*, *55*, *83*, *91*, *92*, *94*, *99*, *117*, *124* （→ 文脈）
 ~s of gender, race, class, nationality *117*
 cosmic ~ *127*
 The framing ~ of a colony *106*
 a framing of ~ *106*
 historical ~ *128*, *130*

 implications of ~ *94*
Cook, Guy *34*, *37*, *39*
Cooper, Robert
 Pinocchio in Venice *181*
Coote, Edmund, ed.(1596)(1.2) *285*
CORDWAINER と SHOEMAKER（2.4）*308*
Corpus Linguistics（コーパス言語学）*59*, *83*
Coulthard, Malcolm *105*, *114–116*
Coulthard, Margaret *50*
Cressot, Marcel *16*, *17*
Critical Discourse Analysis（CDA）（→ 批評的談話分析）
Critical Linguistics （→ 批評的言語学）
Croce, Benedetto *13*, *14*, *17*
Crystal, David and Derek Davy *7*, *8*, *11*, *27*, *33*
Culler, Jonathan *42*
Cullingford, Elizabeth B. *221*, *222*

D

Dahl, Roald *65*
 The Daily Express *191*
 The Daily Mirror *190*
 The Daily Star *191*
de Balzac, Honoré
 Sarrasine（『サラジーヌ』）*54*
de Beaugrande, Robert-Alain, and Wolfgang U. Dressler *40*
de Beauvoir, Simone *52*
de Buffon, G.-L. Leclerc *10*
de la Mare, Walter
 'The Listeners' *83*, *93*
de Saussure, Ferdinand *13*, *15*
Defoe, Daniel
 Robinson Crusoe *178*
Deirdre, Burton *84*, *103–105*
Derrida, Jacques *128*
Deutschbein, Max *21*, *22*, *25*

Dickens, Charles　31, 58, 59
　　Bleak House　167
　　David Copperfield　31, 49, 167, 179
　　Dombey and Son　166
　　Great Expectations　63, 155, 175
　　A Tale of Two Cities　40
The Dickens Lexicon　59
　　Dickens Lexicon Digital　59
discourse（談話）
　　~colony（談話のコロニー）　84, 85, 105–107, 111
　　~rheme　213
　　~theme　213
disfluency features（→ 通常の非流暢的特徴）
domesticating view of translation（翻訳の同化的視点）　129
Dostoevsky, Fyodor　53
Dulcken, Henry W.
　　~'s translation of a Hans Christian Andersen story　132

E

Eagleton, Terry　52, 53
Eaton, Trevor　68
e.e. cummings　98
Eliot, George
　　Silas Marner　47
Empson, William　146
Enkvist, N. Erik　11
ERA（The English Research Association of Hiroshima）　68
ergon（出来上がったもの）と energeia（創造過程）　13
Estuary English（河口域英語）　189
Exclamatio（感嘆法）　257

F

Fairclough, Norman　39, 51
false start（出だしの誤り，フライング）　193

Faulkner, William
　　'A Rose for Emily'　175
Fielding, Henry
　　Joseph Andrews　47, 178
　　Tom Jones　178
Fiore, Peter A.　270
Firth, J. R.　25, 111
Fish, Stanley　25, 26, 55, 56, 118
Fisiak, Jacek　152
Flaubert, Gustave　19, 20
Fludernik, Monika　46n, 47
Fónagy, Iván　25, 56
foregrounding（前景化）　33, 66, 83, 90, 93, 126, 129
Foucault, Michel　55
Fowler, Alastair　267, 269
Fowler, Roger　4, 5, 11, 25, 33, 39, 51, 52, 56, 57, 59–61, 83, 85, 90, 91, 93, 98, 104, 107, 108, 112, 124n, 126, 129, 132, 134
Fowler, Roger and Frederick W. Bateson　83, 91
Freeman, Donald C.　25, 86, 99, 100, 125–129, 131, 133, 136
Freud, Sigmund　44n
Fuami, Kayoko（浮網佳代子）　59
Funada, Saoko（舩田佐央子）　63

G

Garvin, Paul　90
Gavins, Joanna　64
Genette, Gérard　45, 47
Ghost Implicature（亡霊の含意）　200
Gimson, Alfred C.　189, 190
Golding, William
　　The Inheritors　56, 101
Goldsmith, Oliver　220
　　The Vicar of Wakefield　48
Görlach, Manfred　246
Gower, Sir John
　　Confessio Amantis（『恋人の告白』）　147

Mirour de l'Omme（『夢想者の鏡』） *147*
Great Vowel Shift　*246*
Greimas, Algirdas J.　*41*, *44*
Grice, Paul　*38*
Guiraud, Pierre　*12*, *13*, *18*, *20*
Gumperz, John J.　*50*

H

Hall, Geoff　*65*, *67*, *68*
Halliday, M. A. K.　*25*, *56*, *57*, *91*, *101*, *107*, *203*
　〜 transitivity system　*105*
　〜の意味システム　*84*
　〜の機能言語学　*85*, *213*
　〜の体系機能文法　*56*
　Hallidayan transitivity　*104*, *110*
Halliday, M. A. K. and Ruqaiya Hasan　*39*
Halliday, M. A. K. and James R. Martin　*52*
Hamel, Mary　*240*
Harris, Zelig　*50*
Hausenblas, Karel　*57*
h-dropping（h 音脱落）　*155*, *156*
Hecimovich, Gregg A.　*217*
Helsinki Corpus 1500–1570　*246*
Hemingway, Ernest
　'Cat in the Rain'　*43*, *84*, *101–105*
Hendricks, William O.　*39*
HERB は「薬草・香草」よりも広い意味の語（2.5）　*308*
Herman, David　*47*
Herman, David, Manfred Jahn and Marie-Laure Ryan　*47*
Hoey, Michael　*84*, *85*, *105–107*
Holmes, James S.　*124*, *128*
holocaust poetry　*138*
Hopkins, Gerard M.　*98*
Horace　*129*
Hori, Masahiro（堀　正広）　*25*, *58*, *165–168*
Hughes, Rebecca　*49*, *65*, *193*, *194*
Hughes, Ted

'Hawk Roosting'（「憩う鷹」）　*60*
Humboldt–Saussure–Bally の流れ　*14*
Humboldt–Vossler–Spitzer の流れ　*14*

I

ideological bias（イデオロギー上の偏見）*51*
Ihwe, Jens　*39*
Il Piccolo della Sera　*220*
Imahayashi, Osamu（今林　修）　*25*, *155–158*
improvisation（即興性）　*131*
indeterminacies（不確定性）　*86*, *118*
inkhornism（学者気取りの学術用語）　*262*
intentions（意図）
　the author's 〜, the reader's interpretation　*91*
　intentional　*104*, *105*, *112*
　intentionality　（→ 意図性）
The International Association of Literary Semantics（IALS）　*68*, *209n*
interpretation(s)（解釈）　*37*, *90*, *92–94*, *104*, *109*, *212*
　the author's intentions, the reader's 〜（→ intentions）
　meaning and 〜　*83*, *91*
　subjective 〜　*117*
intertextual（間テクスト的，テクスト相互的）　*40*, *85*
intertextuality　*229*
Invention（題材の発見）　*257*
irony（アイロニー）　*102*
　conscious and intentional speaker 〜　*112*
Iser, Wolfgang　*26*, *56*
Ishiguro, Kazuo
　The Remains of the Day　*181*
Ito, Hiroyuki（伊藤弘之）　*167*

J

Jacobs, Roderick A. and Peter S. Rosenbaum　*36*

Jakobson, Roman　*i, 25, 26, 33–36, 66, 83, 86, 90, 91, 124, 127, 130, 134, 146, 182, 187*

Jakobson, Roman and Lawrence G. Jones　*35, 91*

Jakobson, Roman and Claude Lévi-Strauss　*35, 36*

Jakobson, Roman and Linda R. Waugh　*185*

James, Henry　*47, 113*
　The Turn of the Screw　*44n*

Jensen, Wilhelm
　Gradiva　*44n*

Jespersen, Otto　*58*

Jimura, Akiyuki（地村彰之）　*25, 152–155, 162*

Jimura, Akiyuki（地村彰之）, Yoshiyuki Nakao（中尾佳行）, Masatsugu Matsuo（松尾雅嗣）, Norman F. Blake, and Estelle Stubbs　*58*

Jobert, Manuel　*56, 67*

Jones, Daniel　*189*

Jones, Francis R.　*86, 130, 131*

Jones, Richard F.　*243*

Journal of Literary Semantics: An International Review　*68*

Joyce, James
　Dubliners　*iii, iv, 28, 209, 210, 214, 216, 217, 228*
　Finnegans Wake　*229*
　A Portrait of the Artist as a Young Man　*iii, iv, 47, 214–216, 228*
　'The Sisters'　*209–212, 214, 215, 217*
　'Two Gallants'　*28*
　Ulysses　*iii, iv, 30, 31, 209–211, 214, 216–226, 228, 229*

K

Kate, Clark　*85, 109, 110*

Kawabata, Yasunari　（→ 川端康成）

Keats, John
　'Ode to Autumn'　*108*

Kelman, James
　How Late it was, How Late　*181*

Kenner, Hugh　*226, 227*

Ker, William P.　*276*

Kersey, John, ed.（1702）（1.10）　*292*

Kesey, Ken
　One Flew Over the Cuckoo's Nest　*62, 104*

Kikuchi, Shigeo（菊池繁夫）　*57, 103, 198–205, 209*

King's English　*188, 189*

Knapp, John V.　*68*

Koguchi, Keisuke（髙口圭轉）　*40*

L

Labov, William　*44*
　〜流のナラティブの分析　*44*

Labov, William and Joshua Waletzky　*38, 43, 44*

Lakoff, George and Ronald Langacker　*25*

Lakoff, George and Mark Turner　*60, 62*

Lakoff, Robin　*52, 153*

The Lancaster-Oslo / Bergen Corpus（LOB Corpus）　*144, 144n*

Langacker, Ronald W.　*176*

Language and Literature　*68, 133*

langue（ラング）
　〜 vs parole（パロール）　*15, 16*

Lanser, Susan S.　*46*

Larkin, Philip
　'First Sight'　*84, 98*

Lass, Roger　*246*

Lawrence, D. H.
　Lady Chatterley's Lovers　*175*
　Sons and Lovers　*108*

Leech, Geoffrey　*i, iii, 25, 66, 68, 82, 83, 89–95, 144n*

Leech, Geoffrey N. and Mick H. Short　*6, 7, 46n, 60, 65, 84, 89, 102, 168, 170*

Leigh, Mike
   Secrets and Lies　*193*
Lévi-Strauss, Claude　*35*, *43*, *44*
Levý, Jiří　*131*
Lewis, C. S.　*iv*, *270*, *274*
literariness　*38*　(→ 文学)
   〜-inducing presuppositions　*134*
   a cline of 〜（文学性の連続）　*83*, *92*
Louw, William　*85*, *110*–*112*
Lowell, Robert
   'Home After Three Months Away'　*120*
   Life Studies　*120*
   'Skunk Hour'　*85*, *117*–*121*

M

MacMahon, Barbara　*64*
Madeleva, Sister M.　*143*
Malmkjaer, Kirsten　*86*, *87*, *131*–*133*
Malory, Sir Thomas　(→ マロリー)
Marouzeau, Jules　*10*, *12*, *16*, *17*
Martindale, Charles　*278*
Mason, Ellsworth and Richard Ellmann　*220*
Masui, Michio（桝井迪夫）　*25*, *58*, *139*–*143*
Mathesius, Vilém　*203*
Matsutani, Midori（松谷　緑）　*61*
Matsuura, Kazuko（松浦加寿子）　*58*
McGonagall, William　*91*
McIntyre, Dan　*67*
ME, Early ModE の 2 言語／3 言語辞書に見る英語の 1 番目と 3 番目の季節の呼称（3.1.1）　*321*
ME West Midland　*149*
mediation（媒介）　*43*, *213*, *218*
Melia, Daniel　*99*
metaphor（メタファー）
   dead 〜s　*109*
   metaphorized modality（メタファー化された法性）　*67*
Miller, Arthur
   Death of a Salesman　*175*

Mills, Sara　*52*
Milne, Alan A.
   Winnie-The-Pooh　*40*
Milton, John　*134*
   Paradise Lost　*5*, *28*, *29*, *267*–*280*
   Paradise Regained　*28*, *29*
mind style　(→ style)
modality（法性）　*51*, *52*
   epistemic 〜（認知的法性）*61*
   foregrounded 〜（前景化された法性）　*63*
   metaphoraized（メタファー化された法性）〜　*67*
Morte Arthure（MA）　*240*, *241*, *247*
Mukařovský–Jakobson 理論　*33*
Mukařovský, Jan　*33*, *83*, *90*, *124*, *126*, *129*, *134*
Munday, Jeremy　*124*
Murdoch, Iris
   Under the Net　*175*
mystification（あいまい化）　*51*

N

Nakagawa, Ken（中川　憲）　*143*–*146*
Nakao, Masayuki（中尾雅之）　*61*
Nakao, Yoshiyuki（中尾佳行）　*147*–*151*
Nakao, Yoshiyuki（中尾佳行）and Yoko Iyeiri, Yoko（家入葉子）　*60*
narrator（ナレーター）
   a dominating 〜（支配的ナレーター）　*52*
Nash, Walter　*32*, *83*, *92*, *194*
The Nation　*183*
Nelson, Gerald　*193*
the New Criticism movement　*91*
Nicholson, Colin and Ranjit Chatterjee　*117*
Nishio, Miyuki（西尾美由紀）　*58*
Norman Conquest　*147*
North American linguistics　*90*

O

OE 詩学　*233*

Ogden-Richards 235
Ohmann, Richard M. 126
Ohno, Hideshi（大野英志） 58
one の総称性 168
Orwell, George
    Animal Farm 52
    〜の 'a defining feature of his personal voice' 61
Owen, Wilfred
    'Futility' 182–188
Oxford English Dictionary（*OED*）
    OED On-line 9, 31, 32, 229
    OED^2 191
    OED^2 *on CD-ROM* 165
    OED の autumn と spring の初例 324

P

Pagnini, Marcello 25, 58
Parks, Tim 135
The Paston Letters（『パストン家書簡集』） 48
Pearsall, Derek 54, 55
PEOPLE ARE PLANTS metaphor 62
Perryman, Kevin 135
Petöfi, János S. 39
phallocentric（男性中心主義的） 52
Phillips, Edward, ed. (1658) (1.8) 289
PHILOSOPHY (2.7.1) 315
    〜, SCIENCE 及び ART (2.7) 314
    〜の和訳「哲学」の問題点 (2.7.5) 318
Pilkington, Adrian 63, 64
Plath, Sylvia
    The Bell Jar 104
PNEUMA—SPĪRITUS—SPIRIT への流れ (2.6.3) 311
poetic design（詩的デザイン） 86
    Freeman's 〜 126, 129, 133, 136
poetic language fallacy 92
poeticity（詩性） 135
The Poetics and Linguistics Association（PALA） 26, 32, 68, 126n
point of view（視点） 60, 66, 85, 112
Pomorska, Krystyna and StephenRudy 35
post-Bloomfieldian structuralism 90
Pragmatics（語用論） 82
    Literary 〜（文学語用論） 57
the Prague School 93
    〜 School of functional structuralism 90
Prague Structuralists 123
Pratt, Mary L. 25, 92
Presentation （→ 表出）
Prévost, Abbé
    Manon Lescaut 45
Prince, Gerald 38
Propp, Vladimir 41–44
    〜流の線形モデル 43
PROVERBS (1.11.10) 302

Q

Quirk, Randolph 56, 192, 193

R

reader's response 93
    〜（読者反応）理論 83
recreative（再創造的） 86, 130
rhetoric（レトリック） 9, 13
    〜 of text 66
    classical 〜 67
Richards, Ivor A. 43, 91
Richardson, Samuel
    Pamela 178
Richmond, Emma
    His Temporary Mistress 195
Rieser, Hannes 39
Riffaterre, Michael 36, 86, 124, 125, 128–130, 134
Rissanen, Matti 158, 160, 161
Le Roman de la Rose / *The Romaunt of the Rose*（『薔薇物語』） 147–149
The Romance of the Rose 233, 245

Rosewarne, David *189*
Ross, Alan S. C. *196*
Ross, John R. *38*
RP（容認発音）
　advanced ～ *190*
　advanced U-～ *190*
　conservative ～ *190*
　conservative U-～ *190*
　general ～ 190
　U-～（upper-crust ～） *190*
Russian Formalists *123* （→ ロシアフォルマリズム）

S

Sacks, Harvey *50*
Saito, Yoshifumi（斎藤兆史） *47, 65, 177–182*
Sakauchi, Hiroyuki（坂内宏行） *52*
Salinger, Jerome D.
　The Cather in the Rye *48*
Sapir, Edward *25, 60*
Sapir, Edward and Benjamin L. Whorf *104*
Saussure–Bally の流れ *13, 14*
Schulte, Rainer and John Biguenet *128*
SCIENCE（2.7.2） *316*
　～と ART（2.7.3） *317*
Scott, Jeremy *68*
Searle, John R. *40*
Sebeok, Thomas A. *26, 82, 90*
seeming という概念 *201n*
Seidensticker, Edward G. *58, 172*
Sell, Roger D. *25, 57, 58*
semantic（意味論的）
　～analysis of sentences *104*
　～classification of roles（Agent, Affected, Instrument, etc.） *108*
　～prosodies *85, 110–112*
Semino, Elena *25, 64*
Semino, Elena and Jonathan Culpeper *60*
Semino, Elena and Mick H. Short *68*
Semino, Elena and Kate Swindlehurst *60, 62, 63*
semiotics of literary translation（文学的翻訳の記号論） *86, 128*
Shakespeare, William *ii, 7, 19, 35, 46n, 48, 125, 158–165, 196, 198–205*
　As You Like It *164*
　'Th'Expence of Spirit' *35*
　Hamlet *57, 159, 198–205, 318–320*
　Henry 5 *159*
　King Lear *160*
　Merchant of Venice *161*
　1 Henry 4 *163–164*
　Othello *198–201, 203*
　Romeo and Juliet *158, 160*
　Sonnet 129 *91*
　Sonnet 73 *62*
　The Winter's Tale *160*
　2 Henry 4 *164*
Shaw, George Bernard *220*
Shelley, Percy B.
　'Prometheus Unbound' *29*
Sheridan, Richard B. *220*
Shirley, Charles G., Jr *154*
Short, Mick *25, 45, 46, 46n, 65–68, 95*
Short, Mick, Elena Semino and Jonathan Culpeper *83, 93*
Sidney, Sir Philip （→ シドニー）
Simpson, Paul *68, 85, 112–114*
Sinclair, John McH. *84, 91, 98–100, 110, 111*
Sinclair, John McH, I. J. Forsyth, R. Malcolm Coulthard, and Michael C. Ashby *50*
Skinner（1671）に見出し語 Autumn がないこと（3.1.3） *324*
Sloane Ranger の英語 *190*
sparse NP *103*
Speech （→ 発話）
Sperber, Dan and Deirdre Wilson *63, 64*
Spitzer, Leo *12, 14, 18–20, 19n, 25, 151*

Spring よりも時を要した autumn の一般語化
    （3.1.5.3） *327*
Stanzel, Franz *47*
Staten, Henry *30*
Steadman, John M. *278*
Steinthal, Heymann *21*
Sterne, Lawrence
    The Life and Opinions of Tristram Shandy, Gentleman *178*, *179*
Stevens, Wallace *108*
Stockwell, Peter *25*, *60*, *117*
Stockwell, Peter and Sara Whiteley *67*
strikingness（きわ立ち） *102*
Strohmeyer, Fritz *21*, *25*
style（→ 文体）
    mind ～（精神的文体） *59*, *62*, *104*, *107*, *111*, *126*, *134*
le style est l'homme meme *10*
stylistic（文体（論）的）
    ～choice （→ choice）
    ～deviation *18*
    ～differences *63*
    ～features *9*
    ～parallelisms *134*
    OED の定義としての～ *9*
Stylistics *i*, *3* et passim （→ 文体論）
    ～ and stranslation *124–138*
    Cognitive ～ *59*
    contextualised ～ *109*, *132*
    comparative ～ *123*
    history of ～ *89*
    New ～ *126*
    Roger Flower の new ～ *90*
    steam ～ *126*
    Translational ～（翻訳的文体論） *86*, *131*, *132*
The Sun *51*, *85*, *109*, *110*
suprasegmental phonology（超分節音韻論） *111*
The Survey of English Usage（SEU） *192*

Svartvik, Jan and Randolph Quirk *192*

T

tabloid（タブロイド）
    Britain's ～ press *110*
    British ～ newspaper *109*
Tanaka, Toshiro（田中逸郎） *31*
Tannen, Deborah F. *52*
Target *130*, *133*
Taylor, Davis *161*
Taylor, Talbot J. and Michael Toolan *24*, *56*
Tennyson, Alfred *58*
Teranishi, Masayuki（寺西雅之）, Aiko Saito（齋藤安以子）and Kiyo Sakamoto（坂本輝世） *65*
text（テクスト）
    ～ of texts（いくつかのテクストから成るテクスト） *85*, *106*
    autonomy of the ～ *83*, *91*, *92*
Thackeray の *Barry Lyndon* *61*
Thatcher, Margaret *118*
Thomas, Dylan *86*, *98*, *126*, *127*
    'A Refusal to Mourn' *127*
    ～'s poetics *127*
    ～'s syntax *86*, *126–128*
Thomas, Margaret *35*
Thomas, Ronald S.
    'A Life' *135*
    'Remembering' *135*
Thorne, James P. *36*, *84*, *100*, *101*
Thought Indirect ～ （→ 思考）
Thynne's *The Works*（of Chaucer）（1532） *233*, *245*
The Times *190*
Todorov, Tzvetan *41–44*
Toolan, Michael *iii*, *5*, *25*, *35*, *46*, *50*, *51*, *64*, *66–68*, *82*, *84–86*, *94*
Townsend, Sue
    The Queen and I *190*
transference（移動）

one-to-one 〜　*131*
translation（翻訳）
　literary 〜 as 'creative transposition'　*130*
　stylistics and 〜　（→ Stylistics）
Trudgill, Peter　*162*
Tyalor, Davis　*154*
Tyndale, tr. 1534 Jude 12 での変化（3.1.5.2）*327*

U

U, non-U　*196*
Uchida, Seiji（内田聖二）　*64*
University College London　*89*
Uspensky, Boris　*107*, *112*

V

van Dijk, Tuen A.　*33*, *38*, *39*
van Peer, Willie　*83*, *93*
Venuti, Lawrence　*124*, *128*, *129*, *131*
Verdonk, Peter　*11*, *12*, *25*, *60*, *61*, *83*, *92*, *93*
Vices and Virtues（V and V）　*148*
Vinaver, Eugène　*241–243*, *246*
Vinay, Jean-Paul and Jean Darbelnet　*123*, *132*
VITAL SPIRITS（2.6.5）　*313*
vocabulary patterns（語彙的パターン）　*98*
voiced affricate [dʒ]（有声破擦音）　*85*, *119*
voiceless affricate [tʃ]（無声破擦音）　*85*, *119*
von Humboldt, Wilhelm　*12*, *13*, *15*, *21*, *25*

von Lerch, Eugen
　〜の 'ästhetische'（美学的）, 'soziale'（社会的）および 'historische'（歴史的）な視点　*20*
Vossler, Karl　*10*, *12*, *14*, *17*, *18*, *25*
　〜の観念論（idealism）*18*, *20*
Vossler–Spitzer のライン　*14*, *18*, *21*, *25*
　〜の観念的言語学　*18*
　〜の観念的文体論　*24*

W

Wales, Katie　*4*, *4n*, *68*, *83*, *84*, *93*, *168*, *190*
Warton, Thomas　*250*
Weber, Jean J.　*26*, *55*
Wells, John C.　*189*, *190*
Werth, Paul　*35*, *64*, *83*, *91*
Widdowson, Henry G.　*51*, *65*
Wilde, Oscar　*220*
Wilson, Edmund　*44n*
Wimsatt, Jr., William K.　*91*
Woolf, Virginia　*52*, *168–170*
　Mrs Dalloway　*169*
　To the Lighthouse　*180*
Wordsworth, William
　'Daffodils'（「水仙」）　*64*
　The Prelude　*143–146*
Wundt, Wilhelm　*21*, *23–25*

Y

Yeats, William B.　*98*, *220*

執筆者紹介 (＊は編者)

菊池繁夫 (きくち しげお)＊
関西外国語大学教授．近代英語協会会長．Harvard 大学 (言語学科) Fulbright 客員研究員 (Fulbright Program 1998–1999)
専門：英語文体論，文学語用論
主要業績：*Essays on English Literary Discourse: Medieval and Modern* (The Philologia Association, 2007); Katie Wales (著)『英語文体論辞典』(共訳，三省堂，2000)

上利政彦 (あがり まさひこ)＊
佐賀大学名誉教授．Cambridge 大学 Robinson College Bye-Fellow (1977–)
専門：ミルトンとルネサンス文芸論
主要業績：*Formula, Rhetoric and the Word——Studies in Milton's Epic Style* (Peter Lang, 1996); *Inversion in Milton's Poetry* (Peter Lang, 2001);『トテル詩選集 歌とソネット 1557』(訳，九州大学出版会，2010); *Archaism in Tottel's Songes and Sonettes* (渓水社，2011)

和田　章 (わだ あきら)
山口大学名誉教授
専門：英語学
主要業績：中島文雄・忍足欣四郎 (共編)『岩波新英和辞典』(編集協力，岩波書店，1981); 'Some specimens of divided usage in Thomas Deloney's English'. In: Imahayashi, O, Nakao, Y and Ogura, M (eds) *Aspects of the History of English Language and Literature* (Peter Lang, 2010)

Geffrey Leech　(–2014)
Lancaster 大学 Linguistics and English Language 学科 Research Professor Emeritus, British Academy フェロー，Academia Europaea 会員，British National Corpus の創始者のひとり
専門：English grammar, semantics, pragmatics, corpus linguistics, stylistics
主要業績：*Style in Fiction* (M Short と共著，Longman, 1981); *A Comprehensive Grammar of the English Language* (R Quirk, S Greenbaum, J Svartvik と共著，Longman, 1985)

Michael Toolan
Birmingham 大学 English Language and Applied Linguistics 学科教授．*Journal of Literary Semantics* 編集長
専門：stylistics, narrative studies, critical discourse analysis
主要業績：*Narrative: A Critical Linguistic Introduction* (Routledge, 2001); *Total Speech: An Integrational Linguistic Approach to Language* (Duke University Press, 1996)

Jean Boase-Beier
East Anglia 大学 Literature, Drama and Creative Writing 学科 Emeritus Professor. 同大学の MA in Literary Translation を創設．Visible Poets series (Arc Publications) の編集委員
専門：translation, style and poetry (特に Holocaust poetry の翻訳)
主要業績：*A Critical Introduction to Translation Studies* (Bloomsbury, 2011); *Translating the Poetry of the Holocaust* (Bloomsbury, 2015)

英語文学テクストの語学的研究法

2016年4月15日　初版発行

　編　者　　菊池繁夫・上利政彦
　発行者　　五十川直行
　発行所　　一般財団法人　九州大学出版会
　　　　　〒814-0001　福岡市早良区百道浜 3-8-34
　　　　　九州大学産学官連携イノベーションプラザ 305
　　　　　電話　092-833-9150
　　　　　URL　http://kup.or.jp/
　　　　　印刷・製本　研究社印刷株式会社

© Shigeo Kikuchi, 2016　　　　　　ISBN 978-4-7985-0176-5

トテル詩選集 歌とソネット 1557

上利政彦 訳注

菊判　500頁　定価 6,600 円

Tottel's Miscellany の名称で知られる *SONGES AND SONETTES*（1557）はヘンリー八世治下，近代人文主義の影響を受け，古典神話をはじめこれまでにない題材からなる新しい詩の世界を見せる。本書は，ワイアットやサリーらによるソネットが初めて英詩に登場したこと，本書中一の人文主義詩人グリモールドの詩が初めてまとまった形で掲載されたことでも知られる。この英国最初の名歌集に歴史的解説と原文・注釈を付け，本邦初の全訳をもって紹介する。

修辞学の技術

トマス・ウィルソン 著／上利政彦・藤田卓臣・加茂淳一 訳

A5判　298頁　定価 3,800 円

英語による最初の総合的修辞学書である本書は，エリザベス朝期前夜に出版され，やがて迎える英国文芸の隆盛に多大の影響を与えたと言われる。歴史的に重要な本書は古典修辞学にならい，話題の発見，配列，表現法，記憶術，演説法の5項目を豊富な例を挙げて詳述する。弁論述と詩学の両面で本書がもつ意義は大きく，特に16世紀英国において広く利用されたこの英国修辞学の源泉を，わが国で初めて翻訳し，解説を付して紹介する。

（定価税別）　　　　　　　　　　　　　　　　　　　九州大学出版会